DATE DUE

PRINTED IN U.S.A.

Auth
& Art
for Yo
Ad

ISSN 1040-5682

Authors & Artists for Young Adults

VOLUME 22

Thomas McMahon
Editor

GALE

DETROIT · NEW YORK · TORONTO · LONDON

Thomas McMahon, *Editor*

Joyce Nakamura, *Managing Editor*

Hal May, *Publisher*

Diane Andreassi, Ken Cuthbertson, Ronie-Richele Garcia-Johnson, Marian C.
Gonsior, Janet L. Hile, David Johnson, J. Sydney Jones,, Irene McKnight-Durham,
Nancy Rampson, Megan Ratner, Peggy Saari, Pamela L. Shelton, Kenneth R.
Shepherd, Tracy J. Sukraw, and Kathleen Witman,
Sketchwriters/Contributing Editors

Victoria B. Cariappa, *Research Manager*
Cheryl L. Warnock, *Project Coordinator*
Gary J. Oudersluys and Maureen Richards, *Research Specialists*
Laura C. Bissey and Sean R. Smith, *Research Associates*

Susan M. Trosky, *Permissions Manager*
Maria L. Franklin, *Permissions Specialist*
Michele Lonoconus, *Permissions Associate*
Edna Hedblad, *Permissions Assitant*

Mary Beth Trimper, *Production Director*
Deborah Milliken, *Production Assistant*

Randy Bassett, *Image Database Supervisor*
Mikal Ansari, *Macintosh Artist*
Robert Duncan, *Imaging Specialist*
Pamela A. Reed, *Photography Coordinator*

(∞)™ The paper used in this publication meets the minimum requirements of
American National Standard for Information Sciences—Permanence Paper
for Printed Library Materials, ANSI Z39.48-1984.

Library of Congress Catalog Card Number 89-641100
ISBN 0-7876-1673-7
ISSN 1040-5682

10 9 8 7 6 5 4 3 2 1

Printed in the United States of America

Authors and Artists for Young Adults

TEEN BOARD

The staff of *Authors and Artists for Young Adults* wishes to thank the following young adult readers for their teen board participation:

Contents

Introduction

Authors and Artists for Young Adults is a reference series designed to serve the needs of middle school, junior high, and high school students interested in creative artists. Originally inspired by the need to bridge the gap between Gale's *Something about the Author,* created for children, and *Contemporary Authors,* intended for older students and adults, *Authors and Artists for Young Adults* has been expanded to cover not only an international scope of authors, but also a wide variety of other artists.

Although the emphasis of the series remains on the writer for young adults, we recognize that these readers have diverse interests covering a wide range of reading levels. The series therefore contains not only those creative artists who are of high interest to young adults, including cartoonists, photographers, music composers, bestselling authors of adult novels, media directors, producers, and performers, but also literary and artistic figures studied in academic curricula, such as influential novelists, playwrights, poets, and painters. The goal of *Authors and Artists for Young Adults* is to present this great diversity of creative artists in a format that is entertaining, informative, and understandable to the young adult reader.

Entry Format

Each volume of *Authors and Artists for Young Adults* will furnish in-depth coverage of twenty to twenty-five authors and artists. The typical entry consists of:

—A detailed biographical section that includes date of birth, marriage, children, education, and addresses.

—A comprehensive bibliography or filmography including publishers, producers, and years.

—Adaptations into other media forms.

—Works in progress.

—A distinctive essay featuring comments on an artist's life, career, artistic intentions, world views, and controversies.

—References for further reading.

—Extensive illustrations, photographs, movie stills, cartoons, book covers, and other relevant visual material.

A cumulative index to featured authors and artists appears in each volume.

Compilation Methods

The editors of *Authors and Artists for Young Adults* make every effort to secure information directly from the authors and artists through personal correspondence and interviews. Sketches on living authors and artists are sent to the biographee for review prior to publication. Any sketches not personally reviewed by biographees or their representatives are marked with an asterisk (*).

Highlights of Forthcoming Volumes

Among the authors and artists planned for future volumes are:

Tim Allen
Julia Alvarez
Greg Bear
Margaret Buffie
Michael Cadnum
Chris Carter
Willa Cather
C. J. Cherryh
Salvador Dali
Samuel R. Delaney
Charles Dickens
Greg Evans

F. Scott Fitzgerald
Jodie Foster
Mary Downing Hahn
Joseph Heller
M. E. Kerr
Daniel Keyes
E. L. Konigsburg
George Lucas
Mary E. Lyons
Geraldine McCaughrean
Margaret Mitchell
Walter Dean Myers

Beverly Naidoo
Richard Peck
Tamora Pierce
Colby Rodowsky
Carl Sandburg
Robert Silverberg
Steven Spielberg
Robert Louis Stevenson
Bram Stoker
Oprah Winfrey
Patricia Windsor
Paul R. Yee

Contact the Editor

We encourage our readers to examine the entire *AAYA* series. Please write and tell us if we can make AAYA even more helpful to you. Give your comments and suggestions to the editor:

BY MAIL: The Editor, *Authors and Artists for Young Adults*, Gale Research, 835 Penobscot Building, 645 Griswold St., Detroit, MI 48226-4094.

BY TELEPHONE: (800) 347-GALE

BY FAX: (313) 961-6599

BY E-MAIL: CYA@Gale.com@GALESMTP

Authors & Artists for Young Adults

Michael Bedard

Book Award, and Young Adult Canadian Book Award runner-up, both 1991, International Board on Books for Young People (IBBY) Honor List, 1992, all for *Redwork*; National Chapter of Canada IODE Violet Downey Book Award, 1991, for *The Nightingale*.

■ Personal

Born June 26, 1949, in Toronto, Ontario; married to Martha; four children. *Hobbies and other interests:* Collecting books, particularly stories of the supernatural, cooking vegetarian meals, baseball.

■ Addresses

Home—Toronto, Ontario, Canada. *Agent*—Linda McKnight, Westwood Creative Artists.

■ Career

Full-time writer, 1982—. Library assistant, St. Michael's College Library, Toronto, Canada, 1971-78; pressman at a small press, 1978-81.

■ Awards, Honors

Book of the Year, Canadian Library Association, Governor General's Literary Award for Text, 1990, National Chapter of Canada IODE Violet Downey

■ Writings

FOR CHILDREN

Woodsedge and Other Tales, Gardenshore Press, 1979.
Pipe and Pearls: A Gathering of Tales, Gardenshore Press, 1980.
The Tinderbox (retelling), illustrated by Regolo Ricci, Oxford University Press, 1990.
The Nightingale (retelling), illustrated by Regolo Ricci, Oxford University Press, 1991.

JUVENILE FICTION

A Darker Magic, Atheneum, 1987.
The Lightning Bolt, illustrated by Regolo Ricci, Oxford University Press, 1989.
Redwork, Lester, 1990, Atheneum, 1990.
Painted Devil, Lester, 1994.

BIOGRAPHY

Emily, illustrated by Barbara Cooney, Lester, 1992, Doubleday, 1992.

The Divide, illustrated by Emily Arnold McCully, Doubleday, 1997.

Glass Town, illustrated by Laura Fernandez and Rick Jacobson, Atheneum, 1997.

■ Sidelights

"We sat there spellbound as it flowed and eddied about the room, transforming all it touched." In his stories for children and young adults, Michael Bedard uses vivid, sometimes disturbing prose, as in this description of a magician's spell in *A Darker Magic.* Bedard's work is filled with mystery and magic as he investigates themes of freedom, self-determination, and imagination. His novels often investigate the supernatural, but they don't fit neatly into one category. They have been variously described as "realistic," "fantasy," "dark-fantasy," "mystery," "psychological thriller" and "mystical prose-poetry." Joanne Findon explains in *Canadian Children's Literature* that Bedard masters a number of difficult ideas in a sophisticated manner. "One of the most intriguing aspects of Bedard's work is his richly textured representation of evil," Findon says. "In fact, Bedard prefers to speak of "darkness"—a term which expands his symbolic range considerably and allows him to deploy a series of double-edged images throughout his novels."

His major works include *A Darker Magic, Redwork,* and *Painted Devil.* In *Redwork,* his main characters are an alchemist and two teenagers who form an unlikely friendship. In *A Darker Magic* and *Painted Devil* the protagonists face demonic characters. Bedard has also written several picture books reworking the traditional folk and fairy tales of Hans Christian Andersen and the Brothers Grimm with endings that evoke much more optimism than the originals.

Bedard's work has been heavily influenced by Emily Dickinson's poetry and exhibits a keen focus on extremes and what lies beneath the surface of things. Bedard's fiction, picture books, and retellings of fairy tales and folk stories have earned him a reputation as an important writer of fiction for children, but because his writing is detailed it is sometimes viewed as challenging for young readers.

Bedard is best known for writing suspense novels for young adults, a natural audience for some-

one who has been around children all his life. He was born the oldest of five children and was raised in Toronto, Canada, where he still lives. Stories became a fascination for him when he was four, and he pored over Currier and Ives prints and later through comic books that he lugged with him wherever he went. Books were a scarce commodity in Bedard's household, so when he was a young boy he was thrilled to inherit six books from an uncle. These classics sent him on adventures with Tom Sawyer, Huck Finn, Long John Silver and Tarzan. They were the seeds from which his writings would grow. "It was not until I was seventeen or so and fell under the spell of poetry that I first began to write," Bedard explains in *Seventh Book of Junior Authors and Illustrators.* "We had a teacher that year with a passion for poetry that proved infectious. . . . By the end of the year I had begun to write. I knew right then what I wanted to do with the rest of my life."

"The subtlety of Bedard's handling of relationships represents maturity missing in a great deal of adult fiction, not to speak of the plethora of superficiality aimed at teens. Michael Bedard is worth reading."

—Laurence Steven

He went on to attend the University of Toronto and earned a Bachelor of Arts degree in English and Philosophy, graduating in 1971. The next several years he worked at a university library and began a family. Bedard later took a job as a pressman at a small printing shop and while working there published two collections of original fairy tales for children, *Woodsedge and Other Tales* and *Pipe and Pearls: A Gathering of Tales.* All the while he seemed to be building a foundation for his lifetime passion of becoming a full-time writer, which he realized in 1982.

First Novel Casts Compelling Spell

In his first novel, *A Darker Magic,* Bedard tells a story about a magician who takes away children's souls. It centers around an elderly teacher, Miss Potts, who fifty years earlier, as a young girl, persuaded her parents to take her to a magic show in the waiting room of a railway depot. A magician, Professor Mephisto, materializes on the makeshift stage; his performance has deadly results. Five decades later, a handbill appears in one of the schoolroom desks where Miss Potts teaches, announcing there will be a show by Professor Mephisto in the old railway depot. As the date of the show draws closer, Miss Potts begins to remember what happened that fateful night when she was a young girl. Miss Potts and one of her students, Emily Endicott, must work together to thwart Mephisto's evil plans.

Bedard's debut novel was well-received by critics. According to a reviewer in *Children's Book News*, "*A Darker Magic* is rich in imagery and unexplained incident all woven together to make a totally captivating story which will engross—and probably frighten—its readers. It's not a book to be missed." David Gale, writing in *School Library Journal*, similarly stated that the author's "well-paced narrative is rich in language and riveting in tone; it brims with a sense of foreboding that is sustained throughout." Other reviewers questioned the appropriateness of the work for children. In *Books in Canada*, Welwyn Wilton Katz opined that "All of the children of this book are either victims or potential victims," adding, "There is no light in *A Darker Magic*."

Bedard drew from his own upbringing when creating the characters for *A Darker Magic*. In an interview with Marie C. Davis in *Canadian Children's Literature*, Bedard says the relationship between Emily and her younger brother Albert paralleled his family life. "I was often called upon to watch the younger kids because there is a seventeen-year gap between me and the youngest. . . . The younger sibling offers a reminder of where you came from and is helpful in developing where you are going to go."

Two years after *A Darker Magic* was published, Bedard's *The Lightning Bolt* was released. In this reversal on Grimms' tale of *The Fisherman and His Wife*, Bedard features an old, poor woman who frees a little man from a tree in the woods. He gives her a stick that grants wishes and a cap that reveals others' secret thoughts. Quietly keeping the cap, she gives her bullying husband the stick and he greedily obtains more and more gifts. Her husband continues to mistreat her and decides to kill her, but because she has the cap she

knows his secret thoughts and saves herself by returning the gifts to the little man. Finally, the wicked husband is returned to the roots of the tree where the woman found the little man.

> *"It was not until I was seventeen or so and fell under the spell of poetry that I first began to write. . . . I knew right then what I wanted to do with the rest of my life."*
> —Michael Bedard

A year later Bedard retold another story, *The Tinder Box* by Hans Christian Andersen. In this tale, a soldier finds a witch's magical tinder box and with it reaps fortune and the hand of a beautiful princess. The soldier understands that his wealth attracts false friends, but instead of being bitter, he remembers his poor beginnings and makes donations to the poor. "Bedard's satisfyingly zestful narrative allows us to enjoy the soldier's successes without letting us forget the unsavoury greed that motivates him, for the soldier is not a perfect hero," according to Ulrike Walker in *Canadian Children's Literature*.

Writing Style Evolves

There is a similarity between writing fairy tales and writing novels, Bedard explains to Davis: "I began my work by writing poetry and fairy tales. I think perhaps that is still what I'm doing. The form has changed, but the intent is the same. . . . That is what moves us in a piece of poetry, a fine sculpture, a beautiful dance; we see the harmony of inward and outward, the finite and the infinite, eternity and time." Critics believe Bedard achieved this harmony in his second novel, *Redwork*, which was published in 1990 and is generally considered his most accomplished work. "There is simply too much that is good here to cover in a review," according to Laurence Steven in *Canadian Children's Literature*. The story unfolds as fifteen-year-old Cass and his single mother, Alison, move into an unkept old house. Their landlord is Mr. Magnus, a reclusive World War I veteran, who lives on the floor below. Meanwhile, Cass feels a strange bond between the house and

Mr. Magnus. Cass and his new friend Maddy discover that Mr. Magnus is an alchemist and take part in his quest to make a philosopher's stone.

Patrick Jones declares in *Voice of Youth Advocates* that in *Redwork*, "Everything is described with detail, every point is made with dialogue, and each scene is fleshed out considerably." The theme of the novel, like many of his other works, delves into the dark roads people must take during life's travels, which reflects William Blake's writings. This influence is most obvious in *Redwork*, but the idea of descending into death is also present in Bedard's *A Darker Magic* and *Painted Devil*. Despite the dark images in his stories, Bedard says he believes that childhood is a time of innocence. "The child's vision is one of wonder and awe," he tells Davis. "The child is fully imaginative. As the child becomes more accommodated to the world and more self-conscious—around ten, eleven, twelve—some of their initial lights begin to go out. Suddenly it is not enough to just be themselves; it is very important how they are perceived. So these original openings that the child had are curbed or curtailed."

Bedard's next work, *The Nightingale*, is adapted from the original classic written by Hans Christian Andersen. Bedard "uses descriptive and colorful language to relate the ancient tale of a Chinese emperor who ruled over a huge empire and lives in the most magnificent palace in the world," according to Gwen Maguire in a review for *CM: A Reviewing Journal of Canadian Materials for Young People*. Visitors come from around the world to see the palace and city where the emperor ruled. They are impressed with what they see, but they are enraptured by the song of a nightingale. When the emperor learns this, he has the bird captured and kept in a cage. A mechanical, bejeweled bird patterned after the real nightingale is sent as a gift from a Japanese emperor and is equipped to sing one of the songs sung by the real nightingale. The emperor soon cherishes this replica more than the real one. By the story's end, however, it is the real nightingale that gives the dying emperor life.

In his next work, *Emily*, Bedard incorporates two passions, one for reclusive poet Emily Dickinson, and the other for his unquenchable thirst to explore new areas of knowledge. After researching Dickinson's life, "the idea for the picture book *Emily* came to me, as I imagined what it might

---

If you enjoy the works of Michael Bedard, you may also want to check out the following books and films:

Michael Cadnum, *Calling Home*, 1991.
Jackie French Koller, *The Last Voyage of the Misty Day*, 1992.
Margaret Mahy, *The Changeover*, 1984.
The Uninvited, Paramount, 1944.

---

be like for a young child to move in across the street from this remarkable woman," Bedard explains in the *Seventh Book of Junior Authors and Illustrators*. In *Emily*, a young girl's mother is invited to play the piano at Dickinson's house. A brief encounter between Emily and the child involves an exchange of gifts—lily bulbs for a bit of paper with a handwritten poem.

"The story is very quiet but beautifully crafted, with a clarity of observation and a delicately tart edge, that creditably emulate Emily herself," according to a contributor in *Kirkus Reviews*. Bedard explains in the Davis interview that Dickinson was elusive: "The embodiment of mystery. But, she teaches you very deep lessons. On the surface she lived a very limited life in a very limited world. But she opened that out in incredible ways. She saw into the small things of life with a passion and a depth that someone in a larger world might not have seen comparably."

It is precisely that same eye for detail that Stephanie Zvirin refers to in a *Booklist* review. She explains that Bedard "knows how to create chilling atmosphere," in his novel *Painted Devil*. "Recurring imagery and precise descriptions are part of his technique, and he's a master at manipulating tension," Zvirin says. *Painted Devil* centers around Alice, who accepts a summer job helping produce a Punch and Judy puppet show at the library. Alice's parents are preoccupied with her mother's troubled pregnancy and leave a lot of the care of little Lela to her. Frightening events occur as the puppet show is about to begin and only Alice's Aunt Emily (Emily Endicott from *A Darker Magic*), who is odd and secretive, knows that these happenings are part of an ancient satanic spirit's unrelenting plot, and that the only way to avoid doom is to destroy the devil puppet. A reviewer in *Publishers Weekly* comments: "Bedard's intensely dark, moody yet handsomely wrought prose lends itself well to this sophisticated thriller. . . ." Zvirin adds that the author "invokes a sense of mystery and foreboding so vividly that the story is hard to put down."

Bedard tapped on his experience working in a library, as he sets the plot around the home and local public library. He states in the Davis interview that he must be able to see a scene to describe it to the reader. "When I stop being able to see the scene, I must stop writing," he says. "I'm not a writer who can somehow prompt the scene by the acting of writing the words." According to the critics, the format works. "*Painted Devil* is a well-written novel that depicts good and evil forces at play, and the positive results that ensue when fears (real or imagined) are met and conquered," according to Irene E. Aubrey in a *Quill and Quire* review. "Bedard successfully creates a mood of unease and foreboding, and his complex characters capture the reader's imagination." Steven sums up Bedard's writing simply: "the subtlety of Bedard's handling of relationships represents maturity missing in a great deal of adult fiction, not to speak of the plethora of superficiality aimed at teens. Michael Bedard is worth reading."

Bedard explains in his interview with Davis that there is an important relationship between him and the reader. "The reader is really a co-creator," Bedard says. "It is not up to me to detail everything to such an extent that I put the reader's imagination out. It's rather up to me to sketch things and to touch on detail to the extent that I bring the piece alive, but beyond that the reader comes in and fleshes it out."

■ Works Cited

Aubrey, Irene E., review of *Painted Devil*, *Quill and Quire*, April, 1994, pp. 38-39.

Bedard, Michael, *A Darker Magic*, Atheneum, 1987.

Bedard, Michael, autobiographical essay in *Seventh Book of Junior Authors and Illustrators*, edited by Sally Holmes Holtze, H.W. Wilson, 1996.

Review of *A Darker Magic*, *Children's Book News*, Winter, 1987, p. 11.

Davis, Marie C., "An Interview with Michael Bedard," *Canadian Children's Literature*, Number 82, 1996.

Review of *Emily*, *Kirkus Reviews*, December, 1992, p. 26.

Findon, Joanne, "Darkness in the Novels of Michael Bedard," *Canadian Children's Literature*, Number 82, 1996.

Jones, Patrick, review of *Redwork*, *Voice of Youth Advocates*, December, 1990, p. 293.

Katz, Welwyn Wilton, review of *A Darker Magic*, *Books in Canada*, April, 1988, p. 36.

Maguire, Gwen, review of *The Nightingale*, *CM: A Reviewing Journal of Canadian Materials for Young People*, October, 1991, p. 306.

Review of *Painted Devil*, *Publishers Weekly*, March 14, 1994, p. 74.

Steven, Laurence, "Excellent Alchemy," review of *Redwork*, *Canadian Children's Literature*, Number 63, 1991, pp. 72-73.

Walker, Ulrike, "Mixing Fantasy and Reality: Four Picture Books," review of *The Tinderbox*, *Canadian Children's Literature*, Number 63, 1991, pp. 83-87.

Zvirin, Stephanie, review of *Painted Devil*, *Booklist*, March 1, 1994, p. 1249.

■ For More Information See

BOOKS

Twentieth-Century Children's Writers, 4th edition, edited by Laura Standley Berger, St. James Press, 1995, p. 78.

PERIODICALS

Books in Canada, December, 1992, pp. 30-32.

Canadian Children's Literature, Number 70, 1993, pp. 92-94; Number 82, 1996, pp. 69-79.

CM: A Reviewing Journal of Canadian Materials for Young People, May, 1988, p. 85; January, 1993, p. 20.

Horn Book, May-June, 1990, p. 367; January-February, 1993, pp. 72-73.

In Review: Canadian Books for Children, October, 1979, pp. 30-31; February, 1980, p. 34; August, 1981, p. 28.

Junior Bookshelf, August, 1990, pp. 164-65; August, 1991, p. 141.

Kirkus Reviews, November 1, 1990, p. 1528; March 1, 1992, p. 320.

Quill and Quire, November, 1989, p. 15; August, 1990, p. 14; September, 1990, p. 20; December, 1992, p. 26.

School Librarian, August, 1991, p. 99.

School Library Journal, October, 1990, p. 139; November, 1992, p. 88.

Voice of Youth Advocates, April, 1993, p. 34.

—Sketch by Diane Gale Andreassi

Mary Cassatt

Palais, Paris, France. *Gallery Collections:* Adelson Galleries, New York City; Carnegie Museum of Art, Pittsburgh, PA; Hirschl & Adler Galleries, New York City; Kennedy Galleries, New York City; Knoedler & Company, New York City.

■ Awards, Honors

French Legion of Honor, 1904.

■ Sidelights

Through her artwork and her extensive encouragement of other collectors, artist Mary Cassatt was a primary conduit for the introduction of impressionism to America. Cassatt worked hard to develop her craft, expanding her work to incorporate pastels, engraving, and printmaking. Like the paintings of the French impressionists who were her friends and influences, Cassatt's work attempted to show ordinary scenes from contemporary life: short brush strokes, primary colors, odd angles, and reflected rather than artificial light were combined to convey a less formal, more real version of the painted scene. Cassatt's focus was distinctive, her emphasis on women in domestic settings, especially with their children. Her later work shows a strong influence from Japanese prints. Her portraits share a similar intimacy, the figures set against little background detail; Cassatt used techniques similar to photography, homing

■ Personal

Full name, Mary Stevenson Cassatt; born May 22, 1844, in Allegheny, PA; died June 14, 1926; daughter of Robert Simpson (a real estate and banking investor) and Katherine Kelso Johnston Cassatt. *Education:* Studied at Pennsylvania Academy, Philadelphia, 1861-65; also studied under various artists in France and Italy.

■ Career

Artist. Masterworks include *Reading Le Figaro,* 1878; *Little Girl in a Blue Armchair,* 1878; *Five O'clock Tea,* 1880; *The Loge,* 1882; *Alexander Cassatt and His Son Robert,* 1884-85; *Girl Arranging Her Hair,* 1886; *The Letter,* 1890-91; *The Bath,* 1891-92; *The Boating Party,* 1893-94; *Feeding the Ducks,* 1894; *Breakfast in Bed,* 1897; and *Child with Red Hat,* 1901. *Major Museum Collections:* Chicago, IL; Philadelphia, PA; Washington, DC. *Other Collections:* Baltimore, MD; Birmingham, AL; Boston, MA; Cincinnati, OH; Cleveland, OH; Flint, MI; Kansas City, KS; Pasadena, CA; St. Louis, MO; Seattle, WA; Wichita, KS; Glasgow, Scotland; Louvre and Petit

The Boating Party, a painting from 1893-94, is considered one of Cassatt's masterworks.

in on her subjects to observe the specifics of their relationships. She treated everyday details and small moments with gravity, expressing her feminism in the carefully observed moments of women's lives.

The fifth child of a well-to-do Pennsylvania family, Cassatt was born outside Pittsburgh. By the time Cassatt was five, the family had moved to Philadelphia, the city she regarded as her American home. A successful real estate and banking investor, Cassatt's father moved the family to Europe when Cassatt was seven. From 1851 through 1855 her family lived in Paris; the city left an indelible impression on the young girl. Eager to ensure that their children profit from this experience, Cassatt's parents arranged excursions to museums and other cultural institutions. The

children were also tutored in French. Subsequently, the family moved to Germany but returned to Philadelphia a few months later because of the death of Mary's elder brother, Robbie.

At sixteen, Cassatt enrolled in the Pennsylvania Academy of the Fine Arts, one of the few art and museum schools open to women at the time. To do so went against the wishes of her family. Like other women of her social standing, Cassatt was not expected to pursue a career, but instead take-up the duties of wife and mother. Cassatt stayed at the Academy only two years, ultimately becoming frustrated with the tradition-bound curriculum and the condescension of her fellow male students and teachers. She decided that the only sure way to continue learning would be to go to Europe.

Influential Friends

Cassatt returned to Paris in 1866, where she spent the next two years taking private art lessons and copying masterpieces in the Louvre. Among her favorites were the sixteenth-century Italian painter Correggio, his contemporary, the German painter Holbein and Velazquez, the seventeenth-century Spanish court painter. Cassatt painted the French countryside and was for a short period in Rome.

Through its Academy of Fine Arts, the French government sponsored salon exhibitions which became the first step in any materially successful art career. A few of Cassatt's paintings were accepted in the 1868 and 1870 exhibitions but she had already begun to move away from the formal styles favored by the establishment to embrace the ideas of the impressionists whose work she had begun to see. With their emphasis on modern life and their rejection of the more stylized tradition of symmetry in paintings, Jean Courbet, Edouard Manet and especially Edgar Degas exerted an enormous influence on Cassatt. The direction of her work changed to accommodate these new ideas.

Returning to the United States in 1870 to escape the French/Prussian war, Cassatt moved in with her parents in rural Pennsylvania. Two bleak years followed this move, as her father refused to finance her work. Additionally, several of the canvasses she had brought to sell in Chicago were consumed in the great fire of 1871. Finally, in 1872, a bishop in Philadelphia commissioned her to make copies of two religious paintings by Correggio in Parma. It was during her sojourn in this Northern Italian city that Cassatt first painted babies, later a dominant subject and one that made her instantly recognizable.

Having earned enough to return to Paris, Cassatt moved there later in 1872. Her work appeared in that year's Salon and again two years later. It was here that Degas saw her work; they met in 1877, a friendship that became both a personal and a professional boon to both of them. He invited her to exhibit in an alternative show, organized in 1879 by his group, who were by then dubbed the impressionists. Cassatt rejected this term, preferring "independents." Cassatt and Degas became very close, often painting the same scenes in dance halls and theaters in Paris. In the *Atlantic*

Monthly, Nancy Caldwell Sorel described their affinity, based on a shared obsession with art: "On occasion they quarreled, reconciled, quarreled again—never as lovers, which they were not, but always as fierce independents." The freedom from a more academic style became evident in Cassatt's *The Loge*, an 1882 painting of two women in a theater box. Her palette incorporated pastels, and she and Degas experimented with engraving, which led Cassatt to a detailed study of printmaking. Many critics have acknowledged Cassatt as a master of this discipline.

If you enjoy the works of Mary Cassatt, you may also want to check out the following:

The works of the Impressionists, particularly Edgar Degas, Claude Monet, Pierre-Auguste Renoir, Edouard Manet, and Camille Pizarro.

The works of Correggio, a sixteenth-century Italian painter, and Diego Velazquez, a seventeenth-century Spanish court painter, both of whom Cassatt studied.

Women artists were still very much the exception in Cassatt's lifetime. She maintained friendships with her contemporaries, including Berthe Morisot and Eva Gonzalez, and these artists played an important part in her development as a painter. Unlike many of her male colleagues, Cassatt preferred portraits to urban or rural scenes and she paid special attention to women in the home, generally with their children.

Family obligations forced Cassatt to cease painting at several points during the 1870s and 1880s. Her parents had joined her in Paris in 1877, but both her sister and her mother fell ill in quick succession and Cassatt had to run the household. She did not stop entirely, however, and she continued to experiment with new effects. The development of surer brushwork and a more controlled composition can be seen in *Girl Arranging Her Hair* (1886).

Aside from expanding her own work, Cassatt strove to convince her family and American friends to buy impressionist paintings. She convinced her brother, Alexander, to purchase work by Claude Monet, Pierre-Auguste Renoir, Camille Pissarro, and Degas. Alexander eventually became the first important collector of this work. Cassatt also played a pivotal role in her friend Louisine Elder Havemeyer's acquisition of impressionist art. The Havemeyer collection, one of the earliest of impressionism and other French art of the late nineteenth century, was eventually donated to the Metropolitan Museum of Art in New York. During the 1890s, Cassatt became a popular figure for the many American artists who made their way to Paris.

Cassatt's Forte: The Tenderness of Motherhood

In 1890, Cassatt and Degas visited an exhibition of Japanese woodcuts that had a profound effect on her work. Prime examples of this include *The Letter* (1890-91), *The Boating Party* (1893-94), and *Feeding the Ducks* (1894). Inspired by the Japanese

This portrait of Cassatt, circa 1880-84, was painted by Edgar Degas, a close friend who also served as a creative inspiration.

prints, Cassatt made her own series, often considered to be her most beautiful work. Upon viewing these, Degas was reported to remark, "I am not willing to admit that a woman can draw that well."

It was at this time that she embarked on the paintings for which she is best known, her series of mothers and children. In her review of Nancy Mowll Mathews' *Cassatt: A Retrospective*, Genevieve Stuttaford describes the artist as a "hardworking, lonely idealist" whose paintings of mothers and children "radiate maternal tenderness but also bristle with humor and penetrating irony." Cassatt used the observational skills she had learned from Degas to show women's daily lives. Her paintings treated the simplest tasks—sealing a letter, reading a paper, sitting in a garden, sewing—with respect. In particular, she focused on the quiet, often unseen moments of intimacy between a mother and child. This concern is evident in her 1910 pastel, *Sleepy Baby*, which shows a contemporary woman and her sleeping child, but whose composition brings to mind Renaissance Madonna and Child paintings. Cassatt's portraits are characterized by a lack of sentimentality, a directness that was influenced by the impressionists' insistence that modern life be shown as it was, unidealized. Cassatt did more than simply modernize the Madonna and Child portrait: she showed actual gestures, sometimes even awkward positions, that conveyed the emotional and physical connections between mother and child.

The portraits seem spontaneous and unplanned, but in fact Cassatt planned each one extensively, sometimes pairing unrelated women and children in order to achieve a desired effect. In *Agatha and Her Child* (1891), for example, Cassatt shows the baby squirming against the mother's lap, yet their right arms parallel each other and emphasize the connection between the two figures. In 1892, author Paul Durand-Ruel wrote that, although Cassatt's work suggested a modern Holy Family: "It is no longer a matter of ecstatic virgins holding without affection, on rigid knees, a child aware of his destiny and who already goest on his way. These are infinitely human and loving mothers who squeeze against their own bosom the rosy flesh of certainly lively babies who have no care except for their mother's caresses."

Cassatt earned enough to afford a house in a small town near Paris. In 1893, the World's

Domestic life was one of Cassatt's recurrent subjects, as in this pastel work, *Mother and Infant*.

Columbian Exhibition in Chicago commissioned a mural. Despite her success in Europe, Cassatt remained little known in the United States and she saw the commission as a chance to increase her visibility. Unfortunately, because she wasn't in Chicago her design proved unusable. Her disappointment was somewhat mitigated by a solo exhibition later that year in New York which met with critical success. Her work prompted one reviewer, quoted in *Artists: From Michelangelo to Maya Lin*, to note that: "No painter has seen so much feeling, nor has anyone, with such convincing art, translated into canvas the poem of the family."

Her mother's death in 1895 deeply distressed Cassatt. She had nursed her parent for several years and suddenly found herself alone in the world. She devoted less time to her work and became more fixed in her ideas. She had managed to keep her work fresh by being open, allowing herself to be influenced by experimentation. But Cassatt did not respond to the new ideas of dabs of color championed by Paul Cézanne, Henri Matisse, and Monet. Her own work suffered from stodginess, the forms static, the brush strokes thick and inelegant.

Cassatt spent more time advising American art collectors. As well, she undertook several ambitious travels, including a trip to Egypt with her brother and his family in 1910. Impressed by the colors and art, Cassatt found her confidence in her own work ebbing away. Her brother's illness and sudden death upon their return contributed to her further decline. Not long after this, the double cataracts brought on by her diabetes began to affect Cassatt's eyesight.

Cassatt remained dedicated to feminist ideals and she was an active supporter of women's suffrage, going so far as to donate the proceeds from a late-life exhibition in New York to the cause. Having lived through World War I, she hoped that giving women the vote would end warfare.

As an American artist living in France, Cassatt garnered respect and fame in her adopted country despite less recognition in the United States. In 1904, the French government awarded her the Legion of Honor. In 1928, two years after her death at age eighty-two in France, Cassatt's work appeared in four exhibitions in the United States. Art historian John Wilmerding has termed Cas-

satt's 1895 pastel *Portrait of Mrs. Havemeyer and Her Daughter Electra* "the best double female portrait by an American artist," fitting tribute to an artist who ultimately managed to gain the recognition of her country people that eluded her in life.

■ Works Cited

Butler Institute of American Art, Youngstown, OH, catalogue entry on *Agatha and Her Child*, http://www.butlerart.com/cassatt.htm.

Ergas, G. Aimee, "Mary Cassatt," *Artists: From Michelangelo to Maya Lin*, UXL, 1995.

Sorel, Nancy Caldwell, "First Encounters: Edgar Degas and Mary Cassatt," *Atlantic Monthly*, November, 1993, p. 137.

Stuttaford, Genevieve, review of *Cassatt: A Retrospective*, *Publishers Weekly*, October 7, 1996, p. 55.

Vogel, Carol, "The Shelburne Splurges," *New York Times*, December 13, 1996, p. C34.

■ For More Information See

BOOKS

Brooks, Philip, *Mary Cassatt: An American in Paris*, F. Watts, 1995.

Bullard, E. John, *Cassatt: Oils and Pastels*, [New York], 1972.

Breuning, Margaret, *Cassatt*, [New York], 1944.

Carson, Julia, *Cassatt*, [New York], 1966.

Cassatt, [Haverford, PA], 1939.

Effeny, Alison, *Cassatt*, Studio Editions, 1993.

Forbes, Watson, *Cassatt*, [New York], 1932.

Getlein, Frank, *Cassatt: Paintings and Prints*, [New York], 1980.

Getlein, Frank, *Cassatt: Prints and Drawings*, [New York, NY, and London], 1988.

Hale, Nancy, *Cassatt* (biography), [New York], 1975.

Lindsay, Suzanne G., *Cassatt and Philadelphia*, [Philadelphia, PA], 1985.

Love, Richard, *Cassatt, the Independent*, [Chicago, IL], 1980.

Mathews, Nancy Mowll, editor, *Cassatt and Her Circle: Selected Letters*, [New York], 1984; [London], 1988.

Mathews, Nancy Mowll, *Cassatt*, [New York], 1987.

Mathews, Nancy Mowll, *Mary Cassatt: A Life*, Villard Books, 1994.

Muhlberger, Richard, *What Makes a Cassatt a Cassatt?*, Metropolitan Museum of Art, 1994.

Plain, Nancy, *Mary Cassatt, an Artist's Life*, Dillon Press, 1994.

Pollock, Griselda, *Cassatt*, [London], 1980.

Roudebush, Jay, *Cassatt*, [Naefels, Switzerland and New York], 1979.

Segard, Achille, *Cassatt, un peintre des enfants et de meres*, [Paris], 1913.

Sweet, Frederick A., *Miss Mary Cassatt, Impressionist from Pennsylvania*, [Norman, OK], 1966.

Valerio, Edith, *Cassatt*, [Paris], 1930.

EXHIBITION CATALOGUES

Cassatt Among the Impressionists, text by Adelyn D. Breeskin, [Omaha, NE], 1969.

Cassatt, [Washington, DC], 1970.

Cassatt: A Catalogue Raisonné of the Oils, Pastels, Watercolors, and Drawings, text by Adelyn D. Breeskin, [Washington, DC], 1970.

Cassatt: Pastles and Color Prints, text by John E. Bullard, [Washington, DC], 1978.

The Graphic Work of Cassatt: A Catalogue Raisonné, text by Adelyn D. Breeskin, [New York], 1948, as *A Catalogue Raisonné of the Graphic Work*, {Washington, DC], 1979.

Sargent, Whistler and Cassatt, text by Frederick A. Sweet, [Chicago, IL], 1954.*

—Sketch by C. M. Ratner

John Christopher

time writer, 1958—. *Military service:* British Army, Royal Signals, 1941-46.

■ Personal

Pseudonym of Christopher Samuel Youd; also writes as Samuel Youd, Hilary Ford, William Godfrey, Peter Graaf, Peter Nichols, and Anthony Rye; born April 16, 1922, in Knowsley, Lancashire, England; married Joyce Fairbairn, October 23, 1946 (marriage ended); married Jessica Valerie Ball, December 24, 1980; children: (first marriage) Nicholas, Rose, Elizabeth, Sheila, Margret. *Education:* Attended Peter Sy-monds School, Winchester, England. *Politics:* Tory Radical.

■ Addresses

Home—One Whitefriars, Rye, East Sussex TN31 7LE, England; and c/o Society of Authors, 84 Drayton Gardens, London SW10 9SB, England.

■ Career

Freelance writer, 1946-48; worked in and eventually headed the Industrial Diamond Information Bureau of the Diamond Corporation, 1949-58; full-

■ Awards, Honors

Rockefeller Foundation grant, 1946-48; International Fantasy Award runner-up, 1957, for *The Death of Grass;* American Library Association Notable Book award, c. 1967, for *The White Mountains;* Guardian Award runner-up, 1969, and George G. Stone Center for Children's Books Recognition of Merit Award, 1977, both for the "Tripods" trilogy; Christopher Award, 1970, and Guardian Award for children's fiction and Jugendbuchpreis (Germany), both 1971, all for *The Guardians;* Parents' Choice Award, Parents' Choice Foundation, 1983, for *New Found Land.*

■ Writings

JUVENILE FICTION

The White Mountains (first book in "Tripods" trilogy; also see below), illustrated by John Raynes, Macmillan (New York City), 1967, second edition, Collier (New York City), 1988.

The City of Gold and Lead (second book in "Tripods" trilogy; also see below), Macmillan, 1967, second edition, Collier, 1988.

The Pool of Fire (third book in "Tripods" trilogy; also see below), Macmillan, 1968, second edition, Collier, 1988.

The Lotus Caves, Macmillan, 1969, second edition, Collier, 1992.

The Guardians, Macmillan, 1970, second edition, Collier, 1992.

The Prince in Waiting (first part of "Sword of the Spirits" trilogy; also see below), Macmillan, 1970, second edition, Collier, 1989.

Beyond the Burning Lands (second part of "Sword of the Spirits" trilogy; also see below), Macmillan, 1971, second edition, Collier, 1989.

The Sword of the Spirits (third part of "Sword of the Spirits" trilogy; also see below), Macmillan, 1972, second edition, Collier, 1989.

In the Beginning (adult reader), illustrated by Clyde Pearson, Longmans, Green, 1972, expanded for children as *Dom and Va*, Macmillan, 1973.

Wild Jack, Macmillan, 1974.

Empty World, Hamish Hamilton (London), 1977, Dutton (New York City), 1978.

The Tripods Trilogy (includes *The White Mountains*, *The City of Gold and Lead*, and *The Pool of Fire*), Macmillan, 1980.

The Sword of the Spirits Trilogy (includes *The Prince in Waiting*, *Beyond the Burning Lands*, and *The Sword of the Spirits*), Macmillan, 1980, as *The Prince in Waiting Trilogy*, Penguin (London), 1983.

Fireball (first book in "Fireball" trilogy), Dutton, 1981.

New Found Land (second book in "Fireball" trilogy), Dutton, 1983.

Dragon Dance (third book in "Fireball" trilogy), Dutton, 1986.

When the Tripods Came (prequel to "Tripod" trilogy), Dutton, 1988.

A Dusk of Demons, Macmillan, 1994.

FICTION FOR ADULTS

The Twenty-second Century (short stories), Grayson, 1954, Lancer, 1962.

The Year of the Comet, M. Joseph (London), 1955, published as *Planet in Peril*, Avon (New York City), 1959.

No Blade of Grass, Simon & Schuster, 1956, published as *The Death of Grass*, M. Joseph, 1956.

The Caves of Night, Eyre & Spottiswoode (London), 1958, Simon & Schuster, 1959.

A Scent of White Poppies, Simon & Schuster, 1959.

The White Voyage, Simon & Schuster, 1960, published as *The Long Voyage*, Eyre & Spottiswoode, 1960.

The Long Winter, Simon & Schuster, 1962, published as *The World in Winter*, Eyre & Spottiswoode, 1962.

Sweeney's Island, Simon & Schuster, 1964, published as *Cloud on Silver*, Hodder & Stoughton, 1964.

The Possessors, Simon & Schuster, 1965.

A Wrinkle in the Skin, Hodder & Stoughton, 1965, published as *The Ragged Edge*, Simon & Schuster, 1966.

The Little People, Simon & Schuster, 1967.

Pendulum, Simon & Schuster, 1968.

NOVELS FOR ADULTS; AS SAMUEL YOUD

The Winter Swan, Dobson (London), 1949.

Babel Itself, Cassell (London), 1951.

Brave Conquerors, Cassell, 1952.

Crown and Anchor, Cassell, 1953.

A Palace of Strangers, Cassell, 1954.

The Opportunist, Harper (New York City), 1955, published as *Holly Ash*, Cassell, 1955.

The Choice, Simon & Schuster (New York City), 1961, published as *The Burning Bird*, Longmans, Green (London), 1964.

Messages of Love, Simon & Schuster, 1961.

The Summers at Accorn, Longmans, Green, 1963.

NOVELS; UNDER PSEUDONYM HILARY FORD

Felix Walking, Simon & Schuster, 1958.

Felix Running, Eyre & Spottiswoode, 1959.

Bella on the Roof, Longmans, Green, 1965.

A Figure in Grey (juvenile), World's Work (Kingswood, England), 1973.

Sarnia, Doubleday (Garden City, NY), 1974.

Castle Malindine, Harper, 1975.

A Bride for Bedivere, Hamish Hamilton, 1976, Harper, 1977.

NOVELS; UNDER PSEUDONYM WILLIAM GODFREY

Malleson at Melbourne, Museum Press (London), 1956.

The Friendly Game, M. Joseph, 1957.

NOVELS; UNDER PSEUDONYM PETER GRAAF

Give the Devil His Due, Morrow (New York City), 1957, published as *Dust and the Curious Boy*, M. Joseph, 1957.

Daughter Fair, Washburn (New York City), 1958.

The Sapphire Conference, Washburn, 1959.

The Gull's Kiss, P. Davies (London), 1962.

UNDER PSEUDONYM PETER NICHOLS

Patchwork of Death (novel), Holt, 1965.

Piedmont and the English (nonfiction), Evelyn (London), 1967.

UNDER PSEUDONYM ANTHONY RYE

(Self-illustrated) *The Inn of the Birds* (poetry), J. Cape (London), 1947.

Giant's Arrow (novel), Gollancz, 1956, published under name Samuel Youd, Simon & Schuster, 1960.

To a Modern Hero (poetry), Gainsborough (London), 1957.

Poems from Selborne, Sidgwick & Jackson (London), 1961.

Gilbert White and His Selborne (nonfiction), Kimber (London), 1970.

OTHER

Contributor to various anthologies and to periodicals, including *Astounding Stories, Esquire, Cricket, Playboy, Ellery Queen, New Worlds, Fantasy and Science Fiction, Galaxy,* and *Encounter.*

Adaptations

No Blade of Grass was made into a film produced and directed by Cornell Wilde, c. 1970; "The Tripods Trilogy" was adapted as a television series produced by Richard Bates and broadcast by both the British Broadcasting Corporation and the Public Broadcasting Service, and was also optioned for film by Fields & Hellman Company in 1994; *The Caves of Night* has been made into a film by Wilde; *The Guardians* (a six-part serial) and *Empty World* (a ninety-minute teleplay) have been adapted for German television.

Many of Christopher's books have been published in Braille and as talking books. *The Guardians* has been translated into German.

■ Sidelights

Cloaking his true identity beneath a variety of pseudonyms, British writer Samuel Youd has been most highly acclaimed for the science fiction novels he has written for younger readers under the pen name of John Christopher. Among these are the popular "Tripods," "Sword of the Spirits," and "Fireball" trilogies. Because of the high personal standards that Youd has placed on his written work for young people—detailed character development, believable dialogue, and a foundation in significant issues of personal and social development—he has been credited with almost single-handedly raising the reputation of science fiction novels for young readers well above the "pulp" level of the genre's comic book beginnings. Calling Youd "the first important English writer of science fiction specifically for young adults," *Twentieth-Century Young Adult Writers* contributor Gwyneth Evans praised the author as "a skilled writer with a strong social conscious who uses the genre . . . to explore concerns about the direction of social and technological change, and the dangers presented by the fallibility of human nature."

In addition to his trilogies, Youd is the author of such award-winning children's novels as *The Guardians* and *No Blade of Grass*, a highly praised novel for adults that posits a world in which famine threatens to decimate life on earth after all grass is killed off by an uncontrollable virus. Although many of his books are set in the future, Youd objects to being "classified as a science fiction writer because," as he told interviewer John Gough in *Children's Literature in Education*, "I regard science fiction as having strayed from extrapolation into error: there seems to me no credible means of exploring beyond the solar system; and the solar system, of course, we now know to be barren and uninteresting." Youd's books, which he dubs "speculative" rather than "science" fiction, instead reveal an interest in history, his futuristic societies echoing ancient Greece and Rome, Medieval Europe, or Britain during the age of the legendary King Arthur. While some critics of Youd's writing express frustration over his lack of emphasis on "hard" science, Youd is quick to maintain that speculating about advanced technology is not one of his main considerations. "I am more concerned with what happens inside the individual than what happens to society as a whole," he wrote in an essay for *Something about the Author Autobiography Series* (SAAS).

Early Love of Science

Youd was born in Knowsley, Lancashire, England, a suburb of Liverpool, in April of 1922. Ten years later he moved with his family to Hampshire, where he attended the Peter Symonds School. It was here that he would develop his early love of science, first through the study of physics and later of chemistry. While poor marks in science classes—mostly because the teacher was disgusted by Youd's inscrutable scrawl—destined the budding scientist to concentrate his studies in the area of literature instead, science would remain a fascination for Youd. He fed his interest in science by voraciously reading stories in the many science fiction magazines that were published during the 1930s.

After graduating from school, sixteen-year-old Youd obtained work at a local government office, moving from there to a job in industry where he remained until enlisting in Great Britain's Army Signal Corps after the outbreak of World War II. Before the war, his writing was confined to the articles, poems, and short stories that he published in his own *The Fantast* magazine and other periodicals. "In the first winter of the war," the author recalled in *SAAS*, "I had my first short story published professionally, in *Lilliput*, and wrote part of a novel, fairly heavily derived from the fiction of Aldous Huxley which I then intensely admired."

> *"What I have learned is that writing for children is at least as exacting and concentration-demanding as writing for adults. But one can add another word: stimulating. It is the form of writing which I can now least imagine giving up."*
>
> —John Christopher

After his unit was demobilized in 1946, Youd submitted his as-yet unfinished novel to the judges for the Rockefeller Foundation's Atlantic Awards in Literature, hoping to win a grant worth £250. When the award committee requested that Youd submit a more recent example of his writing, he sent them the first chapters of what would later become his novel *The Winter Swan*. These few chapters garnered Youd the grant, which enabled him to write steadily for about a year without the need for other income.

After his grant money ran out, Youd found a steady job that would support him while he pursued a career as a writer. Drawing upon his early interest in science and technology, he began producing short stories, which he submitted to science fiction magazines like *Galaxy* and *Astounding* under the pseudonym John Christopher, thus reserving his real name for mainstream novels. These magazines, and many others, were in need of fiction to respond to a post-World War II boom in interest in science fiction. This interest, which was born of the horrors of the war, addressed many people's concerns and speculations about the future of humankind after its marriage to such deadly technology as the atomic bomb. The 1950s, which has since been judged the "Golden Age of Science Fiction," provided the prolific author a broad readership for *The Twenty-second Century*, a short story collection that centers on the adventures of interstellar businessman Max Larkin. "At this stage in his career Christopher's narrative craft is nearly mature," maintained critic John R. Pfeiffer in *Twentieth-Century Science-Fiction Writers*. Discussing the author's publications during this period, Pfeiffer added that Youd "does not experiment with style. He tells stories with pace, suspense, sanity, and clarity. Moreover, unlike that of many writers, his strength is not in the short story but in the longer narrative work." Many of the stories in *The Twenty-second Century* would prove to be the seeds for Youd's later fiction, including the novel *The Year of the Comet*.

By this point in his career, Youd had taken on the responsibilities of breadwinner in a growing family—he and his young wife would eventually have five children. Knowing that his family could no longer be supported by a job that was not only low paying but also offered no chance of advancement, Youd shackled himself to his typewriter during the evenings and weekends, devoting every free moment to his craft. In addition to science fiction he produced light comedies, detective thrillers, and several mainstream novels, "using a different pen name for each genre, regarding it as only fair that a reader should know what he might reasonably expect under a particular label," as he told *SAAS*.

Youd's first great success came with the 1956 publication of the adult science fiction novel *The Death of Grass*, which was later serialized for American audiences in the *Saturday Evening Post* as *No Blade of Grass*—because his New York publisher thought the original title "sounded like something out of a gardening catalogue." The novel would later be adapted into a motion picture by Metro-Goldwyn-Mayer. From then until the late 1960s, Youd concentrated primarily upon science fiction and mainstream novels, but never received more than tepid reviews. "This was the point at which another publisher suggested I try my hand at writing for children," Youd recalled. "What he wanted was science fiction, on which the small reputation I possessed was founded. But during the preceding years I had tired of this . . . : the past interested me more. I wondered if it might be possible to blend his requirement with my inclinations."

The Birth of the Tripods

Influenced, as he would later realize, by H. G. Wells' classic *The War of the Worlds*, Youd decided to write about a futuristic world in which human society had become as primitive as that of the calamitous Middle Ages. The cataclysm he chose around which to center what would become his "Tripods" trilogy—*The White Mountains*, *The City of Gold and Lead*, and *The Pool of Fire*, as well as the prequel *When the Tripods Came*—was a science fiction classic: an invasion from outer space. In Youd's novel, the invading space aliens take control of the human race by "capping"—controlling people's thoughts and, therefore, their actions by implanting metal caps over the scalps of all humans who have reached adolescence. To keep humans even more firmly under their control, the alien Masters impose a feudal system modeled after that of medieval Europe, wherein younger, more physically fit humans are sent to the Masters' domed cities to serve as house servants, while the rest of the human race is left to labor mindlessly in the fields surrounding the now-destroyed remnants of a once-great human culture.

In *The White Mountains*, the first novel taking place within this futuristic setting, thirteen-year-old Will Parker and friends Beanpole and Henry resolve to escape their fate and search for a community of uncapped freedom fighters rumored to be living in the White Mountains (the Swiss Alps). As the boys gain confidence, they develop a plan to free the human race from its alien conquerors. Disguising himself as a capped human slave and winning an athletic contest designed to weed out the most qualified slaves, Will enters the aliens' climate-controlled headquarters in *The City of Gold and Lead*. In this second novel, while witnessing first hand the aliens' exploitation and mistreatment

of healthy young men in this alien city, Will learns of the Masters' plans to turn the human race into an extinct species after terraforming the planet to suit their own needs. He also finds a chink in the Masters' armor. With this news he returns to the camp of the White Mountain resistance forces. The rush to prepare to do battle for the future of mankind on earth serves as the plot of *The Pool of Fire*, the final novel in the trilogy.

"[The 'Sword of the Spirits' trilogy] echoes the love/hate feelings about technology which many people have today."

—John Christopher

The "Tripod" trilogy, which was praised by a *Bulletin of the Center for Children's Books* critic as a "beautifully developed" concept with its suspense "masterfully maintained," would be one of Youd's most enduringly popular works. Adapted as a television series by the BBC and later optioned for film, it has remained in publication since its introduction in the early 1970s. In 1988 *When the Tripods Came* was published. It serves as an introduction to the "Tripods" trilogy. In the novel thirteen-year-old Lawrence Cordray and his family stumble upon the first Tripod ship during a camping trip. Witnessing the Masters' initial descent to Earth, they hasten to inform the press, which spreads the news. Then, suddenly, all information about the invading alien force ceases. Suspicious, Lawrence and his family flee to the Swiss Alps where they begin to form the underground resistance group that will later help Will and his friends suppress the alien tripod forces in the "Tripod" novels.

Youd recalled the steps involved in channeling the first volume of the series, *The White Mountains*, from manuscript to its 1967 publication. After submission to Macmillan, Youd received notice that the publisher was interested, but asked that he revise the novel's later chapters because while they liked the opening, the story fell apart after the first few chapters. "I was forced to realize . . . that this almost certainly derived from my having tackled the book with the feeling, subconsciously possibly but no less important for that, that it was 'only a juvenile,'" Youd admitted in *A Sense of Story: Essays on Contemporary Writers for Children*. "One did not need to give it such concentrated attention as one would an adult novel. Once I saw this I . . . wrote the book again, part of it a third time."

Successive Trilogies Merge Past and Future

Such extensive rewrites would not be necessary in the remaining "Tripods" segments. In Youd's later trilogies—including the "Sword of the Spirit" trilogy and the "Fireball" trilogy—the author uses similar settings that resemble the past, but also interjects elements of fantasy into his science-based fiction. While noting that Youd was "asking much of a young reader to require him to keep his excitement at a suitable temperature for another year or two" after the introduction of the first of a three-part series, a *Times Literary Supplement* reviewer added that such patience would be well rewarded by novels "richly and consistently imaginative and written with a confident panache."

Retaliation by an abused planet forces survivors of an earth-bound apocalypse to regress into a second Dark Age in the "Sword of the Spirit" trilogy, which encompasses *The Prince in Waiting*, *Beyond the Burning Lands*, and *The Sword of the Spirits*, and which Youd counts among his favorite self-penned works. First published between 1970 and 1972, the trilogy revolves around a world dramatically altered by the effects of earthquakes, volcanoes, and other natural disasters, as well as increasing levels of solar radiation that are blamed by the survivors on the unwise use of technology in the past. The few traces of pre-apocalypse technology that remain are reined in by religious dogma and social structures dating back to ancient Greece with shadows of Arthurian Britain.

The land is divided between antagonistic city-states ruled by joint councils of priests and military leaders. The high levels of radiation have caused wide-scale mutation of both humans and other life forms; society is now structured according to one's degree of "wholeness". Those born grossly mutated are destroyed, while other mutants are classified as Polymufs and are enslaved. Dwarves, who still closely resemble modern man

except for their short stature, are allowed to engage in limited commerce, while the remaining "true men" serve as the highest social class.

The saga taking place on this blighted earth begins with *The Prince in Waiting*, narrated by an upper-class teen named Luke. Suddenly finding himself in line to become the future prince of his city, Luke is sent to help unite the warring city-state factions. During his adventures, however, he learns that a body of technological knowledge is secretly held by the priests, or Seers, who are using this science to awe and frighten their subjects while they await a leader who will be wise enough to use such knowledge for good rather than evil. Luke is chosen by the Seers to be this person: the Prince in Waiting. But, impetuous, angry, and jilted in love, the teen ultimately rejects the cautious wisdom of the priests and harnesses the power of science to wage war on neighboring city-states, using conquest rather than peaceful means to stabilize society in his world.

Through the non-heroic actions of his protagonist, Youd "seems to imply that history repeats itself in cycles, and [Luke's] destructive use of technology will again eventually lead to disaster, and the rejection of all scientific knowledge," commented Evans. As Youd himself noted in *SAAS*, the "Sword of the Spirits" trilogy "echoes the love/hate feelings about technology which many people have today. And although in the trilogy it is machines in general that are anathematized, it reflects my personal view that the most sinister threat lies in advanced communications, and that diminution of the individual which they inevitably bring about."

If Ancient Civilizations Still Held Sway . . .

In the "Fireball" trilogy, which was published between 1981 and 1986, Youd uses the device of a doorway into a parallel reality to transport two cousins to an alternative history where ancient empires never fell. The Roman Empire now rules all of Europe, Aztecs have extended their domination into North America, and China is held sway by a group of warlords who master a form of magic. Brad and Simon, cousins from opposite sides of the Atlantic who are disgruntled over having to spend the summer in one another's company, discover a glowing fireball in a field near Simon's home in Surrey that proves to be a portal into this alternate world. Passing through, they find themselves trapped in a society known for its harshness. Brad becomes the slave of a wealthy Christian who treats the boy as a son, while less fortunate Simon is put into training as a gladiator before being rescued by Brad's owner. Once reunited, the teens begin to recognize many social inequities and vow to make some positive changes. Brad recalls enough of his ancient British history lessons to introduce the saddle stirrup and the long-bow to the downtrodden Christian underclass, thus enabling the peasants, under the guidance of the Bishop of Londinium, to free themselves from the tyranny imposed by the Roman emperor Julian. Unknown to the teens, the Bishop is the head of a powerful segment of zealous Christians who, upon gaining power, begin to tyrannize the peasants in a different but equally inequitable manner as the Romans did before them. Disheartened over their role in this rebellion gone awry, Simon and Brad flee to North America, accompanied by two of Simon's fellow gladiators.

In the novel *New Found Land*, Simon and Brad continue to leap from the frying pan into the fire. Escaping a tribe of hostile, coastal dwelling Algonquin Indians on a handmade raft, the travelers find themselves befriended by residents of a Viking settlement located on the island of Nantucket. However, all is not what it seems, as the boys learn from Lundiga, the daughter of the Viking chief. Informed by the young woman that the highlight of the upcoming New Year's festival will be the ritual sacrifice of their life blood to the god Odin, the cousins and their companions strike-out for the West Coast, where they cross paths with the Aztecs. Never known as a gentle people, the Aztecs have grown substantially in power compared to their stature in Simon and Brad's history books. (This is primarily due to the non-existence of the European Age of Exploration that caused Cortez and Pizarro to plot a course for their destruction.) Their meeting with Simon and Brad bodes ill for the teens, who must escape this new, bloodthirsty enemy that now controls much of the North American continent.

A trip to China in *Dragon Dance* provides an escape from the Aztecs but results in a meeting with medieval scholar Roger Bacon, who has become something of a mystic. Simon and Brad also encounter palace intrigue, revolution, and civil war in a novel that a *Publishers Weekly* reviewer called "vintage Christopher; he introduces provocative ideas and their practical consequences in the course of a lively, colorful adventure." The "Fireball" trilogy, while notable among Youd's works for being the first to include strong female characters, was, however, deemed by most other critics—as well as the author himself—to be without the intensity or depth of his former novels due to its concern with background material over the development of its two protagonists into likeable, believable characters.

The Guardians Proves an Award-Winner

In addition to his trilogies, Youd has also written several popular novels under the John Christopher pseudonym. *Wild Jack* transplants a Robin Hood character into twenty-third-century England where energy resources rather than gold must be wrestled from the hands of the privileged few and dispersed among the multitudes living in desolation on the Outlands. *A Dusk of Demons*, which Youd published in 1994, finds fourteen-year-old Ben in search of his family after a group of demons, minions of the Dark One who controls this future society in which overpopulation and overreliance on technology have all but destroyed the human race, lay waste to his home.

Youd's fifth novel for children, *The Guardians*, which won both the Christopher Award and the Guardian award in Youd's native England, is the story of a world that suffers from a socioeconomic rift resulting in two distinct classes. While one set of residents lives in squalor, with overpopulation in its violence-ridden industrial cities—called Conurbs—the other group of residents live like Edwardian aristocrats in a region called the County. Protagonist Rob flees the Conurbs for the County, where he insinuates himself into the good graces of the more privileged segment of society. All is not what it seems, however, and Rob soon discovers that this graceful world is maintained by the efforts of an elite group known as the Guardians, who censor the actions of the aristocracy and lobotomize anyone found to speak against their wishes. Given the chance to join the Guardians in their efforts to enforce sameness, Rob instead rebels and joins forces with a small group of insurrectionists bent on destroying the Guardians' control of County residents.

The Guardians was originally intended to be an adult book, but its author grew dissatisfied at the way it was shaping up. Unlike "The Sword Trilogy," I didn't feel it translated altogether happily," Youd commented during his interview with Gough. "It didn't surprise me that it was the one of my books to receive literary awards, but it does always slightly surprise me when I get letters from children praising it." Despite its author's misgivings, the novel drew praise from children's book reviewers, with Baird Searles of the *New York Times Book Review* calling the novel "sparsely written, exciting, and based on valid social trends." And a critic in the *Times Literary Supplement* agreed, noting that in *The Guardian*, Youd has created "a more likely, and a much more scaring, prospect that all the world disasters and Lords of the Galaxy dreamed up by S.F. writers of the main stream."

The Struggle to Preserve Freedom

A characteristic theme of Youd's novels for both adults and children is the importance of preserving individual freedom of thought in the face of technology-based mind control or brainwashing through other means. As John Rowe Townsend phrased it in his *A Sense of Story: Essays on Contemporary Writers for Children*, it is a choice between "painful freedom and comfortable submission to authority." In the case of the "Tripods" trilogy, for example, although humans serve the aliens, it is a benign servitude because the servants have lost all capacity for decision-making or creative thought. And the aliens in *The Guardians*—who take over the Earth with a form of surgical mind control similar to that in the "Tripods" novels—also offer their human captives a stress-free way of life. Yet Youd's protagonists—most of-

ten, young boys on the threshold of adulthood—struggle to win their freedom to make their own choices, even if it means hard work and a loss of security about the future. In discussing the issue of personal freedom, Youd explained to Gough that "freedom of thought is perhaps the greatest good, and needs to be fought for and sacrificed for. I suppose it's something of a reverse of the conventional Eden story: the apple which tempts my characters is one that will remove the knowledge of good and evil. As to free will versus determinism, . . . I have an instinctive belief in free will probably because I feel that a life excluding that belief would not be worth living."

Over the years Youd has continued to build upon his success as the author of the popular "Tripods" trilogy, and now has dozens of adult and children's books to his credit. Commenting on his work as a writer for children whose novels continue to gain him new readers, Youd stated in Townsend's *A Sense of Story* that, "What I have learned is that writing for children is at least as exacting and concentration-demanding as writing for adults. But one can add another word," continued the prolific novelist: "stimulating. It is the form of writing which I can now least imagine giving up."

■ Works Cited

Review of *The City of Gold and Lead, Bulletin of the Center for Children's Books,* January, 1968, p. 76.

Review of *Dragon Dance, Publishers Weekly,* June 27, 1986, p. 92.

Evans, Gwyneth, essay in *Twentieth-Century Young Adult Writers,* St. James Press, 1995, pp. 122-24.

Review of *The Guardians, Times Literary Supplement,* April 16, 1970, p. 417.

Pfeiffer, John R., essay in *Twentieth-Century Science-Fiction Writers,* second edition, St. James Press, 1986.

Review of *The Prince in Waiting, Times Literary Supplement,* December 11, 1970, p. 1460.

Searles, Baird, review of *The Guardians, New York Times Book Review,* September 10, 1970.

Townsend, John Rowe, *A Sense of Story: Essays on Contemporary Writers for Children,* Lippincott, 1971, pp. 48-55.

Youd, Samuel, interview with John Gough, in *Children's Literature in Education,* summer, 1984, pp. 93-102.

Youd, Samuel, essay in *Something about the Author Autobiography Series*, Volume 6, Gale, 1988, pp. 297-312.

■ For More Information See

BOOKS

Amis, Kingsley, *New Maps of Hell: A Survey of Science Fiction*, Harcourt, 1960.

Arbuthnot, May Hill, and Zena Sutherland, *Children and Books*, 4th edition, Scott, Foresman, 1972, p. 260.

Children's Literature Review, Volume 2, Gale, 1976.

Crouch, Marcus, *The Nesbit Tradition: The Children's Novel in England, 1945-1970*, Benn, 1972, pp. 51-52.

Fisher, Margery, *Who's Who in Children's Books: A Treasury of the Familiar Characters of Childhood*, Holt, 1975, pp. 306, 309.

Moskowitz, Samuel, *Seekers of Tomorrow: Masters of Modern Science Fiction*, World Publishing, 1966.

Silvey, Anita, editor, *Children's Books and Their Creators*, Houghton, 1995.

Townsend, John Rowe, *Written for Children: An Outline of English-Language Children's Literature*, Lippincott, 1974, pp. 215-16.

PERIODICALS

Booklist, June 1-15, 1994, p. 1803.

Books and Bookmen, February, 1965.

Books for Keeps, July, 1981, pp. 14-15.

Bulletin of the Center for Children's Books, December, 1967, p. 57; April, 1970, p. 1042; July, 1970, p. 173; February, 1972, p. 88; July/August, 1972, pp. 166-67; February, 1975, pp. 90-91; May, 1986, p. 163.

Chicago Tribune, July 1, 1962.

Children's Book Review, February, 1971, pp. 18-19; June, 1971, pp. 77-79; September, 1971, pp. 122-23; September, 1972, p. 113; December 1973, pp. 176-77; winter, 1974-75, p. 150.

Christian Science Monitor, November 7, 1968.

Fantastic Universe, June, 1958.

Horn Book, December, 1969, pp. 673, 675; December, 1971, p. 619; August, 1972, pp. 374-55.

Junior Bookshelf, February, 1968, p. 59; February, 1971, pp. 51-52; December, 1973, p. 402; February, 1975, p. 58.

Kirkus Reviews, September 15, 1967, p. 1143; August 1, 1968, pp. 823-24; July 1, 1969, pp. 672-73; October 15, 1970, pp. 1160-61; March 15, 1973, p. 324; August 1, 1974, pp. 803-4.

New York Times Book Review, August 13, 1967, p. 26; October 13, 1968, p. 26; April 26, 1981, pp. 60, 62.

Publishers Weekly, May 1, 1967, p. 58; September 8, 1969, p. 57.

Saturday Evening Post, April 27, 1957.

School Librarian, June, 1971, p. 155.

School Library Journal, September, 1968, p. 131; November, 1970, p. 115; April, 1981, p. 122; September, 1983, p. 131; September, 1986, p. 142; July, 1994, p. 102.

Signal, January, 1971, pp. 18-23.

Space Voyager, June/July, 1984, pp. 52-54.

Times (London), May 25, 1967.

Times Educational Supplement, March 25, 1983, p. 31.

Times Literary Supplement, November 30, 1967, p. 1160; April 16, 1970, p. 417; December 11, 1970, p. 1460; July 2, 1971, p. 767; April 28, 1972, p. 480.

Voice of Youth Advocates, December, 1981, p. 38; October 1983, p. 213; August 1988, p. 138.

Writer, June, 1966; November, 1968.*

—*Sketch by Pamela L. Shelton*

James Fenimore Cooper

■ Personal

Born September 15, 1789, in Burlington, NJ; died September 14, 1851, in Cooperstown, NY; son of William (a pioneer speculator and land developer) and Elizabeth (maiden name, Fenimore) Cooper; married Susan De Lancey, January 1, 1811; children: Elizabeth, Susan, Caroline, Anne, Maria, Fenimore, Paul. *Education:* Attended Yale College, 1803-5.

■ Career

Novelist and essayist. *Military service:* Enlisted in the United States Navy, 1808; became midshipman; resigned commission, 1811.

■ Writings

NOVELS

Precaution: A Novel, A. T. Goodrich & Co., 1820.
The Spy: A Tale of the Neutral Ground, Wiley and Halstead, 1821.

The Pioneers; or, The Sources of the Susquehanna: A Descriptive Tale, Charles Wiley, 1823.
The Pilot: A Tale of the Sea, Charles Wiley, 1824.
Lionel Lincoln; or, The Leaguer of Boston, Charles Wiley, 1825.
The Last of the Mohicans: A Narrative of 1757, Carey and Lea, 1826.
The Prairie: A Tale, Carey, Lea, and Carey, 1827.
The Red Rover: A Tale, Carey, Lea, and Carey, 1828.
The Wept of Wish-ton-Wish: A Tale, Carey, Lea, and Carey, 1829.
The Water-Witch; or, The Skimmer of the Seas: A Tale, Carey and Lea, 1830.
The Bravo: A Tale, Carey and Lea, 1831.
The Heidenmauer; or, The Benedictines: A Legend of the Rhine, Carey and Lea, 1832.
The Headsman; or, The Abayye des Vigerons; A Tale, Carey, Lea, and Blanchard, 1833.
The Monikins, Carey, Lea, and Blanchard, 1835.
Homeward Bound; or, The Chase: A Tale of the Sea, Carey, Lea, and Blanchard, 1838.
Home as Found, Lea and Blanchard, 1838.
The Pathfinder; or, The Inland Sea, Lea and Blanchard, 1840.
Mercedes of Castile, 2 volumes, Lea and Blanchard, 1840.
The Deerslayer; or, The First War-Path: A Tale, Lea and Blanchard, 1841.
The Two Admirals: A Tale, Lea and Blanchard, 1842.
The Wing-and-Wing; or, Le Feu-Follet: A Tale, Lea and Blanchard, 1842.
Wyandotte; or, The Hutted Knoll: A Tale, Lea and Blanchard, 1843.

Afloat and Ashore; or, The Adventures of Miles Wallingford, (self-published), 1844.

Afloat and Ashore, second series (later retitled *Miles Wallingford*), Burgess, Stringer, 1844.

Satanstoe; or, The Littlepage Manuscripts: A Tale of the Colony, Burgess, Stringer, 1845.

The Chainbearer; or, The Littlepage Manuscripts, Burgess, Stringer, 1845.

The Redskins; or, Indian and Injin: Being the Conclusion of the Littlepage Manuscripts, Burgess, Stringer, 1846.

The Crater; or, Vulcan's Peak: A Tale of the Pacific, Burgess, Stringer, 1847.

Jack Tier; or, The Florida Reef, Burgess, Stringer, 1848.

The Oak Openings; or, The Bee-Hunter, Burgess, Stringer, 1848.

The Sea Lions; or, The Lost Sealers, Stringer, Townsend, 1849.

The Ways of the Hour: A Tale, G. P. Putnam, 1850.

OTHER

Tales for Fifteen; or, Imagination and Heart, Charles Wiley, 1823.

Notions of the Americans: Picked up by a Travelling Bachelor, Carey, Lea, and Carey, 1828.

A Letter to His Countrymen, John Wiley, 1834.

Sketches of Switzerland, 2 volumes, Carey, Lea, and Blanchard, 1836.

Gleanings in Europe, 2 volumes, Carey, Lea, and Blanchard, 1838.

The American Democrat; or, Hints on the Social and Civic Relations of the United States of America, H. & E. Phinney, 1838.

The Chronicles of Cooperstown, H. & E. Phinney, 1838.

The History of the Navy of the United States of America, Lea and Blanchard, 1839.

Le Mouchoir: An Autobiographical Romance (also appeared as *Autobiography of a Pocket Handkerchief*), Wilson & Co., 1843.

Ned Myers; or, A Life Before the Mast, Lea and Blanchard, 1843.

The Battle of Lake Erie, H. & E. Phinney, 1843.

The Cruise of the Somers, J. Winchester, 1844.

Lives of Distinguished American Naval Officers, Carey and Heart, 1846.

Correspondence of James Fenimore Cooper, 2 volumes, Yale University Press, 1922, 1971.

New York, William Farquhar Payson, 1930.

The Lake Gun, William Farquhar Payson, 1932.

Early Critical Essays, with introduction and headnotes by James F. Beard, Scholar's Facsimiles and Reprints, 1955.

The Letters and Journals of James Fenimore Cooper, edited by James F. Beard, 6 volumes, Harvard University Press, 1960, 1964, 1968.

COLLECTED EDITIONS

Cooper's Works, illustrated by F. O. C. Darley, 32 volumes, W. A. Townsend, 1859-61.

J. Fenimore Cooper's Works, with introduction by Susan Fenimore Cooper, 32 volumes, Hurd and Houghton, 1876-84.

The Works of James Fenimore Cooper, 33 volumes, G. P. Putnam's Sons, 1895-96.

Cooper's work has been translated into the major European languages. The largest collection of his papers is in the Beinecke Rare Book Room and Manuscript Library, Yale University. The New York State Historical Association, at Cooperstown, also has many items dealing with the Cooper family.

■ Adaptations

FILMS

The Last of the Mohicans, Associated Producers, 1920, Mascot Films, 1932, United Artists, 1936, Columbia Pictures, 1947 (movie titled *Last of the Redmen*, based on *Last of the Mohicans*), Hanna-Barbera (feature-length cartoon), 1976, Lucerne Films, 1977, BBC-TV, 1980, Twentieth-Century Fox, 1992; *The Deerslayer*, Lucerne Films, 1978.

Educational filmstrips, television movies, and audio cassettes have also been made for many of Cooper's tales, including an NPR radio broadcast of *The Spy*, 1981.

■ Sidelights

James Fenimore Cooper was a pioneer of American literature. He was not only the first of his countrymen to make a living solely from the pen, but he also legitimized American themes, such as the opening of the wilderness and the costs of progress, in literature. Cooper almost single-handedly altered the conception in the minds of American readers of what made fine literature, or indeed literature in any of its guises. With his Leatherstocking Tales, which include such perennial favorites as *The Last of the Mohicans* and *The Deerslayer*, Cooper created a distinctly American

John Quidor's painting *Leatherstocking Meets the Law* shows Hiram and Jotham vanishing when Natty Bumppo draws his rifle in Cooper's 1823 novel *The Pioneers*.

idiom—not so much in speech as Mark Twain would later do—but in content. With the creation of Natty Bumppo, the protagonist of those tales, Cooper also imagined a character, at once rugged individualist and romantic nature-lover, who has become part of the national consciousness through his clones in movies and on television. In shifting the center of cultural gravity from London to the woods of New York, Cooper fostered the use of new literary material for a new country. Also, in his romances of the sea, such as *The Pilot* and *The Red Rover*, he compassed new literary waters which would shortly thereafter be navigated by Charles Anderson Dana and Herman Melville.

In his lifetime Cooper was an international star, equal in stature with Sir Walter Scott, and his books were translated into French, German, Portuguese, Italian, and Russian. However, in the century and a half since his death, Cooper's stay-ing power as a classic has been tested. No longer part of the college canon, his books are most often considered—if at all—as simply adventure stories for young boys. "Today," notes Stephen Railton in *Dictionary of Literary Biography*, "[Cooper's] popular audience has almost completely disappeared. . . . That is unfortunate: the thirty-two novels he wrote, at least the majority of them, are considerably better than that reputation."

Patrician Upbringing

Born on September 15, 1789, James Cooper was the twelfth of thirteen children born to William and Elizabeth Fenimore Cooper. Only seven of these survived childhood—four older brothers and two older sisters in addition to James (he would not begin using his mother's maiden name until he was twenty-seven). His was a privileged childhood, for his parents were of old Quaker stock, the mother's side even more prominent than William's. In fact, by marrying her, the father William not only moved up the social ladder in the tightly clustered world of the New York patrician families, but also won an heiress whose wealth helped in his speculative and land development schemes. He and a partner purchased the 40,000-acre Croghan Patent adjoining Otsego Lake, northwest of the Catskill Mountains, and developed it into farm parcels to sell to the immigrants flooding the newly founded country. When James Cooper was only fourteen months old, the family

ANTAM CLASSIC · A BANTAM CLASSIC · A BANTAM CLASSIC · A BANTAM CLASSIC · A BANTAM CL

The Last of the Mohicans by James Fenimore Cooper

With an Introduction by
A. B. Guthrie, Jr.

Cooper's best-known frontier adventure tells of the scout Hawkeye and his Mohican friends caught in the bloody French and Indian War.

moved to the settlement near Otsego Lake named in William's honor, Cooperstown.

It was here the young Cooper learned about the frontier first hand. Though the family built a fine brick mansion called Otsego Hall, and though his father was the local judge as well as representative to the U.S. Congress, the hold on civilization was tenuous in the environs of Cooperstown. Cooper grew up wild, along with his brothers, often playing and exploring in the surrounding woods. American Indians, however, were already a thing of the past by the early nineteenth century in upstate New York, and thus the Indian wars were something Cooper could only read about in books. If influenced by the immense world of nature at his doorstep, young Cooper was also equally under the spell of his dominating father. Biographers comment that William was no more honest than he needed to be in business dealings, and was a tough and fiery sort of political opponent, a leading spokesman for the Federalist Party and its fears of mob rule. Cooper would assimilate bits of pieces of each of these formative influences and take them with him into the world of adulthood.

At age eleven, Cooper was sent to boarding school in Albany, and from there, at age thirteen, he entered Yale College, a precocious and still prankish young boy. In fact, it was his prankish nature that got him expelled two years later for blowing in another boy's door with gunpowder. Back in Cooperstown, Cooper spent his time reading novels, until his father determined that he would have a naval career. To that end, Cooper was put aboard a merchant ship, the *Stirling,* for a year's voyage to England and Spain. Sea lore and nautical tall tales became part of his vocabulary thereafter, especially as a result of the several day's chase that a pirate ship gave the *Stirling* off the coast of Portugal.

In 1808, Cooper was rated a midshipman in the Navy and was stationed at Fort Ontario for a time, then to a sloop anchored in New York harbor where he worked in recruitment. With the death of his father in 1809, however, matters changed. He was overnight a very wealthy man, inheriting $50,000 as well as a share in the remaining estate of $750,000. Putting himself on furlough, he saw to the estate and found himself a wife, Susan De Lancey, whom he married on New Year's Day of 1811. Partly due to his wife's

Daniel Day-Lewis starred in the 1992 version of *The Last of the Mohicans*, Cooper's classic tragedy of a vanishing race set in the forests of upper New York state.

promptings, Cooper resigned his naval commission and launched the life of a gentleman farmer.

The Hunger Artist

For the next decade, Cooper and his steadily growing family lived mostly in Westchester County, on Angevine Farm which he built on De Lancey property. Involved in the social life of the region, Cooper also founded agricultural and Bible societies and was quartermaster and paymaster for New York's Fourth Division of Infantry, happily parading in his blue uniform and sword. As yet, there was not a hint of the writer's life that was soon to come. Slowly at first, and then more rapidly, the worth of the Cooper estate dwindled, however. Land values decreased after the War of 1812, and Cooper's brothers continually lived beyond their means and made wrong-headed investments. Things were so bad that by the time of his mother's death in 1818, Otsego Hall had to be sold to pay off debts. By 1819, all of his brothers were dead and not only their debts, but also in some cases the welfare of their offspring, had been left to Cooper to deal with. Cooper's own speculative ventures fared not much better than his brothers', but it was one such "venture" that finally struck oil.

One day in 1819 or early 1820, reading a new novel direct from England, Cooper became exasperated at its lack of artistry. According to his daughter Susan, in her "Small Family Memories," the book "must have been very trashy; after a chapter or two he threw it aside, exclaiming, 'I could write a better book than that myself.'" According to the daughter's account, the mother found this boast a bit absurd, for Cooper did not like to write so much as a letter. But Cooper took up the challenge and the result was his first novel, *Precaution*, a work set in England and reminiscent of Jane Austen's *Persuasion*, dealing with the efforts of an English family to marry off its daughters. Cooper self-published the book to little notice in America and modest sales in England. Reviewers there seemed to believe it was penned by a new British female author. Donald A. Ringe, in his critical study, *James Fenimore Cooper*, calls *Precaution* "a weak book," and one that "no one would recommend . . . to the general reader." But Ringe and others note that the book is important because it gave Cooper confidence to proceed with writing. And proceed he did, using a new model

for his next literary effort, the romances of Sir Walter Scott, to create a more adventuresome, exciting story.

The Spy appeared in 1821 and changed the course not only of Cooper's life but of American letters. A thumpingly nationalistic book, *The Spy* is based on a true account that Cooper had heard that involved the exploits of the fictional Harvey Birch, a peddler behind the lines who serves General Washington during the Revolutionary War. Birch is believed by all the rebels of Westchester Country to be a Loyalist spy and is hunted relentlessly. That he is a spy for the British is seemingly confirmed when he helps a local youth, a soldier on the English side, to escape American custody. Amid the intrigues and battle scenes, Cooper also wove a story of the love of two sisters for soldiers on opposing sides. The author threw in a dash of mystery, as well, with the visitations of a mysterious stranger—who turns out to be none other than Washington himself, visiting *his* master spy, Birch. Here for the first time was truly American fare served up to an American reading public. Using patriotic themes from the Revolutionary War and a local setting, Cooper created with *The Spy* one of the first truly American novels; with Harvey Birch he invented an almost mythic character—the independent-minded and committed American hero.

Ringe notes in his study of Cooper's works that "*The Spy* clearly illustrates Cooper's ability to generate a significant theme from the interplay of setting, characters, and action. . . . [I]t is a thrilling tale of adventure which also conveys an important theme." And best of all, as far as Cooper was concerned, the book was an instant success, establishing him overnight as an important novelist. Royalties from the book began to pour in, saving him from bankruptcy. Cooper had found his niche: Though inspired to write on a dare, he now realized he could actually make a living doing so. And make a living he most desperately had to do.

America's Favorite

Cooper moved his family to New York City, then a town of some 100,000 inhabitants, and took up the mantle of the literary man. For the next decade or so, he could do no wrong as far as the American public thought. He lived in New York

If you enjoy the works of James Fenimore Cooper, you may also want to check out the following books and films:

Conrad Richter, *The Light in the Forest*, 1953.
James Collier Lincoln, *The Bloody Country*, 1976.
Jessamyn West, *The Massacre at Fall Creek*, 1975.
Black Robe, Samuel Goldwyn, 1991.

until 1826, writing and meeting regularly for lunch with the Bread and Cheese Club, a group of writers, painters, merchants, and officers who saw themselves creating a new American cultural sensibility. He worked on his books and lost little time in turning out a third novel, *The Pioneers*, in 1823. The first of what became known as his Leatherstocking Tales, a series of five novels, *The Pioneers* is set late in the life of its protagonist, Natty Bumppo, nicknamed Leatherstocking because of his apparel. The book is, as Railton describes it in *Dictionary of Literary Biography*, a "loosely organized narrative of a year in the life of a frontier settlement."

The year is circa 1793, and the settlement is Templeton, near Otsego Lake (an obvious recreation of the Cooperstown of his own youth), founded by one Judge Marmaduke Temple. Cooper takes the reader through the seasons of such a frontier community, while also telling two major tales. One involves the romance of the Judge's daughter with a young man who turns out to be the rightful heir to much of the property the Judge has purchased; the second deals with the conflict between Judge Temple—representing progress and civilization—and Leatherstocking, the old scout and hunter, who cannot abide the "wicked and wasty ways" of civilization. Leatherstocking makes readers reassess the inevitability and desirability of the westward march of civilization as the virgin forests are levelled to make way for farm land, the deer slaughtered, and fish caught in huge nets. In the end, Leatherstocking, who feels more comfortable among animals and the dispossessed Native Americans than among European settlers, heads off into the setting sun. In his book *James Fenimore Cooper*, Robert Emmet Long comments that "*The Pioneers* is an enormous

leap forward for Cooper. In it he creates a richly authentic world and discovers his great character Natty Bumppo." Ralph Waldo Emerson called the book America's first national novel because of this important theme of the balancing of the needs of the solitary individual in nature and those of progress and civilization for the country as a whole. Cooper, early on, had found one of his most important themes: the settling of the continent and the costs of such settlement.

Cooper followed up this success with a romance of the sea, *The Pilot*, which showcased his own knowledge of nautical matters and helped to establish that genre in American letters. Less successful was *Lionel Lincoln* (1825), which was the first of a projected thirteen novel series about the Revolutionary War as told from the perspective of each of the colonies at the time. The lack of sales or critical encouragement, however, sent Cooper back to the safer ground of his Leatherstocking. Cooper eventually wrote four more books that deal with Natty Bumppo, none of them in the chronological order of the man's life. *The Last of the Mohicans*, Cooper's most widely read book, was published in 1826. Natty was a man in his thirties in that book. Then came *The Prairie* in 1827, featuring an eighty-year-old Natty. Over a decade would lapse until Cooper returned to his protagonist in *The Pathfinder* (1840) and *The Deerslayer* (1841), in which Cooper goes back to Leatherstocking's youth. None of these are viewed with the same critical approval as was the very first of the series, nor, generally, do they tackle such important themes as were dealt with in *The Pioneers*. Cooper fashioned the last four as romantic adventure tales.

With *The Last of the Mohicans*, Cooper depicts Natty—here called Hawkeye—as a scout for the British during the French and Indian War of 1757. The title of the novel refers to two other main characters—Hawkeye's Indian friend Chingachook and his son Uncas—who are Cooper's idealized 'good' Indians, the last of their tribe and representatives of the noble savage. Contrasted to them is the evil Magua and his Mingo or Iroquois brethren who represent the dark side of savagery. Magua twice captures the Munro sisters, Alice and Cora—who are on their way to be reunited with their military father at Fort William Henry—and has designs on making the latter his wife. But Hawkeye, aided by his trusted friends Chingachook and Uncas, save the ladies from this fate

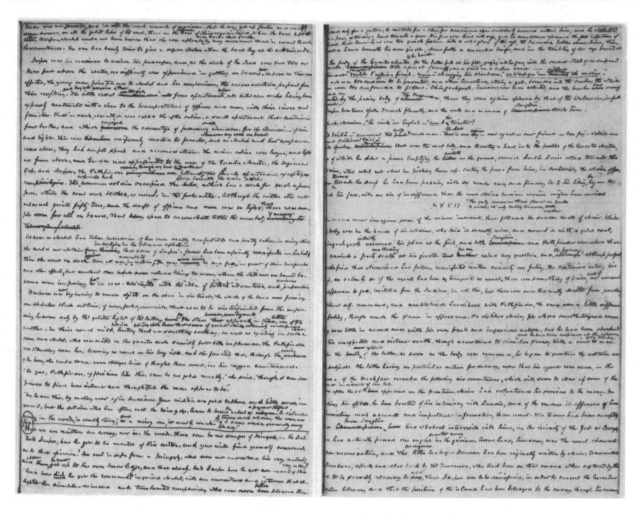

Two manuscript pages from Cooper's 1840 novel *The Pathfinder*, popular for its combination of romance and danger.

worse than death. In the midst of several chase scenes is the violent interlude of the massacre of the British at Fort William Henry by the native allies of the French. In the end, Uncas is killed trying to save Cora, who in turn is also killed, as is Magua. Hawkeye and Chingachook go off into the forest, leaving the civilized world behind.

While many reviewers and critics have noted that Cooper got his facts wrong about which tribe aided who during the French and Indian War, most do agree that he created a great yarn in the adventures of Hawkeye. As Long comments in his book-length study of the author, *The Last of the Mohicans* is "almost continually occupied by action; its movement is rapid, and it is never far removed from and sometimes plunges its charac-

ters suddenly into horror." Long views the entire novel as "an epic struggle between kingdoms of light and darkness" as represented respectively by the graceful Uncas and repulsive Magua. It is this very reliance on action, however, that has convinced some critics to question its artistry. George Dekker, for example, in his book *James Fenimore Cooper: The American Scott,* notes that "*The Last of the Mohicans*, it can be argued, is not an adult work of fiction." James Grossman, in his respected biography *James Fenimore Cooper,* comments that the novel is an example of "the 'pure' adventure story in which in an arbitrarily simplified world everything happens for the sake of the action." Other critics have shown parallels with *Paradise Lost* and *The Iliad,* while still others, such as D. H. Lawrence in his *Studies in Classic American Lit-*

erature, dwell on the theme of miscegenation or interracial marriage and intercourse as depicted in the Cora-Magua-Uncas triangle. "So Fenimore kills them all off," Lawrence writes, "and leaves the white lily [Alice] to carry on the race." Brian Morton, reviewing a reprint of the novel in the *Times Educational Supplement,* declares that in Natty Bumppo, Cooper had created "a character of genuine mythic proportions." And in the end, it is the action and characters that matter. It is the bond between Hawkeye and Chingachook that echoes from the book, for all its technical faults: "Chingachook grasped the hand that, in the warmth of feeling, the scout had stretched across the fresh earth, and in that attitude of friendship these two sturdy and intrepid woodsmen bowed their heads together, while scalding tears fell to their feet, watering the grave of Uncas like drops of falling rain."

European Interlude

Cooper took the manuscript for the next Leatherstocking Tale, *The Prairie,* along with him when he and his family moved to Europe in 1826. He projected a stay on the continent of five years; in the event, he was gone seven. And by the time he returned to his native soil, his fortunes had greatly changed. Settling first in Paris, Cooper completed *The Prairie,* his third Leatherstocking Tale, and the end of the chapter for Natty Bumppo. Having headed westward to the prairie, the old scout, now in his eighties, once again finds the civilized world overtaking him. Borrowing the plotline from *Mohicans, The Prairie* also employs the device of a kidnapped white woman and rival Indian tribes. But the real story here is in theme: the questioning of the rightness of Manifest Destiny. From the old scout's point of view, the prairie should be left pristine; in fact at the end of the book the main characters turn back and re-cross the Mississippi, while Natty is left to die facing the setting sun. The old scout is true to himself to the end: He is a tool of civilized society, perhaps, but not part of it. Most critics agree that both *The Pioneers* and *The Prairie,* in which Natty Bumppo appears in old age, are the strongest thematically of the Leatherstocking Tales. As Long writes: "The sunset imagery of Natty at the beginning and end of *The Prairie* reveals Natty himself unchanged; what changes are the implications of his life, which expand around him to reveal the issue of American destiny."

Two other romances of the sea appeared in these early years abroad: *The Red Rover* (1828), accounted one of Cooper's best sea tales, and *The Water-Witch* (1830). These helped to confirm Cooper as the father of the use of an ocean setting and sailing as proper literary subjects. Soon, however, Cooper's attentions were turning to more political and polemic matters. His friendship with the aged Marquis de Lafayette, hero of the American Revolution, inspired him to write his first nonfiction book, *Notions of the Americans,* a strong defense of American democracy intended primarily for the aristocratic-minded British reading public. Cooper also turned his interests toward European politics, producing a European trilogy of romances in the early 1830s, *The Bravo, The Heidenmauer,* and *The Headsman,* set in Italy, Germany, and Switzerland. Though Cooper's storytelling techniques were at their prime in these, the American public wanted no part of such European romances from the favorite local author. Reviews were bad, sales even worse, and Cooper began to smart at the loss of popularity.

Final Years

Returning to America in 1833, he found his literary position greatly eroded and wrote a farewell letter to his readers, *A Letter to His Countrymen,* in which he chided Americans for their lack of cultural independence and announced that he was putting his pen down. It appeared he meant only that he was quitting fiction, though, for he continued writing, publishing his *History of the Navy of the United States* as well as a treatise on politics, *The American Democrat,* and several travel books recounting his experiences in Europe. Yet his love affair with the American public continued to wane. Involved in a dispute over the rights of public use of Cooper-owned land around Otsego Lake, his own dormant fear of mob rule came to the fore, echoing his father's inherent fears of majority rule. Cooper penned two novels about the Effinghams, thinly disguised Coopers, who battle the tide of rabid democratic tendencies. The tone of these two books, *Homeward Bound* and *Home as Found,* only served to make matters worse. His readership now largely abandoned him. These works brought Cooper back to fiction, finally, but did not restore his former prestige.

When in doubt, Leatherstocking was always handy. In 1840, Cooper resurrected Natty Bumppo

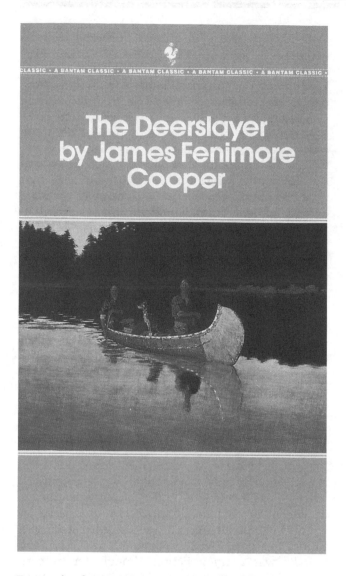

Determined to rescue a captured Indian maiden, Deerslayer and Chingachgook brave enemy tribes and merciless bounty hunters in this 1841 work.

Leatherstocking Tales remain the core of Cooper's achievement, a century and a half after publication. The humorist Mark Twain was one of the first to begin chipping away at the Cooper legend after the author's death. In his biting essay, "Fenimore Cooper's Literary Offenses," Twain punctured the balloon of Cooper's overwriting by editing a sample paragraph of Cooper's prose. Out of a paragraph of 320 words, he was able to cut 100—no mean trick for Twain who himself enormously overwrote to fill up the double-volume prescription of the day. Twain noted also the many tricks Cooper used over and over in his fiction: "Every time a Cooper person is in peril, and absolute silence is worth four dollars a minute, he is sure to step on a twig," Twain wrote. "There may be a hundred other handier things to step on, but that wouldn't satisfy Cooper. . . . In fact, the Leatherstocking series ought to have been called the Broken Twig Series." Yet Twain was only partly correct. Lawrence, in his *Studies in Classic American Literature,* states that "Fenimore Cooper has probably done more than any writer to present the Red Man to the white man," despite the artistry of the tales which describe an arc of a "crescendo of beauty, decrescendo of reality." There are still things for the modern reader to like in the Leatherstocking Tales, according to Richard Brookhiser in the *American Spectator.* "You can read Cooper as a page-turner; you can read him as a mythmaker. . . . You can even read *The Pioneers* as social observation, the ancestor of early James." Reviewing the reprint of the Leatherstocking Tales in uniform edition, a critic in *Time* magazine comments that the series "remain the most diverting westerns available without a VCR." Marie Olesen Urbanski, writing in the *Los Angeles Times Book Review,* notes that the five novels in the Leatherstocking series present "a drama in which right and wrong do exist. Cooper opens the way for the nostalgic to glimpse the Eden that awaited our forebears and to relive its dangers from a comfortable distance."

as a young man for *The Pathfinder,* and the following year penned the final installment in those tales, *The Deerslayer.* These two books relate the earliest adventures of Natty's youth, on the trail of the Mingos with his friend Chingachook. In these two, young Natty is even allowed love interests, though there is never a thought of marriage or of settling down. In both the first of the Leatherstocking Tales, *The Pioneers,* and in the last, *The Deerslayer,* the setting is Lake Otsego, and the five books, taken as a whole, "create a uniquely American mythos," according to Railton in *Dictionary of Literary Biography.* The books of the

Cooper continued to write to the very end of his life. In the early to mid-1840s, there were more nautical tales: *The Two Admirals, Wing-and-Wing,* and *Afloat and Ashore,* and another story of a frontier settlement, *Wyandotte.* Though Cooper continued to earn a living from his writing, he never again felt secure with his American audience. There is no evidence either that he felt in part responsible for such neglect. Increasingly Cooper placed himself on the side of the patricians or old money against the mob—never more so than during the Anti-Rent War of the mid-1840s when the farmers of New York, caught in near feudal conditions, refused to pay their rents. Many even tried intimidating the owners by dressing as Indians and marauding the countryside at night. Cooper was firmly on the side of the patroons, the old landowners such as the Schuylers and Van Rensselaers, so much so that he wrote a trilogy of novels, the Littlepage Manuscripts, to defend their position. The three books follow the fortunes of the Littlepage family from colonial times to the present, with the first in the series, *Satanstoe*, judged to be the best from a fictional point of view. The last two, *The Chainbearer* and *The Redskins*, grew increasingly polemical in tone, almost hysterically in defense of privilege.

As Cooper grew more alienated from society, he dreamed fictions of escaping it altogether, such as *The Crater*, about a man shipwrecked on a Pacific atoll. The 1848 novel, *Jack Tier*, is another nautical story, a realistic tale about a brutal pirate. Late in life, Cooper also converted to the Episcopal Church and wrote two novels with religious themes, *The Oak Openings* and *The Sea Lions*. His final novel, written in 1850, *The Ways of the Hour*, was yet another attempt at educating his reading public, a book that is, according to Railton, "practically all harangue." Cooper had been in failing health for the several years, suffering from a chronic deterioration of his liver. But he continued writing, planning even at the end of his life a history of New York City. He died one day before his birthday, on September 14, 1851.

Cooper's legacy is difficult to assess. For him, as with the settlers of the frontier, it was all open territory. There was no such thing as American letters when Cooper began writing, no rules to judge him by. However, by the time of his death he had established not only the validity of the use of native materials for literature, but had also supplied several of the themes that later writers would gnaw on: the cost of progress, the ethics of Manifest Destiny, the sea as metaphor. His very style of writing would influence later generations. According to Long in his *James Fenimore Cooper*, "In novels such as *Mohicans* he invested the novel with the grandeur of the epic, and thus anticipates the epic form in the novel of *Moby-Dick*." While many modern critics find his language to be overblown, his plots too fantastic, his facts hopelessly wanting, others would place him firmly in the American canon. In the opinion of critic Marius Bewley in his *The Eccentric Design*, "Cooper has been consistently underestimated. He ranks with Hawthorne, James, and Melville as one of the four greatest novelists in the nineteenth century."

■ Works Cited

Bewley, Marius, *The Eccentric Design: Form in the Classic American Novel*, Columbia University Press, 1959, p. 107.

Brookhiser, Richard, review of *The Leatherstocking Tales, American Spectator*, December, 1993, p. 22.

Cooper, James Fenimore, *The Pioneers*, Charles Wiley, 1823.

Cooper, James Fenimore, *The Last of the Mohicans*, Carey and Lea, 1826.

Cooper, Susan, "Small Family Memories," *Correspondence of James Fenimore Cooper*, edited by James Fenimore Cooper (grandson), Yale University Press, 1922, p. 79.

Dekker, George, *James Fenimore Cooper: The American Scott*, Barnes & Noble, 1967, p. 66.

Grossman, James, *James Fenimore Cooper*, Sloan, 1949, p. 43.

Lawrence, D. H., *Studies in Classic American Literature*, Thomas Seltzer, 1923, p. 55.

Review of *The Leatherstocking Tales, Time*, July 1, 1985, pp. 59-60.

Long, Robert Emmet, *James Fenimore Cooper*, Continuum, 1990, pp. 45, 54-55, 74.

Morton, Brian, review of *The Last of the Mohicans, Times Educational Supplement*, January 16, 1987.

Railton, Stephen, "James Fenimore Cooper," *Dictionary of Literary Biography*, Volume 3: *Antebellum Writers in New York and the South*, Gale, 1979, pp. 74-93.

Ringe, Donald A., *James Fenimore Cooper*, Twayne, 1988, pp. 7, 15.

Twain, Mark, "Fenimore Cooper's Literary Offenses," *North American Review*, July, 1895.

Urbanski, Marie Olesen, "The Leatherstocking Tales," *Los Angeles Times Book Review*, August 25, 1985, pp. 3, 6.

■ For More Information See

BOOKS

Boynton, Henry W. *James Fenimore Cooper*, Appleton-Century, 1931.

Clark, Robert, editor, *James Fenimore Cooper: New Critical Essays,* Vision and Barnes & Noble, 1985.

Darnell, Donald G., *James Fenimore Cooper: Novelist of Manners,* University of Delaware Press, 1993.

Dekker, George, *James Fenimore Cooper the Novelist,* Routledge & Paul, 1967.

Fields, Wayne, editor, *James Fenimore Cooper: A Collection of Critical Essays,* Prentice-Hall, 1979.

Kelly, William P., *Plotting America's Past: Fenimore Cooper and the Leatherstocking Tales,* Southern Illinois University Press, 1983.

McWilliams, John P., *The Last of the Mohicans: Civil Savagery and Savage Civility,* Twayne, 1995.

Philbrick, Thomas, *James Fenimore Cooper and the Development of American Sea Fiction,* Harvard University Press, 1961.

Railton, Stephen, *Fenimore Cooper: A Study of His Life and Imagination,* Princeton University Press, 1978.

Spiller, Robert E., *Fenimore Cooper: Critic of His Times,* Minton, Balch, 1931.

Wallace, James D., *Early Cooper and His Audience,* Columbia University Press, 1986.

Waples, Dorothy, *The Whig Myth of James Fenimore Cooper,* Yale University Press, 1957.

PERIODICALS

American Literature, Number 50, 1978, pp. 348-68.

Booklist, February 1, 1977, p. 831; October 15, 1995, p. 421.

Horn Book Guide, July, 1990, p. 83; Fall, 1993, p. 296.

Kliatt, Fall, 1986, p. 39; January, 1988, p. 29; September, 1993, p. 54; November, 1993, p. 59.

Los Angeles Times Book Review, December 6, 1992, p. 14.

Nineteenth-Century Fiction, Number 15, 1961, pp. 313-23.

North American Review, January, 1852, pp. 147-61.

Times Literary Supplement, February 12, 1988, p. 69.

Western American Literature, Fall, 1988, pp. 217-22.

Wilson Library Bulletin, April, 1993, p. 74.*

—Sketch by J. Sydney Jones

Karen Cushman

■ Personal

Born April 10, 1941, in Chicago, IL; daughter of Arthur and Loretta (Heller) Lipski; married Philip Cushman (a professor), June 9, 1969. *Education:* Stanford University, B.A. (English and Greek), 1963; United States International University, San Diego, CA, M.A. (human behavior), 1977; John Kennedy University, Orinda, CA, M.A. (Museum Studies), 1986. *Religion:* Secular humanist. *Hobbies and other interests:* Gardening, reading, medieval music.

■ Addresses

Office—5480 College Ave., Oakland, CA 94618. *Agent*—James Levine, 330 Seventh Ave., New York, NY 10001.

■ Career

John F. Kennedy University, Orinda, CA, adjunct professor in Museum Studies Department, 1986—; writer, 1990—.

■ Awards, Honors

Newbery Honor Book, American Library Association, Carl Sandburg Award for Children's Literature, Golden Kite Book Award, Bay Area Book Reviewers' Association Award for Children's Literature, Best Books citation, *School Library Journal,* Ten Best Books list, Parent's Choice Foundation, Cuffie Award, *Publishers Weekly,* all 1994, Best Books for Young Readers and Recommended Books for Reluctant Readers citations, Young Adult Library Services Association, and Pick of the Lists award, American Booksellers' Association, all 1995, and Honor List, International Board on Books for Young People, 1996, all for *Catherine, Called Birdy;* Best Books citation, School Library Journal, and Newbery Medal, American Library Association, both 1995, both for *The Midwife's Apprentice.*

■ Writings

Catherine, Called Birdy, Clarion, 1994.
The Midwife's Apprentice, Clarion, 1995.
The Ballad of Lucy Whipple, Clarion, 1996.

■ Work in Progress

Matilda Bone (working title), a young adult novel about medieval medicine.

■ Sidelights

"I'm a late bloomer," Karen Cushman told Amy Umland Love of *Publishers Weekly*. "It takes some time, but I always bloom." The Newbery Award-winning author of novels for young people was alluding to the fact that she was fifty-three when her first book was published. That book, *Catherine, Called Birdy*, which is about the adventures of a thirteen-year-old girl as she struggles to live her own life in the medieval world, won several literary awards. The experience of writing it and the success that it enjoyed spurred Cushman to write her second novel in a six-month outburst of creative energy. *The Midwife's Tale*, also set in the Middle Ages, earned its author more honors, including the prestigious 1996 Newbery Medal, one of the highest awards in fiction for young readers. Karen Cushman had come out of nowhere to become a successful author of young adult novels.

The older of two children and the only daughter in her family, Cushman was born in a suburb of Chicago, Illinois, in October 1941. From the beginning, she was an avid reader. In first grade young Karen read all of her books for the entire year the very same day that she got them. Then she cried because she knew she would have to keep those same books for the whole year. Cushman, who attended Catholic school as a girl, felt her education was "more controlled than inspired," as she told J. Sydney Jones in *Something about the Author* (*SATA*). So she looked elsewhere for creative stimulation. "Once I discovered the library, I discovered books," Cushman recalled. "Fiction was my favorite, but I would get these wild passions and read all there was on the Civil War, for instance, or on the physiology of the brain. I guess that kind of curiosity explains my later fascination with the Middle Ages."

Despite her love of books and a realization that her classmates and teachers delighted in the stories, poems, plays, and scripts (even plots for Elvis Presley movies) that she was constantly writing, it never occurred to Cushman to become a writer. "I used to hold plays with my neighborhood friends," she told *SATA*. "One time I got hold of a book on ballet, and I had my friends take a ballet class, gripping the car door handles like a ballet bar as I read to them what to do." At home, her parents were sometimes puzzled by their daughter's behavior. "I come from a work-ing-class Chicago-area family that loved me dearly but often didn't quite know what to make of me," she said in her Newbery Medal acceptance speech. "I used to imagine I was the only child ever kidnapped *from* gypsies and sold to regular people. I didn't know writing was a job, something real people did with their lives, something like being a secretary, or a salesman, or a school crossing guard, like my Grandpa."

Cushman, who was an excellent student, received her primary schooling in Chicago. Then her family moved west, settling in the Los Angeles suburb of Tarzana in 1952. There she attended high school. Being a bright, resourceful, and imaginative girl, Cushman continued to invent stories and plays for herself, and she continued to dream. She recalled to *SATA* how she would sometimes bor-

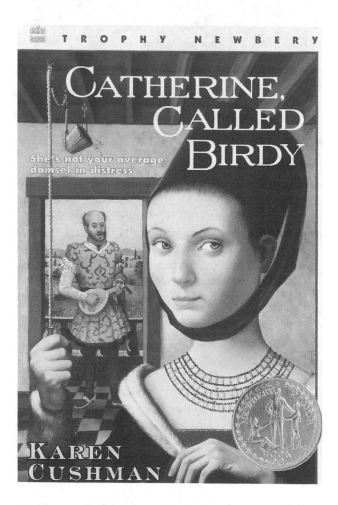

Cushman's lively teenaged heroine Catherine brings life to the year 1290 with her diary about the customs and traditions of medieval times.

row her brother's homemade scooter to take imaginary journeys. "I used to . . . imagine myself going all around the world, which is sort of what I do now, only I travel backwards in time in my writing," she said.

Upon graduating from high school, Cushman won a scholarship that enabled her to attend the university of her choice anywhere in the United States. For no particular reason, she settled on Stanford, where she enrolled as an English major. Then she began studying Greek and dreaming of a career in archeology. As yet, Cushman still had no intentions of earning a living with her pen or her imagination. "I never thought about writing as a profession or as a way to make a living," Cushman explained. "No one I knew made [a] living that way. I thought I might want to take creative writing in college, but that's as far as the ambition went." Stanford had no creative writing program; that was one reason Cushman shelved her writing. But there was another, more compelling one. "Writing was a thing I did to ventilate my feelings or to celebrate," she said. "But at Stanford there were all these semi-intellectual East Coast types who read Camus and I felt very intimidated about sharing my writing with them. To be honest, the whole experience at Stanford was very intimidating."

Museum Job Revives Writing

When Cushman graduated from Stanford in 1963 with her B.A. in Greek and English, it was not in archeology that she found a job. Instead, she became a customer service representative for Pacific Bell in Beverly Hills. That was the first of several menial jobs she held. "I quit. I found other jobs. Quit them all," Cushman wrote in an autobiographical sketch in the *Seventh Book of Junior Authors and Illustrators*. Eventually, she went to work as the assistant clerk-administrator at Hebrew Union College in Los Angeles. In the winter of 1968 she met a young rabbinical student named Philip Cushman. They fell in love and were married on June 9, 1969. When Philip completed his studies, the young couple moved to Oregon. There Philip Cushman found work at a small college and his wife "wove and made blackberry jam and [in 1973] had a daughter, Leah," Cushman recalled.

After two years of this relaxed, idyllic lifestyle, the Cushmans returned to California so both of

them could pursue graduate studies in the field of counselling and human behavior. Cushman received an M.A. degree from the United States International University in San Diego in 1977. Her husband continued on to complete a doctorate in psychology, establish a practice in Oakland, and become a professor of psychotherapy. Meanwhile, his wife's interests took her in another direction. Karen Cushman studied for a second Master's degree, this one in museum studies. In 1986 she earned her degree and joined the faculty of John F. Kennedy University in Orinda, California. As an adjunct professor, Cushman taught classes in museology and material culture, coordinated the Master's project program, and began editing a publication called *Museum Studies Journal*. "Museum studies was an interesting way for me to put together many of the things that interest me in life," Cushman told *SATA*. "I am fascinated about the concept of what artifacts say about a culture, and also which artifacts are saved and why others are not."

Her involvement in the production of the *Museum Studies Journal* put Cushman back in touch with the literary world. As a result, her own dormant interest in writing gradually began to stir once more. As Philip Cushman pointed out in a 1996 article in the *Horn Book*, despite all of the richness and variety in his wife's life, "something was still not right." That something was an unfulfilled desire to use her imagination and storyteller's gift. "Over the years I did a lot of reading of children's books to and with my daughter," Cushman told *SATA*. "When we got to young adult literature, I just stayed there while [Leah] went on to adult books. There is something about the themes of these books that appeal to me—coming of age, the acceptance of responsibility, and development of compassion. I was always coming up with great ideas for books and sharing them with my husband. And finally one day in 1989 when I told him this great idea for a book set in the medieval world, he just told me he didn't want to hear any more about it until it was down on paper." Taking her husband's comments to heart, Cushman drafted a seven-page plot synopsis. Drafting that outline proved to be the easy part. Cushman spent the next three years researching the medieval world to learn all about the daily life of a young woman growing up during that era.

Cushman learned about the craft of writing by reading young adult historical novels by writers whose work she respected, most notably Rosemary Sutcliff and Patricia MacLachlan. Cushman told Love in *Publishers Weekly* that she admired the "simple and polished prose" of these two writers. Cushman also attended meetings of the Society of Children's Book Writers and Illustrators, a strategy that paid off for her one day when she chanced to hear a speaker offer a very simple but valuable bit of advice: "Write from the heart." Embracing that idea as her credo, Cushman took the manuscript she had been working on to Sandy Boucher, a local writer who taught writing classes in Oakland. "I couldn't send it to an agent yet," Cushman told Love. "It was easier working with Sandy, then I felt I could move up."

Many people with whom Cushman talked were skeptical that she would ever find a publisher for her book; as she told Hazel Rochman in *Booklist*, "[They] said nobody wants historical fiction, children don't like diaries, the Middle Ages are dead." Cushman was determined to prove them wrong. When her manuscript was finally complete, her husband took it upon himself to find a publisher. He chanced to meet in the elevator of their building Dorothy Briley, the editor-in-chief of Clarion Publishing. Philip Cushman persuaded her to look at his wife's manuscript. "A couple of days later, [Briley] said, 'We'll take it.' So that's the story. I don't know if it's apocryphal or not," Cushman told Rochman. An editor at Clarion, Dinah Stevenson, worked with Cushman to cut forty pages from the manuscript. The result was a tighter, more compelling story that Cushman was delighted to realize was a perfect reflection of the seven-page outline that she had drafted three years earlier.

Newbery Honors

Cushman's first book, *Catherine, Called Birdy*, was published in 1994. The novel takes the form of a young English noblewoman's diary of the year between September 1290 and September 1291, when at the age of fourteen she is betrothed to an older landowner she calls Shaggy Beard. Since the narrator keeps caged birds in her room, she is known by the nickname Birdy. "The diary is filled with wry comments and presents a candid look at the customs of the times, sparing few appalling details: her mother's long, dangerous labor in giving birth; her father's drinking and consequent suffering from 'ale head'; the total lack

of privacy; the smells of the cesspool and the rushes on the floor fouled with bones and offal and filth of all kinds," reviewer Ann A. Flowers noted in *Horn Book*. The net effect was "fascinating and thought-provoking." Rebecca Barnhouse of *Voice of Youth Advocates* agreed, stating: "The novel succeeds because of the attention to detail in both the historical setting and in the development of the delightful character of Catherine, called Birdy." *School Library Journal* reviewer Bruce Anne Shook termed Catherine "a feminist far ahead of her time" and described Cushman's first book as "superb historical fiction." Some critics were less enthusiastic. Writing in the *Washington Post Book World*, Judy K. Morris said that she found the book had a "hodge podge randomness" to it that was ultimately "unsatisfying." Jane Langton of the *New York Times Book Review* felt "Catherine's wild jokes and confessions are too much like contemporary slapstick. They seem arch rather than true." Most critics did not feel the same way, however, and *Catherine, Called Birdy* won a host of literary awards, including a Newbery Honor Book citation from the American Library Association.

Cushman was so new to the literary world that she raced to a library to find out anything she could about the annual Newbery citations. What she learned is that the awards are among the most prestigious honors in the world of children's literature. Encouraged by this, Cushman immediately began work on a second novel, which grew out of the research she had done for *Catherine, Called Birdy*. Cushman told Rochman that she dashed off the first half of her next novel in a burst of creative passion, then agonized over the latter half for several months before she was finally satisfied that she had gotten it right. *The Midwife's Apprentice*, also set in the Middle Ages, recounts the adventures of an orphan girl named Alyce, who is literally rescued from a dung heap by a sharp-tempered midwife. "Alyce is every child who is parentless, homeless, and hungry, who lives on the edges of our world, who is mocked or excluded for being different," Cushman explained. By the end of this short book, Alyce has learned the invaluable lesson "that trying and failing are not the same as failing without ever trying," as reviewer Rebecca Barnhouse noted in *Voice of Youth Advocates*.

Many critics appreciated *The Midwife's Apprentice*. They praised the book for its lean yet vivid story and its period feel. "Characters are sketched

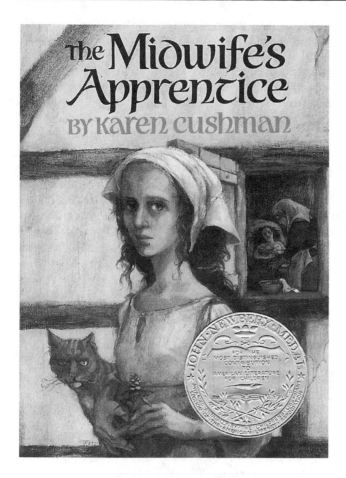

Yanked from a dung heap and apprenticed to a sharp-tongued midwife, a waif from the Middle Ages discovers what she can become.

briefly but with telling, witty detail, and the very scents and sounds of the land and people's occupations fill each page as Alyce comes of age and heart," delared Sara Miller in *School Library Journal*; she went on to describe the book as "a delightful introduction to a world seldom seen in children's literature."A *Kirkus Reviews* critic echoed the praise, describing *The Midwife's Apprentice* as "a rouser for all times." For her efforts, Cushman was named the 1995 winner of the prestigious Newbery Medal for *The Midwife's Apprentice*.

Winning the award was a tremendous boost for Cushman's literary career, but in at least one way it made the actual work of writing more difficult. "I'm still the same person who has to empty the cat box and do the dishes, and it's strange to me that people are standing in line to have me sign my book," Cushman told Sally Lodge of *Publishers Weekly*. "On the other hand, I feel pride and I

feel a certain responsibility. People are now going to seek out my books. And they will come to talks that I'm giving with pens poised above pads of paper, ready to write down what I say. It's a bit scary." After winning the Award, Cushman found that she was in demand for several months as a speaker and as the subject of media interviews. All of this cut into her writing time. Cushman felt relieved that she had already finished her third book before the Newbery Award was announced. "I probably wouldn't have gone back to writing it for a long time after that," she explained.

Cushman's third book, *The Ballad of Lucy Whipple*, represents something of a departure for her. It was another historical novel about a spirited teenager, but this book was set in a California mining town during the Gold Rush of 1849. The novel recounts the adventures of a twelve-year-old girl who is moved by her mother, a sharp-tongued widow, "like a barrel of lard" from her home in Massachusetts to the California boom town of Lucky Diggins. The girl, who is named California Morning Whipple, earns money in anticipation of a move back East by baking dried apple and vinegar pies. In the end, Lucy—as she renames herself—realizes that home is wherever she decides to make it. Cushman has said that part of the inspiration for *The Ballad of Lucy Whipple* came to her one day when she picked up a book about the Gold Rush in a bookshop and began reading the dustjacket. "It said that the gold rush was a movement of men, that fully ninety per cent of the people who came to California to search for gold were men," Cushman told Rochman. "I thought, okay, so what about the other ten per cent, who were probably women and children who didn't choose to come, who weren't marching across the country strumming 'Oh Susannah' on their banjos? They came because of the men. And some of them were happy to do it, but some were unsure, and some were downright reluctant." Later, when Cushman outlined to her husband the plot of her planned novel, he commented that the heroine sounded like Cushman, who had herself been reluctant to move west with her parents. "I think my own life is sort of playing out with somebody else's in this story," she conceded.

Beyond the Middle Ages

The Ballad of Lucy Whipple took two years to write. Ironically, Cushman found it more difficult to find

If you enjoy the works of Karen Cushman, you may also want to check out the following books and films:

Malcolm Bosse, *Captives of Time*, 1987.
Jill Paton Walsh, *A Parcel of Patterns*, 1984.
Anya Seton, *Avalon*, 1965.
Ladyhawke, 20th Century-Fox, 1985.

information about the life of a young woman in the California gold rush than about one in England during the Middle Ages. The reason is simple: apart from a set of letters written to her sister by the wife of a miner, there was very little information available. "Most of what we have on those years we know from miners' journals and letters," Cushman told Lodge in *Publishers Weekly*. "There is virtually nothing about the experiences of women and children. So I ended up extrapolating from the miners' writings—and making some things up." Reviewers liked the result. Elizabeth Devereaux of *Publishers Weekly* praised *The Ballad of Lucy Whipple* as "a coming of age story rich with historical flavor." Linda Perkins, writing in the *New York Times Book Review*, stated that Cushman "re-creates a time and place in gritty detail." Perkins added, "Meticulously researched right down to the slang of the era, including some 50 terms for liquor, Lucy's story is packed with more history than many textbooks."

Despite the critical and commercial success of her books, Cushman insists that she is still learning to write. For that reason, she especially enjoys visiting schools and bookstores, where she can meet the readers who are her primary audience. She particularly likes the energy and passion with which these young people approach their reading. "Writers and young readers feed each other in an important way. As a writer, I whisper in children's ears. And they talk back," she told Lodge. "One day when I was signing books I met a family with three girls. Their mother had read my first two novels aloud, and the youngest child began telling me the story of *The Midwife's Apprentice* as though I'd never heard it. And I began to realize that in her mind, this was not Alyce's story, but the story of the cat that appears in the novel. I realized then what a collaborative effort writing is: not only am I writing the book I think I'm

writing, but I'm also creating a story that kids will see in their own special way."

In her interview with *SATA*, Cushman explained that she has never been "plot-conscious;" she does not sit down at her computer keyboard with a particular structure in mind. Instead, she sets out to tell a good story about a person's life and about how that life changes from day to day. "I don't start a book by thinking of the listener or the reader; I just climb inside a story and write it over and over again until I know what it's about. Then I try to write as clearly and honestly as I can," Cushman said in her Newbery Medal acceptance speech. "I write for the child I was and the child I still am."

■ Works Cited

Barnhouse, Rebecca, review of *Catherine, Called Birdy, Voice of Youth Advocates*, June, 1994, p. 81.

Barnhouse, Rebecca, review of *The Midwife's Apprentice, Voice of Youth Advocates*, August, 1995, p. 155.

Cushman, Karen, "Newbery Medal Acceptance," *Horn Book*, July-August, 1996, pp. 413-19.

Cushman, Karen, *The Ballad of Lucy Whipple*, Clarion, 1996.

Cushman, Karen, autobiographical sketch in *Seventh Book of Junior Authors and Illustrators*, edited by Sally Holmes Holtze, H. W. Wilson, 1996, p. 72.

Cushman, Karen, interview with J. Sydney Jones, *Something about the Author*, Volume 89, Gale, 1997, pp. 44-47.

Cushman, Philip, "Karen Cushman," *Horn Book*, July-August, 1996, pp. 420-23.

Devereaux, Elizabeth, review of *The Ballad of Lucy Whipple, Publishers Weekly*, July 8, 1996, p. 84.

Flowers, Ann A., review of *Catherine, Called Birdy, Horn Book*, July-August, 1994.

Langton, Jane, review of *Catherine, Called Birdy, New York Times Book Review*, August 28, 1994, p. 20.

Lodge, Sally, "A Talk With Karen Cushman," *Publishers Weekly*, August 26, 1996, p. 46.

Love, Amy Umland, "Flying Starts: Seven Talents New to the Children's Book Scene Talk about Their Debuts," *Publishers Weekly*, July 4, 1994, pp. 39-40.

Review of *The Midwife's Apprentice, Kirkus Reviews*, March 15, 1995, p. 380.

Miller, Sara, review of *The Midwife's Apprentice, School Library Journal,* May, 1995, p. 118.

Morris, Judy K., review of *Catherine, Called Birdy, Washington Post Book World,* April 2, 1995, p. 11.

Perkins, Linda, review of *The Ballad of Lucy Whipple, New York Times Book Review,* February 16, 1997, p. 25.

Rochman, Hazel, "The *Booklist* Interview: Karen Cushman," *Booklist,* June 1 & 15, 1996, p. 1701.

Shook, Bruce Anne, review of *Catherine, Called Birdy, School Library Journal,* June 1994, p. 147.

■ For More Information See

PERIODICALS

Booklist, April 15, 1994, p. 1526; April 1, 1995, p. 1399.

Books for Keeps, July, 1997, p. 25.

Horn Book, July-August, 1995, pg. 465-66.

Kirkus Reviews, June 15, 1996.

New York Times, January 23, 1996.

New York Times Book Review, September 24, 1995, p. 29.

School Library Journal, December, 1995, p. 38.

Voice of Youth Advocates, August, 1995, pp. 155-56.*

—*Sketch by Ken Cuthbertson*

Emily Dickinson

■ Personal

Born December 10, 1830, in Amherst, MA; died May 15, 1886, in Amherst; daughter of Edward (a lawyer, later a Congressman, and treasurer of Amherst College), and Emily (maiden name, Norcross) Dickinson. *Education:* Graduated from Amherst Academy, 1847; attended Mount Holyoke Female Seminary, 1847-48.

■ Career

Poet; lived a secluded life in Amherst, MA, except for brief visits to Washington, DC, Philadelphia, PA, and Boston, MA; semi-invalid, 1884-86.

■ Writings

Poems, edited by Mabel Loomis Todd and T. W. Higginson, Roberts Brothers, 1890.

Poems, Second Series, edited by Todd and Higginson, Roberts Brothers, 1891.

Poems, Third Series, edited by Todd, Roberts Brothers, 1896.

The Single Hound: Poems of a Lifetime, edited by Martha Dickinson Bianchi, Little, Brown, 1914.

Further Poems of Emily Dickinson Withheld from Publication by Her Sister Lavinia, edited by Bianchi and Alfred Leete Hampson, Little, Brown, 1929.

Unpublished Poems of Emily Dickinson, edited by Bianchi and Hampson, Little, Brown, 1935.

Bolts of Melody: New Poems of Emily Dickinson, edited by Todd and Millicent Todd Bingham, Harper, 1945.

The Poems of Emily Dickinson, 3 volumes, edited by Thomas H. Johnson, Harvard University Press, 1955.

The Letters of Emily Dickinson, edited by Johnson, Harvard University Press, 1958.

The Complete Poems of Emily Dickinson, edited by Johnson, Little, Brown, 1968.

A Letter to the World: Poems for Young Readers, selected and introduced by Rumer Godden, Bodley Head, 1968.

I'm Nobody! Who Are You?: Poems of Emily Dickinson for Children, introduced by Richard B. Sewall, illustrated by Rex Schneider, Stemmer House, 1978.

A Brighter Garden (poems for young readers), illustrated by Tasha Tudor, Philomel, 1990.

New Poems of Emily Dickinson, edited by William H. Shurr, University of North Carolina Press, 1993.

The Collected Poems of Emily Dickinson, Doubleday, 1997.

Manuscripts from the Bianchi publications are housed in the Houghton Library at Harvard University and the Todd manuscripts are at the Frost Library of Amherst College. There are also other relevant materials in the Margaret Jane Pershing Collection of Emily Dickinson at Princeton University, the Galatea Collection at the Boston Public Library, the Jones Library at Amherst, and the Todd-Bingham Archive at Yale University.

■ Sidelights

"If I read a book and it makes my whole body so cold no fire ever can warm me, I know *that* is poetry. If I feel physically as if the top of my head were taken off, I know *that* is poetry. These are the only ways I know it. Is there any other way?" A rhetorical question, for Emily Dickinson, the lyric poet sometimes known as the New England mystic, knew there was no other way. She spent her life creating an opus of 1,775 poems, only ten of which were published in her lifetime. She knew what made poetry, otherwise she could never have kept writing in the face of such public indifference. Yet this question was still posed in an 1870 letter to the literary editor of the *Atlantic Monthly*, Thomas Wentworth Higginson, a man with whom Dickinson corresponded for many years about her poetry. Higginson, who professed to know exactly what made a good poem, managed to pass over 102 of Dickinson's which she sent to him over the course of their correspondence. He advised the Amherst poet to study her craft further, but never offered to publish one of the poems she sent to him.

After her death in 1886 and with the dedicated sponsorship of her sister Lavinia, Dickinson's poems started to be published. Though the critics complained initially about Dickinson's brief, deceptively simple lyrics and their—at the time—unorthodox use of language, the public made their voice known quite unanimously. The first printing of Dickinson's poems quickly sold-out and was just as quickly supplanted by further printings and further collections. The Dickinson literary mill has been working ever since, for over a hundred years, and Emily Dickinson is now considered one of the great American poets, read by adults and children alike, and translated into the major languages of the world. Critics, including Richard Sewall in his definitive two-volume biography, *The Life of Emily Dickinson*, now compares

her to Walt Whitman for her contribution to American letters, and her poetry has been interpreted by various writers as representing everything from the first bugle call of Modernism to a deconstruction of America's Puritan past. The literary critic Donald F. Connors summed up Dickinson's achievement aptly—quoting the poet in the bargain—when he noted in *College English* that, "Stopping by the landmarks of her poetry, we find ourselves uplifted by her life-poems, moved by her love poems, and taught to see more clearly by her poems on nature and immortality. Within this fourfold circle of experience we perceive the core of Emily's being, and—'This was a poet!'"

A Young Lady of Amherst

Some people are so connected with a place that it has become joined with their name. Henry David Thoreau and Walden Pond are one forever in literary history; the displaced Englishman, Raymond Chandler, had his Los Angeles. So it is for Emily Dickinson and Amherst, Massachusetts. Born December 10, 1830, she was the second of three children of Edward and Emily Dickinson. Named after her mother, young Emily grew up in the small farming town of Amherst, though her family was, as Ruth Miller noted in *Dictionary of Literary Biography*, "at the center of culture and social activity," in the town. Hers was the eighth generation of the family to live and prosper in New England since the large Puritan immigration of the seventeenth century. Amherst College had been founded by her grandfather, Samuel Fowler Dickinson; her father, a lawyer, was also treasurer for the college, a position that her older brother Austin later held as well. Edward Dickinson was a well known local figure, a moderator of the Amherst town meetings for sixteen years, an elected representative of the General Court of Massachusetts, and a one-term member of the U.S. Congress from Massachusetts' Tenth District in 1854 and 1855. Additionally, he was admitted to practice law before the Supreme Court, an honor that set him apart from other local lawyers. It is not surprising that young Emily Dickinson stood in awe of her father, who was somewhat remote, as father's of the time tended to be. He was a proselytizer for the Puritan ideals he himself had received as a child: moderation, hard work, the power of reason over passion, and the virtue of self-denial. Dickinson learned her lessons well:

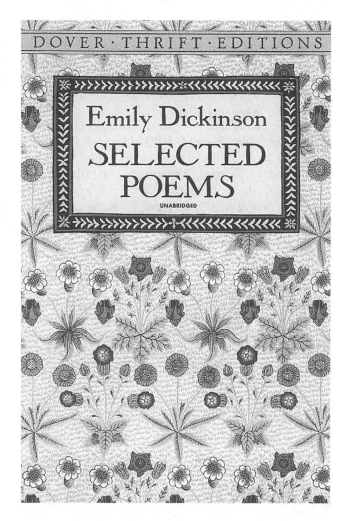

DOVER · THRIFT · EDITIONS

Emily Dickinson
SELECTED POEMS

UNABRIDGED

A selection of over one hundred authoritative versions of her best-loved poems from "I'm Nobody, who are you?" to "The Snake."

"Flowers are so enticing that I fear they are sins—like gambling and apostasy," she once wrote in a letter quoted in Millicent Todd Bingham's *Emily Dickinson's Home*. By the time she was a teenager, Dickinson realized that her father had been the most important influence in her formative years, while her mother was a simpler person, dedicated to the home and family. Like her mother, Dickinson grew up assuming domestic duties as her responsibility, but she also demonstrated an early love of poetry. She copied out poems she read in the newspapers and from collections in her father's library, often attempting to improve on the original.

In 1841 she entered Amherst Academy where she studied French, Latin, history, geology, botany, and philosophy. Illness kept her from regular attendance, though she did graduate in 1847. Though concerned with poetry at an early age, Dickinson was not merely a bookish adolescent, as can be see from the following extract from a letter quoted in *Portrait of Emily Dickinson* by David Higgins: "I am growing handsome very fast indeed!" she wrote. "I expect to be the belle of Amherst when I reach my 17th year. I don't doubt that I shall have perfect crowds of admirers at that age. Then how I shall delight to make them await my bidding, and with what delight shall I witness their suspense while I make my final decision." By all accounts, Dickinson had what could be typified as a normal childhood, with children from the faculty and local profession as friends. She was bright and witty and went to parties like all the other girls. The figure of the reclusive Dickinson was a product of the woman of thirty-something.

For a brief spell after graduating from the academy she was absent from her beloved Amherst while she attended Mount Holyoke Female Seminary in South Hadley, Massachusetts. Though initially homesick, she soon adapted to the new environment and made many new friends among the other 300 girls attending the school. However, Dickinson left the seminary after only one year. Never really healthy, Dickinson was often sick during this year and missed her family. However the greater cause for her departure was that the girls were asked to join the church, and Dickinson wanted no part of that. Reared in a community heavily influenced by Calvinism where such enjoyments as card playing, dancing, and novel reading were frowned on, Dickinson rejected such strictures and was not going to embrace them now that she was approaching adulthood.

Returning to Amherst and the family home called "Homestead," Dickinson settled into the role of oldest daughter and helper to her mother, a role she continued for the rest of her life. Her younger sister, Lavinia, stayed on at home also, a much more practical and down-to-earth sort of young woman as compared to her sister. Like Emily Dickinson, Lavinia never married. Dickinson's brother, Austin, married the daughter of a local tavern keeper and a friend of Emily's, but when the couple proposed to set up life in Chicago, Edward Dickinson intervened, building them a house next door to the family home and making his son partner in his law firm. It appears that Austin's marriage went bad very early on, but his bride, Susan Gilbert, became something of a re-nowned hostess, inviting into her home luminaries such as Emerson and the founder of *Scribner's Magazine*, Dr. Josiah Holland, as well as other editors and legal men. Emily took part in the social life of the vital small community, but also became nursemaid to her mother who was often unwell. She struck-up friendships with students at the college and young instructors, one being the principal of Amherst Academy, Leonard Humphrey, who encouraged her poetry and to whom, in 1850, she wrote a forty-line rhyme as a valentine, a custom much practiced at the time. This led to her first publication, in the Amherst col-

lege magazine, *The Independent*. Another such friendship was made with a law student working as a clerk in her father's law office. Benjamin Franklin Newton apparently encouraged her to go forward with her poetry, sending her the poems of Ralph Waldo Emerson. In 1852, he submitted a poem in the form of a mock valentine she had given him, "Sic Transit," to the *Springfield Republican*, her first publication in that paper. In a letter quoted in Higgins, Dickinson remembered the young law student: "Mr. Newton became to me a gentle, yet grave Preceptor, teaching me what to read, what authors to admire, what was most grand and beautiful in nature, and that sublimer lesson, a faith in things unseen, and in a life again, nobler, and much more blessed—" Newton, like Humphrey, died young, the former in 1850, the latter in 1853, "which enables us to come close to an early dating of the budding career," according to Miller in *Dictionary of Literary Biography*. These two young men were her "masters" as Dickinson referred to them in later letters and poems.

The Budding Poet

Dickinson began writing in earnest in the 1850s, inspired initially by the works of Ralph Waldo Emerson as well as by another Emily, one of the Bronte sisters. Though her formal education was somewhat limited, Dickinson was well versed in models for her writing. She knew the Bible and Shakespeare, and had read Greek and Roman classics in translation. She was also familiar with the other leading American and English authors of the time: Thoreau, Hawthorne, the Brontes and the Brownings, Keats, Ruskin, Tennyson, and George Eliot, whom she much admired. Early publications perhaps spurred her on, but she was that uncommon type—a writer's writer. Public acclaim was not the motivating force to her output; that came from some deeper, inner need. Her life was very uneventful in a worldly way. There were brief visits to Boston, Washington D.C., and Philadelphia in the early part of the decade, and there has been speculation about an unhappy love affair, with any of several men and even one woman named as the unresponsive recipient of Dickinson's love. While visiting her father serving in Congress in 1855, Dickinson and her sister stopped off in Philadelphia where she heard the preaching of the well known clergyman, the Reverend Charles Wadsworth. There was a romantic

SELECTED POEMS OF

EMILY *Dickinson*

SEARING VISIONS OF LIFE, PASSION, DEATH—AND BEYOND.

The Amherst recluse, who only saw ten of her nearly two thousand poems published in her lifetime, revolutionized American poetry.

quality to this figure: an eloquence tempered by a brooding nature. He and Dickinson exchanged letters, mostly of a spiritual nature. Wadsworth was married and a father; Dickinson's letters to him call him "Master" and herself "Daisy." Biographical speculation lists Wadsworth as a possible focus for her love in these years.

At her sister-in-law's house, Dickinson also came into contact with Samuel Bowles, editor of the *Springfield Republican* who published her 1852 poem. Dickinson made it a practice to send along a poem with her letters to friends. Bowles was the recipient of at least fifty-one such gifts, and apparently she was hoping that he would publish more of her work in his newspaper. Bowles is another candidate for the role of "Master," for the recipient of the sentiments in various lines of her poems of the time: "'Tis so much joy! 'Tis so much joy," and "Dare you see a Soul in the White Heat?" Bowles, however, had very different tastes in poetry than Dickinson. He, as most other editors and publishers, appreciated strong rhymes, regular meter, safe and known illusions. Dickinson presented none of this. In fact she was too original for her time.

But Dickinson kept writing. By 1858 she had begun gathering her poems together in packets which she called "fascicles," bound in string. Fifty poems were written in 1858; 100 the next year; sixty-five in 1860; eighty in 1861; and an astounding 366 in 1862. She also continued indirectly submitting her poems to Bowles who, in a 1860 article, derided such poetry as unhealthy and the product of lonely women. Though no names were mentioned, Dickinson took it to heart, and it was about this time that she began her withdrawal from the world. Also at about this same time Wadsworth informed her that he would be moving to the West and thus completely out of her orbit. Whatever the cause, it is generally assumed that Dickinson suffered an emotional trauma at this time and rejected the temporal world for a more spiritual plane. Her poetry reflects this frustration and rejection of worldly love and the acceptance of a new love in Christ and in a sort of celestial harmony. Dickinson's removal from the world was a process that slowly confined her life to her daily household chores and her nightly work on poetry—continually revising and refining poems which she knew would never be read by others. She took to wearing only white; indulged herself with long, solitary walks in the country-side around Amherst. In short, she became something of an eccentric from the point of view of her neighbors.

Lighting the Lamps

Dickinson wrote in poem numbered 883—for she gave no titles to her works, simply gathered them together in her fascicles—that "The Poets light but Lamps— / Themselves—go out— / The Wicks they Stimulate— / If vital Light / Inhere as do the Suns— / Each Age a Lens / Disseminating their / Circumference—" She would spend the rest of her days engaged in this occupation of lamplighting for an indifferent public. Her emotional crisis is thought to have been the inspiration for her awesome output of 1862. That year also she began her communication with Higginson of the *Atlantic Monthly*, encouraged by an article he had written in advise to a prospective poet. Higginson's ultimate rejection of her poetry, however, only served to drive Dickinson farther into her private world. He visited her once, in 1870, an event which he was later to celebrate in print—after Dickinson's death and her discovery by the reading public.

But Dickinson's poetry of the 1860s and beyond leave the old world of poetic form far behind. Suddenly she was experimenting with both language and form. Outwardly the poems maintain the form of the quatrain with generally three iambic feet, a form inspired by the English hymn writer Isaac Watts. Additionally, many of her poems borrow from the rhythms of nursery rhymes. Language and imagery was heavily inspired by the King James version of the Bible as well as by Shakespeare, but increasingly Dickinson was creating her own unique blend of vernacular and poetic language to express her own unique message. She began employing slant or off-rhymes, as well as slant rhythms, which were called deformities by Higginson, but that are now recognized to elicit a power to shock the reader into recognition, as in the lines: "The heart asks pleasure first; / And then, excuse from pain; / And then, those little anodynes / That deafen suffering." As Miller noted in *Dictionary of Literary Biography*, "Conventional rhyme schemes or familiar stanza patterns could not serve poems that were documents of revelation." Dickinson also pared her language down to essentials—creating neologisms such as *gianture* and *diminuet* in the process. Her striving for conciseness often led to what some critics termed ungrammatical writing, as in the lines: "The grass so little has to do / I wish I were a hay." Her use of dashes for pause and capitalization for emphasis were also personal signatures.

The years of the Civil War coincide with Dickinson's greatest output—some 800 poems. The war, however, did not provide inspiration for the poems; that came from inside the poet. After the war, her production of poetry began to trail-off, though her letter writing continued. After the late 1860s, Dickinson never again left the confines of the family's property. The death of Dickinson's father in 1874 was a severe shock to her, and from that time on she never left her house in Amherst. The following year her mother had a stroke, becoming paralyzed, and Dickinson began taking care of her. Her routine was constant: household tasks during the days when she might scribble out some ideas or lines, and then at night her writing and collection of fascicles. The routine was broken somewhat by her relationship with Judge Otis Lord, a man eighteen years her senior, who had been a friend of her father's. This relationship with Lord was perhaps the closest thing Dickinson had to a satisfying love. Dickinson's final years were filled with the death of loved ones: her mother died in 1882, a favorite nephew in 1883, and Lord in 1884. Dickinson suffered an emotional collapse from which she never recovered. In 1886 she was diagnosed as suffering from the kidney disorder known as Bright's disease, and died from it on May 15, 1886.

Publication of the Poems

The ten poems published during Dickinson's lifetime were done so anonymously. After her death, her sister Lavinia, discovered the fascicles containing some 1,800 poems in the top drawer of Emily's dresser, and resolved to see them published. She enlisted the aid of a local woman, Mable Loomis Todd, who had for many years carried on an affair with Austin Dickinson, and was therefore almost part of the family. These two women sought the help of Higginson, who, though he published none of the poems during Dickinson's lifetime, was now helpful in preparing a first volume of *Poems* for publication. His helpfulness, however, extended to 'correcting' some of the originals, re-wording what he felt to be

---

If you enjoy the works of Emily Dickinson, you may also want to check out the following:

The poems of Amy Lowell, including her most famous work, "Patterns."
The poems of Walt Whitman, including *Leaves of Grass.*

---

awkward passages or grammatical slips. Such corrections were later eliminated and the original texts restored. Higginson also helped to secure a publisher for the first volume, though the publisher was so skeptical of the sales potential that he wanted the family to underwrite the cost of publication. But such fears were completely unfounded: *Poems* had to be reprinted twice within two months of publication in 1890, and eventually went through sixteen editions in the next eight years. So popular were the poems, that Higginson and Todd quickly prepared a second volume, again revising what they considered to be rough passages and giving titles to the originally untitled works. The fascicles were completely taken apart and the poems published by subject matter and theme: love, death, nature, and friendship. This second volume, *Poems, Second Series,* again proved popular, and went through five editions by 1893.

In a few short years, Dickinson became, posthumously, a poet of renown. However, the collaborative efforts of Todd and Lavinia soon foundered. Dickinson's sister allied with her sister-in-law, who must have taken umbrage at the power Mrs. Todd wielded not only with her husband—recently deceased—but with the Dickinson name. Lavinia brought suit against Todd to prevent the exchange of a piece of property willed to her by Austin as partial payment for her work on the poems. Scandal ensued, and Mrs. Todd quietly kept the hundreds of manuscript poems still in her possession. Thereafter, Susan Dickinson and her daughter prepared what they believed to be the only remaining poems for publication. Happily, some of these included poems formerly edited by Higginson and Todd and thus the reading public finally was permitted to read Dickinson's unadulterated versions of the poems. By the 1930s what was thought to be a complete edition was published, however, in 1945 the poems Todd had kept, a further 668 works, were added and published in *Bolts of Melody: New Poems of Emily Dickinson* by Todd's daughter, Millicent Todd Bingham. Eventually a definitive edition of all the known poems was published, edited by Thomas H. Johnson, restoring the original manuscript version of the texts, replacing titles with numbers determined by a meticulous reconstruction of Dickinson's fascicles and a handwriting analysis to determine dates of each poem. Letters and diaries were also released, allowing for a closer examination of the poet's life.

The Critical Heritage

Dickinson takes as subject matter for her poems all the standard themes: love, death, and nature. Like Thoreau, she pared down her own life so as to live a creative, inner life. And the materials of her poems are also quite simple and easy to hand: robins, bees, household items, and even domestic chores. But her lyric poems use such common places as metaphors for faith, pain, love, eternity, and the fleeting nature of success. As Michael Myers noted in *Thinking and Writing about Literature*, Dickinson's method is to "reveal the inadequacy of declarative statements by evoking qualifications and questions with images that complicate firm assertions and affirmations." Dickinson herself confirms such a judgment in the lines: "Tell all the truth but tell it slant— / Success in Circuit lies."

The first publication of Dickinson's poems brought not only rapid sales, but fulsome praise. Not incidentally, some of this praise came from the editors themselves, including Higginson, but another early champion was Ella Gilbert Ives who wrote in the *Boston Evening Transcript* about Dickinson's "power of condensation, the rhythmic hammer of her thoughts" being "so phenomenal that it calls for a new system of weights and measures. . . . Many can lull, but few can awake." Other poets also praised Dickinson, including Amy Lowell who felt she was a spiritual sister to her own Imagist poetry. However, some critics looked on Dickinson as perhaps original, but lacking in real poetic technique and depth. Harold Munro, for example, in a 1925 essay in *The Criterion*, noted what he termed Dickinson's "large splendid awkwardness" and questioned exactly how candid she was in her poems. Others, like the critic R. P. Blackmur, originally writing in the *Southern Review*, felt that Dickinson's successes were "accidental,"

that "two-thirds" of her poems were merely exercises, and that she did not have the proper technique to turn such exercises into masterpieces.

The balance of critical opinion, though, is on the side of greatness. As Myers noted in *Thinking and Writing about Literature*, "Dickinson's poetry is challenging because it is radical and original in its rejection of most traditional nineteenth-century themes and techniques. Her poems require active engagement from the reader, because she seems to leave out so much with her elliptical style and remarkable contracting metaphors." On her lasting importance, Paul J. Ferlazzo concluded his study of the poet, *Emily Dickinson*, by noting that her "most important legacy" was the realization "that the human spirit may be rejuvenated, amended, and healed by the perception and application of truth and beauty." Elizabeth Jennings, an English poet and critic, noted in *American Poetry*, that Dickinson's real strength depended on "personal honesty, on the faithful re-creation of a unique experience. . . . It is this power which places her among the great American poets." David T. Porter, in his *The Art of Emily Dickinson's Early Poetry*, pointed out that the distinctive qualities of her art lay in "its bold disregard of conventional shapeliness, the surprise of its novel verbal strategies, its seizure of the significant image, its disconcerting integrity in psychological disclosures, its firm control of powerful emotion." The American novelist and critic, Joyce Carol Oates, perhaps summed up Dickinson's achievement the best when she wrote in *(Woman) Writer: Occasions and Opportunities*, that "No one who has ever read even a few of Dickinson's extraordinary poems can fail to sense the heroic nature of this poet's quest . . . a romance of epic proportions." Oates concluded her passage on Dickinson by noting that the reader takes more than merely artistic method away from a reading of Dickinson. One absorbs more, Oates, wrote: "a quality of personality and vision unlike any other . . . an American artist of words as inexhaustible as Shakespeare."

■ Works Cited

Bingham, Millicent Todd, *Emily Dickinson's Home*, Harper, 1955.

Blackmur, R. P., "Emily Dickinson: Notes on Prejudice and Fact," *Language as Gesture: Essays in Poetry*, Harcourt Brace Jovanovich, 1952.

Connors, Donald F., "The Significance of Emily Dickinson," *College English,* April, 1942, pp. 624-33.

Dickinson, Emily, *The Poems of Emily Dickinson,* edited by Thomas H. Johnson, Harvard University Press, 1955.

Ferlazzo, Paul J., *Emily Dickinson,* Twayne, 1976, p. 151.

Higgins, David, *Portrait of Emily Dickinson,* Rutgers University Press, 1967.

Ives, Ella Gilbert, "Emily Dickinson: Her Poetry, Prose, and Personality," *The Recognition of Emily Dickinson: Selected Criticism since 1890,* edited by Caesar R. Blake and Carlton F. Wells, University of Michigan Press, 1964, pp. 71-78.

Jennings, Elizabeth, "Ideas and Expression in Emily Dickinson, Marianne Moore and Ezra Pound," *American Poetry,* edited by Irvin Ehrenpreis, Edward Arnold Ltd., 1965, pp. 97-113.

Johnson, Thomas H., *Emily Dickinson, An Interpretive Biography,* Belknap Press, 1955.

Miller, Ruth, "Emily Dickinson," *Dictionary of Literary Biography,* Volume 1: *The American Renaissance in New England,* edited by Joel Myerson, Gale, 1978, pp. 34-45.

Munro, Harold, "Emily Dickinson—Overrated," *The Recognition of Emily Dickinson: Selected Criticism since 1890,* edited by Blake and Wells, University of Michigan Press, 1964, pp. 121-22.

Myers, Michael, *Thinking and Writing about Literature,* St. Martin's Press, 1995, pp. 138-44.

Oates, Joyce Carol, "Soul at the White Heat: The Romance of Emily Dickinson's Poetry," *(Woman) Writer: Occasions and Opportunities,* E. P. Dutton, 1988, pp. 163-89.

Porter, David T., *The Art of Emily Dickinson's Early Poetry,* Harvard University Press, 1966, p. 206.

Sewall, Richard B., *The Life of Emily Dickinson,* Farrar, Straus and Giroux, 1974.

■ For More Information See

BOOKS

Anderson, Charles, *Emily Dickinson's Poetry: Stairway of Surprise,* Holt, Rinehart & Winston, 1960.

Bloom, Harold, editor, *Emily Dickinson* (critical essays), Chelsea House, 1985.

Gilbert, Sandra M., and Susan Gubar, *Madwoman in the Attic,* Yale University Press, 1979.

Juhasz, Suzanne, editor, *Feminist Critics Read Emily Dickinson,* University of Indiana Press, 1983.

Weisbuch, Robert, *Emily Dickinson's Poetry,* University of Chicago Press, 1975.

Wolff, Cynthia Griffin, *Emily Dickinson* (biography), Knopf, 1986.

PERIODICALS

Bulletin of the Center for Children's Books, February, 1981, p. 109.

Choice, October, 1986, p. 304; April, 1994, p. 1291.

Horn Book, February, 1981, p. 88.

New York Times Book Review, December 30, 1990, p. 19.

Publishers Weekly, May 16, 1986, p. 75; August 9, 1993, p. 471.

School Library Journal, October, 1990, p. 108; May, 1994, p. 144; February, 1995, p. 104.

Sewanee Review, July-September, 1960, pp. 438-49.

Times Literary Supplement, December 2, 1994, p. 8.

Washington Post Book World, December 4, 1994, p. 19.*

—Sketch by J. Sydney Jones

Walt Disney

■ Personal

Full name, Walter Elias Disney; born December 5, 1901, in Chicago, IL; died December 15, 1966, in Burbank, CA; son of Elias (a building contractor and later a farmer) and Flora (a school teacher; maiden name, Call); married Lillian Bounds (one of his first employees), 1925; children: Diane Marie, Sharon Mae. *Education:* Attended Chicago Academy of Fine Arts, 1917, and Kansas City Art Institute, 1919. *Politics:* Republican. *Religion:* Protestant.

■ Career

Before starting his own cartoon studio, Disney was employed as a mail sorter, factory worker, newspaper deliverer, cartoonist, and commercial artist. His early film projects include "Newman Laugh-O-Grams," 1920-22; "Alice in Cartoonland" series, 1923-1926; "Oswald the Rabbit" cartoons, 1926-1928. Walt Disney Productions (parent company of Walt Disney Music Co., Wonderland Music Co., Buena Vista Distributors, Buena Vista International, MAPO Inc., Walt Disney Travel Co., Walt Disney Educational Media Co., and Walt Disney World), Burbank, CA, president and chairman of the board, 1929-1960, director, 1929-1945, executive producer, 1960-66; Walter Elias Disney (WED) Enterprises (family entertainment and recreational company), founder and owner, 1952-1965, creator (through his company) of the amusement park Disneyland, which opened in Anaheim, CA, 1955, and Disney World, which opened in Orlando, FL, 1971. Disney founded the California Institute of the Arts through the amalgamation of the Los Angeles Conservatory of Music and Chouinard Art Institute in 1961 in Valencia, CA.

Wartime Service: Served in the Red Cross Ambulance Corps as an ambulance driver in France during World War I. Helped in the wartime effort in World War II by involving more than 90% of the facilities of Walt Disney Studios in the production of government-related films, including Armed Forces training films, propaganda films (including "der Fuhrer's Face," which won an Academy Award), the 1943 feature film "Victory Through Air Power," and a number of educational films that were distributed by the U.S. State Department. *Member:* American Society of the French Legion of Honor, Order de Molay, Variety Clubs International, Riviera Club of Santa Monica, Writers and Athletic Clubs of Hollywood; honorary lifetime member of the American Forestry Association, American Guild of Variety Artists, American Institute of Cinematography, Art Workers

Guild of London, Association of Cinematographers of Argentina, California State Park Rangers Association, Izaak Walton League of America, National Association of Children of American Colonists, National Congress of Parents and Teachers, Screen Directors Guild, Society of Motion Picture and Television Engineers, Southern California Academy of Sciences, Sierra Club.

■ Awards, Honors

Over his lifetime, Walt Disney won over 950 awards and citations. He won forty-eight Academy Awards (the first for "Flowers and Trees," the first Technicolor animated film, which he produced in 1932) and seven Emmy Awards. Among the personal and professional awards bestowed on Disney were the Presidential Medal of Freedom, the Irving G. Thalberg Memorial Awards, Legion of Honor from France, Most Noble Order of the Crown of Thailand, National Order of the Southern Cross for Brazil, Order of the Aztec Eagle from the Mexican Ministry of Foreign Affairs, Cross of Merit from the Federal Republic of Germany, Cecil B. DeMille Award, Outstanding Achievement Award from the Freedoms Foundation, and Ambassador of Freedom Award from the Freedoms Foundation. Disney also received honorary degrees from Harvard University, Yale University, Chouinard Art Institute, University of Southern California, and University of California at Los Angeles. The U.S. Post Office also issued a commemorative stamp in his honor.

■ Credits

FILMS AS DIRECTOR, ANIMATOR, AND PRODUCER

"Newman Laugh-O-Grams" series, 1920.
Cinderella; The Four Musicians of Bremen; Goldie Locks and the Three Bears; Jack and the Beanstalk; Little Red Riding Hood; and *Puss in Boots,* all 1922.
Alice's Wonderland; Tommy Tucker's Tooth; and *Martha,* all 1923.

"ALICE IN CARTOONLAND" SERIES

Alice and the Dog Catcher; Alice and the Three Bears; Alice Cans the Cannibals; Alice Gets in Dutch; Alice Hunting in Africa; Alice's Day at Sea; Alice's Fishy Story; Alice's Spooky Adventure; Alice's Wild West Show; Alice the Peacemaker; Alice the Piper; and *Alice the Toreador,* all 1924.
Alice Chops the Suey; Alice Gets Stung; Alice in the Jungle; Alice Loses Out; Alice on the Farm; Alice Picks the Champ; Alice Plays Cupid; Alice Rattled by Rats; Alice's Balloon Race; Alice's Egg Plant; Alice's Little Parade; Alice's Mysterious Mystery; Alice Solves the Puzzle; Alice's Ornery Orphan; Alice Stage Struck; Alice's Tin Pony; Alice the Jail Bird; and *Alice Wins the Derby,* all 1925.
Alice Charms the Fish; Alice's Monkey Business; Alice in the Wooly West; Alice the Fire Fighter; Alice Cuts the Ice; Alice Helps the Romance; Alice's Spanish Guitar; Alice's Brown Derby, and *Clara Cleans Her Teeth,* all 1926.
Alice the Golf Bag; Alice Foils the Pirates; Alice at the Carnival; Alice's Rodeo (Alice at the Rodeo); Alice the Collegiate; Alice in the Alps; Alice's Auto Race; Alice's Circus Daze; Alice's Knaughty Knight; Alice's Three Bad Eggs; Alice's Picnic; Alice's Channel Swim; Alice in the Klondike; Alice's Medicine Show; Alice the Whaler; Alice the Beach Nut; and *Alice in the Big League,* all 1927.

"OSWALD THE LUCKY RABBIT" SERIES

Trolley Troubles; Oh, Teacher; The Ocean Hop; All Wet; The Mechanical Cow; The Banker's Daughter; Great Guns; Rickety Gin; Empty Socks; Harem Scarem; and *Neck 'n Neck,* all 1927.
The Ol' Swimmin' 'ole; Africa before Dark; Rival Romeos; Bright Lights; Sagebrush Sadie; Ozzie of the Mounted; Ride 'em Plow Boy!; Hungry Hoboes; Oh, What a Knight; Sky Scrappers; Poor Papa; The Fox Chase; Tall Timber; Sleigh Bells; and *Hot Dog,* all 1928.

FILMS AS HEAD OF WALT DISNEY PRODUCTIONS; CO-DIRECTED WITH UB IWERKS

"MICKEY MOUSE" SERIES

Steamboat Willie (first synchronized sound cartoon; voice of Mickey Mouse provided by Walt Disney), 1928.
Plane Crazy (made as silent, 1928, but released with synchronized sound); *The Gallopin' Gaucho* (made as silent, 1928, but released with synchronized sound); *The Barn Dance; The Opry House; When the Cat's Away; The Barnyard Battle; The Plow Boy; The Karnival Kid; Mickey's Choo Choo; The Jazz Fool; Jungle Rhythm;* and *The Haunted House,* all 1929.

The Barnyard Concert (sole director); *Just Mickey (Fiddling Around)* (sole director); and *The Cactus Kid* (sole director), all 1930.

"SILLY SYMPHONIES" SERIES

The Skeleton Dance; El Terrible Toreador; and *The Merry Dwarfs* (sole director), all 1929.
Night (sole director), 1930.
The Golden Touch (sole director), 1935.

ANIMATED FEATURE FILMS AS HEAD OF WALT DISNEY PRODUCTIONS

Snow White and the Seven Dwarfs, 1937.
Pinocchio, 1940.
Fantasia (with live action sequences featuring the Philadelphia Orchestra conducted by Leopold Stokowski), 1940.
The Reluctant Dragon (with live action sequences featuring Robert Benchley), 1941.
Dumbo, 1941.
Bambi, 1942.
Saludos Amigos (with live action sequences featuring Walt Disney), 1943.
Victory Through Air Power (with live action), 1943.
The Three Caballeros, 1945.
Make Mine Music, 1946.
Song of the South (with live action sequences featuring starring James Baskett and Bobby Driscoll), 1946.
Fun and Fancy Free (with live action), 1947.
Melody Time, 1948.
So Dear to My Heart (with live action sequences featuring starring Burl Ives and Beulah Bondi), 1948.
Ichabod and Mr. Toad, 1949.
Cinderella, 1950.
Alice in Wonderland, 1951.
Peter Pan, 1953.
Lady and the Tramp, 1955.
Sleeping Beauty, 1959.
101 Dalmatians, 1961.
The Sword and the Stone, 1963.
The Jungle Book, 1967.

LIVE ACTION FILMS AS HEAD OF WALT DISNEY PRODUCTIONS

Treasure Island, 1950.
The Story of Robin Hood, 1952.

The Sword and the Stone, 1953.
Rob Roy, the Highland Rogue, 1954.
20,000 Leagues Under the Sea, 1954.
The Living Desert, 1954.
The Vanishing Prairie, 1954.
Davy Crockett, King of the Wild Frontier, 1955.
The Littlest Outlaw, 1955.
The African Lion, 1955.
The Great Locomotive Chase, 1956.
Davy Crockett and the River Pirates, 1956.
Westward Ho the Wagons, 1956.
Secrets of Life, 1956.
Johnny Tremain, 1957.
Perri, 1957.
Old Yeller, 1957.
The Light in the Forest, 1958.
Tonka, 1958.
White Wilderness, 1958.
Darby O'Gill and the Little People, 1959.
The Shaggy Dog, 1959.
Third Man on the Mountain, 1959.
Toby Tyler, or, Ten Weeks with a Circus, 1960.
Kidnapped, 1960.
Polyanna, 1960.
Ten Who Dared, 1960.
The Swiss Family Robinson, 1960.
The Sign of Zorro, 1960.
Jungle Cat, 1960.
Babes in Toyland, 1961.
The Absent-Minded Professor, 1961.
The Parent Trap, 1961.
Nikki, Wild Dog of the North, 1961.
Greyfriars Bobby, 1961.
Big Red, 1962.
Moon Pilot, 1962.
Bon Voyage, 1962.
Almost Angels, 1962.
The Legend of Lobo, 1962.
In Search of the Castaways, 1962.
Son of Flubber, 1963.
The Miracle of the White Stallions, 1963.
Savage Sam, 1963.
Summer Magic, 1963.
The Incredible Journey, 1963.
The Misadventures of Merlin Jones, 1964.
A Tiger Walks, 1964.
The Three Lives of Thomasina, 1964.
The Moon Spinners, 1964.
Mary Poppins, 1964.
Emil and the Detectives, 1964.
Those Calloways, 1965.
The Monkey's Uncle, 1965.
That Darn Cat, 1965.
The Fighting Prince of Donegal, 1966.

Follow Me, Boys, 1966.
The Ugly Dachsund, 1966.
Lt. Robin Crusoe, U.S.N., 1966.
Monkeys, Go Home, 1967.
The Gnome-Mobile, 1967.
The Adventures of Bullwhip Griffin, 1967.

Many hundreds of artists, animators, story men, and technicians contributed to the achievement of Walt Disney Studios. Some of the major animators included: Ub Iwerks, Disney's earliest collaborator, the designer of Mickey Mouse, and the man responsible for many of the studio's technical innovations (including the multiplane camera technique), Ward Kimball, Les Clark, Frank Thomas, Milt Kahl, John Lounsbery, Ollie Johnston, Marc Davis, Woolie Reitherman, Eric Larson, Norm Ferguson, Art Babbitt, Grim Natwick, Ham Luske, Freddy Moore, Bill Tytla, Fred Spencer, and Preston Blair.

The Disney Studios produced short subjects on a regular basis through the mid-1950s, reaching a total of some 600 films, in addition to many more 16mm films and filmstrips for educational use, advertising purposes, and for television presentation.

TELEVISION

Walt Disney produced a weekly one-hour series, including drama, cartoons, mystery, action-adventure, educational programs, comedy, and nature and science. The program had various titles. On ABC-TV: *Disneyland,* October, 1954 to September, 1958; *Walt Disney Presents* (three rotating series: "The Nine Lives of Elfago Baca," starring Robert Loggia and Robert Simon; "The Swamp Fox," starring Leslie Nielsen and Barbara Eiler; and "Texas John Slaughter," starring Tom Tryon and Harry Carey, Jr.), September, 1958 to June, 1959; *Walt Disney's Adventure Time,* September, 1958 to September, 1959; *Walt Disney's World,* October, 1959 to September, 1961; on NBC-TV: *Walt Disney's Wonderful World of Color,* September, 1961 to September, 1981; on CBS-TV: *Walt Disney,* beginning September, 1981.
Mickey Mouse Club, October, 1955 to September, 1959, ABC TV, daily one-hour series of varied entertainment for children, live and filmed, with Disney cartoons and episodic series (like "Spin and Marty" and "The Hardy Boys") produced in both 30- and 60-minute versions, hosted by

Jimmy Dodd and featuring a cast of forty-four "Mouseketeers," including Annette Funicello, Kevin Corcoran, Tommy Kirk, Johnny Crawford, and Tim Considine.
Zorro, September, 1957 to September, 1959, ABC-TV, weekly 30-minute dramatic series, starring Guy Williams, Richard Anderson, and Annette Funicello.

■ Adaptations

Hundreds of books have been adapted from Disney films, including *Mickey and the Beanstalk* (from the film *Fun and Fancy Free;* illustrations adapted by Campbell Grant), Grosset, 1947; *Donald Duck in the High Andes* (from the film *Saludos Amigos*), Grosset, 1943; *Pinocchio,* Random House, 1939; *Bambi,* Simon and Schuster, 1941; and *Lady and the Tramp* (illustrations adapted by Claude Coats), Simon & Schuster, 1955.

■ Sidelights

He is a man who lifted America's spirits through the Great Depression and two World Wars, and he is still present in spirit today as his company, Walt Disney Productions, continues to define family entertainment in the United States. The legacy of Walter Elias Disney strongly impacts the movie industry, toys, children's clothing and accessories like backpacks and toothbrushes, books and music, and vacation destinations. In *Children's Books and Their Creators,* Terri Payne Butler writes that "Nearly three decades after his death, 'Disney' is no longer a name, but a conjuring word, summoning collective memories of poisoned apples, pumpkined carriages, and raucous blue genies."

Although his accomplishments are many, Disney is best known as the creator of the character Mickey Mouse, as the producer of a myriad of films for children and adults, and as the creator of the theme parks Disneyland and Disney World. In his lifetime, he also created and endowed a new university, the California Institute of the Arts, a professional school for the creative and performing arts.

Walt Disney was born in Chicago, Illinois, in 1901, the fourth son in a family of five from a lower middle class family. His father, Elias, who was Canadian, was an unsuccessful farmer, carpenter, and businessman, and his mother, Flora Call, was a patient women who supported her husband through his numerous pursuits. Although it appears that his early life was not marked by harmony and stability, a happy family life is a recurrent theme in all of Disney's work.

In 1906, the Disneys moved from Chicago to a farm near Marceline, Missouri. Later, Disney would remember the friendliness of rural life, but also the hard work that he and his family were forced to perform in order to get the farm established. When his two older brothers left the farm and returned to Chicago, the farm began to fail. It was on the farm that Disney's interest in art began to show itself; he and his sister Ruth would take sticks dipped in tar and paint on the side of the family's white house. In *The Disney Version: The Life, Times, Art and Commerce of Walt Disney,* Richard Schickel quotes Disney as saying, "I recall when I was about seven. The doctor had a very fine stallion which he asked me to sketch. He held the animal while I worked with my homemade easel and materials. The result was pretty terrible, but both the doctor and his wife praised the drawing highly, to my great delight." Disney also used some of the farm animals as the basis for the animated animals that later appeared in his films. His mother taught him to read at home, but Disney's interest in classwork was minimal.

When the farm failed, the family moved to Kansas City, Missouri. It was 1910, and Elias Disney

Disney's most famous creation, Mickey Mouse, who nearly missed fame and fortune by initially being named Mortimer Mouse in 1928.

began to manage a paper route with the help of Walt, who was nine years old at the time. Again, the work was grueling, and Disney remembered delivering newspapers in the morning and evening in summer heat and winter snowstorms. He was not a good student, but his teachers at the Benton Grammar School in Kansas City encouraged Disney's interest in drawing. When his sister Ruth became ill, Disney designed a flip book in which figures appeared to move; this was his first effort in the world of animation. He also began to read the classics and enrolled in children's art classes at the Kansas City Art Institute.

The family moved again in 1917 when Elias Disney invested in a jelly factory in Chicago. Disney graduated from Benton Grammar School in June of that year, spent the summer working for the railroad selling refreshments to passengers, and met his family in Chicago in September, where he enrolled at McKinley High School and began to take art classes at the Chicago Institute of Art. But after a year of high school, Disney was restless and anxious to see more of the world. He was too young to join the military but decided, with his mother's permission, to join the Red Cross Ambulance Corps and become an ambulance driver. He spent most of his tour of duty delivering relief supplies and working in the motor pool; by the time he went overseas, World War I had virtually ended.

Partners With Iwerks

After the war, Disney headed to Kansas City. He decided to use his artistic talent to get a job, and he soon found work in advertising as an apprentice at a commercial art studio. It was there that he met a Dutch cartoonist named Ub Iwerks. Together, they left to form their own art studio, but it soon failed. Next, the pair went to work for the Kansas City Film Ad Company, where they learned the basics of animation as they also created one-minute animated cartoon commercials. They created the concept of Laugh-O-Grams, which were short cartoons that combined a gag and a commercial announcement. Disney and Iwerks left to form Laugh-O-Gram Films in 1922, and the popularity of these Laugh-O-Grams caused them to be prosperous for a while. While at Laugh-O-Gram Films, they also produced several seven-minute animated cartoons based on fairy tales.

Because they had no experience in distribution, this company failed; however, Disney was determined to succeed, and he persuaded his brother Roy to invest in his third company, which would produce a series known as "Alice in Cartoonland." In this series, a live young girl appeared in adventures along with animated creatures and backgrounds. This company failed, too, and Disney and Iwerks declared bankruptcy.

By 1923, Disney was still determined to produce animated films. He moved to Hollywood and revived Laugh-O-Grams and the "Alice" series. Then, he convinced his brother Roy and Iwerks to join him in Hollywood and he formed Disney Brothers Studios. It was here that Disney began to demonstrate a remarkable ability to delegate responsibility to his staff. He became the main idea man behind stories, characterization, and film development. Iwerks took over the art department, and Roy Disney became the business manager. Iwerks was later replaced by a large staff of artists, but Roy and Walt Disney stayed in these respective positions throughout their careers. After this time, Disney never performed the actual tasks involved in cartooning and animation again; he found that he had a gift for creating visionary master plans and for directing others into seeing them through.

As his professional life became more settled, Disney's personal life did as well. In 1925, his company hired an inker and painter named Lillian Bounds. They fell in love, married that summer, and later had two daughters—Diane Marie, who was born in 1933, and Sharon Mae, who was born in 1936. Their marriage appeared to be happy and lasted until Disney's death.

The early years of Disney Brothers Studio were busy ones, as the company produced fifty-six "Alice in Cartoonland" shorts. By 1927, Disney began collaborating with Universal Studios to produce cartoons featuring the character "Oswald the Lucky Rabbit." Using new techniques for producing these films, the company created ten Oswald shorts in 1927 and sixteen in 1928. The humor was slapstick and the plots were simplistic, but the Oswald series was a popular one. When Disney attempted to negotiate a new contract with Universal Studios, he discovered that the studio actually owned the Oswald character. At this point, Disney vowed never again to work on a property that he did not own.

The Mouse

Next, Disney created his own star, which would become the most famous of all his characters. There are many myths about how the character of Mickey Mouse was created: some say that Disney dreamed up the character when he was working on the drawing board in Kansas City, and others say that the character was created by Disney on the train ride home after the Oswald dispute with Universal. The truth is that the development of the character was a collaboration between Disney, who developed the idea, and Iwerks, who drew the character and created his form. Disney wanted to call him Mortimer Mouse, but his wife thought that the name Mickey would be better. In *The Story of Walt Disney*, his daughter Diane Disney Miller remembers the conversation this way:

> "'I think I've got something,' Father told Mother. 'It's a mouse. I'll call him Mortimer. Mortimer Mouse. I like that, Don't you?'
> "Mother thought it over and shook her head. 'I like the mouse idea,' she said, 'but Mortimer sounds wrong. Too sissy.'
> "'What's wrong with it?' Father asked. "Mortimer Mouse, Mortimer Mouse. It swings, Lilly.'
> "But Mother didn't buy it. She couldn't explain why 'Mortimer' grated on her. It just did.
> "'All right,' Father said. 'How about Mickey? Mickey Mouse?'"

In this way, the world's most famous cartoon character was born. In 1928, the studio produced three animated shorts using their new character Mickey. He was soon joined by a number of supporting characters, including Minnie Mouse, Pluto, Horace Horsecollar, and Donald Duck.

Although Donald Duck is also a popular character, Mickey, whose voice was done by Disney himself, retains a special place in the hearts of people everywhere. According to M. Thomas Inge, writing in *Dictionary of Literary Biography*, Disney once said, "Mickey's a nice fellow who never does anybody any harm, who gets in scrapes through no fault of his own but always manages to come up grinning. . . ."

Mickey Mouse and friends became popular around the world, but Disney Brothers Studios was still experiencing financial problems. In his book *The Disney Version: The Life, Times, Art and Commerce of Walt Disney*, Richard Schickel quotes Disney as describing the problems in this way: "Each film we finished just about paid for getting out the next one. I kept adding new people to our staff, but in spite of that, I had to work over-time night after night myself."

Because Disney owned this group of characters that he had created, he licensed them for use in hundreds of products, including books, games, toys, and watches. Two comic strips were created—an adventure strip based on Mickey that was developed by cartoonist Floyd Gottfredson and was published in daily newspapers from 1930 to 1950, and a Carl Barks' series about Donald Duck, Uncle Scrooge, and Donald's nephews that was published in Dell Comic Books from 1943 to 1945.

After his first six Mickey Mouse shorts were produced, Disney began working on his next project, a film known as *The Skeleton Dance*, which was produced in 1929. In this film, which is the first in the "Silly Symphony" series, the bony residents of a graveyard dance to "The Dance of the Dwarfs." In the next of the "Silly Symphonies," *Flowers & Trees*, Disney added color to the film. In November of 1932, he received an award for this animated cartoon from the Academy of Motion Picture Arts and Sciences.

By 1933, Disney had released his thirty-sixth film in the "Silly Symphony" series. This film was a popular one, primarily because of its upbeat message during the Depression and the memorable theme song "Who's Afraid of the Big Bad Wolf?" In addition to making the nation happy, *The Three Little Pigs* also made Disney wealthy when it grossed $125,000 in its first year.

Big Risk Pays Off

At this point, Disney decided to produce a feature-length animated film. This project was an ambitious one that would involve creating seven reels of action in Technicolor. To create this film, Disney introduced the multiplane camera, a machine that was able to photograph characters and settings through several planes, giving the animated cartoon a multidimensional effect. The film that Disney chose to produce was *Snow White and the Seven Dwarfs*, one of the best loved fairy tales from the Brothers Grimm.

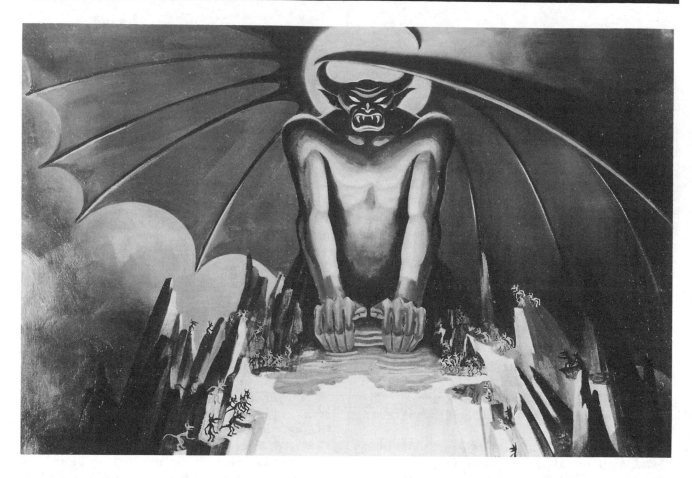

A revolutionary visualization of classical music, the 1940 production of *Fantasia* **included this scene from Moussorgsky's "Night on Bald Mountain" of Chernabog, Lord of Evil and Death.**

Disney realized the gamble he was taking when he set out to work on *Snow White*. In *The Disney Version: The Life, Times, Art and Commerce of Walt Disney,* Richard Schickel quotes Disney as saying: "We've got to be sure of it before we start, because if it isn't good we will destroy it: If it is good, we shall make at least a million." The story was trimmed down, and much of the horror was eliminated from the original tale. The Disney film, which had an optimistic tone, was released a few days before Christmas in 1937. The film premiered at the Carthay Circle Theater in Hollywood, and later appeared at Radio City Music Hall in New York City. Thousands of moviegoers flocked to theaters to see the film, and *Snow White* earned $8 million, putting Disney Studios on solid financial ground for the first time. Although *Snow White* might have looked as though it was easy to produce, it took four years of hard work involving hundreds of talented people. The film won a spe-

cial Academy Award in 1939, in the form of one large Oscar statue and seven little Oscar statuettes—one for each of the film's dwarfs.

Encouraged by the financial and critical success of his first feature-length animated film, Disney and his staff began working on *Pinocchio*, another full-length animated film. Taking a classic children's story written by Carlo Collodi in the late nineteenth century, Disney reworked the tale of a puppet who came to life and turned it into a Disney masterpiece that combines comedy, terror, artistry, and memorable music.

Pinocchio was still in production when Disney Studios began working on *Fantasia,* a revolutionary integration of imaginative visuals and some of the great works of classical music. In an August 1941 interview with *Who* magazine, Disney described his interest in *Fantasia* this way: "It seems I'm just finding out about music. . . . I never liked this highbrow stuff. It bored me. Honest, I just couldn't listen to it. But I can now. It seems to mean a little more to me. Maybe 'Fantasia' can do the same for other people." The film was released in 1940, nine months after *Pinocchio*, but *Fantasia* was not as popular as Disney had hoped and only came into its own as it was re-released over the years.

The years that directly followed the release of these two films were not as magical for Walt Disney. Production costs on both films had been high, and *Fantasia* was basically a commercial failure. When World War II began, foreign film markets were closed. Additionally, Disney felt betrayed when many of his employees went out on a labor strike in 1941. The films *Dumbo* and *Bambi* were released in 1941 and 1942, respectively, but most of the work on these projects had been completed before problems set in at the studio. Both *Dumbo*, the story of a flying elephant that contains the surrealistic "Pink Elephants on Parade" segment, and *Bambi*, the rendering of the Felix

Visitors to the Disney-MGM Studios in Florida watch animators at work in 1990.

Salten novel about the life of a fawn and life in the forest, were popular with moviegoers.

Disney took on many government contracts during the war years. He produced animated training films for all branches of the armed forces. At first, the treasury department did not like the idea of using Donald Duck to represent the average taxpayer in these films. In Diane Disney Miller's *The Story of Walt Disney*, Disney is quoted as saying: "You wanted me to get this message over, so I've given you Donald. At our studio, that's like MGM giving you Clark Gable. The Duck is well known to the American public and they'll go to theaters to see him. I can promise that they won't walk out on him and I wouldn't promise that they won't take a walk on your Mr. Taxpayer." Later, in a film designed to support a good neighbor policy with South America (*The Three Caballeros*, 1945), Disney combined live action and animation; this technique was so effective that it was later used in *Song of the South* (1946), a film collection of selected stories by Joel Chandler Harris. This film included some Old South stereotypes, but it did use some innovative film techniques to tell the stories of Brer Rabbit, Brer Bear, and Brer Fox.

Disney Diversifies

In the years directly following the war, Disney continued to produce anthologies (*Make Mine Music*, 1946, and *Melody Time*, 1948), films that combined animation with music (*Fun and Fancy Free*, 1947) and films that retold old stories (*Ichabod and Mr. Toad*, 1949, *The Wind in the Willows*, 1949, and *So Dear to My Heart*, 1948). Disney Studios also continued to produce a number of short films, including cartoons featuring the popular characters Mickey Mouse, Donald Duck, Pluto, and Goofy. About 180 short films were produced in the 1930s, 150 in the 1940s, 90 in the 1950s, and 12 in the 1960s as theater managers lost interest in this medium. In addition to being shown in theaters, these films were also used when Disney introduced his first television special in 1951 and initiated his weekly show *Disneyland* in 1954. *The Mickey Mouse Club*, which was the most widely loved children's program of the 1950s, was introduced in 1955. Disney himself became a television personality when he served as host for *Disneyland* (which became the *Wonderful World of Color* in 1961).

If you enjoy the works of Walt Disney, you may also want to check out the following:

Katsuhiro Otomo's *Akira*, an animated film produced in Japan in 1988.
Watership Down, an animated film based on the novel by Richard Adams, 1978.
Yellow Submarine, an animated fantasy based on the music of The Beatles, 1968.

In 1950, Disney Studios began to produce adaptations of classic fairy tales and children's stories, including *Cinderella* (1950), *Alice in Wonderland* (1951, based on the book by Lewis Carroll), *Peter Pan* (1953, based on the play by Sir James M. Barrie), *Lady and the Tramp* (1955, based on the story by Ward Greene), *Sleeping Beauty* (1959), *101 Dalmations* (1961, based on the book by Dodie Smith), *The Sword and the Stone* (1963, inspired by T. H. White's retelling of the Arthurian legends), and *The Jungle Book* (1967, inspired by Rudyard Kipling's *Mowgli* stories). *The Jungle Book* was the last film that Disney actually supervised.

At the same time, Disney Studios was also hard at work producing a number of live action films, including *Treasure Island*, *20,000 Leagues Under the Sea*, *Kidnapped*, and *Mary Poppins*. In a sixteen-year period, Disney oversaw the production of sixty-three live-action films. These films are considered great family entertainment and were generally box-office hits, but few of them are recognized as classics. Some exceptions include *Treasure Island* and *20,000 Leagues Under the Sea*, which are considered the best of these films, and *Mary Poppins*, which, in 1964, was nominated for thirteen Academy Awards and received five of them.

As might be expected, Disney is not without detractors. In 1965, Dr. Max Rafferty, California's superintendent of public instruction, wrote an article in which he described Disney as "the greatest educator of this century." This claim created a backlash, as educators and critics around the country described the way that Walt Disney had mishandled fairy tales and children's classics. Frances Clarke Sayers, who was director of children's services for the New York Public Library, wrote a letter to the *Los Angeles Times* in response to Dr. Rafferty's article. In it she said that Disney had "scant respect for the integrity of the original creations . . . manipulating and vulgarizing everything for his own ends. His treatment of folklore is without regard for its anthropological, spiritual, or psychological truths." "I call him to account for his debasement of the traditional literature of childhood, in films and in the books he publishes," she wrote. She also commented, "the acerbity of *Mary Poppins,* unpredictable, full of wonder and mystery, becomes . . . one great marshmallow-covered cream-puff" and added that Disney "transformed *Pinocchio* into a slapstick sadistic revel." Author and illustrator Maurice Sendak, however, writing in his 1988 collection of essays *Caldecott & Co.,* praises Disney's *Pinocchio.* "Collodi's book is of interest today," Sendack writes, "chiefly as evidence of the superiority of Disney's screenplay." Writing in *People* in 1992, Ralph Novak also gives *Pinocchio* high marks. "While modern kids may find the ending too low-key or the whole production too low-tech, the film is to children what *Casablanca* is to adults," he writes. As might be expected, Disney did not try to recreate fairy tales or children's classics faithfully. In the *Horn Book,* Betsy Hearne writes that Disney once said to one of his story men assigned to work on *The Jungle Book,* "The first thing I want you to do is not to read it," adding later, "You can get all bogged down with these stories."

One of Disney's proudest achievements was Disneyland, the amusement park that he built in Anaheim, California, in 1955. At the dedication, Disney said, "Disneyland will never be completed as long as there is imagination left in the world." In Diane Disney Miller's *The Story of Walt Disney,* she quotes her father as saying: "The germ of Disneyland was planted in my mind when you and your sister Sharon were little and I took you to amusement parks and to zoos on Saturdays and Sundays. Those days were among the happiest of my life. . . ." Although he planned it, he did not live to see Disneyworld, which was completed in Orlando, Florida, in 1971. (Disney died of lung cancer in 1966.) Nearly sixteen years after his death, Epcot Center, Disney's vast vision of a combination world's fair, theme park, and dream factory, opened in Orlando, Florida, at a cost of $900 million.

In a 1993 interview with *Entertainment Weekly,* Adriana Caelotti, who was the original voice in *Snow White,* describes Disney this way: "To me, he was just about the greatest man artistically. He seemed to understand what was correct with any-

thing that had to do with art, with music. And I feel that he will never die."

Among his many accomplishments, Disney is best remembered for bringing about these magical family amusement parks and for bringing animation to a new level of accomplishment. Today, his financial and cultural empire is secure, and young animators continue to bring forth new feature films every year. Disney characters are known throughout the world and Disney's influence is felt throughout society. Few have influenced popular culture more than Walt Disney.

■ Works Cited

Butler, Terri Payne, *Children's Books and Their Creators,* edited by Anita Silvey, Houghton Mifflin, 1995, pp. 204-5.

Disney, Walt, interview in *Who* Magazine, August, 1941.

Hearne, Betsy, "Disney Revisited, Or, Jiminy Cricket, It's Musty Down Here!," *Horn Book,* March/April, 1997, pp. 137-46.

Inge, M. Thomas, "Walt Disney," *Dictionary of Literary Biography,* Volume 22: *American Writers for Children, 1900-1960,* Gale, 1983, pp. 124-35.

Miller, Diane Disney, *The Story of Walt Disney,* Curtis, 1956.

"Not So Happily, After All," *Entertainment Weekly,* July 9, 1993, p. 59.

Novak, Ralph, review of *Pinocchio, People,* July 6, 1992, pp. 14-15.

Sayers, Frances Clarke, "Walt Disney Accused," *Horn Book,* December, 1965, pp. 602-11.

Schickel, Richard, *The Disney Version: The Life, Times, Art and Commerce of Walt Disney,* Avon Books, 1968.

Sendak, Maurice, *Caldecott & Co.: Notes on Books & Pictures,* Michael Di Capua Books/Farrar, Straus, 1988.

■ For More Information See

BOOKS

Bailey, Adrian, *Walt Disney's Wonderful World of Fantasy,* Dodd, Mead, 1985.

Beard, Richard R., *Walt Disney's EPCOT Center: Creating the New World of Tomorrow,* Abrams, 1985.

Cole, Michael D., *Walt Disney: Creator of Mickey Mouse,* Enslow, 1996.

DiFranco, Joann, *Walt Disney: When Dreams Come True*, Dillon, 1985.

Disney, Walt, *Sketch book/Walt Disney*, Applewood, 1993.

Eliot, Marc, *Walt Disney: Hollywood's Dark Prince*, Harper, 1994.

Fanning, Jim, *Walt Disney*, Chelsea House, 1994.

Finch, Christopher, *The Art of Walt Disney: From Mickey Mouse to the Magic Kingdoms*, Abrams, 1995.

Fisher, Maxine P., *Walt Disney*, F. Watts, 1988.

Ford, Barbara, *Walt Disney: A Biography*, Walker, 1989.

Greene, Katherine, *The Man Behind the Magic: The Story of Walt Disney*, Viking, 1991.

Italia, Bob, *Mickey Mouse*, Abdo & Daughters, 1991.

Jachnin, Boris, *Walt Disney*, ASF, 1990.

Jackson, Kathy Merlock, *Walt Disney: A Bio-Bibliography*, Greenwood Press, 1993.

Korman, Justine, *Walt Disney's Sleeping Beauty and the Prince: A Book About Determination*, Golden Book, 1988.

Mosley, Leonard, *Disney's World: A Biography*, Stein & Day, 1985.

Schomp, Virginia, *Walt Disney: Making Dreams Come True*, Dillon Press, 1992.

Selden, Bernice, *The Story of Walt Disney: Maker of Magical Worlds*, G. Stevens, 1996.

Sinyard, Neil, *The Best of Disney*, Twin Books, 1988.

Thomas, Bob, *Walt Disney: An American Original*, Hyperion, 1994.

Tietyen, David, *The Musical World of Walt Disney*, H. Leonard Publishers, 1990.

Uelmen, Amelia J., *Seeing the U.S.A.: The Landscapes of Walt Disney*, Georgetown University Press, 1991.

West, John, *The Disney Live-Action Productions*, Hawthorne & Peabody, 1994.

PERIODICALS

American Legion, September, 1996, p. 72.
Boy's Life, October, 1994, p. 15.
Entertainment Weekly, April 2, 1993, p. 57.
Gentlemen's Quarterly, January, 1996, p. 105.
Journal of American History, June, 1995, p. 84.
Life, Fall, 1990, p. 26.
New York, October 22, 1990, p. 116.
New Yorker, January 6, 1992, p. 14.
People, July 6, 1992, p. 14; November 21, 1994, p. 142.
Variety, April 19, 1993, p. 63; November 7, 1994, p. 142; September 9, 1996, p. 124.

■ Obituaries

PERIODICALS

National Review, January 10, 1967.
Newsweek, December 26, 1966.
New York Times, December 18, 1966.
Time, December 23, 1966.*

—Sketch by Irene Durham

E. L. Doctorow

■ Personal

Born Edgar Laurence Doctorow, January 6, 1931, in New York, NY; son of David Richard (a music store proprietor) and Rose (a pianist; maiden name, Levine) Doctorow; married Helen Esther Setzer (a writer), August 20, 1954; children: Jenny, Caroline, Richard. *Education:* Kenyon College, A.B. (with honors), 1952; Columbia University, graduate study, 1952-53.

■ Addresses

Home—New Rochelle, NY. *Office*—c/o Random House Publishers, 201 East 50th Street, New York, NY 10022; New York University English Department, New York, NY 10003-6607.

■ Career

Columbia Pictures Industries, Inc., New York City, script reader; New American Library, New York City, senior editor, 1959-64; Dial Press, New York City, editor-in-chief, 1964-69, vice-president, 1968-

69; Sarah Lawrence College, Bronxville, NY, member of faculty, 1971-78; New York University, New York City, Glucksman Professor of English, 1982. University of California, Irvine, writer-in-residence, 1969-70; Yale School of Drama, creative writing fellow 1974-75; University of Utah, visiting professor, 1975; Princeton University, visiting senior fellow, 1980-81. *Military service:* U.S. Army, Signal Corps, 1953-55. *Member:* American Academy and Institute of Arts and Letters, Authors Guild (board director), PEN (director), Writers Guild of America, East, Century Association.

■ Awards, Honors

National Book Award nomination, 1972, for *The Book of Daniel;* Guggenheim Fellowship, 1973; Creative Artists Service fellow, 1973-74; National Book Critics Circle Award, American Academy, and Arts and Letters award, National Institute of Art, both 1976, both for *Ragtime;* L.H.D., Kenyon College, 1976, and Brandeis University, 1989; Litt. D., Hobart and William Smith Colleges, 1979; National Book Award Nomination, 1980, for *Loon Lake;* American Book Award, 1986, for *World's Fair;* Edith Wharton Citation of Merit for Fiction and NY State Author, 1989-91; one of 13 Best Books of 1989 selection, *New York Times Book Review,* for *Billy Bathgate;* PEN/Faulkner Award for Fiction, National Book Critics' Circle Award, and William Dean Howells Medal, American Academy and Institute of Arts and Letters, all 1990, all for *Billy Bathgate.*

■ Writings

NOVELS

Welcome to Hard Times, Simon & Schuster, 1960, reprinted, Fawcett, 1988, published in England as *Bad Man from Bodie*, Deutsch, 1961.

Big as Life, Simon & Schuster, 1966.

The Book of Daniel, Random House, 1971, reprinted, Fawcett, 1987.

Ragtime, Random House, 1975.

Loon Lake, Random House, 1980.

World's Fair, Random House, 1985.

Billy Bathgate, Random House, 1989.

The Waterworks, Random House, 1994.

E. L. Doctorow: Three Complete Novels (includes *Billy Bathgate*, *World's Fair*, and *Loon Lake*), Wings Books, 1994.

OTHER

(Contributor) Theodore Solotaroff, editor, *New American Review 2*, New American Library, 1968.

Drinks Before Dinner (play; first produced Off-Broadway at Public Theater, November 22, 1978), Random House, 1979.

American Anthem, photographs by Jean Claude Suares, Stewart, Tabori, 1982.

Daniel (screenplay based on author's *The Book of Daniel*; film starring Timothy Hutton), Paramount Pictures, 1983.

Lives of the Poets: Six Stories and a Novella, Random House, 1984.

The People's Text: A Citizen Reads the Constitution, wood engraving by Barry Moser, Nouveau Press for the Mississippi Civil Liberties Union, 1992.

Jack London, Hemingway, and the Constitution: Selected Essays, 1977-1992, Random House, 1993; published in England as *Poets and Presidents: Selected Essays, 1977-1992*, Macmillan, 1994.

Also author (with Don Henley and Robert Bly) of *Heaven is Under Our Feet: A Book for Walden Woods*. Contributor of articles to periodicals including *Architectural Digest*, *Harper's*, *Nation*, *Times*, and *New York Times Book Review*.

■ Adaptations

Welcome to Hard Times was adapted for film starring Henry Fonda, Metro-Goldwyn-Mayer, 1968; *Ragtime* was adapted for film with a screenplay by Michael Weller, directed by Robert Altman, and starring Howard Rollins, Jr., and James Cagney, 1981; *Billy Bathgate* was adapted for film by Touchstone Pictures, with a screenplay by Tom Stoppard, directed by Robert Benton, and starring Dustin Hoffman and Nicole Kidman, 1991.

■ Sidelights

"It was juggling that had got me where I was. . . . I practiced my juggling. I juggled anything, Spaldeens, stones, oranges, empty green Coca-Cola bottles, I juggled rolls we stole hot from the bins in the Pechter Bakery wagons, and since I juggled so constantly nobody bothered me about it except once in a while just because it was something nobody else could do, to try to interrupt my rhythm by giving me a shove, or to grab one of my oranges out of the air and run with it, because it was what I was known to do, along the lines of having a nervous tic, something that marked me but after all wasn't my fault."

So speaks the title character and narrator of E. L. Doctorow's novel *Billy Bathgate*, hailed by Anne Tyler as "a wonderful new addition to the ranks of American boy heroes" in the *New York Times Book Review*. Counted among the most important living writers in the United States, Doctorow is also an editor, teacher, short story writer, dramatist, and essayist. His unique contribution to American literature has been to re-create historical figures and events in his fiction. Exploring times and spaces in American history that traditional history books have ignored, Doctorow narrates his stories with colorful and engaging prose.

Doctorow's novels, which are frequently set in New York City, feature the experiences of boys coming of age and take place in time periods from the early to mid-twentieth century. Nevertheless critics note that his work speaks to all Americans. As Stephen Fender observed in *Times Literary Supplement*, "the project of Doctorow's fiction has been to deconstruct crucial episodes in American political history and to rebuild them out of . . . his own speculative imagination." Boyd Tonkin wrote in *New Statesman and Society* that "E. L. Doctorow has already made his fortune as a mythographer of the 20th century, his chronicles too full of dragons and miracles for a sober historian to trust." In a review in the *Listener*, Andrew Clifford stated that "Doctorow's trademark of using historical fact to brew up brilliantly imaginative fiction has helped him stake a claim to be the present-day Great American Novelist."

Yet Doctorow is known for more than his literary vision. His prize-winning novels, like *Ragtime* and *Billy Bathgate*, have been adapted for film, thus increasing his exposure and popularity. Serving on the boards of influential writers' organizations has also given Doctorow an opportunity to express his opinions on political and social issues. In addition, he writes commentaries on American literature and culture for various periodicals. Surveying Doctorow's career in an article in the *Christian Science Monitor*, Merle Rubin described him as a "winner of prestigious prizes, predictably to the left in politics, comfortably ensconced in the anti-establishment, first as an influential editor, then as a still more influential author with all the subsidiary academic honors and appointments." Doctorow is a committed social critic and artist, Rubin said, adding that he "even looks like a writer."

Speaking with Donna Seaman in an interview for *Booklist*, Doctorow claimed he got his first name as a result of his father's interest in literature: His father "loved Poe's work. He loved James Fenimore Cooper, too." So Doctorow was named Edgar, after Poe. He developed a love for literature at an early age while he was growing up in New York City. In fact, as he told Johnathan Yardley in an interview for the *Miami Herald*, he decided to be a writer when he was in third grade. After attending the Bronx High School of Science, Doctorow went to Kenyon College in Ohio. At Kenyon he studied criticism and philosophy. He was also involved in acting, which he continued to study at Columbia after graduating with a bachelor's degree. However, he left Columbia without completing a graduate degree and joined the army. While he was in the service he wrote plays during his spare time.

From Script-Reader to Novel-Writer

After leaving the army Doctorow worked as a script reader and summarizer for Columbia Pictures where, he told Yardley, he had "to suffer one lousy Western after another." Finally, when he was in his late twenties, Doctorow decided he

Filmed in 1981 by Paramount Pictures, *Ragtime* weaves the lives of black and white, privileged and immigrant, into vivid 1906 events.

"could lie about the West in a much more interesting way." He wrote his own Western, *Welcome to Hard Times.* Unlike most Westerns, the novel addressed the conflict between good and evil, and it received favorable reviews from critics.

In 1959 Doctorow began a career as an editor at the New American Library, and he went on to become the editor-in-chief at Dial Press in the mid-1960s. He still found time to write another novel, *Big as Life,* a science fiction work that opens with two naked, human giants emerging from New York harbor. Like *Welcome to Hard Times,* the book won praise from reviewers. Doctorow remained at Dial Press until he became a writer-in-residence at the University of California at Irvine. In 1971 he began a long career as an English professor.

Doctorow's third novel, *The Book of Daniel,* is a work of historical fiction that portrays the story of Julius and Ethel Rosenberg. The Rosenbergs were communists who were convicted of conspiracy to commit treason against the United States and later executed. *The Book of Daniel* depicts the emotions of the Rosenbergs and their children, especially their son Daniel. Critics were charmed by the book, and some even praised it as a great American novel. As Doctorow pointed out to John F. Baker in *Publishers Weekly, The Book of Daniel* "got me on the map critically and introduced me to a wider audience." Doctorow also wrote the screenplay for the movie version of the novel, entitled *Daniel.* Starring Timothy Hutton, the film was released in 1983.

Doctorow had a difficult time beginning his next novel. He revealed to Seaman that he became desperate and began to write about the wall he was facing from his desk. The result was *Ragtime,* which became a best-seller and a hit movie. *Ragtime* features famous historical figures and fictional characters from the 1920s, as well as historical events and fictional moments from 1902 to 1917. Doctorow linked all these elements together in a convincing story set in New York. Fictional characters include a family who recently emigrated to the United States, a wealthy Prostestant family, and a family headed by a black musician. Among the actual historical figures are scholar Booker T. Washington, inventor Thomas Edison, industrialist Henry Ford, magician Harry Houdini, banker J. P. Morgan, anarchist Emma Goldman, and psychoanalyst Sigmund Freud.

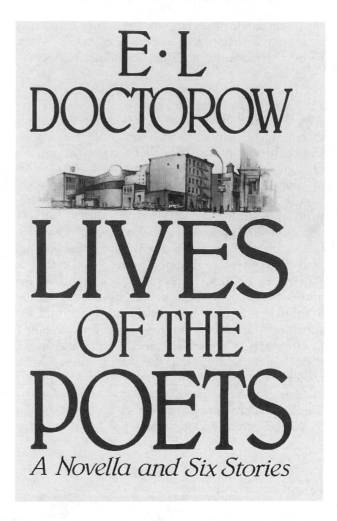

The novella that follows the mysterious short stories in this 1984 work details the mundane life and disturbed imagination of their supposed writer.

Yardley noted that *Ragtime* was "hugely successful." It moved Bantam Books to pay a record sum—$1.85 million—for the paperback rights and attracted the attention of Hollywood movie stars. "The book seems to have somehow laid something down in the public consciousness in this country at this time that I haven't even begun to analyze," Doctorow admitted to Yardley. Although Doctorow wrote a screenplay for a film version of the novel for director Robert Altman, the script was rejected for being too long. The movie was eventually made and starred James Cagney in what happened to be the legendary actor's last screen performance.

Doctorow's next novel, *Loon Lake,* takes place during the Great Depression. Its main characters include a wealthy industrialist, his aviatress wife, some gangsters, a poet, and a drifter. In the words of Christopher Lehmann-Haupt of the *New York Times*, the book provides "a complex and haunting meditation on modern American history." While the novel's unusual narrative style was criticized by some reviewers, others appreciated *Loon Lake* as Doctorow's most ambitious work.

Loon Lake was followed by *World's Fair*. A reviewer for *Publishers Weekly* hailed it as Doctorow's "most powerful book to date." With hints of autobiography, *World's Fair* tells the story of Edgar Altschuler, who is growing up in the Bronx in the 1930s during the Great Depression and the war in Europe. Events in the novel portray Edgar's experiences in learning to deal with his family and the outside world. According to the *Publishers Weekly* reviewer, "the book should immediately become a classic." *World's Fair* won the prestigious American Book Award.

Boy-Hero *Billy Bathgate*

Following the success of *World's Fair*, Doctorow's next novel, *Billy Bathgate*, was greatly anticipated. The book more than met the expectations of readers and critics alike. Set in New York in the 1930s, *Billy Bathgate* was praised for a realistic portrayal of a young boy's perspective and for a myth-making treatment of American gangsters. Based in part on the story of an actual gang-leader, Dutch Schultz, the novel begins as Billy, the fifteen-year-old title character, watches the execution of a man from a boat in New York harbor. Readers learn that Billy, who is fatherless, took up with Schultz's gang after Schultz admired his juggling. The gang serves as a family for Billy, and Schultz is a kind of father to him. Thus it is surprising when the young man has an affair with Schultz's girlfriend. After Schultz and his gang are gunned down, Billy is the only one clever enough to interpret their last words. In the end he finds money they stashed away.

At the conclusion of the book, Billy reveals that he is writing his story years later, after completing an Ivy League education, serving in the military, and making his own fortune. "Billy unrolls before us the most complex and oddly beautiful New York street scenes, full of grime and energy and color," Anne Tyler observed in the *New York Times Book Review*. Richard Eder commented in the

Los Angeles Times Book Review that the "novel makes full and loving use of the manners, the artifacts, the savors and the rhythms of the '30s. He [Doctorow] is marvelously skillful at getting into the thoughts and the lingo of the time." Salman Rushdie also praised *Billy Bathgate* in a review in the *Observer*: "The gangsters in Doctorow's novel . . . draw their self-belief, their sense of solidity and permanence, from the metropolis itself, which suggest that only those who can believe in the permanence of the city are able to survive its transformations . . . because it's that belief that keeps you one step ahead, with money in your pocket and the world at your feet, until you come up against somebody who believes even harder than you."

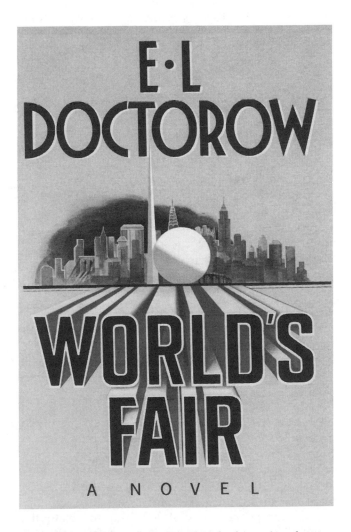

Considered to be autobiographical, this tale of 1930s New York City as seen through a child's eyes was published in 1985 and received the American Book Award in 1986.

If you enjoy the works of E. L. Doctorow, you may want to check out the following books and films:

James Lincoln Collier, *My Crooked Family*, 1991.
Jack Finney, *Time and Again*, 1970.
Robert Lehrman, *The Store That Mama Built*, 1992.
Miller's Crossing, Circle Films, 1990.

Some critics, however, found it difficult to reconcile the vocabulary of the narrator with the "fact" that he is a boy. As reviewer Michael Wood pointed out in *Times Literary Supplement*, "Billy seems to have swallowed not the dictionary but several portions of Ulysses and most of Faulkner, along with, conceivably, a dash of García Márquez." Others said it was hard to believe that such a boy could view violence without much emotion. While several reviewers noted the absence of a complex plot, many were willing to overlook the deficiency. For instance, Anne Tyler argued in the *New York Times Book Review* that "What the novel loses in authenticity, it gains in eloquence. Kindly agree to grant Billy his gift of language and you'll be rewarded with passages of writing so intense, so breathtakingly vivid, that you'll trust the story in spite of yourself. . . ." Merle Rubin, writing in the *Christian Science Monitor,* was not so enthusiastic. He noted that "this story has little more depth than a B-movie." *Listener* contributor Clifford agreed: "Although beautifully written, with his [Doctorow's] usual painstaking establishment of each scene and many excellent set pieces, the novel fails to climb the usual heights."

Doctorow explained to Seaman in a *Booklist* interview that his next novel, *The Waterworks,* evolved from a dream that he had turned into a short story of the same name. In the story, a man approaching a reservoir sees a child's boat sinking in the water. When he enters the waterworks, he finds a boy's body. Doctorow described the lingering image and how it led him to create the novel: "Another man who is observing this sees the first man wrap up the body and race off with it. And the observer is left to wonder exactly what he's seen. And I was wondering, too." The image

stuck in Doctorow's mind until he recalled that New York had once had a reservoir in the middle of town. He then found some photos of the reservoir as well as other scenes around New York. Although the story developed from there, Doctorow told Seaman he "also looked at old newspapers and read about the newspaper business in the nineteenth century and, of course, about medicine, medical practice. . . ."

The Waterworks Makes a Splash

The Waterworks was highly praised by critics. Characterizing the novel as a long poem "written in a supple and subtle, multi-claused and premodernist prose," John Whitworth of the *Spectator* found it totally engrossing: "*The Waterworks* is a marvellous book, gathering such momentum that I read the last 120 pages in one go at four o'clock in the morning." As Whitworth and other reviewers noted, however, *The Waterworks* provides more than a thrilling reading experience.

Many remarked on the similarity of *The Waterworks* to nineteenth-century detective and mystery stories. "On the surface, the novel has all the suspense and the appeal of a period detective melodrama, complete with fainting beauties, lovely impoverished widows, cold-blooded villains, and wonderfully spooky set pieces," Francine Prose wrote in the *Washington Post Book World.* Ted Solotaroff observed in a review for the *Nation* that "Hints and glints of Poe are embedded in its twinned interests in mystery and science, its detective-story format, its necrological overlay, its protagonist—a brilliant, noir, disinherited literary journalist—its man-about-New York ambiance, even a mansion named Ravenwood." According to William Hutchings in *World Literature Today,* "the foremost literary precedents for *The Waterworks* are the stories of Arthur Conan Doyle: McIlvane's investigation proceeds with Holmes-like logic. . . . Dr. Sartorius, [is] a Moriarty-like evil genius. . . ."

The Waterworks was also recognized as a social commentary on America—both past and present. According to Will Blythe in *Esquire*, the novel "is most of all a suspenseful inquiry into the relationship in America between power, evil, and the growth of the city, in this case Manhattan in the 1870s, the era of Boss Tweed. The novel implies that beneath the decorous surface of nineteenth-

Fifteen-year-old Billy Bathgate, mascot and apprentice to gangsters of Depression-era New York City, introduces a memorable cast of underworld characters in this acclaimed 1989 work.

century America, there were plenty of ungodly energies bubbling away." Writing in the *New York Times Book Review,* Simon Schama observed, "Almost all of Mr. Doctorow's novels have been, to some degree, documents of New York history. . . . But in 'The Waterworks,' New York is no longer a setting . . . it *is* the action, the principal character, the presiding genius and the trap of history." Schama continued, "Mr. Doctorow's postbellum Gehenna is plainly held up as a mirror in which we are meant to see our own time and manners." Andrew Delbanco of the *New Republic* described *The Waterworks* as a "fantastic novel . . . a sort of moral prehistory of our own age." Doctorow, he said, "concentrates his pity and horror into images rather than arguments" and creates "a persuasive portrait of an era akin to our

own . . . in which, for the first time, human beings had become indistinguishable from litter."

Not all critics enjoyed the emphasis on New York's history or the elements of social criticism in *The Waterworks.* "Doctorow's troubles begin where the ambition swells and etudes get inflated into historical novels—mournful fanfares given a social/historical spin. That was the problem with 'Ragtime'; so it is with "The Waterworks,'" Mark Shechner pointed out in a review in the Chicago *Tribune Books.* Others found *The Waterworks* less impressive than Doctorow's previous fiction. "Readers of this book will wait in vain for the irony and sensuality of 'Ragtime,' the sumptuous prose and vivid characters of 'Billy Bathgate,' the viscerality of 'The Book of Daniel,'" lamented Jonathan Franzen in the *Los Angeles Times Book Review.*

Having developed a reputation as a vocal, outspoken writer, Doctorow has never simply let his novels explain his beliefs about American culture and society. His essays, speeches, articles, and reviews have been published in collections, yet this work has received less attention than his novels. Among the collections are *Jack London, Hemingway, and the Constitution* and *Poets and Presidents.* In "the best of these essays," wrote a *New York Times* critic about *Jack London,* the "the spirit moving here" "is a beguiling blend of gravity and humor." *Times Literary Supplement* reviewer Stephen Fender appreciated Doctorow's essays in *Poets and Presidents.* Fender noted that they provide "a key to the author's own work in a way that no other criticism by a contemporary novelist does." In any case, as Doctorow explained to Baker in *Publishers Weekly,* reviews of *Jack London, Hemingway and the Constitution* had "been 98% favorable."

Doctorow has also expressed his views on topics ranging from politics to publishing in various forums around the country. When he won the American Book Award in 1986, Baker reported in *Publishers Weekly,* he announced he would donate much of the $10,000 prize he had won to help free writers from prison or exile. Michael Kilian also reported in the *Chicago Tribune* that when Doctorow was awarded the PEN/Faulkner Award for Fiction, he took the opportunity to voice his opinions about politicians. Doctorow joined other prominent writers in 1989 to defend the exiled novelist Salman Rushdie, who was under sentence of death in Iran for writing a book that was critical of the Islamic religion. In 1991 Doctorow and several fellow writers and PEN members—among them Allen Ginsberg, Edward Said, and Susan Sontag—sent a letter to the *New York Times* to protest the detention of a Palestinian activist.

During the mid-1990s Doctorow continued to write. He also taught creative writing at New York University, where, as Baker noted in *Publishers Weekly*, he advised his students "to read plenty of poetry." Doctorow was involved in some interesting projects as well. According to Deirdre Carmody in a *New York Times* article, he and several other investors, including actor Paul Newman and the *Nation* magazine editor Victor S. Navasky, acquired the *Nation*. In addition, Doctorow started a highly publicized project, "Booknet," the first book-oriented cable channel. The twenty-four-hours-a-day channel was to feature readings, profiles, news stories, and book reviews. Doctorow was enthusiastic about the project. As he told Baker, "Booknet is an essential way to combine *our* [print] culture with today's electronic culture.

■ **Works Cited**

Baker, John F., "American Book Awards: Back to Their Roots," *Publishers Weekly*, November 28, 1986, p. 15.

Baker, John F., "E. L. Doctorow," *Publishers Weekly*, June 27, 1994, pp. 51-52.

Blythe, Will, "Dirty Secrets of the Rich," review of *The Waterworks*, *Esquire*, June, 1994, p. 148.

Carmody, Deirdre, "Editor in Deal for *Nation* Magazine," *New York Times*, January 14, 1995, p. A-41.

Clifford, Andrew, "True-ish Crime Stories," review of *Billy Bathgate*, *Listener*, September 14, 1989, p. 29.

Delbanco, Andrew, "Necropolis News," review of *The Waterworks* and *Jack London, Hemingway, and the Constitution*, *New Republic*, July 18 & 25, 1994, pp. 44-48.

Doctorow, E. L., *Billy Bathgate*, Random House, 1989.

Doctorow, E. L., Allen Ginsberg, Larry McMurtry, Arthur Miller, Edward Said, and Susan Sontag, "War Covers Crackdown on Palestinians," *New York Times*, February 18, 1991, p. A-22.

Doctorow, E. L., interview with Donna Seaman, *Booklist*, October 1, 1994, pp. 238-39.

Eder, Richard, "Siege Perilous in the Court of Dutch Schultz," review of *Billy Bathgate*, *Los Angeles Times Book Review*, March 5, 1989, p. 3.

Fender, Stephen, "The Novelist as Liar," review of *Poets and Presidents* and *The Waterworks*, *Times Literary Supplement*, May 27, 1994, p. 20.

Franzen, Jonathan, "Where Our Troubles Began," review of *The Waterworks*, *Los Angeles Times Book Review*, June 19, 1994, pp. 1, 8.

Hutchings, William, review of *The Waterworks*, *World Literature Today*, Winter, 1992, pp. 138-39.

Review of "Jack London, Hemingway and the Constitution," *New York Times*, November 4, 1993, p. C-24.

Kilian, Michael, "Doctorow Wins PEN/Faulkner Prize in Fiction," *Chicago Tribune*, May 14, 1990, p. 14.

Lehmann-Haupt, Christopher, review of *Loon Lake*, *New York Times*, September 12, 1980.

Prose, Francine, "Nightmares in Old Gotham," review of *The Waterworks*, *Washington Post Book World*, June 5, 1994, pp. D-1, 9.

Rubin, Merle, "Bathgate: Technique Surpasses Tale," review of *Billy Bathgate*, *Christian Science Monitor*, March 22, 1989, p. 13.

Rubin, Merle, "Doctorow's Nightmarish, 19th-Century Metropolis," review of *The Waterworks*, *Christian Science Monitor*, June 13, 1994, p. 13.

Rushdie, Salman, "Billy the Streetwise Kid," review of *Billy Bathgate*, *Observer*, September 10, 1989, p. 51.

Schama, Simon, review of *The Waterworks*, *New York Times Book Review*, June 19, 1994, p. 1.

Shechner, Mark, "A 'Gothic fantasia' from E. L. Doctorow," review of *The Waterworks*, *Tribune Books* (Chicago), July 10, 1994, p. 3.

Solotaroff, Ted, "Of Melville, Poe and Doctorow," review of *The Waterworks*, *Nation*, June 67, 1994, pp. 784-90.

Tonkin, Boyd, "A Round Table Story," review of *Billy Bathgate*, *New Statesman and Society*, September 15, 1989, p. 37.

Tyler, Anne, "An American Boy in Gangland," review of *Billy Bathgate*, *New York Times Book Review*, February 26, 1989, pp. 1, 46.

Whitworth, John, "A Wonderful Town, Even Then," review of *The Waterworks* and *Poets and Presidents: Selected Essays, 1977-1992*, *Spectator*, May 28, 1994, p. 33.

Wood, Michael, "Light and Lethal American Romance," review of *Billy Bathgate*, *Times Literary Supplement*, September 15, 1989, p. 997.

Review of *World's Fair*, *Publishers Weekly*, September 13, 1985, p. 124.

Yardley, Jonathan, "E. L. Doctorow: Mr. 'Ragtime,'" *Miami Herald*, December 21, 1975, pp. 88-89.

■ For More Information See

BOOKS

Fowler, Douglas, *Understanding E. L. Doctorow,* University of South Carolina Press, 1992.

Morris, Christopher D., *Models of Misrepresentation: On the Fiction of E. L. Doctorow,* University Press of Mississippi, 1991.

Parks, John G., *E. L. Doctorow,* Continuum, 1991.

PERIODICALS

American Literature, March, 1978.

Architectural Digest, November, 1992, p. 31.

Booklist, April 15, 1994; October 1, 1994, p. 238.

Detroit News, November 10, 1985.

Entertainment Weekly, June 17, 1994, p. 46; July 15, 1994, p. 58.

Esquire, June, 1994, p. 148.

Glamour, March, 1989, p. 190.

Interview, February, 1989, p. 96.

Journal of Popular Culture, Fall, 1989.

Kirkus Reviews, August 15, 1993, p. 1045.

Locus, July, 1994, p. 37.

Los Angeles Times Book Review, March 5, 1989; June 19, 1994, p. 1; November 24, 1995.

Modern Fiction Studies, Summer, 1976.

Nation, June 2, 1979; September 27, 1980; November 17, 1984; November 30, 1985; April 3, 1989, p. 454; October 2, 1989; June 6, 1994, pp. 784-90.

National Review, August 15, 1975; March 14, 1986; May 5, 1989, p. 52; December 27, 1993, p. 72.

Newsweek, June 7, 1971; July 14, 1975; November 4, 1985; February 13, 1989, p. 76; June 27, 1994, p. 53.

New Yorker, December 9, 1985; March 27, 1989, p. 112; June 27, 1994, p. 195.

New York Times Book Review, September 25, 1960; July 4, 1971; July 6, 1975; September 28, 1980; December 6, 1984; November 10, 1985; February 26, 1989, p. 1; December 3, 1989, p. 69; June 19, 1994, p. 1.

People, March 20, 1989, p. 33; July 4, 1994, p. 28.

Rolling Stone, October 17, 1991, p. 53.

Time, February 27, 1989, p. 76.

Village Voice, July 7, 1975; July 14, 1975; August 4, 1975; December 4, 1978; September 22, 1980; November 26, 1985; December 18, 1985; February 27, 1989, p. 76; June 20, 1994, p. 66.*

—Sketch by R. Garcia-Johnson

Alexandre Dumas

■ Personal

Full name, Alexandre Dumas Davy de la Pailleterie; born July 24, 1802, in Villers-Cotterets, France; died December 5, 1870, in Puys, France; buried at Villers-Cotterets; son of Thomas Alexandre Dumas (a general in Napoleon's army) and Marie-Louise-Elizabeth (Labouret) Davy de la Pailleterie; married Ida Ferrier, 1849; children: Alexandre, Marie Alexandrine, Henry Bauer, Micaella Cordier. *Education:* Attended school for a short while, but was largely self-taught and educated at home by family members. *Politics:* Republican.

■ Career

Novelist and playwright. Apprenticed to a local notary at age fifteen. Went to Paris to work for the Duc d'Orleans, first as a clerk and then as a librarian, 1923-30. Aided LaFayette when revolution threatened France in 1830, and became a local hero until exiled by the new king, Louis Philippe (the former Duc d'Orleans). *Military service:* Fought with Garibaldi in the attack on Sicily and Naples, 1860, in the battle to unify Italy.

■ Writings

NOVELS

La Salle d'armes (three stories: "Pauline", "Pascal Bruno," and "Murat"), Dumont, 1838, translations published separately as *Pauline: A Tale of Normandy,* J. Winchester, 1842, *Pascal Bruno,* Colburn, 1837, and *Murat,* Methuen, 1907.

(With Adrien Dauzats) *Le Capitaine Paul* (based on James Fenimore Cooper's novel, *The Pilot*), Dumont, 1838, translation published as *Captain Paul the Pirate: A Tale of the Sea,* G. Pierce, 1848.

La Comtesse de Salisbury, Dumont, 1839.

Acte, Dumont, 1839, translation by Henry W. Herbert published as *Acte of Corinth; or, The Convert of St. Paul,* E. P. Williams, 1847.

Aventures de John Davys, Dumont, 1840.

Maitre Adam le Colabrais, Dumont, 1840, translation by Harry A. Spurr published as *Master Adam the Calabrian,* R. F. Fenno, 1902.

Othon l'archer, Dumont, 1840, translation published as *Otho the Archer,* H. Lea, 1869.

Le Maitre d'armes, Dumont, 1840, translation by G. Griswold published as *The Fencing Master; or, Eighteen Months in St. Petersburg,* Stretton & Burnard, 1850.

Le Capitaine Pamphile, Dumont, 1840, translation by Douglas Munroe with illustrations by William Papas published as *Captain Pamphile's Adventures,* Oxford University Press, 1971.

La Chasse au chastre (also see below), [Paris], 1841, translation published as *The Bird of Fate,* Methuen, 1906.

Jehanne la pucelle, 1429-1431, Magen & Cormon, 1842, translation published as *Joan the Heroic Maiden,* J. S. Pratt, 1847.

Aventures de Lyderic, Dumont, 1842, translation published as *Lyderic, Count of Flanders,* R. B. Johnson, 1903.

Albine, C. Maquardt, 1842, reissued as *Le Chateau d'Eppstein,* de Potter, 1844, translation published as *The Spectre Mother,* Clarke, 1864.

Georges, Dumont, 1843, translation by G. J. Knox published as *George; or, The Planter of the Isle of France,* Simms & MacIntyre, 1846.

(With Paul Meurice) *Ascanio,* Petion, 1843-44, translation published as *Ascanio,* Simms & MacIntyre, 1861.

(With Auguste Maquet) *Le Chevalier d'Harmental* (also see below), Dumont, 1843, translation by H. L. Williams published as *The Orange Plume; or, The Bride of the Bastille,* E. D. Long, 1860.

(With Meurice) *Amaury,* H. Souverain, 1844, translation published as *Amaury,* Harper, 1854.

Cecile, Dumont, 1844, translation published as *Cecile,* Methuen, 1904.

Gabriel Lambert, H. Souverain, 1844, translation published as *Gabriel Lambert,* Methuen, 1904.

Fernande, Dumont, 1844, translation published as *Fernande,* Methuen, 1904.

Les Freres Corses (also see below), Cans, 1844, translation by Gerardus van Dam published as *The Corsican Brothers,* G. Munro, 1883.

(With Maquet) *Sylvandire* (also see below), Dumont, 1844, translation by T. Williams published as *The Disputed Inheritance,* Clarke, 1847, translation published as *Sylvandire: A Romance of The Reign of Louis XIV,* Little, Brown, 1897.

(With Maquet) *Les Trois Mousquetaires* (also see below), Baudry, 1844, translation by William Robson published as *The Three Musketeers,* Routledge, 1853, translation by William Barrow, Pan Books, 1974.

(With Maquet) *Le Comte de Monte Cristo* (also see below), Petion, 1844-45, translation by William Thiese published in two parts as *Edmond Dantes, The Count of Monte Cristo* and *The Count of Monte Cristo; or, The Revenge of Edmond Dantes,* M. J. Ivers, 1892, new edition illustrated by Bill Sokol published as *The Count of Monte Cristo,* Platt & Munk, 1968.

La Fille de regent, Cadot, 1845, translation by Charles H. Town published as *The Regent's Daughter,* Harper, 1845.

(With Maquet) *La Reine Margot* (also see below), Garnier Freres, 1845, translation published as *Marguerite de Valois,* R. Griffin, 1850, translation published as *Queen Margot,* Routledge, 1856.

(With Maquet) *Vingt ans apres* (also see below), Baudry, 1845, translation by Barrow published as *Twenty Years After; or, The Further Feats and Fortunes of a Gascon Adventurer,* Bruce & Wyld, 1846, new edition, Collins, 1962.

La Guerre des femmes (also see below), de Potter, 1845-46, translation published as *Nanon,* Routledge, 1867, translation published as *The War of Women,* Little, Brown, 1895.

(With Maquet) *Le Chevalier de Maison-Rouge* (also see below), Cadot, 1846, translation published as *Marie Antoinette; or, The Chevalier of the Red House: A Tale of the French Revolution,* G. Pierce, 1845, translation published as *The Chevalier de Maison Rouge,* G. Munro, 1877.

(With Maquet) *La Dame de Monsoreau* (also see below), Petion, 1846, translation published as *Chicot the Jester,* Clarke, 1857, new edition, Collins, 1956.

(With Meurice) *Les Deux Diane,* Cadot, 1846-47, translation published as *The Two Dianes,* Simms & MacIntyre, 1857.

(With Maquet) *Le Batard de Mauleon,* Cadot, 1846-48, translation published as *The Bastard of Mauleon,* Appleyard, 1848, translation by L. Lawford published as *The Half Brothers,* Routledge, 1858.

(With Maquet) *Memoires d'un medecin: Joseph Balsamo* (also see below), Cadot, 1846-48, translation published as *Memoirs of a Physician,* Clarke, 1854.

(With Maquet) *Les Quarante-cinq,* Cadot, 1848, translation published as *The Forty-Five Guardsmen,* Clarke, 1861, translation published as *The Forty-Five,* Little, Brown, 1984.

(With Maquet) *Le Vicomte de Bragelonne; ou, Dix ans plus tard* (also see below), M. Levy Freres, 1848-50, translation published as *The Vicomte de Bragelonne; or, Ten Years Later,* Routledge, 1857, translation by H. L. Williams published in three volumes: *The Vicomte de Bragelonne, the Son of Athos; or, Ten Years Later, Louise de La Valliere; or, The Love of Bragellone,* and *The Man in the Iron Mask,* F. M. Lupton, 1892 (*The Man in the Iron Mask,* illustrated by E. Legrand with an introduction by A. Maurois, published separately, Limited Editions, 1965).

(With Paul Bocage) *Les Mille et un fantomes: Une Journee a Fonlenay-Aux-Roses* (stories about the occult), Cadot, 1849, translation published as *Tales of the Supernatural, Tales of Strange Adventure,* and *Tales of Terror,* Methuen, 1907-09.

(With Maquet) *Le Collier de la reine,* Cadot, 1849-50,

translation published as *The Queen's Necklace*, Clarke, 1861, new edition with illustrations by Cyril Arnstam, Limited Editions, 1973.

(With Bocage) *Les Mariages du Pere Olifus*, Cadot, 1850, translation published as *The Marriages of Pere Olifus*, Methuen, 1907.

(With Maquet and Paul Lacroix) *La Tulipe noire*, Baudry, 1850, translation published as *Rosa; or, The Black Tulip*, Clarke, 1861, new edition published as *The Black Tulip*, Mayflower, 1970.

Le Testament de Monsieur de Chauvelin, Cadot, 1850, translation by Mary Stuart Smith published as *Monsieur de Chauvelin's Will*, G. Munro, 1900.

Le Trou de l'enfer, Cadot, 1850-51, translation published as *The Mouth of Hell*, Methuen, 1906.

(With Lacroix) *La Femme au collier de velours*, Cadot, 1851, translation by Smith published as *The Woman with the Velvet Collar*, G. Munro, 1900.

La Colombe, Cadot, 1851, translation published as *The Dove*, Methuen, 1906.

Dieu dispose, Cadot, 1851-52, translation published as *God's Will Be Done*, Methuen, 1909, translation by Alexandre Dumas (fils) published as "The Pigeon Prize," *Golden Book Magazine*, September, 1930.

(With Lacroix) *Olympe de Cleves*, Cadot, 1852, translation published as *Olympe de Cleves*, Little, Brown, 1893.

Conscience l'innocent, Cans, 1852, translation published as *The Conscript: A Tale of War*, T. B. Peterson, 1863.

Les Drames de la mer (sea stories), Cadot, 1852.

La Maison de Savoie, C. Perrin, 1852-56.

Le Pasteur d'Ashbourne, Cadot, 1853.

L'Horloger, 1853, translation published as *The Watchmaker*, Clarke, 1862.

Isaac Laquedem, Marchant, 1853.

(With Maquet) *Ange Pitou*, Cadot, 1853, translation published as *Six Years Later; or, Taking the Bastille*, G. Munro, 1878, translation published as *Ange Pitou*, Little, Brown, 1890.

La Comtesse de Charny, Cadot, 1853-55, translation published as *The Countess de Charny*, Lea, 1860.

Catherine Blum (also see below), Cadot, 1854, translation published as *The Foresters*, D. Appleton, 1854.

Le Salteador, Cadot, 1854, translation published as *The Brigand*, Dent, 1897.

La Princesse de Monaco, Cadot, 1854.

(With Lacroix) *Ingenue*, Cadot, 1854, translation published as *Ingenue; or, The Socialists of Paris*, G. Munro, 1878.

(With Bocage) *Les Mohicans de Paris* [et] *Salvator* (also see below), Cadot, 1854-59, translations published separately as *The Mohicans of Paris*, T. B. Peterson, 1859, and *Salvator*, G. Munro, 1882.

Le Page du Duc de Savoie, Cadot, 1855, translation published as *Emmanuel Philibert; or, The European Wars of the Sixteenth Century*, D. Appleton, 1854, translation published as *The Page of the Duke of Savoy*, G. Munro, 1878.

Madame de Deffand, Cadot, 1856-57, reissued as *Memoires d'une Aveugle* [et] *Confessions de la Marquise*, M. Levy Freres, 1862.

Les Compagnons de Jehu (also see below), Cadot, 1857, translation by Katharine Prescott Wormeley published as *The Company of Jehu*, Estes & Lauriat, 1894.

Le Meneur de loups, Cadot, 1857, translation by A. Allinson published as *The Wolf-Leader*, Methuen, 1904, reissued with illustrations by Mahlon Blaine, Prime Press, 1950.

Le Capitaine Richard, Cadot, 1858, translation by Williams published as *The Twin Lieutenants; or, The Soldier's Bride*, Peterson Brothers, 1862.

Black (also see below), Cadot, 1858, translation published as *Black: The Story of A Dog*, Little, Brown, 1895.

L'Horoscope, Cadot, 1858, translation published as *The Horoscope: A Romance of the Reign of Francois II*, Little, Brown, 1897.

Herminie, Cans, 1858, reissued as *Une Aventure d'Amour*, M. Levy Freres, 1863.

Ammalat-Bey, Cadot, 1859, reissued as *Sultanetta*, M. Levy Freres, 1862, translation by Allinson with illustrations by F. Adams published as *Sultanetta*, Methuen, 1904.

Charles le temperaire, M. Levy Freres, 1859, translation published as *Charles the Bold*, Hodgson, 1860.

L'Histoire d'un cabanon et d'un chalet, Meline, Cans, 1859, reissued as *Monsieur Coumbes: Roman Marseilles*, M. Levy Freres, 1869, translation published as *The Convict's Son*, Methuen, 1905.

Les Louves de Machecoul, Cadot, 1859, translation by Wormeley published as *The Last Vendee; or, the She-Wolves of Machecoul*, Estes & Lauriat, 1894.

La Princess Flora, Meline, Cans, 1859.

Ainsi soit-il!, Meline, Cans, c. 1859, reissued as *Madame de Chamblay* (also see below), Cadot, 1862, translation published as *Madame de Chamblay*, Turner Brothers, 1869.

La Chasseur de sauvagine, Cadot, 1859, translation published as *The Wild Duck Shooter*, Methuen, 1906.

Marianna, Meline, Cans, 1859, translation published as *Marianna*, Methuen, 1905.

Le Medecin de Java, c. 1859, reissued as *L'Ile de Feu*, M. Levy Freres, 1879, translation published as *Doctor Basilius*, Routledge, 1860.

Jane, Meline, Cans, 1859, translation published as *Jane*, Methuen, 1903.

La Maison de glace, M. Levy Freres, 1859, translation published as *The Russian Gipsy; or, The Palace of Ice*, Clarke, 1861.

Le Pere la ruine, M. Levy Freres, 1860, translation published as *Pere la Ruine*, Methuen, 1905.

Jacquot sans oreilles, Meline, Cans, 1860, translation by Allinson with illustrations by G. Browne published as *Crop-Eared Jacquot*, Methuen, 1905.

Les Drames galants, M. Levy Freres, 1860.

Une Nuit a Florence sous Alexandre de Medicis, M. Levy Freres, 1861.

La Boule de neige, M. Levy Freres, 1862, translation by Allinson with illustrations by F. Adams published as *The Snow Ball*, Methuen, 1904.

La Dame de Volupte: Memoires de Mademoiselle de Luynes, M. Levy Freres, 1863.

Les Deux reines, M. Levy Freres, 1864.

La Peche aux filets, [Paris], 1864, translation published as *Netting the Waters*, Methuen, 1904.

La San-Felice [et] Emma Lyonna, M. Levy Freres, 1864-65, translation by Williams published as *The Lovely Lady Hamilton; or, The Beauty and the Glory* [London], 1903, published as *The Neapolitan Lovers [and] Love and Liberty*, S. Paul, 1916-18.

(With Charles Nodier) *Les Blancs et les bleus* (also see below), M. Levy Freres, 1867-68, translation by Wormeley published as *The First Republic; or, The Whites and the Blues*, Estes & Lauriat, 1894.

La Terreur Prussienne, M. Levy Freres, 1867, translation by R. S. Garnett published as *The Prussian Terror*, S. Paul, 1915.

(With Gaspard de Cherville) *Parisiens et provinciaux*, M. Levy Freres, 1868.

The Count of Moret (translated from the French by Williams), Peterson Brothers, 1868.

Le Docteur mysterieux, M. Levy Freres, 1872.

La Fille du marquis, M. Levy Freres, 1872.

Le Prince des voleurs (also see below), M. Levy Freres, 1873, translation by Allinson with illustrations by Adams published as *The Prince of Thieves*, Methuen, 1904.

Robin Hood le proscrit, M. Levy Freres, 1873, translation by Allinson with illustrations by Adams published as *Robin Hood the Outlaw*, Methuen, 1904, translation by Lowell Blair published as *Robin Hood, Prince of Outlaws*, Dell, 1965.

Also contributed articles to the *Revue des Deux Mondes*.

PLAYS

(With Adolphe de Leuven and P. J. Rousseau) *La Chasse et l'amour* (title means "The Chase and Love"; one act; produced in Paris, 1825), Duverois, 1825.

La Noce et l'enterrement (title means "The Wedding and the Burial"; three acts; produced in Paris, 1826), Bezou, 1826.

Henry III et sa cour (title means "Henry III and his Court"; five acts; produced in Paris, 1829), Vezard, 1829.

Christine; ou, Stockholm, Fontainebleau, et Rome (five acts; produced in Paris, 1830), J. N. Barba, 1830.

Napoleon Bonaparte; ou, Trente ans dans l'histoire de France (title means "Napoleon Bonaparte; or, Thirty Years in the History of France"; six acts; produced in Paris, 1831), Tourachon, Molin, 1831.

Antony (five acts; produced in Paris, 1831), A. Auffray, 1831, translation by H. A. Spurr published as *Antony*, Tuten, 1904.

Charles VII chez ses grands vassaux (title means "Charles VII and his Chief Vassals"; five acts; produced in Paris, 1831), Lemesle & la Veuve Bechet, 1831.

Richard Darlington (three acts; produced in Paris, 1831), J. N. Barba, 1832.

(With August Anicet-Bourgeois) *Teresa* (five acts; produced in Paris, 1832), C. Lemesle, 1832.

Le Mari de la veuve (title means "The Widow's Husband"; one act; produced in Paris, 1832), A. Auffray, 1832.

(With Frederic Gaillardet) *La Tour de Nesle* (five acts; produced in Paris, 1832), J. N. Barba, 1832, translation by A. L. Gowans published as *The Tower of Nesle*, Gowans & Gray, 1906.

Le Fils de l'emigre (four acts; title means "The Son of the Emigrant"), produced in Paris, 1832.

Perinet Leclerc; ou, Paris en 1418 (five acts; produced in Paris, 1832), J. N. Barba, 1832.

Angele (five acts; produced in Paris, 1833, Charpentier, 1834.

La Venitienne (title means "The Venetian Woman"; five acts; produced in Paris, 1834), J. N. Barba, 1834.

Catherine Howard (five acts; produced in Paris, 1834), Charpentier, 1834, translation by W. D. Suter published as *Catherine Howard*, Lacy's Plays, 1859.

La Tour de Babel (title means "The Tower of Babel"; one act; produced in Paris, 1834), Marchant, 1834.

(With E. C. H. Cordellier-Delanoue) *Cromwell et Charles I* (five acts; produced in Paris, 1835), Marchant, 1835.

(With M. E. G. Theaulon de Lambert and E. Rousseau) *Le Marquis de Brunoy* (five acts; produced in Paris, 1836), J. N. Barba, 1836.

Don Juan de Marana; ou, La Chute d'un ange (title means "Don Juan of Marana; or, The Fall of an Angel"; five acts; produced in Paris, 1836), Marchant, 1836.

(With Theaulon de Lambert) *Kean; ou, Desordre et genie* (five acts; produced in Paris, 1836), J. N. Barba, 1836, translation published as *Edmund Kean; or, The Genius and the Libertine*, Vickers, 1847.

(With Gerard de Nerval) *Piquillo* (three-act opera; music by Hippolyte Monpou; produced in Paris, 1837), Marchant, 1837.

Caligula (five acts; produced in Paris, 1837), Marchant, 1838.

(With Romand) *Le Bourgeois de Gand: ou, Le Secretaire du Duc D' Albe* (title means "The Man from Ghent; or, the Duke of Alba's Secretary"; five acts; produced in Paris, 1838), [Paris], 1838.

Paul Jones (five acts; produced in Paris, 1838), Marchant, 1838.

(With Maquet) *Bathilde* (three acts; produced in Paris, 1839), Marchant, 1839.

Mademoiselle de Belle Isle (three acts; produced in Paris, 1839), Dumont, 1839.

(With de Nerval) *L'Alchimiste* (title means "The Alchemist"; five acts; produced in Paris, 1839), Dumont, 1839.

(With de Nerval) *Leo Burckart* (five acts; produced in Paris, 1839), J. N. Barba, 1839.

(With Charles Lafont) *Jarvis l'honnete homme; ou, Le Marchand de Londres* (title means "Jarvis the Gentleman; or, The Merchant of London"; two acts; produced in Paris, 1840), Henriot, 1840.

Un Mariage sous Louis XV (five acts; produced in Paris, 1841), Marchant, 1841, translation by S. Grundy published as *A Marriage of Convenience: Period Louis XV*, Lacy's Plays, 1899.

(With Eugene Bourgeois) *Jeannil le Breton; ou, Le Gerant responsable* (title means "Jeannil the Breton; or, The Responsible Manager"; five acts; produced in Paris, 1841), Beck, 1842.

Lorenzino (five acts; produced in Paris, 1842), Marchant, 1842.

(With C. Lafont) *Le Seducteur et le mari* (title means "The Seducer and the Husband"; three acts; produced in Paris, 1842), Marchant, 1842.

Halifax (three acts; produced in Paris, 1842), Marchant, 1842.

(With de Leuven and Leon Lherie) *Le Mariage au tambour* (title means "Marriage to Drumbeats"; three acts; produced in Paris, 1843), C. Tresse, 1843.

Les Demoiselles de Saint-Cyr (five acts; produced in Paris, 1843), C. Tresse, 1843, translation published as *The Ladies of Saint-Cyr*, Lacy's Plays, 1870.

(With Louis Lefevre) *L'Ecole des princes* (title means "The School of Princes"; five acts; produced in Paris, 1843), C. Tresse, 1843.

(With de Leuven and Lherie) *Louise Bernard* (five acts; produced in Paris, 1843), Marchant, 1843.

(With de Leuven and Lherie) *Le Laird de Dumbicky* (title means "The Laird of Dumbicky"; five acts; produced in Paris, 1843), Marchant, 1844.

(With de Leuven and Lherie) *Le Garde-forestier* (title means "The Forester"; two acts; produced in Paris, 1845), Beck, 1845.

(With de Leuven and Lherie) *Un Conte de fees* (title means "A Fairy Tale"; three acts; produced in Paris, 1845), Beck, 1845.

(With de Leuven and Louis-Emile Vanderburch) *Sylvandire* (four acts; produced in Paris, 1845), Marchant, 1845.

(With Manquet) *Les Mousquetaires* (based on *Vingt ans apres*; five acts; produced in Paris, 1845), Marchant, 1845.

Une Fille du regent (title means "The Regent's Daughter"; five acts; produced in Paris, 1846), Marchant, 1846.

(With Octave Feuillet and Bocage) *Echec et mat* (title means "Check and Checkmate"; five acts; produced in Paris, 1846), Jerome, 1846.

(With Maquet) *La Reine Margot* (title means "Queen Margot"; five acts; produced in Paris, 1847), M. Levy Freres, 1847.

Intrigue et amor (title means "Intrigue and Love"; five acts; based on play by Johann Schiller; produced in Paris, 1847), M. Levy Freres, 1864.

(With Maquet) *Le Chevalier de Maison-Rouge* (title means "The Knight of Maison-Rouge"; five acts; produced in Paris, 1847), M. Levy Freres, 1847.

(With Meurice) *Hamlet, Prince de Danemark* (based on play by William Shakespeare; five acts; produced in Paris, 1847), M. Levy Freres, 1848.

(With Maquet) *Monte-Cristo I* (five acts; produced in Paris, 1848), C. Tresse, 1848.

(With Maquet) *Monte-Cristo II* (five acts; produced in Paris, 1848), C. Tresse, 1848.

(With Maquet) *Catalina* (five acts; produced in Paris, 1848), M. Levy Freres, 1848.

(With Maquet) *La Jeuness des Mousquetaires* (title means "The Youth of the Musketeers"; five acts; produced in Paris, 1849), Dufoyr & Mulat, 1849.

(With Maquet) *Le Chevalier d'Harmental* (title means "The Chevalier of Harmental"; five acts; produced in Paris, 1849), Cadot, 1849.

(With Maquet) *La Guerre des femmes* (title means "The War of Women"; five acts; produced in Paris, 1849), Cadot, 1849.

(With Eugene Grange and Xavier de Montepin) *Le Connetable de Bourbon; ou, L'Italie au seizieme siecle* (title means "Constable Bourbon; or, Italy in the Sixteenth Century"; five acts; produced in Paris, 1849), Cadot, 1849.

(With Jules Lacroix) *Le Testament de Cesar* (title means "The Testament of Caesar"; five acts; produced in Paris, 1849), M. Levy Freres, 1849.

Le Comte Hermann (five acts; produced in Paris, 1849), Marchant, 1849.

(With Eugene Nus) *Le Cachemire vert* (title means "The Green Cashmere"; one act; produced in Paris, 1849), Marchant, 1850.

Trois Entr'actes pour "L'Amour medecin" (title means "Three Intermissions for 'Love the Doctor'"; produced in Paris, 1850), [Paris], 1864.

(With Maquet) *Urbain grandier* (five acts; produced in Paris, 1850), Marchant, 1850.

Le Vingt-quatre Fevrier; ou, L'Auberge de Schwasbach (title means "The Twenty-fourth of February; or, The Tavern of Schwasbach"; one act; based on the play by Zacharias Werner; produced in Paris, 1859), Marchant, 1850.

(With Maquet) *La Chasse au chastre* (three acts; produced in Paris, 1850), Marchant, 1850.

(With Grange and de Montepin) *Pauline* (five acts; produced in Paris, 1850), Dondey-Dupre, 1850.

(With Grange and de Montepin) *Les Chevaliers du Lansquenet* (five acts; produced, in Paris, 1850), Marchant, 1850.

(With Grange and de Montepin) *Les Freres Corses* (title means "The Corsican Brothers"; produced in Paris, 1850), Dondey-Dupre, 1850.

(With Maquet) *Le Vampire* (five acts; produced in Paris, 1851), [Paris], 1865.

(With Maquet) *Le Comte de Morcerf* (title means "The Count of Morcerf"; five acts; produced in Paris, 1851), C. Tresse, 1851.

(With Maquet) *Villefort* (five acts; produced in Paris, 1851), C. Tresse, 1851.

(With Meurice) *La Barriere de Clichy* (title means "The Clichy Gate"; five acts; produced in Paris, 1851), Marchant, 1851.

(With Meurice) *Benvenuto Cellini* (five acts; produced in Paris, 1852), M. Levy Freres, 1852.

La Jeunesse de Louis XIV (title means "The Youth of Louis XIV"; five acts; produced in Brussels, 1854), Kiessling, Schnee, 1854.

(With Lherie and Bocage) *Le Marbrier* (title means "The Marble-Polisher"; three acts; produced in Paris, 1854), M. Levy Freres, 1854.

La Conscience (six acts; produced in Paris, 1854), Taride, 1854.

Romulus (one act; produced in Paris, 1854), Librairie Theatrale, 1854, translation by Barnett Shaw, Samuel French, 1971.

L'Orestie (three acts; produced in Paris, 1856), Librairie Theatrale, 1856.

(With de Montepin) *La Tour Saint-Jacques* (five acts; produced in Paris, 1856), Marchant, 1856.

Le Verrou de la reine (title means "The Queen's Bolt"; three acts; produced in Paris, 1856), M. Levy Freres, 1865.

(With Charles Gabet) *Les Compagnons de Jehu* (title means "Jehu's Companions"; five acts; produced in Paris, 1857), Beck, 1857.

L'Invitation a la valse (title means "The Invitation to the Waltz"; one act; produced in Paris, 1857), Beck, 1857, translation by C. L. Young published as *Childhood's Dreams*, Lacy's Plays, 1881.

L'Honneur est satisfait (title means "Honor is Satisfied"; one act; produced in Paris, 1858), Librairie Theatrale, 1858.

Les Forestiers (based on his novel *Catherine Blum*; five acts; produced in Marseilles, 1858), M. Levy Freres, 1865.

L'Envers d'une conspiration; ou, Le Fils de Donald le Noir (title means "Behind a Conspiracy; or, The Son of Black Donald"; five acts; produced in Paris, 1860), [Paris], 1860.

(With de Leuven) *Le Roman d'Elvire* (title means "The Romance of Elvire"; three acts; produced in Paris, 1860), M. Levy Freres, 1869.

Le Gentilhomme de la montagne (title means "The Gentleman of the Mountain"; five acts; produced in Paris, 1869), M. Levy Freres, 1860.

(With Maquet) *La Dame de Monsoreau* (title means "The Lady from Monsoreau"; five acts; produced in Paris, 1860), M. Levy Freres, 1860.

(With Maquet) *Le Prisonnier de la Bastille: Fin des Mousquetaires* (title means "The Prisoner of the Bastille: End of the Musketeers"; five acts; produced in Paris, 1861), Calmann-Levy, 1861.

(With Bernard Lopez) *La Veillee Allemande* (title means "The German Vigil"; one act; produced in Paris, 1863), E. Dentu, 1864.

(With Bocage) *Les Mohicans de Paris* (title means

"The Mohicans of Paris"; five acts; produced in Paris, 1864), M. Levy Freres, 1864.

(With Amedee de Jallais) *Gabriel Lambert; ou, Gabriel le faussaire* (title means "Gabriel Lambert; or, Gabriel the Forger"; five acts; produced in Paris, 1866), M. Levy Freres, 1866.

Madame de Chamblay (five acts; produced in Paris, 1868), M. Levy Freres, 1868.

Les Blancs et les bleus (title means "The Whites and the Blues"; five acts; produced in Paris, 1869), M. Levy Freres, 1874.

Joseph Balsamo (completed by Alexandre Dumas, fils), produced in Paris, 1878.

Also author of the following plays, neither published nor produced: "Ivanhoe" (three-act); "Fiesque de Lavagna" (five-act); "L'Ecossais" (five-act); "La Jeunesse de Louis XV" (five-act); (with Meurice) "Romeo et Juliet" (five-act); and "La Femme sans amour" (three-act).

WRITINGS FOR CHILDREN

Histoire d'un Casse-Noisette (based on *The Nutcracker and the Mouse King* by Ernst Hoffmann), J. Hetzel, 1845, translation published as *The Story of a Nutcracker*, Chapman & Hall, 1846, translation with illustrations by Else Hasselriis published as *The Nutcracker of Nuremberg*, McBride, 1930.

La Bouille de la Comtesse Berthe, J. Hetzel, 1845, translation published as *Good Lady Bertha's Honey Broth*, Chapman & Hall, 1846.

La Jeunesse de Pierrot; ou, Le roi de Boheme, Coulon-Pineau, 1854, translation by H. A. Spurr with illustrations by Harry Rountree published as "When Pierrot Was Young" in *Fairy Tales by Dumas*, edited by Spurr, F. A. Stokes, 1904.

Le Lievre de mon Grand-Pere, Cadot, 1857.

L'Homme aux contes (fairy tales), Meline, Cans, c. 1858.

Contes pour les grands et les petit enfants (collection of fairy tales), M. Levy Freres, 1860.

HISTORICAL WRITING

Gaule et France, A. Auffray, 1833, translation published as *The Progress of Democracy*, J. & H. G. Langley, 1841.

La Vendee et madam, Guyon & Canel, 1833, translation published as *The Duchess of Berri in La Vendee*, Bull & Churton, 1833.

Isabel de Baviere, Dumont, 1836, translation by W. Barrow published as *Isabel of Bavaria; or, The Chronicles of France for the Region of Charles VI*, Bruce & Wyld, 1846.

Napoleon, Delloye, 1839, translation by John B. Larner published as *Napoleon*, Putnam, 1894.

Crimes celebres, Querard, 1839-40, translation by I. G. Burnham with illustrations by de Los Rios published as *Celebrated Crimes*, G. Barrie, 1895.

Les Stuarts, Dumont, 1840.

L'Armee Francaise, [Paris], 1841-45.

Louis XIV et son siecle, Dufour & Fellens, 1844-45.

Trois maitres, Recoules, 1844-46.

Les Medicis, Recoules, 1845.

L'Histoire des peintres, Cans, 1845.

Souvenirs d'Antony, M. Levy Freres, 1848.

Louis XV et sa cour, Cadot, 1849.

Montevideo; ou, Une nouvelle troie, N. Chaux, 1850.

Louis XVI et la revolution; ou, Louis XVI et Marie Antoinette, Cadot, 1850-51.

Le Drame de Quatre-vingt-treize: Scenes de la vie revolutionnaire, H. Souverain, 1851-52.

Histoire de la vie politique et privee de Louis-Philippe, Dufour & Mulat, 1852.

Le Dernier roi des Francaise, 1771 a 1851, H. Souverain, 1852, translation published as *The Last King; or, The New France*, S. Paul, 1915.

Les Grands hommes en robe de chambre: Henri IV, Louis XIII, et Richelieu, Cadot, 1856.

Le Grands hommes en robe de chambre: Cesar, Cadot, 1857-58.

Les Garibaldiens: Revolution de Sicile et de Naples, M. Levy Freres, 1861, translation published as *The Garibaldians in Sicily*, Routledge, 1861.

Italians et Flamands, M. Levy Freres, 1862.

Les Souvenirs d'une favorite, M. Levy Freres, 1865.

Les Hommes de fer, M. Levy Freres, 1867.

TRAVEL

Impressions de voyage: En Suisse, [Paris], 1833-34, translation by R. W. Plummer and A. Craig Bell published as *Adventures in Switzerland*, Chilton, 1960.

Nouvelles impressions de voyage: Quinze jours au Sinai, Dumont, 1839, translation published as *Impressions of Travel in Egypt and Arabia Petraea*, J. S. Taylor, 1839, reprinted, Art Guild Reprints, 1968.

Nouvelles impressions de voyage: Midi de la France, Dumont, 1841, translation published as *Pictures of Travel in the South of France*, Ingram, 1852.

Excursions sur les bords du Rhin, Dumont, 1841.

Une Anee a Florence, Dumont, 1841.

Le Speronare, Dumont, 1842, translation by K. P. Wormeley published as *The Speronara,* Dent, 1902.

Le Capitaine arena, Dolin, 1842.

Le Corricolo, Dolin, 1843.

La Villa Palmieri, Dolin, 1843.

De Paris a Cadix, illustrated by Gustave Dore, Garnier Freres, 1848, translation by Alma Elizabeth Murch published as *Adventures in Spain,* Chilton, 1959.

Le Veloce; ou, Tanger, Alger, et Tunis, Cadot, 1848-51, translation by Murch published as *Adventures in Algeria,* Chilton, 1959.

Taiti-Marquiese-Califorie; Journal de Madame Giovanni, Cadot, 1856, translation by Marguerite E. Wilbur published as *The Journal of Madame Giovanni,* Liveright Publishing, 1944.

La Caucase, Librairie Theatrale, 1859, translation by Murch published as *Adventures in Caucasia,* Chilton, 1962, reissued, Greenwood Press, 1975.

La Route de Varennes, M. Levy Freres, 1860, translation by A. C. Bell published as *The Flight to Varennes,* Alston Books, 1962.

De Paris a Astrakan: Nouvelles impressions de voyage, A. Bourdilliat, 1860, reissued as *Impressions de voyage: En Russie,* M. Levy Freres, 1865, translation by Murch published as *Adventures in Czarist Russia,* Chilton, 1961.

Un Gil-blas en Californie, M. Levy Freres, 1861, translation by M. E. Wilbur with illustrations by Paul Landacre published as *A Gil Blas in California,* Primavera Press, 1933.

Un Pays inconnu, M. Levy Freres, 1865.

OTHER

Oeuvres completes (286 volumes of novels, short stories, travel sketches, memoires, histories, and essays), 1848-1900.

Mes Memoires, twenty-two volumes, Cadot, 1852-54, translation by E. M. Waller published as *My Memoirs,* ten volumes, with an introduction by Andrew Lang, Methuen, 1907-9, translation by A. C. Bell published as *My Memoirs,* Chilton, 1961.

Une Vie d'artiste, Cadot, 1854, translation by R. S. Barnett published as *A Life's Ambition,* S. Paul, 1924.

L'Art et les artistes contemporains au salon de 1859, A. Bourdelliat, 1859.

Histoires de mes betes, M. Levy Freres, 1868, translation by A. Allinson with illustrations by V.

Lecomte published as *My Pets,* Methuen, 1909, translation by Bell published as *Adventures with My Pets,* Chilton, 1960.

Souvenirs dramatiques, M. Levy Freres, 1868.

Grand Dictionnaire de cuisine, A. Lemerre, 1873, translation by Louis Colman with illustrations by John Jocoby published as *Dictionary of Cuisine,* Simon & Schuster, 1958.

Propos d'Art et de cuisine, M. Levy Freres, 1877.

Petit Dictionnaire de cuisine, A. Lemerre, 1882.

Oeuvres d'Alexandre Dumas pere (38 volumes of novels), 1962-67.

■ Adaptations

MOTION PICTURES

Black, adapted for film as *Where is My Father?,* Exclusive Features, 1916.

Brigand, Columbia, 1952.

Les Compagnons de Jehu, adapted for film as *Fighting Guardsman,* Columbia, 1945.

Le Comte de Monte Cristo, adapted for film as *The Count of Monte Cristo,* Famous Players, 1912; Twentieth Century-Fox, 1922; United Artists (UA), 1934; adapted for film as *The Return of Monte Cristo,* Columbia, 1946; adapted for film as *The Secret of Monte Cristo,* Metro-Goldwyn-Mayer, 1961; adapted for film as *The Story of the Count of Monte Cristo,* Warner Brothers, 1962.

La Dame de Monsoreau, adapted for film as *Chicot the Jester,* Societe Francaise des Films et Cinematographes Eclair, 1914.

Les Freres Corses, adapted for film as *The Corsican Affair,* Universal, 1915; UA, 1941; adapted for film as *The Bandits of Corsica,* UA, 1954.

Kean; ou, Desordre et Genie, adapted for film as *A Stage Romance,* Twentieth Century-Fox, 1922.

Marguerite de Valois, adapted for film as *Queen Margaret,* Pathe, 1915.

Memoires d'un Medecin: Joseph Balsamo, adapted for film as *Black Magic,* UA, 1949.

Le Prince de Voulers, adapted for film as *The Prince of Thieves,* Columbia, 1947.

Les Trois Mousquetaires, adapted for film as *The Three Musketeers,* Edward Laurillard, 1913; Film Attractions Co., 1914; Douglas Fairbanks Pictures Corp., 1921; Mascot (series of twelve episodes), 1933; RKO Radio Pictures, 1935; Twentieth Century-Fox, 1939; Loew's, 1948; Sterling, 1965; Twentieth Century-Fox, 1974; adapted for film as *D'Artagnan,* Triangle Film Corp., 1916; adapted for film as *The Three Must-Get-Theres,*

Allied Producers & Distributors, 1922; adapted for film as *The Lady in the Iron Mask*, Twentieth Century-Fox, 1952; adapted for film as *The Four Musketeers*, Twentieth Century-Fox, 1975; adapted for film as *The Three Musketeers*, Disney, 1993.

Le Vicomte de Bragelonne, adapted for film as *The Iron Mask*, Elton Co., 1929; adapted for film as *The Man in the Iron Mask*, UA, 1939; adapted for film as *The Prisoner of the Iron Mask*, Alta Vista Productions, 1962.

Vingt and apres, adapted for film as *At Sword's Point*, RKO Radio Picures, 1952.

FILMSTRIPS

The Count of Monte Cristo [and] Cyrano de Bergerac (animated; featuring Mr. Magoo; with a teacher's guide), McGraw-Hill, 1972.

The Three Musketeers (animated; featuring Mr. Magoo; with a teacher's guide), McGraw-Hill, 1972.

TELEVISION

Le Comte de Monte Cristo, adapted for television as *The Count of Monte Cristo* (series), Vision Productions, 1955-56; Bell System Family Theater (special), NBC, 1975.

Le Vicomte de Bragelonne, adapted for television as *The Man in the Iron Mask*, Bell System Family Theater (special), NBC, 1977.

■ Sidelights

Towards the end of his ebullient and prolific career, Alexandre Dumas took pen in hand not to dash off one more spell-binding drama or history-filled epic, but to complain to the Emperor of rough handling by the official censor. Over the years many of Dumas's plays had been banned after limited performances; when his *The Mohicans of Paris* was stopped in pre-production, he had had enough. But in writing to the Emperor, Dumas also summed up his own worth. As reported in Herbert Gorman's *The Incredible Marquis: Alexandre Dumas*, Dumas explained that there were three men at the head of French literature: Victor Hugo, Alphonse de Lamartine, and himself. Dumas then went on to note that though he was not exiled as Hugo had been, he was being financially ruined by the censor just as Lamartine

had. "I do not know what malevolence animates the censor against me. I have written and published twelve hundred volumes. It is not for me to appreciate their literary value. Translated into all languages they have gone as far as steam can carry them. Though I am not the least worthy of the three, these works have made me the most popular in the five parts of the world, perhaps because the first is a thinker, the second a dreamer, while I am, myself, only a vulgarizer."

Though Dumas waxed hyperbolic with his output—the actual number of over 300 titles was large enough by all standards—he was spot on with his self-criticism. "Vulgarizer" might be a bit harsh, but received literary criticism has labeled him a popularizer, and this label has kept him in the anteroom of the literary greats ever since his death. Though two of his novels, *The Three Musketeers* and *The Count of Monte Cristo*, are still so widely read that they have become part of a shared mythic history, Dumas and his works "have been largely unappreciated by critics," according to Barbara T. Cooper in the *Dictionary of Literary Biography*. Cooper posited three reasons for such critical neglect in the face of such popular acclaim. First there is the notoriety surrounding the life of Dumas. Because of his enormous output and because also of his enormous appetite for life—his gala parties and the ever-changing mistresses—intellectual critics have assumed that there was little substance to the man. Secondly, his use of collaborators for much of his prodigious output taints his literary fame. And thirdly, his very popularity condemned his writings as nonliterary. The stories of Dumas rip along at a fantastic pace, avoiding complexity for action, character analysis for plot. However, as Cooper notes, "There are, no doubt, works that are more aesthetically self-conscious than Dumas's. It would, however, be a mistake to conclude that texts which reinvent and recount four centuries of French history are artlessly composed and innocent of meaning or that characters whose passions and ambitions have so enthralled generations of readers are psychologically flat."

Popularizer, man about town, workaholic who put in twelve- to fourteen-hour days. These were all parts of the writer Alexandre Dumas. Common knowledge of the man is most usually in error. Thought of as simply the author of historical romances, a sort of French Sir Walter Scott, Dumas in fact first gained renown for his dramas such as *Henri III and his Court, Antony,* and *The Tower of Nesle,* which played to packed houses in Paris from the 1830s on. But he was also an essayist, poet, journalist, travel writer, memoirist, and one of the first of the great cookbook writers.

Provincial Origins

Dumas was born on July 24, 1802, in the village of Villers-Cotterets in the department of Aisne to the west of Paris. His mother, Marie-Louise-Elisabeth Labouret, was the offspring of a local innkeeper, while his father, Thomas-Alexandre Dumas, had been born in Haiti, son of a French marquis, Antoine-Alexandre Davy de la Pailleterie, and of a black slave woman, Louise-Cessette Dumas. That Dumas's father had taken the name of his slave mother rather than the aristocratic title of his father was demonstration of a breach between the two. Thomas-Alexandre, virtually cut off financially after a late-in-life marriage by his father, had joined the army as a junior officer. At Davy de la Pailleterie's insistence, his son had used the name of Dumas upon enlistment, so as not to drag the more noble name "through the mire of the lowest ranks of the army," as Alexandre Dumas recalled in his autobiography, *My Memoirs.* According to Dumas, his father was something out of myths himself, a prototype of the strong and manly heroes who would populate some of the author's works. In a mere twenty months Thomas-Alexandre Dumas rose from a junior officer to one of the highest military offices under Napoleon. But his fall was as precipitous, for he was strong-minded, and his outspoken criticism of Napoleon earned him an involuntarily retirement from the service just after the birth of his third child, Alexandre Dumas. Thomas-Alexandre died four years later, in 1806. His image, however, lived on in Dumas's imagination, informing the young boy's conceptions of the courageous dragoon.

Times were difficult for the Dumas family after the death of the father, yet young Alexandre did manage to attend a local private school, where he learned penmanship, Latin, and reading. By 1814, his mother had finally received her husband's military pension, with which she opened a tobacconist's shop in Villers-Cotterets, while her son began working as an errand boy for a notary. He was also developing a love for the outdoors and for hunting, a passion which later in-

fused many of his books, and which also provided food for the family table. But Dumas was more than a simple provincial lad; by the age of seventeen, he had already formed two other passions—for the ladies and for the theater. With a young Swedish nobleman, Adolphe de Leuven, who spent part of the year in his village, Dumas co-authored some youthful dramas and managed to see plays in Paris and even go backstage to meet a famous actor of his day, Talma, who encouraged the young man from Aisne.

The Stage of Paris

By 1823, Dumas had managed to fulfill one dream of his: he had left the provinces for Paris, where his fine penmanship and family connections secured him a position as a secretarial assistant to the duc d'Orleans. Assured a comfortable annual salary for his labors of copying out correspondence, Dumas set about the hard work of attaining his second dream—that of becoming a writer. One of the assistants with whom Dumas worked set him a strenuous reading course, from Aeschylus to Shakespeare and Moliere, and from Goethe to Cooper and Scott. Carefully analyzing the works of such masters, Dumas learned the rudiments of drama and fiction, and soon, together with his Swedish friend Leuven, and a further collaborator, Pierre-Joseph Rousseau, he wrote a one-act play, *The Chase and Love,* which was staged in 1825. As Dumas recalled in his memoirs, "It was an immense success." While his employer thought such dramatics trifling and that the young man should concentrate on his secretarial work, Dumas plowed ahead with his literary life, founding a poetry review with Leuven and publishing some of his own poems therein. Collaborating with two other authors, he staged another play, *The Wedding and the Burial,* in 1826. Still Dumas continued his dual life of scribe by day, dramatist by night.

Upon seeing a performance of *Hamlet* in 1827, he finally saw the real direction for his drama, and thereafter developed the blending of a certain degree of historical truth with melodrama which would mark all his works. In 1829 he had his first major success with the staging of his five-act historical drama, *Henri III and His Court.* As Cooper stated in the *Dictionary of Literary Biography,* the play "marked not only the true beginning of Dumas's literary career but also a turning point in the history of French drama." With one sweep of the literary broom, Dumas rid the French stage of its neoclassical drama, replacing it with the high passions and action of Romanticism. Set in 1578, when the royal powers of Henri III were being challenged, the play displays many of the techniques and themes Dumas would employ throughout the rest of his career: a portrait of a society smack in the middle of a political upheaval; actual historical personages employed alongside fictional characters; a tragic romance or two; vibrant and exciting action passages; and dialogue that rings true.

There followed a string of theatrical successes for Dumas: *Charles VII at the Homes of his Great Vassals, Richard Darlington,* and *Antony.* The last mentioned, a drama set in contemporary times, has at its center a doomed Byronic hero, one of the first of his kind on the Paris stage. The English critic A. W. Raitt, in his *Life and Letters in France: The Nineteenth Century,* has called *Antony* "the real preface to the past-Romantic theater in France," and indeed the play has proved serviceable to many generations with a new production even in 1990, more than a century-and-a-half after its penning. Dumas's *The Tower of Nesle,* dealing with aristocratic homicide and orgies during the rein of Louis X, was a favorite of audiences of the time, as titillating as good gossip.

Paris was his; praise came from all sides, even from literary competitors such as Victor Hugo. But, like his father, Dumas was an outspoken

This 1974 20th Century-Fox film adaptation of *The Three Musketeers* starred Richard Chamberlain, Oliver Reed, Michael York, and Frank Finlay.

man, and soon his republican sympathies became known to the new king, Louis Philippe. The young dramatist found it prudent to leave France for a time, traveling in Switzerland with his current lover, an actress named Belle Krelsamer with whom he had a daughter. He had also already fathered a son by another mistress in 1824, named after Dumas, who was destined to become a dramatist in his own right with his *The Lady of the Camelias*. The Swiss trip resulted in the first of many travelogues written by Dumas, *The Glacier Land*, which detailed his impressions of the Alpine lands. Throughout the 1830s, Dumas continued his travels in France, along the Mediterranean, and in Belgium, gathering material. At the same time he wrote dramas such as *Keane, The Alchemist*, and *Paul Jones* that continued to play to delighted audiences but scandalized some critics, among them the English novelist William Makepeace Thackeray. Viewing Dumas's 1836 drama, *Don Juan de Marana*, Thackeray was appalled to find that "the indecency, the coarse blasphemy, and the vulgar wit of this piece should find admirers among the public, and procure a reputation for the author. . . . [Dumas] shows heaven, in order that he may carry debauch into it."

Dumas as Novelist—The Literary Factory

By 1840 Dumas began publishing short novels, having tired of writing only plays. He had learned his "two chief qualities" as a writer, as he described them in his memoirs: a gift for dialogue and narrative. Only later would he discover another pair that were equally as valuable: "gaiety and a lively imagination." These early novels were loosely based on history, for they thus provided a "ready made stage upon which to plan my characters," Dumas related in *My Memoirs*. But profligate living was causing difficulties for Dumas. In 1840 he was married to a long-time partner, Ida Ferrier, but the couple were forced to live in Florence for a time for reasons of economy. His first extensive historical novel was published in serial form as *The Chevalier d'Harmental*; it was also Dumas's first collaboration with Auguste Maquet, with whom he would work closely over the years. All the typical Dumas characteristics are present in this early novel: political conspiracy, a doomed romance, gripping action, betrayal and loyalty in equal measures. With this novel, Dumas began his long process of documenting the history of France at various critical moments, this one set in the

Paris of 1718 and 1719 and against the background of a failed conspiracy against the regent. But the years 1844 and 1845 were perhaps the most productive for Dumas, for it was during that period that he and Maquet collaborated not only on *The Three Musketeers*, but also on the equally renowned *The Count of Monte Cristo*. In fact, during the period between 1840 to 1850, Dumas and collaborators produced three renowned series of novels, the "D'Artagnan Romances," which include *The Three Musketeers, Twenty Years After; or, The Further Feats and Fortunes of a Gascon Adventurer*, and *The Viscount of Bragelonne; or, Ten Years Later*; the "Valois Romances," a further trilogy of books dealing with the reins of the last two kings of the Valois line and of the religious wars of their time, including *Marguerite de Valois, Chicot the Jester* (also known as *The Lady from Monsoreau*), and *The Forty-Five Guardsmen*; and the "Balsamo tetralogy," a work chronicling the story of Marie Antoinette, Louis XVI, and the French Revolution, which is comprised of *Joseph Balsamo* (or *Memoirs of a Physician*), *The Queen's Necklace, The Taking of the Bastille*, and *The Countess de Charny*. These works taken together comprise so many pages and adventures and so much invention that Dumas was accused by some of running a literary factory with legions of unknown and poorly paid collaborators. The decade from 1840 to 1850 was the high point of Dumas's career financially; he built a splendid house at Marly-le-Roi with the profits from his books and plays, calling his villa appropriately "Chateau de Monte-Cristo."

All of these novels share a common thread: set from the sixteenth to the nineteenth century, each deals with the struggles of a protagonist against the historical backdrop. At the same time, this crucible historical situation also figures in the success or failure of the individual, in the chances for happiness or love. *The Three Musketeers* was based on a document that was itself more fiction than history, *Memoires de M. d'Artagnan* by Gatien de Courtilz de Sandras. Set during the rein of Louis XIII, the tale recounts the adventures of young D'Artagnan who becomes a musketeer after performing many heroic deeds and is befriended by the three musketeers. Each of these musketeers is representative of a character type: D'Artagnan himself is usually recognized as the man of action and adventure; Aramis is the cunning one, the schemer; Athos is the aristocrat afflicted by melancholia; and Porthos is the muscular type, the boaster. Together the four swashbuck-

The Count of Monte Cristo by Alexandre Dumas

Translated and abridged by Lowell Bair

Falsely imprisoned in a dungeon in the Chateau d'If, Edmond Dantes not only escapes but has his revenge in this famous French novel.

lers experience adventures against the actual historical backdrop of the intrigues involving Louis XIII, Cardinal Richelieu, Anne of Austria, and the duke of Buckingham in sixteenth-century France. Their famous motto, "All for one and one for all," is as familiar as expressions by Shakespeare. Rather than heavily plotted novels, the three books that comprise the musketeer sequence are "emphatically chronicles, slices from the history of the world . . . the dimensions of which are determined merely by the arbitrary will of the carver," according to the literary historian George Saintsbury in the *Fortnightly Review.* "Dumas has the facility," Saintsbury wrote, "of presenting rapid

and brilliant dioramas of the picturesque aspects of history, animating them with really human if not very intricately analyzed passion, and connecting them with dialogue matchless of its kind." As the critic Richard S. Stowe noted in his critical study, *Alexandre Dumas pere,* "If Dumas had written nothing but *The Three Musketeers,* his fame would have been assured."

Published serially in magazines—as most of Dumas's fiction was—*The Three Musketeers* ranges from a quest for diamonds to the wrath of Milady. The first volume in the trilogy opens on an April day in 1625 with the introduction of a young character reminiscent of Don Quixote—D'Artagnan, riding a yellow nag and wearing his father's sword, arrives with a letter of introduction to the captain of the king's elite corps of musketeers. Of course D'Artagnan's road is not an easy one, and his friendship with the three musketeers must be sealed by duels with each in turn. Cardinal Richelieu plays the heavy, commissioning the evil Milady to steal diamonds given to the Duke of Buckingham by the queen, Anne of Austria. Of course the king, who gave Anne the diamonds in the first place, is unaware of her gift to Buck-ingham. The diamonds must somehow be recovered, and this action is only the first of many adventures that pits D'Artagnan against Milady and Richelieu. The tale of adventures and romance was an instant success in Paris and later the "five parts of the world," as Dumas himself wrote. According to Stowe, much of the popularity is due to "Dumas's rich imagination and love of concrete detail; much comes also from his knowledge of the period absorbed from his extensive reading of other—authentic memoirs." Stowe goes on to point out that "Dominance of dialogue and action . . . is a constant" in this novel, as it is in most of Dumas's work.

Later volumes of the adventures deal tangentially with an attempt to rescue Charles I as well as the restoration of Charles II. *Twenty Years After* is the second in the trilogy, and is set against the civil strife in France and England. Both Richelieu and Louis XIII are now dead, and Anne of Austria rules with Cardinal Mazarin in the name of Louis XIV, who is only fourteen. Athos and Aramis are off in England to help Charles I, who is battling Cromwell; meanwhile Porthos and D'Artagnan remain in Paris at the unwilling beck and call of the unpopular Mazarin. Caught in the revolutionary struggles, the quartet must overcome

If you enjoy the works of Alexandre Dumas, you may also want to check out the following books and films:

The novels in Brian Jacques "Redwall" series, including *Redwall, Mattimeo,* and *The Bellmaker,* 1987.
Howard Pyle, *The Merry Adventures of Robin Hood of Great Renown in Nottinghamshire,* 1883.
Mary Stolz, *Bartholomew Fair,* 1990.
Captain Blood, Warner Bros., 1935.
The Princess Bride, 20th Century-Fox, 1987.

arrest on both sides of the Channel. More episodic than *Three Musketeers, Twenty Years After* is also a longer book, but nowhere near the length of the third novel in the cycle, *The Viscount of Bragelonne,* actually two books in one. It also ranges over thirteen years, whereas the first two only covered two or three each. The last installment deals with the years from 1660 when Louis XIV journeys to meet his Spanish bride to 1673 and the death of D'Artagnan. Along the way there are attempts to restore the English king, Charles II, and a love affair of Louis XIV, as well as the tale usually adapted as *The Man in the Iron Mask.* Though large passages of this final book do not even include the Musketeers, the writer Robert Louis Stevenson declared in his *Memories and Portraits* that "no part of the world has ever seemed to me so charming as these pages, and not even my friends are quite so real, perhaps quite so dear, as D'Artagnan." History truly is mere backdrop for the real story—the passions and adventures of the four protagonists who have been taken by some critics to be symbolic of the four staying points of French civilization.

The Count of Monte Cristo was equally as popular and remains so today despite what some critics have referred to as its bloated final volumes. Inspired once again by an actual historical incident and one reported in the *Memoires tires des archives de la police de Paris,* Dumas's tale of the unjust imprisonment of one Edmond Dantes in the Chateau d'If—and of his escape—is ultimately a novel of revenge. When Dantes finds a hidden treasure on the island of Monte-Cristo, he becomes the self-styled count of Monte-Cristo, and is free to seek

vengeance for his unjust imprisonment, employing all matter of disguise for this purpose. Saintsbury, among other critics, noted that the Chateau d'If section of this multi-volume novel was the truest and that the popularity of the book ended with "the first volume." Inspired by a journey Dumas took to the actual island when accompanying young Prince Napoleon on a visit to nearby Elba, the novel quickly took shape in the same period Dumas and Maquet were busy with the Musketeers. Appearing in serial publication, the novel became as popular as *The Three Musketeers,* whose last serialization appeared only the month before the first serial publication of *The Count of Monte Cristo.*

A Man of Many Parts

The decade from 1840 to 1850 was a turbulent one for Dumas in his private life as well as in his career as an author. His marriage to Ida Ferrier ended after only four years, and Dumas once again resumed his usual habit of moving from affair to affair, most usually with much younger women in the theater. Well into his sixties, he was able to scandalize Paris with his liaison with the American actress, Adah Isaacs Menken. His finances also followed the boom-and-bust cycle of Dumas's love life. By 1849 he had poured so much money into his villa that he had to sell it to avoid bankruptcy. In 1850, with the failure of a theater that he had founded, he fled to Brussels, one step ahead of his creditors. There he lived for three years, still writing plays and historical romances. After reaching an agreement on the rest of his debt, Dumas returned to Paris and started a newspaper, the *Mousquetaire,* only one in a long line of such quixotic ventures, including others called *Monte-Cristo* and *D'Artagnan.* These were generally devoted to publishing his own works.

In 1857, Dumas's former collaborator sued the author for unpaid royalties. Though Maquet subsequently lost his case, the affair opened the old questions as to the authorship of works credited to Dumas. The American critic and novelist, Brander Matthews, addressed this question in his *French Dramatists of the 19th Century.* Matthews concluded that while it was probable that Maquet "made researches, accumulated notes, invented scenes even," it was clear that the "mighty impress of Dumas's hand is too plainly visible in every important passage" for there to be any more than a pupil-master relationship in Maquet's service.

Despite this falling out with his collaborator, Dumas continued his prolific career almost to the very end of his life. His interests were not solely literary, for in 1860 he took part in Giuseppe Garibaldi's campaign to unify Italy and translated many of the Italian leader's works. Dumas's eclectic writings continued to include drama, novels, journalism, and essays; he even proposed to an editor no less than a fictionalized history of civilization, from the time of Jesus to his own era. But this monumental work schedule eventually took its toll on the man. In 1870, as the Prussians were preparing to occupy Paris, Dumas went to stay with his son, a successful playwright in his own name by then. There, at his son's home in Dieppe, Dumas died on December 5. In 1872, his body was transferred to the cemetery of his home town, Villers-Cotterets.

Though critical judgment has vacillated over the years, one thing has never been questioned: Dumas is the father of the page-turner, mixing action and romance in a powerful brew. As is fitting, Dumas himself summed up his work best. As reported in *The Titans* by Andre Maurois, Dumas noted that his first desire "is always limitless; my first inspiration is to achieve the impossible. . . . Having discovered a vein of gold in the well of the beginning of the fifteenth century . . . I never doubted . . . that at each well a century nearer our own times, I should find, if not a vein of gold, at least one of platinum or silver."

■ Works Cited

Cooper, Barbara T., "Alexandre Dumas," *Dictionary of Literary Biography*, Volume 119: *Nineteenth-Century French Fiction-Writers: Romanticism and Realism, 1800-1860*, Gale, 1992, pp. 98-119.

Dumas, Alexandre, *My Memoirs*, translated by A. Craig Bell, Peter Owen, 1961.

Gorman, Herbert, *The Incredible Marquis: Alexandre Dumas*, Farrar, and Rinehart, 1939.

Matthews, Brander, "Alexandre Dumas," *French Dramatists of the 19th Century*, 3rd Edition, Scribner's, 1901, pp. 46-77.

Maurois, Andre, *The Titans*, translated by Gerard Hopkins, Harper, 1957.

Raitt, A. W., "Alexandre Dumas pere,: 'Antony'," *Life and Letters in France: The Nineteenth Century*, Scribner's, 1965, pp. 36-42.

Saintsbury, George, "Alexandre Dumas," *Fortnightly Review*, October 1, 1878, pp. 527-42.

Stevenson, Robert Louis, "A Gossip on a Novel of Dumas," *Memoirs and Portraits*, Scribner's, 1912, pp. 212-28.

Stowe, Richard S., *Alexandre Dumas pere*, Twayne, 1976.

Thackeray, William Makepeace, "French Drama and Melodrama," *The Paris Sketchbook of Mr. M. A. Titmarsh*, Estes and Lauriat, 1891, pp. 358-83.

■ For More Information See

BOOKS

Bell, A. Craig, *Alexandre Dumas: A Biography and Study*, Cassell, 1950.

Gribble, Francis, *Dumas: Father and Son*, E.P. Dutton & Co., 1930.

Maurois, Andre, *Alexandre Dumas: A Great Life in Brief* (translated from the French by Jack Palmer White), Knopf, 1955.

Pearce, G. R., *Dumas Pere*, Duckworth, 1934.

Spurr, Harry S., *The Life and Writings of Alexandre Dumas*, F. A. Stokes, 1902.

World Literature Criticism, Gale, 1992.*

—*Sketch by J. Sydney Jones*

Nikki Giovanni

■ Personal

Born Yolande Cornelia Giovanni Jr., June 7, 1943, in Knoxville, TN; daughter of Gus Jones (a probation officer) and Yolande Cornelia (a social worker; maiden name, Watson) Giovanni; children: Thomas Watson. *Education:* Fisk University, B.A. (with honors), 1967; postgraduate studies at University of Pennsylvania School of Social Work and Columbia University School of Fine Arts, 1968.

■ Addresses

Office—English Department, Virginia Polytechnic Institute and State University, Blacksburg, VA 24061.

■ Career

Poet, writer, lecturer. Queens College of the City University of New York, Flushing, assistant professor of black studies, 1968; Rutgers University, Livingston College, New Brunswick, NJ, associate professor of English, 1968-72; Ohio State University, Columbus, visiting professor of English, 1984; College of Mount St. Joseph on the Ohio, Mount St. Joseph, Ohio, professor of creative writing, 1985-87; Virginia Polytechnic Institute and State University, Blacksburg, VA, professor, 1987—; Texas Christian University, visiting professor in humanities, 1991. Founder of publishing firm, NikTom Ltd., 1970; participated in "Soul at the Center," Lincoln Center for the Performing Arts, 1972; Duncanson artist-in-residence, Taft Museum, Cincinnati, 1986; co-chair, Literary Arts Festival for State of Tennessee Homecoming, 1986; appointed to Ohio Humanities Council, 1987; director, Warm Hearth Writer's Workshop, 1988—; member of board of directors, Virginia Foundation for Humanities and Public Policy, 1990-93; featured poet, International Poetry Festival, Utrecht, Holland, 1991; participant in Appalachian Community Fund, 1991-93, and Volunteer Action Center, 1991-94. Has given numerous poetry readings and lectures worldwide and appeared on numerous television talk shows. *Member:* National Council of Negro Women, Society of Magazine Writers, National Black Heroines for PUSH, Winnie Mandela Children's Fund Committee, Delta Sigma Theta (honorary member).

■ Awards, Honors

Grants from Ford Foundation, 1967, National Endowment for the Arts, 1968, and Harlem Cultural Council, 1969; named one of ten "Most Admired

Black Women," *Amsterdam News*, 1969; outstanding achievement award, *Mademoiselle*, 1971; Omega Psi Phi Fraternity Award, 1971, for outstanding contribution to arts and letters; Meritorious Plaque for Service, Cook County Jail, 1971; Prince Matchabelli Sun Shower Award, 1971; life membership and scroll, National Council of Negro Women, 1972; National Association of Radio and Television Announcers Award, 1972, for recording *Truth Is on Its Way*; Woman of the Year Youth Leadership Award, *Ladies' Home Journal*, 1972; National Book Award nomination, 1973, for *Gemini: An Extended Autobiographical Statement on My First Twenty-Five Years of Being a Black Poet*; "Best Books for Young Adults" citation, American Library Association, 1973, for *My House*; "Woman of the Year" citation, Cincinnati Chapter of YWCA, 1983; elected to Ohio Women's Hall of Fame, 1985; "Outstanding Woman of Tennessee" citation, 1985; Post-Corbett Award, 1986; Woman of the Year, NAACP (Lynchburg chapter), 1989. Doctorate of Humanities, Wilberforce University, 1972, and Fisk University; D. Litt., University of Maryland (Princess Anne Campus), 1974, Ripon University, 1974, Smith College, 1975, and Mount St. Joseph on the Ohio, 1983; D.H.L., Mount St. Mary College and Indiana University. Recipient of keys to numerous cities, including Dallas, TX, New York, NY, Cincinnati, OH, Miami, FL, New Orleans, LA, and Los Angeles, CA.

■ Writings

POETRY

Black Feeling, Black Talk (also see below), Broadside Press (Detroit, MI), 1968, 3rd edition, 1970.
Black Judgement (also see below), Broadside Press, 1968.
Black Feeling, Black Talk/Black Judgement (contains *Black Feeling, Black Talk* and *Black Judgement*), Morrow (New York City), 1970, selection published as *Knoxville, Tennessee*, illustrated by Larry Johnson, Scholastic (New York City), 1994.
Re: Creation, Broadside Press, 1970.
Poem of Angela Yvonne Davis, Afro Arts (New York City), 1970.
Spin a Soft Black Song: Poems for Children, illustrated by Charles Bible, Hill & Wang (New York City), 1971, illustrated by George Martins, Lawrence Hill (Westport, CT), 1985, revised edition, Farrar, Straus (New York City), 1987.
My House, foreword by Ida Lewis, Morrow, 1972.

Ego-Tripping and Other Poems for Young People, illustrated by George Ford, Lawrence Hill (Chicago, IL), 1973.
The Women and the Men, Morrow, 1975.
Cotton Candy on a Rainy Day, introduction by Paula Giddings, Morrow, 1978.
Vacation Time: Poems for Children, illustrated by Marisabina Russo, Morrow, 1980.
Those Who Ride the Night Winds, Morrow, 1983.
The Genie in the Jar, illustrated by Chris Raschka, Holt (New York City), 1996.
The Selected Poems of Nikki Giovanni (1968-1995), Morrow, 1996.
The Sun Is So Quiet, illustrated by Ashley Bryant, Holt, 1996.
Love Poems, Morrow, 1997.

Sound recordings by the author of her works include *Truth Is on Its Way*, 1971; *Like a Ripple on a Pond*, 1973; *The Way I Feel*, 1974; and *Legacies: The Poetry of Nikki Giovanni* and *The Reason I Like Chocolate*, both 1976.

OTHER

(Editor) *Night Comes Softly: An Anthology of Black Female Voices*, Medic Press (Newark, NJ), 1970.
Gemini: An Extended Autobiographical Statement on My First Twenty-Five Years of Being a Black Poet, Bobbs-Merrill (Indianapolis, IN), 1971.
(With James Baldwin) *A Dialogue: James Baldwin and Nikki Giovanni*, Lippincott (Philadelphia, PA), 1973.
(With Margaret Walker) *A Poetic Equation: Conversations between Nikki Giovanni and Margaret Walker*, Howard University Press (Washington, DC), 1974.
(Author of introduction) *Adele Sebastian, Intro to Fine* (poems), Woman in the Moon, 1985.
Sacred Cows . . . and Other Edibles (essays), Morrow, 1988.
(Editor, with C. Dennison) *Appalachian Elders: A Warm Hearth Sampler*, Pocahontas Press (Blacksburg, VA), 1991.
(Author of foreword) *The Abandoned Baobob: The Autobiography of a Woman*, Chicago Review Press, 1991.
Racism 101 (essays), Morrow, 1994.
(Editor) *Grand Mothers: Poems, Reminiscences, and Short Stories about the Keepers of Our Traditions*, Holt, 1994.
(Editor) *Shimmy Shimmy Shimmy like My Sister Kate: Looking at the Harlem Renaissance through Poems*, Holt, 1995.

Contributor to numerous anthologies. Contributor of columns to newspapers. Contributor to magazines, including *Black Creation, Black World, Ebony, Essence, Freedom Ways, Journal of Black Poetry, Negro Digest,* and *Umbra.* Editorial consultant, Encore American and Worldwide News.

A selection of Giovanni's public papers is housed at the Mugar Memorial Library, Boston University.

■ Adaptations

Spirit to Spirit: The Poetry of Nikki Giovanni (television film), 1986, produced by Corporation for Public Broadcasting, and Ohio Council on the Arts.

■ Sidelights

One of the best-known African American poets to reach prominence during the late 1960s and early 1970s, Nikki Giovanni has continued to create poems that encompass a life fully experienced. Her unique and insightful verses testify to her own evolving awareness and experiences as a woman of color: from child to young woman, from naive college freshman to seasoned civil rights activist, and from daughter to mother. Frequently anthologized, Giovanni's poetry expresses strong racial pride and respect for family. Her informal style makes her work accessible to both adults and children. In addition to collections such as *Re: Creation, Spin a Soft Black Song,* and *Those Who Ride the Night Winds,* Giovanni has published several works of nonfiction, including *Racism 101* and the anthology *Grand Mothers: Poems, Reminiscences, and Short Stories about the Keepers of Our Traditions.* A frequent lecturer and reader, Giovanni has also taught at Rutgers University, Ohio State University, and Virginia Polytechnic Institute and State University.

Giovanni was born in Knoxville, Tennessee, in 1943, the youngest of two daughters in a close-knit family. Having gained an intense appreciation for her African American heritage from her outspoken grandmother, Louvenia Terrell Watson, Giovanni had a reputation for being strong-willed even as a child. "I come from a long line of storytellers," she once explained in an interview with *Contemporary Authors (CA),* describing how her family influenced her poetry through oral tradi-

tions. "My grandfather was a Latin scholar and he loved the myths, and my mother is a big romanticist, so we heard a lot of stories growing up." This early exposure to the power of spoken language would influence Giovanni's career as a poet, particularly her tendency to sprinkle her verses with colloquialisms such as curse words. "I appreciated the quality and the rhythm of the telling of the stories," she told *CA,* "and I know when I started to write that I wanted to retain that—I didn't want to become the kind of writer that was stilted or that used language in ways that could not be spoken. I use a very natural rhythm; I want my writing to sound like I talk."

When Giovanni was a young child, she moved with her parents from Knoxville, Tennessee, north to a predominantly black suburb of Cincinnati, Ohio. She remained close to her outspoken grandmother, however, spending both her sophomore and junior years of high school at the family home in Knoxville. Encouraged by several schoolteachers, Giovanni enrolled at Fisk University, a prestigious, all-black in college in Nashville, Tennessee. Unaccustomed to Fisk's traditions, the outspoken young woman inevitably came into conflict with the school's dean of women—whom Giovanni characterized as "bitchy"—and was asked to leave. She returned to Fisk in 1964, however, determined to be an ideal student. She accomplished her goal, becoming a leader in political and literary activities on campus during what would prove to be an important era in black history.

Political Outlook Shifts to Left

Giovanni had experienced racism firsthand during her childhood in the South. Random violence that erupted in and near Knoxville "was frightening," she later recalled in an autobiographical essay for *Contemporary Author Autobiography Series (CAAS).* "You always felt someone was trying to kill you. Yet when Giovanni re-entered the freshman class at Fisk she was decidedly conservative in her political outlook. During high school she had been a supporter of Republican presidential candidate Barry Goldwater, as well as an avid reader of books by Ayn Rand, who was famous for her philosophy of objectivism (based on self-assertion and competition). The poet credits a Fisk roommate named Bertha with successfully persuading her to embrace revolutionary ideals. In the wake of the civil rights movement and demonstrations against U.S. involvement in the Vietnam conflict, demands for social and poilitical change were sweeping college campuses around the country. "Bertha kept asking, 'How could Black people be conservative?,'" Giovanni wrote in *Gemini: An Extended Autobiographical Statement on My First Twenty-Five Years.* "'What have they got to conserve?' And after a while (realizing that I had absolutely nothing, period) I came around."

While Giovanni was at Fisk a black renaissance was emerging, as writers and other artists of color were finding new ways of expressing their distinct culture to an increasingly interested public. In addition to serving as editor of the campus literary magazine, *Elan*, and participating in the Fisk Writers Workshop, Giovanni worked to restore the Fisk chapter of the Student Non-Violent Coordinating Committee (SNCC). At that time the organization was pressing the concept of "black power" to bring about social and economic reform. Giovanni's political activism ultimately led to her planning and directing the first Black Arts Festival in Cincinnati, which was held in 1967.

Later that year Giovanni graduated magna cum laude with a degree in history. She decided to continue her studies at the University of Pennsylvania School of Social Work under a grant from the Ford Foundation, and then take classes at Columbia University's School of Fine Arts. This period was punctuated by tragedy, however, when Giovanni's beloved grandmother died. The loss "stirred in her a sense of guilt and shame both for the way in which society had dealt with this strong, sensitive woman, to whom she had been so close and who had deeply influenced her life, as well as for the way she herself had left her alone to die," according to Mozella G. Mitchell in *Dictionary of Literary Biography* (*DLB*).

Publishes First Poetry Collection

Giovanni's first published volume of poetry grew out of her response to the assassinations of such figures as Martin Luther King, Jr., Malcolm X, Medgar Evers, and Robert Kennedy. *Black Feeling, Black Talk* and *Black Judgement* display a strong, almost militant African American perspective as she recounts her growing political and spiritual awareness. These early books, which were followed by *Re: Creation*, quickly established Giovanni

Giovanni directed this 1973 collection of appealing poetry to black youngsters to foster pride in their own cultural history.

as a prominent new African American voice. *Black Feeling, Black Talk* sold over ten thousand copies in its first year alone, making the author an increasingly visible and popular figure on the reading and speaking circuit. Because of Giovanni's overt activism, her fame as a personality almost preceded her critical acclaim as a poet. She gave the first public reading of her work at Birdland, a trendy New York City jazz club, to a standing-room-only audience. Mitchell described the poems Giovanni produced between 1968 and 1970 as "a kind of ritualistic exorcism of former nonblack ways of thinking and an immersion in blackness. Not only are they directed at other black people whom [Giovanni] wanted to awaken to the beauty of blackness, but also at herself as a means of saturating her own consciousness."

Critical reaction to Giovanni's early work focused on her more revolutionary poetry. Some reviewers found her political and social positions to be unsophisticated, while others were threatened by her rebelliousness. "Nikki writes about the familiar: what she knows, sees, experiences," Don L. Lee observed in *Dynamite Voices I: Black Poets of the 1960's*. "It is clear why she conveys such urgency in expressing the need for Black awareness, unity, solidarity. . . . What is perhaps more important is that when the Black poet chooses to serve as political seer, he must display a keen sophistication. Sometimes Nikki oversimplifies and therefore sounds rather naive politically." *DLB* contributor Alex Batman heard in Giovanni's verse the echoes of blues music. "Indeed the rhythms of her verse correspond so directly to the syncopations of black music that her poems begin to show a potential for becoming songs without accompaniment," Batman noted.

Giovanni's first three volumes of poetry were enormously successful, taking into account the relatively low public demand for modern poetry. *Black Judgement* alone sold six thousand copies in three months, almost six times the sales level expected of a book of its type. As she traveled to speaking engagements at colleges around the country, Giovanni was often hailed as one of the leading black poets of the new black renaissance. The prose poem "Nikki-Rosa," Giovanni's reminiscence of her childhood in a close-knit African American home, was first published in *Black Judgement*. As it became her most beloved and most anthologized work, "Nikki-Rosa" expanded her appeal to an audience well beyond fans of her more activist poetry.

In 1969 Giovanni took a teaching position at Rutgers University. That year she also gave birth to her son, Thomas. Her decision to bear a child out of wedlock was understandable to anyone who knew her. Even as a young girl she had determined that the institution of marriage was not hospitable to women and would never play a role in her life. "I had a baby at 25 because I *wanted* to have a baby and I could *afford* to have a baby," she told an *Ebony* interviewer. "I did not get married because I didn't *want* to get married and I could *afford* not to get married."

Despite her success as a poet of the black revolution, Giovanni's work exhibited a shift in focus after the birth of her son. Her priorities had ex-

If you enjoy the works of Nikki Giovanni, you may also want to check out the following books:

Maya Angelou, *I Know Why the Caged Bird Sings*, 1974.
The poetry of Gwendolyn Brooks, including *Annie Allen*, 1949.
Toni Morrison, *The Bluest Eye*, 1969.
Rita Williams-Garcia, *Blue Tights*, 1988.

panded and now encompassed providing her child with the security of a stable home life. As she remarked to an interviewer for *Harper's Bazaar*, "To protect Tommy there is no question I would give my life. I just cannot imagine living without him. But I can live without the revolution." During this period Giovanni produced a collection of autobiographical essays, two books of poetry for children, and two poetry collections for adults. She also made several recordings of her poetry set against a gospel music backdrop. Reviewing these works, Mitchell commented that "We see evidence of a more developed individualism and greater introspection, and a sharpening of her creative and moral powers, as well as of her social and political focus and understanding."

In addition to writing her own poetry, Giovanni sought exposure for other African American women writers through NikTom, Ltd., a publishing cooperative she founded in 1970. Gwendolyn Brooks, Margaret Walker, Carolyn Rodgers, and Mari Evans were among those who benefited from Giovanni's efforts. Travels to other parts of the world, including the Caribbean, also filled much of the poet's time and contributed to the evolution of her work. As she broadened her perspective, Giovanni began to review her own life. Her introspection led to *Gemini: An Extended Autobiographical Statement on My First Twenty-Five Years of Being a Black Poet*, which earned a nomination for the National Book Award.

Gemini is a combination of prose, poetry, and other musings. In the words of a critic writing in *Kirkus Reviews*, it is a work in which "the contradictions are brought together by sheer force of personality." From sunsoaked childhood memories of a supportive family to an adult acceptance of revolutionary ideology and solo motherhood, the work reflected Giovanni's internal conflict and self-questioning. "I think all autobiography is fiction," Giovanni observed in the *CA* interview, expressing amazement that readers feel they learn something personal about an author by reading a creative work. "[T]he least factual of anything is autobiography, because half the stuff is forgotten," she added. "Even if you [write] about something terribly painful, you have removed yourself from it. . . . What you have not come to terms with you do not write." While she subtitled *Gemini* an autobiography, Giovanni denied that it offered a key to her inner self. The essays contained in the volume—particularly one about her grandmother—were personal in subject matter and "as true as I could make it," she commented. But, as Giovanni noted to the *CA* interviewer several decades later, "I also recognize that there are [parts of] the book in which I'm simply trying to deal with ideas. I didn't want it to be considered *the definitive*. It's far from that. It's very selective and how I looked at myself when I was twenty-five."

Poetry Collections for Children

In addition to writing for adults in *Gemini* and other works during the early 1970s, Giovanni began to compose verse for children. Among her published volumes for young readers are *Spin a Soft Black Song, Ego-Tripping and Other Poems for Young People,* and *Vacation Time.* Written for children of all ages, Giovanni's poems are unrhymed incantations of childhood images and feelings. *Spin a Soft Black Song,* which she dedicated to her son Tommy, covers a wealth of childhood interests, such as basketball games, close friends, moms, and the coming of spring. "Poem for Rodney" finds a young man contemplating what he wants to be when he grows up. "If" reflects a young man's daydreams about what it might have been like to participate in an historic event. In a *New York Times Book Review* article on *Spin a Soft Black Song,* Nancy Klein noted, "Nikki Giovanni's poems for children, like her adult works, exhibit a combination of casual energy and sudden wit. No cheek-pinching auntie, she explores the contours of childhood with honest affection, sidestepping both nostalgia and condescension."

Ego-Tripping and Other Poems from Young People contains several poems previously published in *Black Feeling, Black Talk.* Focusing on African American history, the collection explores issues and concerns specific to black youngsters. In "Poem for Black Boys," for example, Giovanni wonders why young boys of color do not play runaway slave or Mau-Mau, thereby identifying with the brave heroes of their own race rather than the white cowboys of the Wild West. "Revolutionary Dreams" and "Revolutionary Music" speak to the racial strife of the 1960s and 1970s and look toward an end to racial tension. Commenting on *Ego-Tripping,* a *Kirkus Reviews* contributor declared: "When [Giovanni] grabs hold . . . it's a rare kid, certainly a rare black kid, who could resist being picked right up."

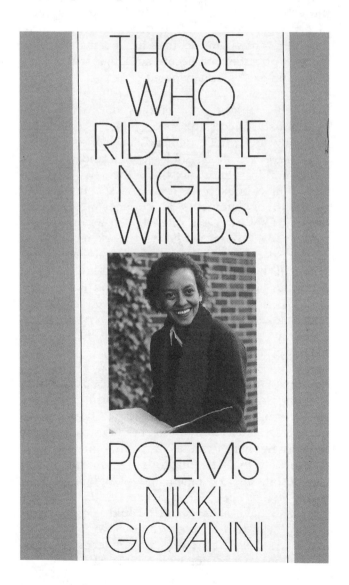

Dedicated to people who made a difference, this book offers Giovanni's views of John Lennon, Billie Jean King, Martin Luther King, Jr., among others.

Vacation Time contrasts with Giovanni's two earlier poetry collections for children by being "a much more relaxed and joyous collection which portrays the world of children as full of wonder and delight," according to Kay E. Vandergrift in *Twentieth-Century Children's Writers*. In *Vacation Time* Giovanni uses more traditional rhyme patterns than in *Spin a Soft Black Song*. Reviewing the work for the *Bulletin of the Center for Children's Books*, Zena Sutherland noted that the rhythms often seem forced and that Giovanni uses "an occasional contrivance to achieve scansion." Yet other critics praised the poet's themes. "In her singing lines, Giovanni shows she hadn't forgotten childhood adventures in . . . exploring the world with a small person's sense of discovery," wrote a *Publishers Weekly* reviewer. Mitchell, too, claimed: "One may be dazzled by the smooth way [Giovanni] drops all political and personal concerns [in *Vacation Time*] and completely enters the world of the child and brings to it all the fanciful beauty, wonder, and lollipopping."

Giovanni's later works for children include *Knoxville, Tennessee*, a free-verse poem about the pleasures of summer originally published in *Black Feeling, Black Talk*, and *The Sun Is So Quiet*, a collection of thirteen poems. As Mary Lystad noted in *Twentieth-Century Young Adult Writers*, "All of Giovanni's works may be enjoyed by the young adult. Those found in the children's section of the library are among her most joyous and lyrical. Young adults will respond to her references of growing up, to her dreams of running faster than any gazelle, outswimming any fish, and beating a falcon up to the top of the mountain."

Giovanni has found writing for children to be particularly fulfilling because she is a mother who reads to her son. "Mostly I'm aware, as the mother of a reader, that I read to him, she observed in the *CA* interview. "I think all of us know that your first line to the child is going to be his parent, so you want to write something that the parent likes and can share." According to Mitchell, the children's poems have "essentially the same impulse" as Giovanni's adult poetry—namely, "the creation of racial pride and the communication of individual love. These are the goals of all of Giovanni's poetry, here directed toward a younger and more impressionable audience."

Throughout the 1970s and 1980s Giovanni's popularity as a speaker and lecturer increased along with her success as a poet and children's author. She received numerous awards for her work, including honors from the National Council of Negro Women and the National Association of Radio and Television Announcers. She was featured in articles for such magazines as *Ebony*, *Jet*, and *Harper's Bazaar*. She also continued to travel, making trips to Europe and Africa.

Maturity Prompts an Evaluation of the Past

In *My House* Giovanni began to exhibit increased sophistication and maturity. Her viewpoint had broadened beyond a rigid black revolutionary consciousness to balance a wide range of social concerns. Her rhymes had also become more pronounced, more lyrical, more gentle. The themes of family love, loneliness, and frustration, which Giovanni had defiantly explored in her earlier works, find much deeper expression in *My House*. In a review for *Contemporary Poets*, Jay S. Paul called the book "a poetic tour through . . . a place rich with family remembrance, distinctive personalities, and prevailing love." And in the foreword to *My House*, Ida Lewis observed that Giovanni "has reached a simple philosophy more or less to the effect that a good family spirit is what produces healthy communities, which is what produces a strong (Black) nation." Noting the focus on self-discovery throughout *My House*, critic John W. Conner suggested in *English Journal* that Giovanni "sees her world as an extension of herself . . . sees problems in the world as an extension of her problems, and . . . sees herself existing amidst tensions, heartache, and marvelous expressions of love." "*My House* is not just poems," added Kalumu Ya Salaam in *Black World*. "*My House* is how it is, what it is to be a young, single, intelligent Black woman with a son and no man. It is what it is to be a woman who has failed and is now sentimental about some things, bitter about some things, and generally always frustrated, always feeling frustrated on one of various levels or another."

When Giovanni published *Cotton Candy on a Rainy Day*, critics viewed it as one of her most somber works. They noted the focus on emotional ups and downs, fear and insecurity, and the weight of everyday responsibilities. Batman also sensed the poet's sense of frustration at aims unmet. "What distinguishes *Cotton Candy on a Rainy Day* is its poignancy," the critic maintained. "One feels

Giovanni reading from her *Gennie in the Jar* at the First Baptist Church in Charlottesville, Virginia.

throughout that here is a child of the 1960s mourning the passing of a decade of conflict, of violence, but most of all, of hope."

During the year *Cotton Candy* was published, Giovanni's father suffered a stroke. She and her son immediately left their apartment in New York City and returned to the family home in Cincinnati to help her mother cope with her father's failing health. When he was removed to a convalescent home and later died of cancer, Giovanni and her son continued to stay in Cincinnati with her aging mother. She thus built the same secure, supportive, multi-generational environment for Tommy that she had enjoyed as a child.

The poems in *Vacation Time* reflect, perhaps, the poet's growing lightness of spirit and inner sta-

bility as she enjoys her family. Similarly, *Those Who Ride the Night Winds* reveals "a new and innovative form," according to Mitchell, who adds that "the poetry reflects her heightened self-knowledge and imagination." *Those Who Ride the Night Winds* tends to echo the political activism of Giovanni's early verse as she dedicates various pieces to Phillis Wheatley, Martin Luther King, Jr., and Rosa Parks. In *Sacred Cows . . . and Other Edibles* she presents essays on a wide range of topics: African American political leaders, national holidays, and termites all come under her insightful and humorous scrutiny. Such essays as "Reflections on My Profession" and "An Answer to Some Questions on How I Write" are described by *Washington Post Book World* critic Marita Golden as "quintessential Nikki Giovanni—sometimes funny, nervy and unnerving with flashes of wisdom."

Later Work Reflects Personal Growth

As Giovanni moved through her middle years, her works continued to reflect her changing concerns and perspectives. *The Selected Poems of Nikki Giovanni*, which spans the first three decades of her career, was heralded by *Booklist* critic Donna Seaman as a "rich synthesis [that] reveals the evolution of Giovanni's voice and charts the course of the social issues that are her muses, issues of gender and race." Twenty of the fifty-three works collected in *Love Poems* find the writer musing on subjects as diverse as friendship, sexual desire, motherhood, and loneliness, while the remainder of the volume includes relevant earlier works. "Funny yet thoughtful, Giovanni celebrates creative energy and the family spirit of African American communities," Frank Allen wrote of *Love Poems* in a *Library Journal* review.

Giovanni continues to supplement her poetry with occasional volumes of nonfiction. In *Racism 101* she looks back over the past thirty years as one who has influenced the civil rights movement and its aftermath. Characterized by a *Publishers Weekly* reviewer as "fluid, often perceptive musings that beg for more substance," this collection of essays touches on diverse topics. Giovanni gives advice to young African American scholars who are just starting an academic career, and she reflects on her own experiences as a teacher. She also provides a few glimpses into her personal life—for instance, she admits to being a confirmed "Trekkie." The book is a rich source of impressions of other black intellectuals, including writer and activist W. E. B. DuBois, writers Henry Louis Gates, Jr. and Toni Morrison, Supreme Court Justice Clarence Thomas, and filmmaker Spike Lee. "Giovanni is a shrewd observer and an exhilarating essayist," maintained Seaman in *Booklist*, "modulating her tone from chummy to lethal, hilarious to sagacious as smoothly as a race-care driver shifts gears." In addition to publishing original writings, Giovanni has edited poetry collections like the highly praised *Shimmy Shimmy Shimmy like My Sister Kate*. A compilation of works composed by African American writers during the Harlem Renaissance of the early twentieth century, *Shimmy* helps students of black writing to gain an understanding of the past.

"Most writers spend too much time alone; it is a lonely profession," Giovanni explained in the *CA* interview. "I'm not the only poet to point that out.

Unless we make ourselves get out and see people, we miss a lot." Teaching, lecturing, sustaining close family ties, and remaining active in her community have allowed the poet to balance the loneliness of writing with a myriad of life experiences. "[Teaching] enriches my life, I mean it keeps reminding all of us that there are other concerns out there," Giovanni said. "It widens your world. . . . I have certain skills that I am able to impart and that I want to, and it keeps me involved in my community and in a community of writers who are not professional but who are interested. I think that's good."

"Writing is . . . what I do to justify the air I breathe," Giovanni wrote, explaining her choice of a vocation in *CAAS*. "I have been considered a writer who writes from rage and it confuses me. What else do writers write from? A poem has to say something. It has to make some sort of sense; be lyrical; to the point; and still able to be read by whatever reader is kind enough to pick up the book." Giovanni believes one of her most important qualities is to have experienced life and to have been able to translate those experiences into her work—"apply the lessons learned," as she terms it in *CAAS*. "Isn't that the purpose of people living and sharing? So that others will at least not make the same mistake, since we seldom are able to recreate the positive things in life." She continues to look back on her contributions to American poetry with pride. "I think that I have grown; I feel that my work has grown a lot," she told the *CA* interviewer. "What I've always wanted to do is something different, and I think each book has made a change. I hope that the next book continues like that. Like all writers, I guess, I keep looking for the heart. . . ." She concluded, "Human beings fascinate me. You just keep trying to dissect them poetically to see what's there."

■ Works Cited

Allen, Frank, review of *Love Poems*, *Library Journal*, February 1, 1997, p. 84.

Batman, Alex, *Dictionary of Literary Biography*, Volume 5: *American Poets Since World War II, Part I: A-K*, Gale, 1980.

Conner, John W., review of *My House*, *English Journal*, April, 1973, p. 650.

Review of *Ego-Tripping and Other Poems*, *Kirkus Reviews*, January 1, 1974, p. 11.

Review of *Gemini: An Extended Autobiographical Statement on My First Twenty-Five Years of Being a Black Poet, Kirkus Reviews,* September 15, 1971, p. 1051.

Giovanni, Nikki, interview in *Ebony,* February, 1972, pp. 48-50.

Giovanni, Nikki, interview in *Harper's Bazaar,* July, 1972, p. 50.

Giovanni, Nikki, interview in *Contemporary Authors New Revision Series,* Volume 18, Gale, 1986, pp. 187-94.

Giovanni, Nikki, essay in *Contemporary Authors Autobiography Series,* Volume 6, Gale, 1988, pp. 151-64.

Golden, Marita, review of *Sacred Cows . . . and Other Edibles, Washington Post Book Review,* February 14, 1988, p. 3.

Klein, Nancy, review of *Spin a Soft Black Song, The New York Times Book Review,* November 28, 1971, p. 8.

Lee, Don L., "Nikki Giovanni," *Dynamite Voices I: Black Poets of the 1960's,* Broadside Press, 1971, pp. 68-73.

Lewis, Ida, introduction to *My House,* Morrow, 1972.

Lystad, Mary, "Nikki Giovanni," *Twentieth-Century Young Adult Writers,* St. James Press, 1994, pp. 245-46.

Mitchell, Mozella G., essay in *Dictionary of Literary Biography,* Volume 41: *Afro-American Poets since 1955,* Gale, 1985, pp. 135-51.

Paul, Jay S., "Nikki Giovanni," *Contemporary Poets,* St. James Press, 1996, pp. 390-91.

Review of *Racism 101, Publishers Weekly,* December 13, 1993, p. 54.

Salaam, Kalumu Ya, review of *My House, Black World,* July, 1974.

Seaman, Donna, review of *Racism 101, Booklist,* December 1, 1993, p. 658.

Seaman, Donna, review of *The Selected Poems of Nikki Giovanni (1968-1995), Booklist,* December 15, 1995, p. 682.

Sutherland, Zena, review of *Vacation Time: Poems for Children, Bulletin of the Center for Children's Books,* October 1980, p. 31.

Review of *Vacation Time: Poems for Children, Publishers Weekly,* May 23, 1980, p. 77.

Vandergrift, Kay E., essay in *Twentieth-Century Children's Writers,* 4th edition, St. James Press, 1995, p. 388.

■ For More Information See

BOOKS

Authors in the News, Volume 1, Gale, 1976.

Black Literature Criticism, Gale, 1992.

Children's Literature Review, Volume 6, Gale, 1984.

Contemporary Literary Criticism, Gale, Volume 2, 1974, Volume 4, 1975, Volume 19, 1981, Volume 64, 1991.

Evans, Mari, editor, *Black Women Writers, 1950-1980: A Critical Evaluation,* Doubleday, 1984.

Fowler, Virginia, *Nikki Giovanni: An Introduction to Her Life and Works,* 1992.

Tate, Claudia, editor, *Black Women Writers at Work,* Crossroads Publishing, 1983.

PERIODICALS

America, February 19, 1972.

Black World, December, 1970; January, 1971; February, 1971; April, 1971; August, 1971.

Booklist, May 1, 1972, p. 770.

Bulletin of the Center for Children's Books, October, 1980.

Choice, May, 1972; March, 1973; September, 1974; January, 1976.

Christian Science Monitor, June 4, 1970; June 19, 1974.

Ebony, August, 1972.

Horn Book, September/October, 1994, pp. 575-76.

Jet, April 4, 1994, p. 29.

Kirkus Reviews, January 1, 1974, p. 11.

Library Journal, February 15, 1988, p. 169; January 1996, p. 103.

Los Angeles Times, December 4, 1985.

New York Times Book Review, November 7, 1971; November 28, 1971, p. 8; February 13, 1972, pp. 6, 26; May 5, 1974, p. 38.

Publishers Weekly, November 13, 1972; May 23, 1980; December 18, 1987, p. 48; December 18, 1995, pp. 51-52; October 21, 1996, p. 83.

School Library Journal, April, 1994, p. 119; October, 1994, p. 152.

Time, April 6, 1970; January 17, 1972.

Voice of Youth Advocates, October 1996, pp. 229-30.

Washington Post Book World, May 19, 1974; March 8, 1981.

Writer's Digest, February 1989, pp. 30-34.*

—Sketch by Pamela L. Shelton

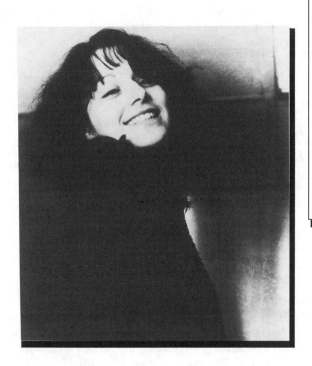

Amy Heckerling

■ Awards, Honors

American Film Institute fellow, 1975; People's Choice Award for Best Comedy, for *Look Who's Talking.*

■ Personal

Born May 7, 1954, in New York, NY; daughter of an accountant; married second husband, Neal Israel (a film director and screenwriter), July, 1984 (marriage ended); children: (second marriage) Mollie Sara. *Education:* New York University, B.A., 1975; attended the American Film Institute.

■ Addresses

Agent—Creative Artists, 9830 Wilshire Blvd., Beverly Hills, CA 90212.

■ Career

Director, writer, and producer. Director of feature films, including *Fast Times at Ridgemont High,* Universal, 1982, *National Lampoon's European Vacation,* Warner Brothers, 1985, and *Clueless,* Paramount, 1995. Author of screenplays, including *Look Who's Talking,* Tri-Star, 1989. Producer for films, including *Look Who's Talking Now,* 1994, and for television, including *Fast Times* (series), CBS, 1986.

■ Credits

FILM DIRECTOR

Fast Times at Ridgemont High, Universal, 1982.
Johnny Dangerously, Twentieth-Century Fox, 1984.
National Lampoon's European Vacation, Warner Brothers, 1985.
Look Who's Talking, Tri-Star, 1989.
Look Who's Talking, Too, Tri-Star, 1990.
Clueless, Paramount, 1995.

Also director of several short films, including *Modern Times, High Finance,* and *Getting It Over With,* 1974.

OTHER FILM WORK

Ship's waitress (cameo appearance), *Into the Night,* Universal, 1985.
Co-producer, *Look Who's Talking Now,* 1994.

TELEVISION WORK

Supervising producer and episodic director, *Fast Times* (series), CBS, 1986.

Supervising producer, *Tough Cookies* (series), CBS, 1986.

Producer, *Life on the Flipside* (pilot; also known as *Flipside*, *Homeward Bound*, and *Pop Rock*), NBC, 1988.

Executive producer, episodic director, and writer, *Clueless*, ABC, 1996.

Also director of episodes for *Twilight Zone*.

■ Writings

SCREENPLAYS

Look Who's Talking, Tri-Star, 1989.
(With Neal Israel) *Look Who's Talking, Too*, Tri-Star, 1990.
Clueless, Paramount, 1995.

TELEVISION SERIES

Fast Times, CBS, 1986.
Clueless, ABC, 1996.

OTHER

(With Pamela Pettler) *The No-Sex Handbook*, illustrated by Jack Ziegler, Warner Books, 1990.

■ Adaptations

The television series *Baby Talk*, ABC, 1991, was based on the films *Look Who's Talking* and *Look Who's Talking, Too*. The television series *Clueless*, ABC, 1996, was based on the film *Clueless*.

■ Work in Progress

Producer of film *A Night At the Roxbury*, scheduled for 1998 release.

■ Sidelights

Amy Heckerling is one of just a handful of women directors who has made a career for herself in the male-dominated world of the American movie industry. She rose to prominence as the director of a raunchy teenage comedy called *Fast Times at Ridgemont High*, which became one of the surprise box office hits of 1982. In the years since,

Heckerling's directorial credits have included such "low-brow" but commercially successful movies as *National Lampoon's European Vacation*, *Clueless*, *Look Who's Talking*, and *Look Who's Talking, Too* (she also wrote screenplays for the latter three films). In addition, Heckerling has occasionally worked in television, dabbled in acting, and co-authored a book of humor entitled *The No-Sex Handbook* with Pamela Pettler. However, she remains best known as a writer-director, a vocation in which she feels very much at home. "I'd rather be on a different schedule than the rest of the world and lead a daydreaming life," she told Richard Cohen of *Rolling Stone* in a 1995 interview. "I like to sleep late, avoid the phone, goof with my kid, exercise, and then after dinner I start in."

Heckerling is a native of New York City, where she attended the High School of Art and Design. Heckerling graduated from New York University in 1975 with a B.A. degree. It was during her student days that she saw a 1973 film called *Mean Streets* by fellow New Yorker Martin Scorsese; the experience changed her life. "I worshiped [that film]," Heckerling recalled to Cohen. "Before, it felt like movies were these big splashy things filled with stars that came out of Hollywood. Suddenly there was this movie where I could understand what everybody was saying. I understood their motives, and there was music and energy, and the shooting was cuckoo, and I was going, 'Wow. Movies are for me now.'" As a result, Heckerling enrolled in courses at the American Film Institute, where she learned the art of directing by making a series of short films such as *Modern Times*, *High Finance*, and *Getting It Over With*. This latter effort, a comedy about a nineteen-year-old woman's efforts to lose her virginity, helped Heckerling land a contract at Metro-Goldwyn-Mayer (MGM) studios. Unfortunately for Heckerling, her first project at MGM was aborted by the 1980 Hollywood actors' strike.

She got another chance when she was hired by Universal Studios the following year to direct *Fast Times at Ridgemont High*, the movie version of a novel by Cameron Crowe, who also wrote the screenplay. This low-budget, R-rated comedy chronicled a year in the life of a group of California teenagers. The story focused on the adventures of Ridgemont High senior Brad Hamilton, played by the then-unknown Judge Reinhold, and his younger sister Stacy, who was played by Jennifer Jason Leigh. Other up-and-coming young stars in the talented ensemble cast included Phoebe Cates, Forest Whitaker, Eric Stoltz, and Nicolas Cage. However, it was Sean Penn as a stoned surfer named Jeff Spicoli who was the movie's "real scene stealer," as *New York Times* critic Janet Maslin noted. In her review, she described *Fast Times at Ridgemont High* as "a jumbled but appealing teen-age comedy with something of a fresh perspective on the subject." In *New York*, David Denby described the film as "in memory, [standing] out from the *Porky's* era of teen exploitation like a diamond glistening in the trash." Pulitzer Prize-winning critic Roger Ebert of the Chicago *Sun-Times* was less impressed, giving the film a very definite thumbs down. Ebert described *Fast Times at Ridgemont High* as "sexist," adding that the plot contained "erratic, offensive material that hasn't been thought through. . . ." Although several critics shared Ebert's opinion, *Fast Times at Ridgemont High* was successful at the box of-

fice, where it became a cult hit with youthful audiences.

Sophomore Slump

Fast Times's domestic gross alone totaled more than $27 million; that kind of commercial success attracted attention in Hollywood, where Heckerling was suddenly tabbed as one of America's first commercially successful female film directors. But her next film, which she made in 1984 for the Twentieth-Century Fox studio, did little to enhance that reputation. *Johnny Dangerously* was a comedy spoof of 1930s gangster films, starring a talented cast that included Michael Keaton, Joe Piscopo, Maureen Stapleton, and Peter Boyle. Despite Heckerling's best efforts, the film was a flop with audiences and critics alike when it was released in the busy pre-Christmas season. "The movie

An unexpected box office hit, *Fast Times at Ridgemont High*, a 1982 teenage comedy which featured Sean Pean and Ray Walston, was Heckerling's first Hollywood production.

National Lampoon's European Vacation, starring Chevy Chase, was another hit for Heckerling, making $12.3 million its first weekend in theaters.

wants to do for gangster films what *Airplane!* did for *Airport,* and *Top Secret!* did for spy movies. It has its work cut out," Roger Ebert wrote. Ralph Novak of *People* was one of the few reviewers who had anything positive to say, hailing *Johnny Dangerously* as a "good-natured, relaxed parody."

Heckerling did not let the negative press affect her career. She bounced back in 1985 with *National Lampoon's European Vacation,* a comedy that starred Chevy Chase and Beverly D'Angelo. The movie provided fresh proof of Heckerling's deft commercial touch; *National Lampoon's European Vacation* made more than $12.3 million dollars in its first weekend in theaters and went on to become one of the summer's hits, despite indifferent reviews. David Ansen of *Newsweek* said the movie was a "tacky-looking, mildly amusing, episodic comedy." Janet Maslin of the *New York Times* described it as "a retread" of *National Lampoon's Vacation,* a 1981 hit that had been directed by Harold Ramis.

The same year that *National Lampoon's European Vacation* was released, Heckerling and her second husband, screenwriter-director Neal Israel, had a daughter they named Mollie Sara. Heckerling has said her pregnancy and the birth of her daughter were the inspiration for her next two films. "Anything good that's happened to me in the last five years is because of my kid," she told Richard Lacayo of *People* in a 1991 interview. Heckerling spent the next three years between 1985 and 1988 raising her child and working in television, both as a producer and occasionally as the director of episodes of the *Twilight Zone* and *Fast Times,* a short-lived CBS series that was a spin-off of the film *Fast Times at Ridgemont High.* During this period she also began writing her first movie screenplay. She explained to Daniel Cerone of the *Los Angeles Times,* "When I had Mollie, she would sit on the table in this baby seat and just endlessly look around. . . . My husband and I started to put words in her mouth, what she might be thinking based on her expressions." The end result was a script that became the basis for Heckerling's biggest box office hit, the movie *Look Who's Talking*. That 1989 comedy recounted a baby's humorous thoughts and feelings from the time he was in the womb until he was about two years old.

Look Who's Directing

Bruce Willis provided the voice for Mikey, a wise-cracking infant who is intent on finding a husband for his unmarried mom, played by Kirstie Alley of *Cheers* television sitcom fame. Heckerling wrote the role of the New York cab driver who eventually marries Mikey's mother especially for her friend John Travolta, whose career was at a low point; he had not had a hit in several years. Although the *Look Who's Talking* plot was predictable and the humor sometimes silly, audiences loved the movie and it became a huge hit, breaking box office records for a film opening in the fall, earning Heckerling a People's Choice Award for Best Comedy, and breathing new life into Travolta's career. The reasons were obvious; as Roger Ebert put it in the Chicago *Sun-Times*, "as a silly entertainment [it] is full of good feeling, and director Amy Heckerling finds a light touch for her lightweight material." Other critics were less kind. "This flabby comedy . . . deserves only one thing: to fall on its fat one," wrote a reviewer for *Rolling Stone*. Suzanne Moore, writing in *New Statesman & Society*, concurred, stating, "*Look Who's Talking* is as yucky as babyfood."

Yucky or not, *Look Who's Talking* spawned a 1990 sequel called *Look Who's Talking, Too* and a 1991 television sitcom titled *Baby Talk*. (There was also a 1994 movie called *Look Who's Talking Now*, which Heckerling co-produced. That film also starred John Travolta and Kirstie Alley in the same roles they had played in the earlier films, but this time there were talking dogs rather than babies.) Neither *Look Who's Talking, Too* nor *Baby Talk* achieved the level of commercial success enjoyed by *Look Who's Talking*. *Look Who's Talking, Too* follows the adventures of the John Travolta and Kirstie Alley characters after they married. Heckerling again wrote the screenplay, this time in cooperation with Israel, whose earlier writing credits included co-authorship of the phenomenally successful 1984 comedy *Police Academy*. Working on the premise that if audiences loved a talking baby the first time out, they'd love more of the same a second

time around, Heckerling and Israel gave Mikey a baby sister, whose voice was supplied by comedian Roseanne Barr. Several other new characters were thrown into the mix for good measure, with Damon Wayans and comic legend Mel Brooks providing the voices. Most critics liked *Look Who's Talking, Too* even less than they liked its predecessor. A reviewer for *Variety*, the entertainment industry weekly newspaper, panned *Look Who's Talking, Too* as a "vulgar sequel" that "overemphasizes toilet humor and expletives. . . ." Ralph Novak of *People* felt much the same way: "Whatever limited charm there was in the original centered on the notion of giving voice to a baby's thoughts. If [*Look Who's Talking*] offered a childish pleasure or two, though, this one is just infantile."

Heckerling not only directed but also wrote the screenplay for *Look Who's Talking* and its sequel, *Look Who's Talking, Too*, both of which starred John Travolta and Kirstie Alley.

Modeled on Jane Austen's *Emma*, *Clueless* was rejected as a television sitcom pilot but turned into Heckerling's most acclaimed movie.

Clued In

Heckerling's next movie is arguably her best. *Clueless*, which appeared in 1995, was a modern-day version of English writer Jane Austen's classic 1816 novel *Emma*, about a well-intentioned know-it-all matchmaker who is constantly interfering in other people's lives. Heckerling originally wrote the story as a television sitcom pilot for Fox. But when the network rejected it, she followed her agent's advice and turned the story into a film which she also directed. Heckerling told Cohen of *Rolling Stone*, "I needed a story a girl could go through. I wanted a comedy of manners—so I thought about Jane Austen and remembered how much I loved *Emma* in college. The plot is perfect for any time. Here's a girl, she's rich, she's manipulating people and thinks she knows what's going on but is so into her own world, she doesn't see what everybody else can see." Heckerling set her plot in a Beverly Hills high school in 1995. Emma becomes a hip fifteen-year-old named Cher, played by Alicia Silverstone.

That audiences loved the film was clear, for it made more than $20 million in the first week after its release. Critics too were impressed, praising Heckerling's screenplay and direction and lauding Silverstone's performance. In the Chicago *Sun-Times*, Roger Ebert described *Clueless* as a "smart and funny movie" and noted that "Heckerling walks a fine line between satire and put-on, but she finds it, and her dialogue could be anthologized." Reviewer Peter Travers of *Rolling Stone* declared, "Silverstone is a winner. And so is the movie." Ironically, after the success of the big screen version of *Clueless*, the characters and the concept returned to television, the medium for which they were originally intended. Heckerling, acting as executive producer, episodic director, and writer, sold ABC-TV a short-lived weekly half-hour sitcom of the same name. The show aired briefly in 1996.

Noting that it had been five years between feature films for Heckerling, Cohen asked if *Clueless* felt like a "comeback" movie for her. Heckerling

If you enjoy the works of Amy Heckerling, you may also want to check out the following books and films:

Betsy Byars, *Bingo Brown, Gypsy Lover*, 1990.
Rachel Vail, *Do-Over*, 1992.
Dazed and Confused, Gramercy Pictures, 1993.

---

reacted strongly to the question. "I hate that," she said. "I didn't retire. These things take time. It takes a year writing and developing and then getting [passed] over and going somewhere else and redeveloping, then finding a crew and shooting and editing, and the next thing is 'Hello, I'm back.' I didn't go anywhere." With *Clueless* signaling her "artistic rebirth," as Glenn Kenny termed it in *Entertainment Weekly*, Heckerling is sure to be around for some time to come.

■ **Works Cited**

Ansen, David, review of *National Lampoon's European Vacation, Newsweek*, August 12, 1985, p. 71.

Cerone, Daniel, interview with Amy Heckerling, *Los Angeles Times*, October 13, 1989.

Cohen, Richard, "High School Confidential," *Rolling Stone*, September 7, 1995, p. 53.

Denby, David, review of *Clueless, New York*, August 7, 1995, p. 71.

Ebert, Roger, review of *Look Who's Talking, Sun-Times* (Chicago), October 13, 1989.

Ebert, Roger, review of *Fast Times at Ridgemont High*, Microsoft Cinemania 1994 CD.

Ebert, Roger, review of *Johnny Dangerously*, Microsoft Cinemania 1994 CD.

Ebert, Roger, review of *Clueless, Sun-Times* (Chicago), July 19, 1995.

Kenny, Glenn, "High School Confident," *Entertainment Weekly*, December 8, 1995, pp. 76-78.

Lacayo, Peter, "Look Who's Not Paying For Her Ticket," *People*, Spring, 1991, p. 48.

Review of *Look Who's Talking, Rolling Stone*, October 19, 1989, p. 29.

Review of *Look Who's Talking, Too, Variety Movie Guide*, Prentice Hall, 1991, p. 357.

Maslin, Janet, review of *Fast Times at Ridgemont High, New York Times*, September 3, 1982.

Maslin, Janet, review of *National Lampoon's European Vacation, New York Times*, July 27, 1985, p. 13.

Moore, Suzanne, review of *Look Who's Talking, New Statesman & Society*, April 13, 1990, p. 45.

Novak, Ralph, review of *Johnny Dangerously, People*, January 28, 1985.

Novak, Ralph, review of *Look Who's Talking, Too, People*, January 21, 1991.

Travers, Peter, review of *Clueless, Rolling Stone*, October 8, 1995.

■ **For More Information See**

BOOKS

Contemporary Authors, Volume 139, Gale, 1993.

Contemporary Theatre, Film, and Television, Volume 10, Gale, 1993.

Katz, Ephram, *The Film Encyclopedia*, Harper Perennial, 1994, p. 610.

PERIODICALS

Chicago Tribune, December 17, 1990.

Entertainment Weekly, October 25, 1996, p. 98.

Los Angeles Times, October 26, 1989.

Ms., November, 1985, p. 62.

New York, August 7, 1995, p. 71.

New York Times, October 13, 1989; October 25, 1989; December 1, 1989.

People, May 13, 1985; August 12, 1985, p. 10; February 19, 1990; January 21, 1991, p. 21; July 31, 1995, p. 20.

Rolling Stone, October 19, 1989, p. 29.

Time, July 31, 1995, p. 65.

Washington Post, October 13, 1989; December 14, 1990.*

—*Sketch by Ken Cuthbertson*

Alfred Hitchcock

■ Personal

Full name, Alfred Joseph Hitchcock; born August 13, 1899, in London, England; came to the United States in 1939; naturalized U.S. citizen, 1955; died of kidney failure in Los Angeles, CA, April 29, 1980; son of William (a poultry dealer, greengrocer, and fruit importer) and Emma (Whelan) Hitchcock; married Alma Reville (an assistant film director and screenwriter), December 2, 1926; children: Patricia (Mrs. Joseph O'Connell). *Education:* Attended Salesian College, Battersea, London, 1908; St. Ignatius College, Stamford Hill, London, 1908-13; School of Engineering and Navigation, 1914; and drawing and design classes under E. J. Sullivan at London University, 1917.

■ Career

Film director, 1925-76. W. T. Henley Telegraph Co., London, England, technical estimator, advertising artist, 1914-19; Famous Players-Lasky Co. (now Paramount Pictures Corp.), Islington, began as silent picture title card writer and artist, became scriptwriter, art director, and assistant director to Graham Cutts, 1920-22; Gainsborough Pictures, Islington, began as scenario writer, became art director, production manager, and assistant director, 1923-25, produced and directed first film, 1925; director of motion pictures for Michael Balcon in Germany, 1925-27; director of motion pictures for studios in England, including British International Pictures, 1927-33, Elstree Studio Centre, 1927-39, Lime Grove Studios, 1934-39, and Gaumont-British Studios, 1935-38; director of motion pictures for studios in the United States, including Selznick International, Hollywood, CA, 1940-48, Warner Brothers, Inc., Burbank, CA, 1948-54, Paramount Pictures Corp., Beverly Hills, CA, 1954-60, and Universal Pictures, Universal City, CA, 1960-80. Executive producer, host, and occasional director, "Alfred Hitchcock Presents," Columbia Broadcasting System, Inc., 1955-60, retitled "The Alfred Hitchcock Hour," National Broadcasting Co., Inc., 1960-65; Shamley Productions, founder and production supervisor of television series "Suspicion," 1957, and series of programs for "Ford Star Time," 1960.

■ Awards, Honors

Best Director, New York Film Critics, 1938, for *The Lady Vanishes;* Academy Award for Best Picture, 1940, for *Rebecca;* Academy Award Best Director nominations, 1940, for *Rebecca,* 1944, for *Lifeboat,* 1945, for *Spellbound,* 1954, for *Rear Window,* and 1960, for *Psycho;* Milestone Award, Producers

Guild of America, Inc., 1954; Golden Globe Award for best television show, Hollywood Foreign Press Association, 1958, for *Alfred Hitchcock Presents;* Chevalier, Legion of Honor, 1962; D. W. Griffith Award, Directors Guild of America, 1968; Irving G. Thalberg Memorial Award, Academy of Motion Picture Arts and Sciences, 1968; D.F.A., University of California, Santa Cruz, 1968; Officier des Arts et des Lettres, 1969; Cecil B. De Mille Award, Hollywood Foreign Press Association, 1972; D.H.L., Columbia University, 1972; Commander, National Order of Arts and Letters, 1976; Life Achievement Award, American Film Institute, 1979; Knight Commander of the Order of the British Empire, 1980.

■ Film, Stage, and Television Work

FILM DIRECTOR

(And adapter with others) *Blackmail* (based on the play by Charles Bennett), Sono-Art, 1929.

(And scriptwriter with Alma Reville) *Juno and the Paycock* (based on the play by Sean O'Casey; also known as *The Shame of Mary Boyle*), Wardour, 1929.

(And scriptwriter with Alma Reville) *The Skin Game* (based on the play by John Galsworthy), British International, 1931.

(And co-scriptwriter with Alma Reville and Rodney Ackland) *Number Seventeen* (based on the play and novel by J. Jefferson Farjeon), Wardour, 1932.

(And co-scriptwriter with Alma Reville and Val Valentine) *Rich and Strange* (based on a novel by Dale Collins; also known as *East of Shanghai*), Power, 1932.

Waltzes from Vienna (based on the musical *Great Waltz* by Heinz Reichert, A. M. Willner, and Ernst Marischka; also known as *Strauss's Great Waltz* and *The Great Waltz*), Gaumont, 1933.

The Man Who Knew Too Much (based on a story by Charles Bennett and D. B. Wyndham-Lewis), Gaumont, 1935.

The Thirty-Nine Steps (based on the novel by John Buchan), General Films, 1935.

Secret Agent (based on the play by Campbell Dixon from the stories "Triton" and "The Hairless Mexican" in the book *Ashenden* by W. Somerset Maugham), Gaumont, 1936.

Sabotage (based on the novel *The Secret Agent* by Joseph Conrad; also known as *The Woman Alone*), Janus, 1936.

Young and Innocent (based on the novel *A Schilling for Candles* by Josephine Tey; also known as *The Girl Was Young*), Gaumont, 1937.

The Lady Vanishes (based on the novel *The Wheel Spins* by Ethel Lina White), Metro-Goldwyn-Mayer, 1938.

Jamaica Inn (based on the novel by Daphne du Maurier), Paramount, 1939.

Rebecca (based on the novel by Daphne du Maurier), United Artists, 1940.

Foreign Correspondent, United Artists, 1940.

Mr. and Mrs. Smith, RKO, 1941.

Suspicion (based on the novel *Before the Fact* by Frances Iles), RKO, 1941.

(And author of story) *Saboteur,* Universal, 1942.

Shadow of a Doubt (based on a story by Gordon McDonnell), Universal, 1943.

Life Boat (based on the story by John Steinbeck), Fox, 1944.

Spellbound (based on the novel *The House of Dr. Edwards* by Francis Beeding), United Artists, 1945.

(And producer and author of story) *Notorious,* RKO, 1946.

The Paradine Case (based on the novel by Robert Hichens), United Artists, 1947.

(And producer with Sidney Bernstein) *Rope* (based on the play *Rope's End* by Patrick Hamilton), Warner Brothers, 1948.

(And producer with Sidney Bernstein) *Under Capricorn* (based on the play by John Colton, Margaret Linden, and the novel by Helen Simpson), Warner Brothers, 1949.

(And producer) *Stage Fright* (based on the stories "Man Running" and "Outrun the Constable" by Selwyn Jepson), Warner Brothers, 1949.

(And producer) *Strangers on a Train* (based on the novel by Patricia Highsmith), Warner Brothers, 1951.

(And producer) *I Confess* (based on the play *Nos Deux Consciences* by Paul Anthelme), Warner Brothers, 1953.

(And producer) *Dial M for Murder* (based on the play by Frederick Knott), Warner Brothers, 1954.

(And producer) *Rear Window* (based on the novel *It Had to Be Murder* by Cornell Woolrich), Paramount, 1954.

(And producer) *To Catch a Thief* (based on the novel by David Dodge), Paramount, 1954.

(And producer) *The Trouble with Harry* (based on the story by Jack Trevor Story), Paramount, 1954.

(And producer) *The Man Who Knew Too Much* (remake of the 1935 film of the same title), Gaumont, 1955.

(And producer) *The Wrong Man* (based on "The True Story of Christopher Emmanuel Balestrero" by Maxwell Anderson), Warner Brothers, 1956.

(And producer) *Vertigo* (based on the novel *D'entre les morts* by Pierre Boileau and Thomas Narcejac), Paramount, 1957.

(And producer) *North by Northwest*, Metro-Goldwyn-Mayer, 1959.

(And producer) *Psycho* (based on the novel by Robert Bloch), Paramount, 1960.

(And producer) *The Birds* (based on the story by Daphne du Maurier), Universal, 1963.

(And producer) *Marnie* (based on the novel by Winston Graham), Universal, 1964.

(And producer) *Torn Curtain* (based on the story by Brian Moore), Universal, 1966.

(And producer) *Topaz* (based on the novel by Leon Uris), Universal, 1969.

(And producer) *Frenzy* (based on the book *Goodbye Piccadilly, Farewell Leicester Square* by Arthur LaBern), Universal, 1972.

(And producer) *Family Plot* (based on the novel *The Rainbird Pattern* by Victor Canning), Universal, 1976.

Also director of uncompleted silent film *Number Thirteen* (also known as *Mrs. Peabody*), 1922; director, with Seymour Hicks, of silent film *Always Tell Your Wife*, 1923. Director of silent films *The Pleasure Garden* (also known as *Irrgarten der Leidenschaft*), 1926; *The Mountain Eagle* (also known as *Der Bergadler* and *Fear o' God*), 1926; *The Lodger*, 1926; (and co-scriptwriter) *A Story of the London Fog* (also known as *The Case of Jonathan Drew*), 1926; *Easy Virtue*, 1926; *Downhill* (also known as *When the Boys Leave Home*), 1927; (and scriptwriter) *The Ring*, 1927; (and scriptwriter) *The Farmer's Wife*, 1928; (and adapter) *Champagne*, 1928; *The Manxman*, 1928; (co-director) *Elstree Calling*, 1930; (and co-adapter with Alma Reville and Walter C. Mycroft) *Murder!* (based on the play *Enter Sir John* by Clemence Dane and Helen Simpson; released in Germany as *Mary* and *Sir John greift ein!*, 1931), 1930; *An Elastic Affair* (short film), 1930. Director of short films *Bon Voyage*, 1944, and *Aventure Malgache* (also known as *The Malgache Adventure*), 1944.

(Producer) *Lord Camber's Ladies* (based on *The Case of Lady Camber* by Horace Annesley Vachell), British International, 1932.

Also inter-title designer of *The Great Day*, 1920; *The Call of Youth*, 1920; *The Princess of New York*, 1921; *Appearances*, 1921; *Dangerous Lies*, 1921; *The Mystery Road*, 1921; *Beside the Bonnie Brier Bush* (also known as *The Bonnie Brier Bush*), 1921; *Three Live Ghosts*, 1922; *Perpetua* (also known as *Love's Boomerang*), 1922; *The Man from Home*, 1922; *Spanish Jade*, 1922; *Tell Your Children*, 1922. Co-screenwriter, assistant director, art director, and editor of *Woman to Woman*, 1923; art director and editor of *The White Shadow* (also known as *White Shadows*), 1923; co-screenwriter, assistant director, and art director of *The Passionate Adventure*, 1924; assistant director and art director of *The Prude's Fall*, 1924; assistant director and art director of *The Blackguard* (also known as *Die Prinzessin under der Geiger*), 1925; director of additional scenes for *The House Across the Bay*, 1940; re-editing and dubbing for U.S. version of *Men of the Lightship* (short film), 1940; supervisor of re-editing for U.S. version for *Target for Tonight*, 1941; producer of *The Directors*, 1963.

FILM APPEARANCES

Hitchcock's trademark was his many cameo appearances in his own films, including *A Story of the London Fog, Blackmail, Murder, The Thirty-Nine Steps, Young and Innocent, The Lady Vanishes, Rebecca, Foreign Correspondent, Mr. and Mrs. Smith, Saboteur, Shadow of a Doubt, Life Boat, Spellbound, Notorious, The Paradine Case, Rope, Stage Fright, Strangers on a Train, I Confess, Dial M for Murder, Rear Window, To Catch a Thief, The Trouble with Harry, The Man Who Knew Too Much, The Wrong Man, Vertigo, North by Northwest, Psycho, The Birds, Marnie, Torn Curtain, Topaz, Frenzy,* and *Family Plot.*

Also did voice of man on telephone telling Glenn Ford how to dispose of a corpse in *The Gazebo*, 1960, and made an appearance in *The Directors*, 1963. Hitchcock also appeared in the documentary *Makin' It*, 1970, and as an interviewee in *Once Upon a Time . . . Is Now*, 1977.

■ Writings

EDITOR

Suspense Stories, Dell, 1945.
Bar the Doors: Terror Stories, Dell, 1946.
Fireside Book of Suspense, Simon & Schuster, 1947.

Fear and Trembling: Shivery Stories, Dell, 1948.

Alfred Hitchcock Presents: Stories They Wouldn't Let Me Do on TV, Simon & Schuster, 1957.

Alfred Hitchcock Presents: My Favorites in Suspense, Random House, 1959, published as *Alfred Hitchcock Presents: Fourteen of My Favorites in Suspense*, Dell, 1959.

(And author of introduction) Henry Slesar, *Clean Crimes and Neat Murders*, Avon, 1960.

Alfred Hitchcock Presents: Stories for Late at Night, Random House, 1961.

Alfred Hitchcock Presents: Thirteen More Stories They Wouldn't Let Me Do on TV, Dell, 1961.

Haunted Houseful, illustrated by Fred Banbery, Random House, 1961, new edition illustrated by Anthony Colbert, Reinhardt, 1962.

Ghostly Gallery: Eleven Spooky Stories for Young People, illustrated by Fred Banbery, Random House, 1962.

Alfred Hitchcock Presents: Sixteen Skeletons from My Closet, Dell, 1963.

Alfred Hitchcock Presents: Stories My Mother Never Told Me, Random House, 1963.

Solve-Them-Yourself Mysteries, illustrated by Fred Banbery, Random House, 1963.

Alfred Hitchcock Presents: Stories Not for the Nervous, Random House, 1965.

Alfred Hitchcock's Monster Museum, illustrated by Earl E. Mayan, Random House, 1965.

Alfred Hitchcock's Sinister Spies, illustrated by Paul Spina, Random House, 1966.

Alfred Hitchcock Presents: Stories That Scared Even Me, Random House, 1967.

Alfred Hitchcock's Spellbinders in Suspense, illustrated by Harold Isen, Random House, 1967.

Alfred Hitchcock Presents: A Month of Mystery, Random House, 1969, published as *Alfred Hitchcock Presents: Dates with Death*, Dell, 1976.

Murders I Fell in Love With, Dell, 1969.

Death Can Be Beautiful, Dell, 1972.

A Hearse of a Different Color, Dell, 1972.

Alfred Hitchcock Presents: Stories to Be Read with the Lights On, Random House, 1973.

Alfred Hitchcock's Supernatural Tales of Terror and Suspense, illustrated by Robert Short, Random House, 1973.

Alfred Hitchcock Presents: Stories to Be Read with the Door Locked, Random House, 1975.

Alfred Hitchcock Presents: Stories That Go Bump in the Night, Random House, 1977.

Alfred Hitchcock's Witch's Brew, illustrated by Stephen Marchesi, Random House, 1977.

Alfred Hitchcock Presents: The Master's Choice, Random House, 1979.

■ Sidelights

"I am out to give the public good, healthy, mental shake-ups," the late great film director Alfred Hitchcock once said back in 1936. The quote is taken from *Hitchcock on Hitchcock: Selected Writings and Interviews*, a collection of interviews, essays, and speeches edited by Sidney Gottlieb. The director continued, "Civilization has become so screening and sheltering that we cannot experience sufficient thrills at first hand. Therefore, to prevent our becoming sluggish and jellified, we have to experience them artificially, and the screen is the best medium for this." This was a vision he would maintain throughout his life. That Hitchcock, who was sometimes simply called "Hitch" for short, was an accomplished and highly influential director of thrillers is beyond question, even among his most stalwart critics. Years after his death in 1980, his name is still familiar to young and old as the creative hand behind such films as *Psycho, The Birds, North by Northwest, Rear Window, Vertigo, The Man Who Knew Too Much*, and many more.

During a career that spanned five decades, Hitchcock directed fifty-three feature films. He has been both hailed as a master technician and lambasted for caring too much about technique and not enough about the characters in his film. Despite the praise and many awards he has received, Hitchcock, for some critics, falls short of being "an artist." As William S. Pechter averred in his *Twenty-four Times a Second*, "[Hitchcock's] films veer schizophrenically toward empty entertainment on the one hand, and something like art on the other." Other critics, however, have looked more deeply into the director's films to find a unifying and fascinating preoccupation. Robin Wood, writing in the *International Directory of Films and Filmmakers*, asserted that in Hitchcock there is "so much more than the skillful entertainer and master-craftsman he was once taken for. His films overall represent an incomparable exposure of the sexual tensions and anxieties (especially *male* anxieties) that characterize a culture built upon repression, sexual inequality, and the drive to domination." In addition to the sexual tones in many of his films, however, are the distinctive preoccupations with feelings of guilt and fear. Still other experts have simply acknowledged, as Andrew Sarris did in *The American Cinema: Directors and Directions, 1929-1968*, that "Hitchock's art is full of paradoxes."

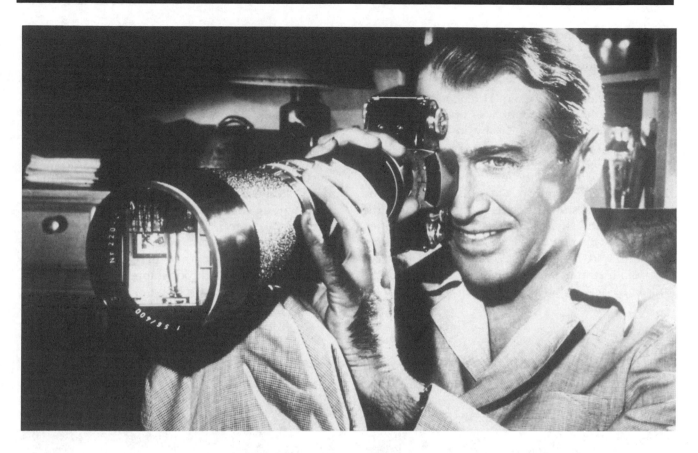

Suspense builds in *Rear Window,* about a housebound newspaper photographer, played by Jimmy Stewart, determined to solve a murder.

Early Years

Alfred Joseph Hitchcock was born in London, England, in 1899. His family loved to go to the theater, and so young Alfred was exposed early to the entertainment world, even before movies. Raised in a Catholic family, he attended the Jesuit school of St. Ignatius College in London. "It was probably during this period with the Jesuits," Hitchcock said in Francois Truffaut's *Hitchcock,* "that a strong sense of fear developed—moral fear—the fear of being involved in anything evil. Why? Perhaps out of physical fear. I was terrified of physical punishment. In those days they used a cane made of very hard rubber. I believe the Jesuits still use it." This sense of fear was combined with a love of crime stories. "I was reading . . . all the real-life crime stories I could get hold of," he recalled in a *Sight and Sound* article by John Russell Taylor, "but it never occurred to me as a practical possibility that my professional life might take that turn."

Instead, Hitchcock at first planned to be an engineer, and so his parents obligingly sent him to the School of Engineering and Navigation, where he studied mechanics, electricity, acoustics, and navigation. After leaving school, Hitchcock got a job at Henley Telegraph Company, where he became a technical estimator at the young age of nineteen. At the same time, however, he was also studying art at the University of London. Both his studies in engineering and art would prove helpful in his later film career.

Though his parents' early influence on him led to a fondness for the theater, Hitchcock was even more drawn to movies. "I preferred the movies and was more attracted to American films than to the British . . . ," he said in Truffaut's book. "I was very keen on pictures and the stage and very often went to first nights by myself. From the age of sixteen on I read film journals. Not fan or fun magazines, but always professional and trade papers. And since I was studying art at the

University of London, Henley's transferred me to the advertising department, where I was given a chance to draw."

The year was 1920 when Hitchcock read in a trade paper that Paramount was opening a branch studio of Famous Players-Lasky in Islington, London. Seeing an opportunity, he read one of the books that the studio was planning to turn into a movie. This was still the era of silent films, and dialogue and narration was displayed on the screen as titles shown between scenes to help the audience follow the story. These titles were often illustrated with pictures. Hitchcock took his drawing skills and designed several pictures to serve as title illustrations. Submitting his work to the studio, he got a job as a title designer, and his first job was doing the titles for the 1920 film *The Great Day*.

"At this time," Hitchcock recalled in Truffault's book, "I met several American writers and I learned how to write scripts. And sometimes when an extra scene was needed—but not an acting scene—they would let me shoot it. However, the pictures made by Famous Players in England were unsuccessful in America. So the studio became a rental studio for British producers." Practicing his scriptwriting abilities, Hitchcock wrote an adaptation for the screen based on a serial novel published in a magazine. Upon showing his work to a British company that had taken over the Islington studio, Hitchcock impressed the filmmakers enough to land a job as an assistant director.

Ray Milland, Grace Kelly, and Robert Cummings star in *Dial M for Murder*, about a husband who plots to murder his rich wife.

When another company came to the studio in 1922 to film an adaptation of the play *Woman to Woman*, Hitchcock offered to write the screenplay. Not only did he become co-screenwriter, he also worked on that film as assistant director, art director, and editor.

The British and German Films

Michael Bacon, the man who formed the company Hitchcock was working for, offered the young assistant his first chance to direct an entire film with *The Pleasure Garden* in 1925. Hitchcock went on to direct ten silent features. *The Lodger*, the 1926 film about a man accused of being Jack the Ripper, was a thriller that was a sensation in England. Even more important of these early films was 1929's *Blackmail*, in which the unique Hitchcock style—and his interest in the theme of guilt—first becomes truly discernible. Though originally without sound, *Blackmail* later had a soundtrack added to it, allowing Hitchcock to display more of the inventiveness he had already begun to show in his imagery. Hitchcock called his technique "subjective sound." In *Blackmail*, the story of a woman who has stabbed her seducer to death, he uses subjective sound to slowly distort dialogue until only the word "knife" can be heard, thus focusing in on the woman's sense of guilt and anxiety.

The Pleasure Garden and Hitchcock's second film, *The Mountain Eagle*, were shot in German studios. In the 1920s, German film was highly influenced by Expressionism. Expressionism, as Robin Wood explains in the introduction to his book *Hitchcock's Films*, "evades simple definition, but a central impulse was clearly the attempt to 'express' emotional states through a distortion or deformation of objective reality, 'expression' taking precedence over representation." Hitchcock's interest in showing his audiences subjective views of reality as expressed through various cinematic techniques thus begins in Germany. A second early influence on the director came when he first saw films from the Soviet Union, which introduced him to the technique of montage, or piecing together various elements of a film to convey a certain impression. From the Soviet filmmakers, Hitchcock learned that skillful editing can be used "for deceiving the spectator, for playing tricks with time and space." As Wood noted, Hitchcock learned that showing images in certain sequences can lead the audience to impose emotions onto a scene. For example, if

a picture of an actor's face is shown, followed by a picture of a bowl of soup, the audience might think that the actor is hungry, even if he isn't trying to convey that feeling.

By the time *Blackmail* was released, Hitchcock was already developing a reputation as a fine director of thrillers. Yet in the 1930s he was still honing his skills, and, consequently, some of his early works were not successful. Films such as *The Skin Game* and *Number Seventeen* were damaged by ridiculous villains or even boring plots (such as in the stultifying musical piece, *Waltzes from Vienna*). On the other hand, movies such as the spy thrillers *The Thirty-Nine Steps*, *Secret Agent*, and 1935's *The Man Who Knew Too Much*, which Hitchcock remade in 1955, rewarded audiences with strong acting and flashes of brilliant directing. Of Hitchcock's English films, David Thomson wrote in *A Biographical Dictionary of Film*, "The English films are playful, and sometimes facetious or silly. But they have dark moments and there are stirrings of sexual menace. The comic adventure of *The Lady Vanishes*, for instance, turns into a parable on appeasement, in which stock English fools get hurt. The first *Man Who Knew Too Much* is startlingly grim and cruel, and *Sabotage* is not unworthy of Conrad's novel *The Secret Agent*." Still, Hitchcock was not satisfied with the limitations of working in English studios. He had always admired American cinema more than British, and so it did not take much for producer David O. Selznick to lure Hitchcock to Hollywood in 1939.

Hitchcock in Hollywood

Thomson credits Selznick with teaching Hitchcock something about the importance of character and plausible plots in films. The director being a good student, his first American film, *Rebecca*, proved an auspicious beginning to his new life. The film, based on the Daphne du Maurier novel, won an Academy Award for best picture and received wonderful reviews from critics. Selznick had expected Hitchcock to make another spy film, but the director surprised him with a psychological thriller instead. *Rebecca* is the story of a young woman who becomes the second wife of the rich widower Mr. de Winter. Upon arriving at her husband's mansion, she discovers that the staff hates her for replacing the beloved, deceased Rebecca. Especially nasty is the housekeeper, Ms.

Anderson, who torments the new Mrs. de Winter to the brink of insanity. Later, it is revealed that the late Mrs. de Winter was actually a horrible person who cheated on and tormented her husband, and that she wanted to destroy him. Her death at Mr. de Winter's hand is shown to be accidental, and the horrible Ms. Anderson dies when the mansion catches fire.

Although *Rebecca* is not typical of Hitchcock's films, it does contain characteristic elements, especially when it comes to the question of whether Mr. de Winter is guilty of killing his wife. The question of guilt is a central strain in the director's oeuvre, a theme that is often laced with sexual implications. Interestingly, the male characters in his films are usually innocent of any crimes in which they are suspects (with very few exceptions, such as *Shadow of a Doubt*), while his female characters are often guilty of murder, conspiracy, or sexually immoral acts such as adultery.

Shadow of a Doubt, released in 1943, is often considered one of Hitchcock's best works, and it was also one of his personal favorites. Based on a real-life murderer, Earle Leonard Nelson, who strangled several women during the 1920s, Hitchcock created an urbane and witty villain who kills his victims in a small, middle-class town. Charming villains and violence in ordinary settings are two Hitchcock trademarks, for the director enjoyed doing anything to catch his audience off balance. Instead of keeping the murderers' identities a secret—Hitchcock was not interested in mysteries, wanting instead to create suspenseful thrillers—he made them unsettlingly appealing. Having a murder occur in an ordinary household instead of a back alley or gloomy mansion was equally disturbing to most audiences. But Hitchcock particularly liked *Shadow of a Doubt* because he was able to blend character so well with action.

More typical of his early films, however, are movies such as *Suspicion* (1941) and *Spellbound* (1945), in which the hero might be a killer but proves in the end not to be (the studio did not want the film's star, Cary Grant, to be a villain). Grant plays Johnnie Aysgarth, a man whose wife suspects him of murder, and who fears that he will kill her too. However, in the end he actually saves her life and proves his love. *Spellbound* is another psychological thriller. Here, Gregory Peck plays psychiatrist John Ballantine, whose odd behavior makes him the suspect of a murder. Dr. Peterson,

played by Ingmar Bergman, becomes convinced that his peculiar actions are caused by some kind of trauma, which turns out to be the time when Ballantine accidentally caused his brother's death.

During the 1940s, Hitchcock was still evolving as a director. *Foreign Correspondent* (1940), *Saboteur* (1942), and *Notorious* (1946) are spy thrillers; *Under Capricorn* (1949) was considered a failure; and in 1941 Hitchcock even uncharacteristically tried his hand at comedy with *Mr. and Mrs. Smith* (he also later tried black comedy in *The Trouble with Harry*, a flop about a natural death mistaken for a murder, and *Family Plot*, one of his most successful works). Though still not viewed as his most brilliant period, Hitchcock was assuredly coming into his own. *Lifeboat* (1944) is an intense drama in which several passengers from an American ship are stuck on a lifeboat with a German submarine captain after both vessels have sunk. *Rope* (1948), a film in which two homosexual men strangle another friend to death just for the thrill of it, is unique in that Hitchcock filmed it so that the entire movie appeared to be one continuous shot with all the action occurring in real time. With such films, Hitchcock was always proving himself an inventive director, thinking up new tricks to add visual impact to his films. In *Suspicion*, for example, Hitchcock placed a lit lightbulb within a glass of milk to make it glow ominously because the wife suspects her husband has poisoned the drink.

On Themes, Technique, and Actors

It was with 1951's *Strangers on a Train* that some critics feel Hitchcock reached the top of his form. In this movie, Hitchcock mixes a concoction of fear, anxiety, and dread into one of his most suspenseful potions. After meeting for the first time on a train, as the title implies, Bruno Antony, a young playboy with rich parents who has been expelled from three colleges, makes an unusual proposal to Guy Haines, a tennis pro who is trying to start a career in politics. Bruno hates his father, whom he feels is too demanding, and promises that if Guy will murder Mr. Antony, then he, in turn, will kill Guy's money-grubbing wife. When Guy calls the plan ridiculous, Bruno backs off. But then he begins to pursue Guy, repeatedly insisting that he murder Bruno's father. When Bruno actually kills Guy's wife, the suspense

Based on an actual crime, *Psycho* deals with a female thief, a psychopathic transvestite, and a new Hollywood level of horror.

builds even more until the final climactic confrontation between Bruno and Guy.

Some movie critics, who had felt that Hitchcock had been in somewhat of a slump since *Shadow of a Doubt*, felt that the director had regained his stride with *Strangers on a Train*. As Richard Winnington remarked in *Sight and Sound*, "Strangers on a Train . . . recalls the old virtuoso of the art of suspense. Here again fear and paranoia are let loose in the open against normal backgrounds." Guilt, too, is central to the story. Guy wished to be rid of his wife, and when Bruno actually kills her Guy must question his own involvement. Is he guilty—through his association with Bruno—of the murder, too? "Strangers on a Train," remarked Wood in *Hitchcock's Films*, "draws together many themes already adumbrated in earlier films, which will be taken further in later ones: the theme of what Conrad calls the 'sickening assumption of

common guilt' (developed especially in *Psycho*); the theme of the search for identity (*Vertigo*); the theme of the struggle of a personality torn between order and chaos (perhaps the most constant Hitchcock theme); and, in close conjunction with this, the notion of experience-therapy—the hero purged of his weaknesses by indulging them and having to live out the consequences (*Rear Window*)."

Though Hitchcock's heroes often suffer through some sort of emotional or moral crisis, they are seldom guilty of a crime. But this is not the case with the heroines in the director's movies. Women are guilty of murder in films such as *The Paradine Case*, or conspiracy to murder, as in *Vertigo*, or, if not murder, then adultery, as in *Dial M for Murder*, or theft, as in *Psycho*. Wood argued in the *International Directory of Film and Filmmakers* that Hitchcock's tendency to make his female characters guilty of crimes has a distinct sexual connotation, especially when one considers how the male characters are often drawn toward and "contaminated" by the females' guilt. "On the whole," wrote Wood, "it is the guilty woman films that are the more disturbing . . . ; here, the potentially threatening and subversive female sexuality . . . erupts to demand recognition [and], is answered by an appalling violence." It is these films, concluded Wood, that are Hitchcock's most disturbing.

Whether or not these trends in his films were conscious decisions on Hitchcock's part is a matter for debate. What is much more certain, however, is the director's interest in technique to get the best reaction from his audience. "I don't want to film a 'slice of life,'" he told Truffault, "because people can get that at home, in the street, or even in front of the movie theater. . . . Making a film means, first of all, to tell a story. . . . The next factor is the technique of film-making, and in this connection, I am against virtuosity for its own sake. Technique should enrich the action. One doesn't set the camera at a certain angle just because the cameraman happens to be enthusiastic about that spot. The only thing that matters is whether the installation of the camera at a given angle is going to give the scene its maximum impact. The beauty of image and movement, the rhythm and the effects—everything must be subordinated to the purpose."

Because he felt each shot was so important, Hitchcock was known for his obsessive planning before any scene was filmed. "The secret," he told Pete Martin in the *Saturday Evening Post*, "is the way in which the story is pieced together. With me, all the little bits of business and the situations must be planted and established before the camera rolls. Sometimes I plan as many as six hundred camera setups before I begin to shoot." Actress Janet Leigh, who played Marion in *Psycho*, recalled in an *American Film* article by Stephen Rebello: "His camera was absolute. . . . Every move was planned. . . . He said, 'You can do almost anything with Marion and I won't interfere, so long as it's within my concept.'" Leigh later added, "Hitchcock's films had so little cutting, he told me, because he had learned the hard way. . . . Before he had the clout to have his pictures the way he wanted, someone else would cut them their own way. . . . He learned to preplan so precisely to not give them extra material, be-

cause it was either going to work or not. If it worked, he didn't want anybody to muck it up."

Hitchcock had a reputation for not only being meticulous with his camera, but also for his sense of wit he deployed in his shots. For example, in one scene in *Marnie* Hitchcock films a kind of split screen shot, with Marnie on one side stealing the contents of her boss's safe and, on the other, a maid cleaning up the boss's office. Some critics have seen the director's wit as being integral to his ability to create suspense. In *Films in Review*, for example, Steve Sondheim remarked "Hitchcock's brilliance is his wit, and his flawless technique for using that wit to support and counterpoint suspense. When his wit fails, his suspense fails."

Hitchcock was not only known for his cleverness on camera, but also off, when he would indulge in practical jokes, although he later told Martin: "I have pretty much outgrown that now. And I'm afraid that if I tried to describe them to you, they'd seem pretty flat and contrived." One trick Hitchcock was particularly noted for on camera, however, was his penchant for cameo appearances. Usually these are simple bits, such as Hitchcock playing a passerby in *The Thirty-nine Steps* or as a man standing in a railway station in *The Lady Vanishes*. At other times, he would add a little humor, such as when he played a man who misses a bus in *North by Northwest*.

Despite this sense of humor, Hitchcock was also notorious for his poor treatment of his actors and for other people with whom he worked. He saw actors not as fellow artists who could contribute something to his films but, rather, as props to be used. "Hitchcock's thing about actors was very strange," said Joseph Stefano in Rebello's article. Stefano was a screenwriter who worked on *Psycho* and who commented that Hitchcock viewed actors as "spoiled children. . . . It was as though he really didn't live in the same world with them—or they in his." The director sometimes treated his coworkers with similar contempt. He often did not give others credit for contributing to his films, a deliberate omission that gave the false impression that Hitchcock did more work on his films than he actually did. He could also hold heavy grudges. For example, when screenwriter John Michael Hayes, who had done the writing for famous Hitchcock films like *Rear Window* and *The Man Who Knew Too Much*, refused to write the script for *The Wrong Man* for free, the director threatened to end their partnership. Hayes recalled in *Premiere*, "He said, 'If you don't do this, I'll never speak to you again,'" and he never did.

The 1950s and 1960s

Many of Hitchcock's most well-known and talked-about films were made from the mid-1950s through the mid-1960s, including *Rear Window, Vertigo, North by Northwest, Psycho,* and *The Birds.* Each is a very distinct work that convey different ideas. *Rear Window,* which debuted in 1954 and starred Jimmy Stewart, who had been in other Hitchcock films such as *Rope,* is about a magazine photographer who takes to observing his neighbors through a pair of field glasses while he is convalescing from a broken leg. One night, unable to sleep, he sees his neighbor, Mr. Thorwald, doing something suspicious. Thorwald's wife has disappeared, and the photographer begins to suspect that Thorwald has killed her. The theme of voyeurism in the film is clear, and, since the audience is watching Stewart watching his neighbor, that sense of voyeurism is also implied on the audience's part. Francois Truffaut, writing in his *The Films in My Life,* felt that in *Rear Window* one can see by implication the director's opinion of humanity—his audience—because everything the photographer sees shows people at their worst. "*Rear Window,* wrote Truffaut, "is a film about indiscretion, about intimacy violated and taken by surprise at its most wretched moments; a film about the impossibility of happiness, about dirty linen that gets washed in the courtyard." Truffaut compared the courtyard in the film to "the world, the reporter/photographer is the film maker, the binoculars stand for the camera and its lenses. And Hitchcock? He is the man we love to be hated by."

Stewart also starred in 1957's *Vertigo.* Stewart plays John "Scottie" Ferguson, a policeman who develops a severe case of acrophobia (a fear of heights) and a sense of dizziness and disorientation (vertigo) after almost falling to his death while pursuing a criminal on the roof of a building. Retiring from the force, Scottie agrees to help his old college friend Gavin keep track of his wife, Madeleine, who has been acting peculiarly. Madeleine is obsessed with the idea that she is possessed by the spirit of an ancestor who killed herself. Scottie follows Madeleine for some time

and begins to fall in love with her. When Madeleine climbs to the top of a tower and leaps to her death, Scottie is torn by guilt because his vertigo prevented him from following her. Later, he meets Judy Barton, who bears an uncanny resemblance to Madeleine. Scottie becomes obsessed with Judy and insists she change her appearance to look like Madeleine. Actually, Judy is, in fact, Madeleine, having played the role as a favor to Gavin to cover up the real murder Gavin committed. Realizing he has been duped, Scottie, enraged, drags Judy to the top of a church bell tower. He has overcome his vertigo, but he can't bring himself to murder Judy. Judy, however, is accidentally startled when a nun suddenly appears, and she falls to her death.

Vertigo falls into the category of one of Hitchcock's "guilty women" films. However, Judy is highly sympathetic because she falls in love with Scottie, who can't return that love because he is obsessed with Madeleine. Often acclaimed as one of the director's most fascinating films, the most common criticism of *Vertigo* is that Hitchcock reveals too soon the fact that Judy and Madeleine are the same person (something the French novel *D'entre les morts,* upon which the film is based, does not do until the end). Hitchcock explained in David Zinman's *50 from the 50's: Vintage Films from America's Mid-Century* that *Vertigo* is a prime example of his intention not to surprise viewers so much as to create a suspenseful plot. The suspense lies in the question of what Scottie will do once he finds out Judy is Madeleine. "I felt that the second part of the novel was written as if nothing came next," said Hitchcock.

Hitchcock followed *Vertigo* with 1959's *North by Northwest,* starring Cary Grant as Roger Thornhill. *North by Northwest* is a spy/chase film like 1955's *The Man Who Knew Too Much,* and a good example of Hitchcock's love of putting ordinary people in extraordinary situations. *The Man Who Knew Too Much,* the film Hitchcock liked so much he made it twice, places two tourists (played by Doris Day and, again, Stewart) in Morocco, where they unwittingly stumble into a spy ring, kidnappers, and murderers. *North by Northwest* features an advertising executive who is mistaken for another man and kidnapped because he is suspected of being a spy. While *North by Northwest* is an exciting chase film tinged with Hitchcock's black sense of humor, his movie *The Wrong Man* (1956), which also has the theme of mistaken identity, is much bleaker. In this film, Manny, played by Henry Fonda, is accused of murder. Manny is imprisoned, and his wife, unable to cope, is committed to a sanatorium. Though the real criminal is eventually found and Manny is released, he loses his wife to her mental disorder. Audiences found *The Wrong Man* disturbingly bleak, and so it was not as popular as the more upbeat *North by Northwest* and *The Man Who Knew Too Much*.

Psycho, The Birds, and *Marnie*

Psychological disturbance was a theme Hitchcock had touched on in several of his films—most notably, *Shadow of a Doubt* and *Strangers on a Train*—but it was later in his career that he made his most famous film on the subject, *Psycho*. *Psycho*, whose murderous psychopath character is based on the real-life Ed Gein, a cannibal and murderer who lived in Wisconsin, has everything one could expect of a Hitchcock film: the guilty woman stealing money from her boss, sexual overtones and voyeurism (a la *Rear Window*) with Norman Bates (Anthony Perkins) looking through the peephole at Marion Crane (Janet Leigh), and brilliant camera work (the famous shower scene in which Marion is stabbed to death). *Psycho* also begins with a scene—very controversial for its time—in which Marion (appearing in her undergarments) is having a hotel tryst with her lover, Sam. Sam, who is in debt and has to pay his ex-wife alimony, says he can't afford to get remarried. Marion, desperate to make a new life for herself, steals money from her boss and leaves town. She stops at the Bates motel, where she meets Norman, a shy young man who seems like he is suppressed by his domineering mother, whom Marion is not allowed to meet. That night, while Marion (who has decided to return the money) is taking a shower, the curtain is drawn back and a figure wearing a dress stabs her.

Marion's sister, Lila, worried about her sister's disappearance, contacts Sam and a detective. The detective, checking motels in the area where Marion was last seen, enters the Bates motel and is killed by the same figure in a dress. Lila and Sam next go to the hotel, where Sam distracts Norman while Lila goes to talk to Norman's mother. To her horror, she finds that Norman's mother is a corpse. Just then, the figure in a dress comes in to attack Lila, but Sam enters, pulls away the wig and reveals that Norman is the

murderer. Norman, who killed his mother and her lover years ago in a fit of jealousy, has become insane.

Psycho was a sensation when it was released in 1960. Critics called it ingeniously grizzly, and audiences flocked to see it. Theaters created more interest with certain tricks, as Danny Peary remarked in *Cult Movies 3:* "In 1960, theaters wouldn't let you in if you missed the beginning of *Psycho* (a gimmick that attracted enormous crowds) and it's a good thing because the opening scene in the hotel is vital." There is much sexual tension in the film. Marion, as the opening scene shows, is uncomfortable with her sexuality; Norman is a sexually repressed voyeur; Norman's mother was puritanical and controlling. It is thus Norman's pent-up sexual anxieties that lead him to murder both his mother (and her lover) and Marion. His killing of the detective, however, is more the result of his fear of being found out.

The violence, of course, is the most disturbing part of the film. Hitchcock keeps his audience off balance by having the murders occur when they are least expected: in a well-lit shower; in a comfortable, ordinary room; and on a staircase, well before the detective reaches the door to Mrs. Bates' room. Ernest Callenbach, writing in *Film Quarterly*, called *Psycho* "the sickest film ever made. It is also one of the most technically exciting films of recent years." Of course, there were also critics who did not like the film. Dwight Macdonald asserted in his *D. M. on Movies* that *Psycho* was "third-rate Hitchcock," calling it "a reflection of a most unpleasant mind, a mean, sly, sadistic little mind."

The next film Hitchcock made, 1963's *The Birds*, was also a horror film, but of a very different sort. The first color feature Hitchcock ever made, it is based on a story by Daphne du Maurier, who also wrote the novel *Rebecca* that the director adapted. In *The Birds* Hitchcock juxtaposes tense human relationships with the bizarre and completely unexplained attack of thousands of birds upon the citizens of Bodega Bay. When Melanie Daniels (played by Tippi Hedren), a spoiled young socialite, arrives in town in pursuit of her love interest, lawyer Mitch Brenner (played by Rod Taylor), tensions grow between her and Mitch's former girlfriend and his mother. The reason for the birds' sudden attack on the town has been a

If you enjoy the works of Alfred Hitchcock, you may want to check out the following:

Cape Fear, Universal, 1991.
The films of Brian DePalma, including *Dressed to Kill*, 1980, *Blow Out*, 1981, and *Body Double*, 1984.
Silence of the Lambs, Orion, 1991.
The Spy Who Came in from the Cold, Salem, 1965.

matter of debate. In *Hitchcock's Films*, author Robin Wood addresses three possibilities: "1) *The birds are taking revenge for man's persecution of them.* . . . 2) *The birds are sent by God to punish evil humanity.* . . . 3) *The birds express the tensions between the characters.*" Of the first two, Wood feels that the events in the film are not supportive, whereas the third choice "is more interesting, and seems to gain some support when one considers the original attack on Melanie by the seagull [when she is about to meet Mitch to give him a present of love birds]. But objections soon pile up: the birds attack innocent schoolchildren and kill Dan Fawcett, of whose possible tensions we know nothing."

Another theory expounded upon by John Thomas in *Film Society Review* is that the birds simply represent the irrationality of the world: "The birds . . . are but an analogue for those violent irrational forces that Hitchcock sees underlying our civilized world." Peter Bogdonavich, writing in *Film Culture*, favored the theory that *The Birds* "is a modern fable about the complacency of Man and the uncertainty of his position in the universe." The critic praised the film for its disturbing, Hitchcockian combination of horrible events within an ordinary setting. "There are sequences in *The Birds* that will literally leave you limp," Bogdonavich reported. Other critics, however, have been disappointed by *The Birds*. Comparing *The Birds* to *Psycho*, Callenbach said that *The Birds* does not build-up tension the way *Psycho* does: "*The Birds* uses up its excitement early, then tries to rise to what is only an anticlimax—the escape of the four individuals in the sports car." Wood, too, did not like the film—but only before gaining a better appreciation of it: "At first it seemed to me a great disappointment; now, after repeated

viewings, it seems to me among Hitchcock's finest achievements."

Marnie, released in 1964, readdresses Hitchcock's interest in psychological disturbances. Marnie Edgar (played by Tippi Hedren) is a woman who takes jobs at rich firms under various aliases and steals from them. She then gives the money to her mother, who, for some reason, seems to hate Marnie, even though Marnie loves her. Marnie is also troubled by nightmares and becomes unreasonably frightened by thunderstorms and the sight of anything that is the color of blood. When Marnie is hired by Mark Rudland (played by Sean Connery), she does not know he has heard she is a thief. Mark is strangely attracted to Marnie, however, and when he catches her stealing from him, he offers to let her off the hook if she will marry him. Marnie agrees, but it is an uneasy union, for Marnie hates all men. Mark becomes aware that something horrible happened to Marnie in her past that makes her act the way she does. One day, he insists they go to the home of Marnie's mother, where Mark confronts Mrs. Edgar. When Marnie tells him to leave her mother alone, a memory comes to the surface of when she saw her mother, who was once a prostitute, being attacked by one of her clients. Marnie killed the man with a poker from the fireplace. Finally understanding her past, Marnie is able to accept Mark's love.

Marnie once again mixes murder and guilt with themes about sexual transgressions, including a scene where Mark takes advantage of Marnie. It also harkens back to earlier Hitchcock films, such as *Blackmail* and *Notorious*, in which the heroine is "saved" by the male lead. Although *Marnie* was not one of the director's more successful films at the box office, it is a prime example of the Hitchcockian theme of the search for identity. Marnie slips in and out of aliases to hide her identity as a thief, which in itself is an alter ego of the real Marnie—the one who committed murder as a child. "Hitchcock considered *Marnie* an unusual mystery," stated Peary in *Cult Movies 2*, "because the search is not for a criminal but for a criminal's motivations." George Kaplan, writing in *Film Comment,* called *Marnie* "the culmination of Hitchcock's concept of cinema as an artificially fabricated construct; it is also among the films in which one senses him most emotionally engaged. The paradox is only apparent: it is in the nature of Hitchcock's art that it is most intense when it

The Birds pits nature against man in a tense film of pure terror as thousands of birds attack the citizens of Bodega Bay.

leaves daily reality, the 'normal,' behind to explore unnatural relationships and extreme mental states, especially the obsessive compulsive, in a kind of abstraction only cursorily disguised as naturalism."

A Career Draws to a Close

Hitchcock did not break any new ground with his last four films. Indeed, some critics, like Thomas, felt that his color films suffered from "sloppiness" not seen in his earlier black-and-white movies. *Torn Curtain* (1966) and *Topaz* (1969) are spy films, *Frenzy* (1972) is a thriller, and *Family Plot* (1976) is another dark comedy harkening back to *The Trouble with Harry*. *Torn Curtain* was one of the director's least successful films financially, part of which might be due to what has been called poor

casting and acting by stars Julie Andrews and Paul Newman, who plays Professor Michael Armstrong, a nuclear scientist defecting to East Germany to give the enemy a secret formula. Although Wood, writing in *Hitchcock's Films*, called *Torn Curtain* "a remarkably rich film," he also felt it left one with "a certain sense of emptiness. This is partly due to what is in other ways so admirable—the undermining of the morality of what Michael is doing on a political level: we are left wondering what it has all been for, and not finding very much of an answer." *Topaz* again involves East-West international intrigue. Set in the year 1962, while the Soviet Union was sending missiles to Cuba, the plot involves a French spy who is trying to uncover an information leak to the enemy.

Of his final films, *Frenzy,* for which he returned to England for the first time in twenty years, is one of the more successful. Although a reiteration of earlier thrillers, Hitchcock delivers some of his best material in this 1972 feature. The film concerns an ordinary man, Jon Finch, who is falsely accused of murdering his ex-wife and his girl-friend, and a debonair man who is the actual psychopathic rapist and killer. Hitchcock garnishes his movie with a dollop of humor, most notably a chef who insists on serving elaborate cuisine when all Finch really longs for is meat and potatoes. Hitchcock displays a most playful mood with his audience in *Frenzy.* As Joseph Sgammato stated in *Sight and Sound,* "Much of the vitality of *Frenzy* results from this implied relationship between director and audience. Hitchcock plays with our anticipations." Sgammato later added that "*Frenzy* is not about a sex killer; it's about looking at a sex killer. Its manner is its matter." Gabriel Miller, writing in *Film Heritage,* expressed his belief that *Frenzy,* despite its touches of humor, "is Hitchcock's most pessimistic film." It is a pessimism that Miller felt was evident in all of Hitchcock's later features (though it is also present in films like *Rear Window*). "It seems that over the years Hitchcock's belief in the possibilities of man to save himself and his world have diminished." As further evidence, Miller pointed to the conclusion of *The Birds,* in which the menace of the birds remains even at the end, and *Topaz,* in which war has been avoided but humanity is indifferent to its fate.

Hitchcock concluded his career with *Family Plot,* which was second only to *Psycho* in terms of box office sales, earning over seven million dollars. In this film, Hitchcock intertwines two stories: a spiritual medium and her boyfriend are hired by an heiress to locate her heir, and two thieves are planning a kidnapping in order to get a ransom of diamonds. The four characters meet accidentally in a graveyard, and Hitchcock ties them all together in a suspenseful, humorous ride. Although popular with audiences, some critics did not regard it as one of the director's best. "Ultimately," concluded Roger Greenspan in *Film Comment,* "*Family Plot* may be more fun to think about than to see. . . . There are moments of quite stunning intensity. . . . But some of the principle action sequences seem relatively lax and unfocused."

In the latter decades of his life, Hitchcock was known not only for his film directing, but also as the host of the television program *The Alfred Hitchcock Hour* and as the editor of the *Alfred Hitchcock Presents* horror and thriller short story collections. His true fame, however, will always rest with his feature movies. Though his films have been both praised and condemned, there is little question that he gave the world such a unique and memorable theatrical contribution that he is well remembered years after his death in 1980. Hitchcock stands out among other directors for what Wood called in the *International Directory of Films and Filmmakers* the "extreme peculiarity of [his] art." Sometimes criticized for not making films about "real life" or "the human condition," Hitchcock never pretended to be anything other than what he was: a man who delighted in the art of film. As Eric Rhode declared in *Encounter,* "Hitchcock may well be the last commercial director to think of the cinema as a new medium and the camera as a fresh toy." "I'm not interested in content," Hitchcock reiterated in a *Rolling Stone* article by James Toback. "It's the same as a painter not worrying about the apples he's painting—whether they're sweet or sour. Who cares? It's his style, his manner of painting them—that's where the emotion comes from."

■ Works Cited

Bogdanovich, Peter, "'The Birds,'" *Film Culture,* spring, 1963, pp. 69-70.

Callenbach, Ernest, "Film Reviews: 'Psycho,'" *Film Quarterly,* fall, 1960, pp. 47-49.

Callenbach, Ernest, "Film Reviews: 'The Birds,'" *Film Quarterly,* summer, 1963, pp. 44-46.

Gottlieb, Sidney, editor, *Hitchcock on Hitchcock: Selected Writings and Interviews,* University of California Press, 1995.

Greenspan, Roger, "Plots and Patterns," *Film Comment,* May-June, 1976, pp. 20-22.

Kaplan, George, "Alfred Hitchcock: Lost in the Wood," *Film Comment,* November-December, 1972, pp. 46-53.

Macdonald, Dwight, *D. M. on Movies,* Prentice-Hall, 1969, pp. 303-304.

Martin, Pete, "I Call on Alfred Hitchcock," *Saturday Evening Post,* July, 1956.

Miller, Gabriel, "Hitchcock's Wasteland Vision: An Examination of 'Frenzy,'" *Film Heritage,* spring, 1976, pp. 1-10.

Peary, Danny, *Cult Movies 2: 50 More of the Classics, the Sleepers, the Weird, and the Wonderful,* Delta, 1983, pp. 84-87.

Peary, Danny, *Cult Movies 3: 50 More of the Classics, the Sleepers, the Weird, and the Wonderful,* Simon & Schuster, 1988, pp. 187-93.

Pechter, William S., *Twenty-four Times a Second,* Harper, 1971, pp. 177-78.

Rebello, Stephen, "Alfred Hitchcock Goes Psycho," *American Film,* April, 1990, pp. 38-48.

Rhode, Eric, review of *The Birds, Encounter,* October, 1963, p. 44.

Sarris, Andrew, *The American Cinema: Directors and Directions, 1929-1968,* Dutton, 1968, pp. 56-61.

Sgammato, Joseph, "The Discreet Qualms of the Bourgeoisie: Hitchcock's 'Frenzy,'" *Sight and Sound,* summer, 1973, pp. 134-37.

Sondheim, Steve, review of *Rear Window, Films in Review,* October, 1954, p. 427.

Taylor, John Russell, "Surviving: Hitchcock and Cukor," *Sight and Sound,* 1977.

Thomas, John, review of *The Birds, Film Society Review,* September, 1965, pp. 13-14.

Thomson, David, *A Biographical Dictionary of Film,* 3rd edition, Knopf, 1994, pp. 341-43.

Toback, James, "The Great Filmmakers—And Hitchcock," *Rolling Stone,* December 25-January 8, 1981.

"The Trouble with Hitch," *Premiere,* February, 1994, p. 36.

Truffaut, Francois, *Hitchcock,* Simon & Schuster, 1968.

Truffaut, Francois, *The Films in My Life,* Simon & Schuster, 1978.

Wood, Robin, *Hitchcock's Films,* A. S. Barnes, 1966.

Wood, Robin, "Alfred Hitchcock," *International Directory of Film and Filmmakers,* 2nd edition, Volume 2: *Directors,* edited by Nicholas Thomas, St. James Press, 1991, pp. 388-92.

Winnington, Richard, "Reviews: 'Strangers on a Train,'" *Sight and Sound,* August-September, 1951, pp. 21-22.

Zinman, David, *50 from the 50's: Vintage Films from America's Mid-Century,* Arlington House, 1979, pp. 381-87.

■ For More Information See

BOOKS

Arginteanu, Judy, *The Movies of Alfred Hitchcock,* Lerner Publications, 1994.

Bouzereau, Laurent, *The Alfred Hitchcock Quote Book,* Carol Publishing Group, 1993.

Boyd, David, editor, *Perspectives on Alfred Hitchcock,* G. K. Hall, 1995.

Finler, Joel W., *Hitchcock in Hollywood,* Continuum, 1992.

Freeman, David, *The Last Days of Alfred Hitchcock: A Memoir Featuring the Screenplay of "Alfred Hitchcock's The Short Night,"* Overlook Press, 1984.

Gottlieb, Sidney, editor, *Hitchcock: Selected Writings & Interviews,* University of California Press, 1995.

Humphries, Patrick, *The Films of Alfred Hitchcock,* Portland House, 1986.

Hurley, Neil P., *Soul in Suspense: Hitchcock's Fright and Delight,* Scarecrow Press, 1993.

Kapsis, Robert E., *Hitchcock: The Making of a Reputation,* University of Chicago Press, 1992.

LaValley, Albert J., editor, *Focus on Hitchcock,* Prentice-Hall, 1972.

Nevins, Francis M., Jr., and Martin Harry Greenberg, editors, *Hitchcock in Prime Time,* Avon, 1985.

Phillips, Gene D., *Alfred Hitchcock,* Twayne, 1984.

Rohmer, Eric, and Claude Chabrol, *Hitchcock, the First Forty-four Films,* Frederick Ungar, 1979.

Sloan, Jane, *Alfred Hitchcock: A Guide to References and Resources,* G. K. Hall, 1993.

Sloan, Jane, *Alfred Hitchcock: A Filmography and Bibliography,* University of California Press, 1995.

Donald Spoto, *The Art of Alfred Hitchcock: Fifty Years of His Motion Pictures,* Doubleday, 1992.

Taylor, John Russell, *Cinema Eye, Cinema Ear: Some Key Film-Makers of the Sixties,* Hill & Wang, 1964.

Taylor, John Russell, *Hitch: The Life and Times of Alfred Hitchcock,* Da Capo Press, 1996.

PERIODICALS

American Scholar, spring, 1970, pp. 295-304.

Film Culture, winter, 1955, p. 31.

Film Heritage, winter, 1969-70, pp. 17-23; winter, 1972-73, pp. 19-24; February 4, 1974, pp. 17-23.

Film Quarterly, winter, 1962-63, pp. 3-16; summer, 1968, pp. 21-27.

Films and Filming, October, 1974, pp. 51-54.

Nation, January 7, 1939, p. 45; November 10, 1945, p. 506.

New Republic, October 19, 1938, p. 307; February 8, 1943, p. 182; December 3, 1945, p. 477; September 13, 1948, pp. 29-30.

New Yorker, November 22, 1941, p. 98; January 15, 1944, pp. 56-57; November 3, 1945, pp. 69-70.

New York Magazine, April 19, 1976, pp. 84-86.

Saturday Review, June 8, 1940, p. 21.

Sight and Sound, October-December, 1954, pp. 89-90; summer, 1956, pp. 30-31; spring, 1957, p. 211.

Time, September 23, 1935, pp. 44-45.
Village Voice, April 2, 1979, pp. 45-46.

■ Obituaries

PERIODICALS

London Times, April 30, 1980.
New York Times, April 30, 1980.
Washington Post, May 4, 1980.*

—Sketch by Janet L. Hile

Jan Hudson

■ Personal

Born April 27, 1954, in Calgary, Alberta, Canada; died in April, 1990; daughter of Laurie (a school librarian and professor) and Marie (a teacher; maiden name, Haugen) Wiedrick; married in 1977; children: (stepdaughter) Cindy. *Education:* University of Calgary, B.A., 1978; University of Alberta, LL.B. 1983. *Religion:* Society of Friends (Quaker).

■ Career

Legal editor and writer. Legal researcher, administrative assistant, and editor for attorney general of British Columbia. *Member:* Writers Union of Canada (British Columbia/Yukon representative to national council, 1986-87), Canadian Bar Association, Free-Lance Editors Association, Canadian Society of Composers, Authors, Illustrators, and Performers.

■ Awards, Honors

Children's Literature Prize, Canada Council, and Best Children's Book of the Year, Canadian Asso-

ciation of Children's Librarians, both 1984, and Notable Book and Best Book for Young Adults citations, American Library Association, 1989, all for *Sweetgrass;* R. Ross Annett award, 1991, and honorable mention for the Young Adult Canadian Book Award for 1991, both for *Dawn Rider.*

■ Writings

Sweetgrass (juvenile novel), Tree Frog Press, 1984, Philomel Books, 1989.
Dawn Rider (juvenile novel), Philomel Books, 1990.

■ Sidelights

Jan Hudson, a Canadian author of historical fiction, wrote only two novels during her short life. She died at the age of thirty-six in 1990 of respiratory failure due to viral pneumonia. However, she left a lasting message for young girls about overcoming adversity to find their true place in the world. Hudson's two novels, *Sweetgrass* and *Dawn Rider,* exemplify her interest in "social anthropology—the little things that make up most people's lives," as she stated in a 1989 *Publishers Weekly* interview with Bella Stander. She conveyed these details by using the history of the Blackfoot Nation as her background. "Both [novels] are evocative historical works, rich in nuance and resonance, about young women coming of age in the Blackfoot Nation," commented Sandra Martin in *Quill and Quire.* "Underlying this theme is a subtle yet haunting message about the devastating consequences that have resulted from native contact with Europeans." Perhaps the greatest compliment to Hudson's work was written by Sarah Ellis in the *Horn Book:* "We also experience the more complex satisfaction of having genuinely entered another time and the lives of another people." Hudson's hope, more specifically, was to write about the lives of Canadian Indian women of the past who, in her opinion, had been ignored. Through her work, she wanted to provide a tribute to the dignity and heritage of these women.

The world was almost robbed of the works of Jan Hudson because finding a publisher was not an easy job. She completed the first draft of *Sweetgrass* in 1979, but the manuscript spent the next several years in the mail, continuously rejected by American publishers. "I was going to keep rewriting it and keep resubmitting it until someone took it," Hudson told Stander. After *Sweetgrass* was chosen as a finalist in a young people's fiction contest, the house that had agreed to publish the book reneged on its offer, claiming the work was not commercial enough. In 1984, five years after the first draft was completed, Tree Frog Press, a small regional publisher in Canada, finally released *Sweetgrass*. It was another five years before Philomel published the work in the United States. *Sweetgrass* was an immediate success and is now published in eight languages overseas.

A Canadian Upbringing

Hudson was born in Calgary, Alberta, the daughter of Laurie Wiedrick, a school librarian and professor, and Marie Haugen Wiedrick, a teacher. During her childhood she was surrounded by books, and she began writing stories at an early age. In her "Author Gives Thank You's" in the *Canadian Library Journal,* Hudson credited her father with stimulating her interest in becoming a writer: "One thing I remember is that he used to get whole boxes of children's books for reviewing. . . . Sometimes he'd ask what I thought of a book. So I would write him a little book report. On occasion, he would then quote parts of my report in the final review sent in. So you see, ladies and gentlemen, that's how I got my start as a published author." In 1977 Hudson married a Blackfoot Native American man and adopted his daughter, Cindy Lynn. This young girl was the inspiration for Hudson's first book, *Sweetgrass,*

Can a fifteen-year-old girl save her people?

SWEETGRASS
Jan Hudson

SCHOLASTIC

Author of only two books before her untimely death, Hudson won both Canadian and American awards for her tale of a brave Indian girl.

which she dedicated to her stepdaughter (or "almost-daughter" in Blackfoot terms, which the author preferred). "I wanted to write a story about a very brave girl because Cindy taught me a lot about courage," Hudson later told Stander in *Publishers Weekly.*

The following year Hudson received a B.A. degree from the University of Calgary. She was pursuing a law degree when the setting for *Sweetgrass* was born from documents she found on local history. Wanting to familiarize herself with her husband's and daughter's culture, she began reading about Blackfoot history and came upon a description of the smallpox epidemic that killed half the tribe in the harsh winter of 1837. The plight of the Blackfoot nation so moved Hudson that she decided to incorporate their story into her writings. While writing *Sweetgrass*, Hudson spent time with Native American families as part of her research, as well as drawing from historical records. She also used surviving oral history, records of traders, and Blackfoot winter population counts. Just before the publication of *Sweetgrass* in 1983, Hudson received a law degree from the University of Alberta. Besides being a writer, throughout her career Hudson also worked as a legal research editor and served as administrative assistant and editor for the attorney general of British Columbia.

Native American Background

Sweetgrass was well received by critics, who noted Hudson's ability to recreate the past. "In a colorful, lyrical style evoking all the senses, *Sweetgrass* tells with strength and tenderness a dramatic story of coming of age in another time and culture," stated a critic in *Kirkus Reviews*. The novel opens with Sweetgrass, a fifteen-year-old Indian girl, picking strawberries in the summer of 1837. Her friend Pretty-Girl, whose name explains itself, is helping her. Pretty-Girl is only thirteen, yet her parents have given her away in marriage to a man who already has many wives. She will be subject to the most grueling chores because she is the newest bride. Sweetgrass dreams of a better life with an Indian boy named Eagle-Sun, hoping one day he will be able to pay her father for her hand. However, her father, Shabby Bull, has other plans for her—he does not want to give his favorite daughter away easily and he feels she is not yet strong enough to marry. At the annual Sun Dance, Shabby Bull announces that Sweetgrass must prepare twenty-eight buffalo hides alone before spring. At that time he will then consider her ready for marriage. Because Eagle-Sun and Sweetgrass come from different family groups, the end of the summer brings the separation of the two young lovers as they depart for their winter homes.

"Much of this coming-of-age story shows how Sweetgrass learns to value her role in the cultural pattern of her people, the 'beaded design,'" stated a *Publishers Weekly* reviewer. Hudson portrays this

If you enjoy the works of Jan Hudson, you may also want to check out the following books and films:

Kristiana Gregory, *Jenny of the Tetons*, 1989.
Jamake Highwater, *Legend Days*, 1984.
Sollace Hotze, *A Circle Unbroken*, 1988.
Dances with Wolves, Orion, 1991.

role at the beginning of the story, where Sweetgrass and the other young girls gather berries. They also butcher buffalo that the braves have killed, preparing the hides and making pemmican (dried buffalo meat). They perform these tasks as part of an endless cycle in preparation for the long, cold months of winter. As Ellis observed in *Horn Book*, "We are kept close to the story by Hudson's clear descriptions of the details of Blackfoot life."

The Blackfoot families spend the winters in isolation. As food begins to run scarce, Shabby Bull must go on a hunting trip to the snow-filled plains. Sweetgrass is left alone with her twelve-year old brother Otter, two baby siblings, and a demanding stepmother, or "almost-mother." During this time the small pox epidemic strikes, killing the babies and eventually striking both the stepmother and Otter. Sweetgrass becomes the only hope for the survival of her family. She faithfully cares for them. As she tries unsuccessfully to hunt for food, she decides to defy the river demon by catching fish, even though Blackfoot laws forbid the consumption of fish. It was this courage that Hudson wanted to convey. As she explained in *Canadian Library Journal*, "I hope Sweetgrass's courage in facing new realities will be some small source of inspiration to at least a few children today." Sweetgrass's actions impress her brother Otter and her almost-mother, but most importantly she wins the respect of her father. Her perseverance and maturity convince him that she is a woman, and at the end of the book the reader understands that with the return of spring, Sweetgrass will marry Eagle-Sun.

Yvonne A. Frey praised *Sweetgrass* in *School Library Journal*, calling it a book that reluctant readers could enjoy and declaring that "the message is one which is valuable for young readers to consider: maturity is not measured by one's physical growth alone but by the manner in which one faces both the emergencies of life and the ordinary and practical chores of everyday life." A testimony to the success of Hudson's talents are the awards she earned for *Sweetgrass*. Since 1984 it has received the Canadian Library Association Book of the Year for Children Award and the Canada Council Children's Literature Prize, among other honors.

The Coming of the Horse

Hudson's second book, *Dawn Rider*, was published quickly after the success of *Sweetgrass*. Appearing in 1990, it won critical acclaim. A contributor in *Kirkus Reviews* called the book a "beautifully crafted, thought-provoking novel." In a review in *School Library Journal*, Frey described *Dawn Rider* as "a historical native American novel, a romance, and a coming-of-age story, woven in flowing, lyric, descriptive language." Mary L. Adams, in *Voice of Youth Advocates*, observed that *Dawn Rider* is "a well-written historical fiction detailing the coming of the horses to the Northern Plain Indians."

In *Dawn Rider* Hudson again used the Blackfoot Indian women and their culture as a backdrop, this time portraying the trials of a young Indian girl in the 1700s. The main character is Kit Fox, a sixteen-year-old Blackfoot girl who, much like Sweetgrass, has a dream. Her dream, which comes to her in a vision, is to ride one of her father's horses. Horses were new to the prairies at the time, and most members of Kit Fox's tribe are still wary of them. Kit wants to be the first in her tribe to ride the horse, and her extreme feeling of kinship with the animal leads her to challenge the ban against women riders. Not only does she have to overcome the prejudice of her tribe, the Blood Band, against women riding horses, but she must also confront the tribe's fear of the horse itself. Found Arrow, the guardian of the horse, deviously helps Kit learn to ride and soon they become romantically involved. Kit's riding skills are tested when the Blood Band is attacked by the Snakes, an enemy tribe. She must ride to get guns and help, or her tribe will be massacred. Kit Fox's courage saves her people.

Frey observed in *School Library Journal* that the final scene of *Dawn Rider* is "poignant and ironic": Kit Fox and Found Arrow can exchange youthful

hopes for the bright future of the Blackfoot because of the use of guns and horses. In the *Publishers Weekly* interview, however, Hudson indicated that this realization parallels the theme she was trying to develop—"that you expect one thing, but life is another and it is still worth living." *Booklist* contributor Carolyn Phelan praised Hudson's achievement in *Dawn Rider*: "As she did in her extraordinary first novel, *Sweetgrass*, Hudson excels at portraying the changing consciousness of young women as they move into adulthood." Martin commented in *Quill and Quire* that "underneath this story is a sensitive and detailed portrait of the daily life of the Blackfoot people. It is instructional in the best possible sense, a piece of fiction that informs, broadens, and uplifts the reader."

Hudson was in the midst of moving to a "quiet place" to work on her third novel for Philomel at the time of her death. Susan Lehr's observation in *Language Arts* might be considered a summary of the writer's legacy: "Hudson's strength is that she doesn't judge; she illuminates." A perfect example is how, as a reviewer points out in *Kirkus Reviews*, she "recreates the life of a long-ago culture with telling detail and lyrical grace." Hudson told Stander in the *Publishers Weekly* interview, 'I tried to let the universal part of being human shine through a pattern of details of time." It was a task that she accomplished in her short literary career.

■ Works Cited

Adams, Mary L., review of *Dawn Rider*, *Voice of Youth Advocates*, February, 1991, p. 352.

Review of *Dawn Rider*, *Kirkus Reviews*, December 1, 1990, p. 1673.

Ellis, Sarah, review of *Sweetgrass*, *Horn Book*, September-October, 1986, p. 626.

Frey, Yvonne A., review of *Sweetgrass*, *School Library Journal*, April, 1989, p. 102.

Frey, Yvonne A., review of *Dawn Rider*, *School Library Journal*, December, 1990, p. 103.

Hudson, Jan, "Author Gives Thank You's," *Canadian Library Journal*, October, 1984, p. 287.

Lehr, Susan, review of *Sweetgrass*, *Language Arts*, April, 1990, pp. 425-26.

Martin, Sandra, "YA Fiction: Old Hands, Swan Song," *Quill and Quire*, October, 1990, pp. 13, 16.

Phelan, Carolyn, review of *Dawn Rider*, *Booklist*, November 15, 1990, p. 657.

Stander, Bella, "Jan Hudson," *Publishers Weekly*, December 22, 1989, p. 32.

Review of *Sweetgrass*, *Kirkus Reviews*, December 1, 1990, p. 1673.

Review of *Sweetgrass*, *Publishers Weekly*, November 23, 1990, pp. 65-66.

■ For More Information See

BOOKS

Holtze, Sally Holmes, editor, *Seventh Book of Junior Authors & Illustrators*, H. W. Wilson, 1996, pp. 146-47.

PERIODICALS

Booklist, April 1, 1989, p. 1384.
Books for Keeps, March, 1994, p. 12.
Books for Your Children, summer, 1994, p. 23.
Books in Canada, October, 1990, pp. 28-29.
Booktalker, September, 1989, p. 14.
Bulletin of the Center for Children's Books, April, 1989, pp. 196-97; February, 1991.
Canadian Children's Literature, Number 41, 1986, pp. 89-92.
Children's Library Journal, October, 1984, p. 287.
Children's Literature Association Quarterly, winter, 1990, pp. 197-98.
Christian Science Monitor, October 5, 1984, p. B8.
CM: A Reviewing Journal of Canadian Materials for Young People, May, 1991, pp. 153-54, 156.
English Journal, December, 1990, pp. 78-79.
Five Owls, January/February, 1990, p. 37.
Junior Bookshelf, December, 1986, pp. 233-34.
Language Arts, April 1, 1990, pp. 425-26.
Publishers Weekly, November 23, 1990, pp. 65-66.
Quill and Quire, July, 1984, p. 67; August, 1985, p. 30.
Reading Teacher, April, 1990, p. 584.
School Librarian, December, 1986, pp. 362, 365; May, 1994, p. 72.
School Library Journal, April, 1989, p. 102.
Voice of Youth Advocates, June, 1989, p. 102; February, 1991, p. 352.*

—Sketch by Peggy Saari

Elmore Leonard

■ Personal

Full name, Elmore John Leonard, Jr.; born October 11, 1925, in New Orleans, LA; son of Elmore John (a salesman) and Flora Amelia (maiden name, Rive) Leonard; married Beverly Cline, July 30, 1949 (divorced May 24, 1977); married Joan Shepard, September 15, 1979; married Christine Kent, August 19, 1993; children: (first marriage) Jane Jones, Peter, Christopher, William, Katherine. *Education:* University of Detroit, Ph.B., 1950. *Religion:* Roman Catholic.

■ Addresses

Home—Birmingham, MI. *Office*—c/o Michael Siegel and Associates, 8929 Rosewood Avenue, Los Angeles, CA 90048. *Agent*—H. N. Swanson, 8523 Sunset Blvd., Los Angeles, CA 90069.

■ Career

Full-time writer, 1967—. Campbell-Ewald Advertising Agency, Detroit, MI, copywriter, 1950-61; freelance copywriter and author of educational and industrial films, 1961-63; head of Elmore Leonard Advertising Company, 1963-66. *Military service:* U.S. Naval Reserve, 1943-46. *Member:* Writers Guild of America, West, Mystery Writers of America, Western Writers of America, Authors League of America, Authors Guild.

■ Awards, Honors

Hombre was selected as one of the twenty-five best western novels of all time, Western Writers of America, 1977; Edgar Allan Poe Award nominations, Mystery Writers of America, 1978, for *The Switch,* and 1981, for *Spilt Images;* Edgar Allan Poe Award, Mystery Writers of America, 1984, for *La Brava;* Michigan Foundation of the Arts Award, 1985; North American Hammett Prize for Best Crime Book of the Year, International Association of Crime Writers, 1991, for *Maximum Bob;* Grand Master Award, Mystery Writers of America, 1992.

■ Writings

WESTERN NOVELS

The Bounty Hunters, Houghton, 1953, reprinted, Bantam, 1985.
The Law at Randado, Houghton, 1955, reprinted, Bantam, 1985.
Escape from 5 Shadows, Houghton, 1956, reprinted, Bantam, 1985.
Last Stand at Saber River, Dell, 1957, reprinted, Bantam, 1985 (published in England as *Lawless River,* R. Hale, 1959, and as *Stand on the Saber,* Corgi, 1960).

Hombre, Ballantine, 1961, reprinted, 1984.
Valdez Is Coming, Gold Medal, 1970.
Forty Lashes Less One, Bantam, 1972.
Gunsights, Bantam, 1979.

CRIME AND MYSTERY NOVELS

The Big Bounce, Gold Medal, 1969, revised edition, Armchair Detective, 1989.
The Moonshine War (also see below), Doubleday, 1969, reprinted, Dell, 1988.
Mr. Majestyk (also see below), Delacorte, 1974.
Fifty-Two Pickup, Delacorte, 1974.
Swag (also see below), Delacorte, 1976, published as *Ryan's Rules*, Dell, 1976.
Unknown Man, No. 89, Delacorte, 1977.
The Hunted (also see below), Dell, 1977.
The Switch, Bantam, 1978.
City Primeval: High Noon in Detroit (also see below), Arbor House, 1980.
Gold Coast (also see below), Bantam, 1980, revised edition, 1985.
Split Images (also see below), Arbor House, 1981.
Cat Chaser (also see below), Arbor House, 1982.
Stick (also see below), Arbor House, 1983.
LaBrava (also see below), Arbor House, 1983.
Glitz, Arbor House, 1985.
Bandits, Arbor House, 1987.
Touch, Arbor House, 1987.
Freaky Deaky, Morrow, 1988.
Killshot, Morrow, 1989.
Get Shorty, Delacorte, 1990.
Maximum Bob, Delacorte, 1991.
Rum Punch, Delacorte, 1992.
Pronto, Delacorte, 1993.
Riding the Rap, Delacorte, 1995.
Out of Sight, Delacorte, 1996.

OMNIBUS VOLUMES

Elmore Leonard's Dutch Treat (contains *The Hunted, Swag,* and *Mr. Majestyk*), introduction by George F. Will, Arbor House, 1985.
Elmore Leonard's Double Dutch Treat (contains *City Primeval: High Noon in Detroit, The Moonshine War,* and *Gold Coast*), introduction by Bob Greene, Arbor House, 1986.
Three Complete Novels (contains *LaBrava, Cat Chaser,* and *Split Images*), Wings Books, 1992.

SCREENPLAYS

The Moonshine War (based on Leonard's novel of the same title), Metro-Goldwyn Mayer, 1970.

Joe Kidd, Universal, 1972.
Mr. Majestyk (based on Leonard's novel of the same title), United Artists, 1974.
High Noon, Part 2: The Return of Will Kane, Columbia Broadcasting System (CBS), 1980.
(With Joseph C. Stinson) *Stick* (based on Leonard's novel of the same title), Universal, 1985.
(With Jon Steppling) *52 Pick-Up* (based on Leonard's novel of the same title), Cannon Group, 1986.
(With Fred Walton) *The Rosary Murders* (based on the novel by William X. Kienzle), New Line Cinema, 1987.
Desperado, National Broadcasting Corporation (NBC), 1988.
(With Joe Borrelli) *Cat Chaser* (based on Leonard's novel of the same title), Viacom, 1989.

OTHER

(Contributor) Dennis Wholey, editor, *The Courage to Change: Personal Conversations about Alcoholism*, Houghton, 1984.

Also contributor of about thirty short stories and novelettes to *Argosy, Dime Western, Saturday Evening Post, Zane Grey's Western Magazine,* and other publications during the 1950s; author of filmscripts for Encyclopedia Britannica Films, including *Settlement of the Mississippi Valley, Boy of Spain, Frontier Boy,* and *Julius Caesar,* and of a recruiting film for the Franciscans.

■ Adaptations

The novelette *3:10 to Yuma* was filmed by Columbia Pictures, 1957; the story "The Tall T" was filmed by Columbia, 1957; *Hombre* was filmed by Twentieth Century-Fox, 1967; *The Big Bounce* was filmed by Warner Brothers, 1969; *Valdez Is Coming* was filmed by United Artists, 1970; *Glitz* was filmed for television by the National Broadcasting Corporation; *Get Shorty* was adapted as a motion picture of the same title by Metro-Goldwyn-Mayer, 1995; *Pronto* was filmed for television by Showtime, 1997. Several of Leonard's novels have been recorded on audio cassette.

■ Sidelights

Elmore Leonard has been called the greatest living writer of crime fiction. His novels have been compared to the works of the acknowledged masters of the genre, Dashiell Hammett and Raymond Chandler. Critics praise Leonard's uncanny ear for dialogue, and many claim that his best fiction, steeped in the recklessness and violence of criminal America, offers significant commentary on contemporary life. It took thirty years of hard work, however, and the publication of more than twenty novels, before Leonard achieved the recognition that has since become commonplace. His first books were Westerns, which he wrote not out of literary ambition, but as a potentially lucrative form of entertainment. Motivated by the waning interest in Westerns, Leonard took up the subject of crime. His audience grew, and his books are now regularly on best-seller lists. With several film adaptations to his credit, he has become that rare, marketable author whose work transcends the supposed limits of popular fiction. "Elmore Leonard may only write crime stories," observed *Times Literary Supplement* reviewer David Papineau, "but he writes rings around most authors with loftier ambitions."

Leonard was born October 11, 1925, in New Orleans, Louisiana, a city he would revisit in one of his novels. Early in his childhood, Leonard's family relocated to Detroit, Michigan. His interest in writing was sparked while he was in the fifth grade. Inspired by the novel *All Quiet on the Western Front*, Leonard wrote and staged a short play set during the First World War. He continued to write throughout his school years, contributing stories to the school newspaper while a student at University of Detroit High. Shortly after graduating from high school, Leonard joined the U.S. Navy and served in the South Pacific during the Second World War. At the end of the war in 1946, he returned to Michigan, enrolled at the University of Detroit, and began work at an advertising agency. After completing his degree, Leonard continued in advertising and made his first serious attempts at fiction. "I'd get up early, write, then go crank out zingy copy for Chevrolet trucks," Leonard recalled for *Time* magazine reviewer J. D. Reed.

In the early 1950s, Leonard explained to Jean W. Ross in a *Contemporary Authors* interview, he studiously read the novels of Ernest Hemingway. Admiring the author's restrained style, Leonard made up his mind to develop a "kind of lean, deadpan delivery" in his own writing. He experimented with this style by writing Western novels

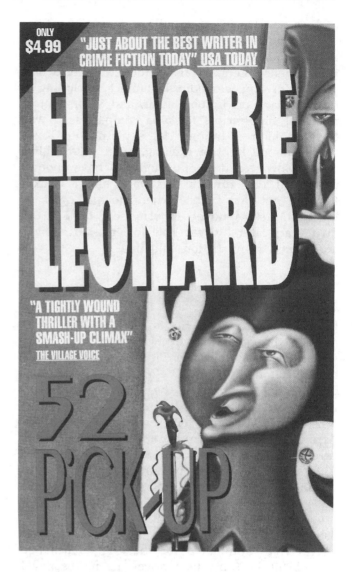

A Detroit businessman seeks revenge on an extortionist in this 1974 novel.

because he "liked Western movies a lot." His first fiction publication, a short novel titled "Apache Agent," sold to *Argosy* magazine for $90. By the end of the 1950s Leonard had published five novels and roughly thirty stories, most in magazines like *Dime Western*. Two of his works, the novel *3:10 to Yuma*, and a short story, "The Tall T," were adapted for film. This marked the beginning of Leonard's ongoing relationship with Hollywood, where producers continue to capitalize on the action, suspense, and quirky characters in his fiction.

Despite his success, Leonard abandoned fiction altogether when the Western craze subsided in the early 1960s. During this lull he worked as a freelance copywriter for several clients in the auto industry and, eventually, opened his own advertising agency. Leonard also wrote educational film scripts for Encyclopedia Britannica, including a documentary on Julius Caesar, and several informational film scripts for area companies. "I was busy making a living," he explained to Ross. "That was all kind of exciting. But I still couldn't wait, really, for an opportunity to have enough money at one time to get back into a book." Leonard got that chance when the film rights to his last Western novel, *Hombre*, sold for $10,000. Two years later he was able to leave advertising and start writing fiction full time.

Becoming A Crime Writer

Leonard's return to fiction in the late 1960s marked the beginning of his career as a crime writer. His first effort, *The Big Bounce*, was rejected by eighty-four publishers before being accepted by Gold Medal. Questioning the wisdom of his move to crime fiction, Leonard wrote two more Westerns, *Valdez Is Coming* and *Forty Lashes Less One*. Again, Hollywood played a pivotal role in his career: film rights to *The Big Bounce* sold for $50,000, giving him the resources and incentive to continue working in his new genre. Leonard produced roughly one book annually for the next several years. By the late 1970s he was an established author of crime fiction. *The Switch* and *Split Images* were nominated for the Edgar Allen Poe Award for best mystery novel. Leonard's novel *Stick*, featuring a car thief caught on the wrong side of the mob, received considerable critical attention. It was also adapted as a film starring and directed by Burt Reynolds. Even though Leonard later said the film version was inaccurate, the movie's popularity boosted interest in his work.

LaBrava, Leonard's next novel, brought him to the foreground of crime fiction. Set in Miami, a favorite Leonard location, the novel tracks the misadventures of Joseph LaBrava, a former IRS and FBI agent who has retired to pursue a career as a freelance photographer. LaBrava's new lifestyle is interrupted when he photographs a murder. While eluding the murderers, he becomes entangled with an ex-movie star. When her plan to defraud the mob goes awry, LaBrava regains his lawman's conscience and makes sure justice is done. Applauding the novel's engrossing plot and

convincing dialogue, reviewers hailed Leonard as a master craftsman. *LaBrava* earned the Edgar Allen Poe Award, which had eluded Leonard on two previous occasions, when the Mystery Writers of America selected it as the best book of 1984.

Critics praised the polished style in *LaBrava*, and they were startled by Leonard's grasp of the criminal mentality. His understanding was built on research conducted in police stations, bars, and courtrooms in and around Detroit. For years, Leonard had been in the habit of inconspicuously listening to the conversations of cops and crooks

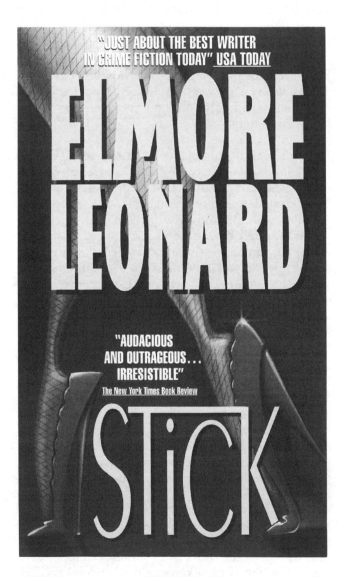

In this 1983 work, an ex-con trying to lead a clean life is tempted by a revenge scheme and targeted by a killer.

to absorb the peculiarities of their speech and vocabulary. Similarly, he employed a researcher to document the cities, through photographs and interviews, where his novels are set. Following *LaBrava*, Leonard applied this technique to Atlantic City, the setting of his first best-seller, *Glitz*.

After a Miami police officer, Vincent, is wounded outside his local supermarket, he travels to Puerto Rico to recuperate. In Puerto Rico he is seen by the homicidal Teddy Magyk, a man he had once arrested. From there the action relocates to Atlantic City, where Vincent and Magyk pursue one another through a carnival of gangsters and gamblers. *Glitz* drew rave reviews from several critics. Author Stephen King, for instance, writing in *New York Times Book Review*, compared Leonard to Charles Dickens, whose depictions of the underworld in nineteenth-century London are considered masterpieces of English literature.

Get Shorty Gets Attention

In the late 1980s Leonard produced four novels that were all well received, but failed to earn the same high marks as *Glitz*. Departing from his typical locales, Leonard set *Get Shorty* in Hollywood. The plot turns on the pursuits of Chili Davis, a loan shark from Miami who travels to Las Vegas to collect a debt from a man who has faked his own death. While in Las Vegas, Chili agrees to help out an old friend by collecting money owed to his friend by Harry Zimm, a former producer of horror films. Once Chili arrives in Hollywood, he discovers that Zimm is also indebted to Bo Catlett, one of the novel's villains. Finding himself caught between Zimm and Catlett, Chili successfully manages a complicated series of double-crosses. All the while, Chili has been bitten by the Hollywood bug, and he attempts to sell his story—that is, the story of a loan shark who comes to Hollywood. To his great amusement, Chili realizes the power brokers of the film industry are not much different from the crooks he has worked for all his life.

"It would be easy to assume that what Mr. Leonard is saying here is that the con men are right at home in the movie business," wrote Nora Ephron in the *New York Times Book Review*, "but it seems to me he's making an even wittier point, which is that even tough guys want to be in the movies." Commenting on Leonard's familiarity

If you enjoy the works of Elmore Leonard, you may also want to check out the following books and films:

The works of mystery grandmasters Ross Macdonald, Raymond Chandler, and Dashiell Hammett.
The writings of Ernest Hemingway, John Steinbeck, and John O'Hara, whom Leonard cites as major influences.
The Maltese Falcon, Warner Bros. 1941.
The Big Sleep, Warner Bros., 1946.
Reservoir Dogs, Miramax, 1992.

with Hollywood in *Los Angeles Times Book Review*, Charles Champlin wrote that *Get Shorty* is "at heart a portrait of the community, less angry than [Nathaneal West's] *Day of the Locusts*, but not less devastating in its tour of the industry's soiled follies and the gaminess beneath the grandeurs." *Publishers Weekly* reviewer Sybil Steinberg announced that "Chili and his story are Leonard's best yet." *Get Shorty* was released as a major motion picture, starring John Travolta in the role of Chili.

With *Maximum Bob*, Leonard returned to the familiar territory of South Florida. The title character, Maximum Bob Gibbs, is a racist circuit court judge feared throughout the county for his unnecessarily stiff sentences. Bob is trying to rid himself of his wife, Leanne, who was traumatized by an alligator and now believes that she has the spirit of a twelve-year-old slave girl, Wanda Grace, living inside her. While Bob concocts schemes to drive away Leanne, former convicts who have suffered under his harsh sentences begin to seek revenge. The female protagonist, public defender Kathy Baker, has been discriminated against by "Maximum Bob." She joins forces with police sergeant Gary Hammond to unravel the mysteries surrounding the judge and his would-be assassins. Christopher Lehmann-Haupt, writing in the *New York Times*, found Kathy Baker "appealing, easy to identify with and apt at the sort of decisive action one expects of an Elmore Leonard hero." He considered the novel generally less successful than its main character, however, noting that "*Maximum Bob* arouses one to feel the minimum." *Times Literary Supplement* reviewer Savkar Altinel was equally critical: "This is low-life America stripped of its despair and turned into a freak show for the amusement of those who are better off." In a review for the *Los Angeles Times Book Review*, Clifford Irving was more complimentary. "Leonard, like any true comic, has a melancholy view of the world and its primitive denizens," Irving wrote. "Without moralizing, he is telling us—no, he is showing us—how rotten life is in the heartland of the USA." Novelist Barry Gifford's review in the *New York Times Book Review* was also laudatory. "Nobody I've ever read sets up pace,

ONLY $4.99

"JUST ABOUT THE BEST WRITER IN CRIME FICTION TODAY" *USA TODAY*

ELMORE LEONARD

"TERRIFIC... LEONARD'S BEST NOVEL SO FAR" *PHILADELPHIA INQUIRER*

LABRAVA

Winner of the 1984 Edgar Allan Poe Award for best mystery, this novel concerns a photographer who witnesses a murder and becomes involved with an ex-movie star.

mood, and sound better than Elmore Leonard," Gifford observed.

Rum Punch A Knockout

Leonard followed *Maximum Bob* with *Rum Punch*, the story of Jackie Burke, a flight attendant who uses her position to smuggle cash into Florida for a gun runner named Ordell. Ordell and his dim-witted partner, Louis, are revived from the earlier Leonard novel, *The Switch*. They are on the verge of making a big score when Jackie is caught by the police. To avoid both jail and Ordell's revenge, Jackie concocts a scam involving a bondsman named Max Cherry. Critic Ann Arensberg, a confessed Leonard convert, wrote in the *New York Times Book Review*: "Outpacing the classic hard-boiled novel, leaving the British detective novel in the dust, Elmore Leonard has compressed *Rum Punch* into almost pure drama, as close to playwriting as novel writing can get." However, the violence of the villains provoked a negative response from other critics. *New Statesman and Society* reviewer John Williams was disturbed by changes in the characters of Ordell and Louis. "In *The Switch* they were good-bad, in *Rum Punch* they're plain evil," he stated. Yet, Michael Dirda noted in *Washington Post Book World* that the novel has a philosophical theme: "Beneath its fast-pacing surface, *Rum Punch* is a novel about growing old, about the way time changes us, about the dream of starting over and its cost."

Leonard's next novel, *Pronto,* recounts the exploits of Harry Arno, a Miami bookmaker who is skimming profits from his boss, Jimmy Capotorto. Harry flees when federal investigators pressure him into squealing on Jimmy by threatening to tell Jimmy about his indiscretions. Harry settles in Rapallo, an Italian city on the Mediterranean, where he had once been stationed during the Second World War. The city was also the scene of Harry's first and only murder, which he committed while he was in the service. He is nostalgic for the war years, and the location holds additional appeal because of his fondness for the poetry of Ezra Pound, who lived there as a dissident. Rapallo is no haven for Harry, however. He is pursued by a pair of hit men and a Stetson-wearing U.S. Marshall, Raylan Givens, who wants to take Harry and his girlfriend Joyce back into protective custody. Dick Lochte of the *Los Angeles Times Book Review* commended *Pronto* for its blend

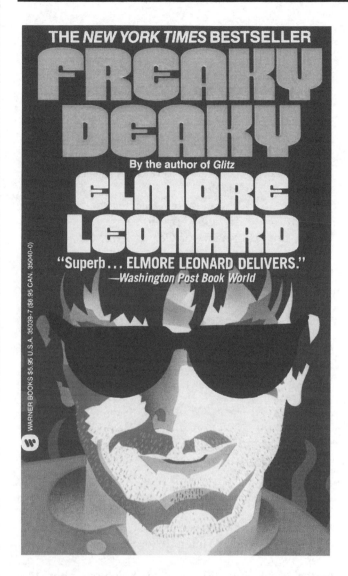

THE *NEW YORK TIMES* BESTSELLER

FREAKY DEAKY

By the author of *Glitz*

ELMORE LEONARD

"Superb... ELMORE LEONARD DELIVERS."
—*Washington Post Book World*

A pair of 1960s radicals reunite to seek revenge against the millionaire who turned them over to the FBI in this 1988 work.

of "the romantic notions of the past, when honor and justice and a woman's love were things to be cherished, with Leonard's particularly adroit insight into the harsh realities and tensions of today." In the *New York Times Book Review* Teresa Carpenter found *Pronto* "fun," but not so appealing as some of Leonard's earlier works. She noted that he fails to evoke Rapallo with the same realism he brings to Detroit and Miami. *Times Literary Supplement* reviewer Karl Miller concluded the novel was not Leonard's most convincing. David Montrose, writing in the *Spectator*, was even harsher, calling *Pronto* "a full-strength letdown." Commenting on an apparent decline in the qual-

ity of Leonard's work, he added: "Expect whispers that the king is dead."

Leonard revived the characters Harry Arno and Raylan Givens in *Riding the Rap*. This time around, Harry has been kidnaped by a couple of would-be terrorists who want to get at his hidden money. Harry's former girlfriend Joyce, who has since become Raylan's companion, prevails on Raylan to find and rescue Harry. Between his regular assignments, Raylan pieces together the clues that eventually lead him to Harry. Along the way Raylan crosses paths with a score of oddball characters, including a mysterious psychic named Reverend Dawn. Impressed by Leonard's depiction of Reverend Dawn, *Los Angeles Times Book Review* critic Leonard Michaels claimed she was unique in literature. "She is absurd, convincing, good, bad, weak, effective, frightened, daring, and the whole plot turns on her actions," Michaels observed. "Whoever plays Reverend Dawn in the movie has a chance to make cultural history." Critiquing *Riding the Rap* in the *New York Times Book Review*, Martin Amis called Leonard a "literary genius." According to Amis, "Mr. Leonard possesses gifts—of ear and eye, of timing and phrasing—that even the most indolent and snobbish masters of the mainstream must vigorously covet."

Salon Magazine reviewer Charles Taylor found *Out of Sight*, a 1996 work, to be "Leonard's most satisfying book in a long time." As the novel opens, Karen Sisco, a Deputy U.S. Marshall dressed in a Chanel suit, is kidnaped by escaped convict Jack Foley. Jack forces Karen into the trunk of her car and climbs in alongside her as one of his accomplices drives. The two become strangely well acquainted in the trunk. When Jack eludes Karen and escapes the law a second time, she becomes part of a team that sets out to apprehend him. She meets him again in Detroit, and they have a brief romantic encounter. However, like an earlier Leonard hero, Joseph LaBrava, Karen puts aside her infatuation in the name of the law and makes sure Jack is returned to prison.

Despite critical acclaim and considerable income generated by book and movie royalties, Leonard and his wife lead a relatively modest life in the Detroit suburb of Birmingham. With more than thirty novels to his credit, the workman-like Leonard continues to please readers with riveting plots and inventive dialogue. As *New Yorker* critic

Whitney Baillett observed, "Book by book (he publishes almost one a year), the tireless and ingenious genre novelist Elmore Leonard is painting an intimate, precise, funny, frightening, and irresistible mural of the American underworld."

■ Works Cited

Altinel, Savkar, review of *Maximum Bob, Times Literary Supplement*, September 27, 1991, p. 24.

Amis, Martin, "Junk Souls," review of *Riding the Rap, New York Times Book Review*, May 14, 1995, p. 7.

Arensberg, Ann, "Elmore Leonard for Beginners," review of *Rum Punch, New York Times Book Review*, August 16, 1992, p. 13.

Balliett, Whitney, "Elmore Leonard in Hollywood," review of *Get Shorty, New Yorker*, September 3, 1990, pp. 106-7.

Carpenter, Teresa, "On the Land in Rapallo," review of *Pronto, New York Times Book Review*, October 17, 1993, p. 39.

Champlin, Charles, "Leonard Cocks a Snook at Hollywood," review of *Get Shorty, Los Angeles Times Book Review*, July 29, 1990, p. 9.

Dirda, Michael, "Dreams Die Hard," review of *Rum Punch, Washington Post Book World*, July 19, 1992, p. 2.

Ephron, Nora, "The Shylock Is the Good Guy," review of *Get Shorty, New York Times Book Review*, July 29, 1990, pp. 1, 28.

Gifford, Barry, "The Alligator Rings Twice," review of *Maximum Bob, New York Times Book Review*, July 28, 1991, pp. 8-9.

Irving, Clifford, review of *Maximum Bob, Los Angeles Times Book Review*, August 4, 1991, pp. 2, 9.

King, Stephen, "What Went Down When Magyk Went Up," review of *Glitz, New York Times Book Review*, February 10, 1985, p. 7.

Lehmann-Haupt, Christopher, "Tough Talk, Shootouts, Auras, and A Loopy Lady," review of *Maximum Bob, New York Times*, July 25, 1991, p. C18.

Leonard, Elmore, interview with Jean W. Ross, *Contemporary Authors New Revision Series*, Volume 28, Gale, 1990, pp. 282-87.

Lochte, Dick, "When Honor and Justice Were Things to Be Cherished," review of *Pronto, Los Angeles Times Book Review*, October 24, 1994.

Michaels, Leonard, "Good Guys Win," review of *Riding the Rap, Los Angeles Times Book Review*, May 14, 1995, pp. 1, 8.

Miller, Karl, "Capo conversations," review of *Pronto, Times Literary Supplement*, November 5, 1993, p. 20.

Montrose, David, "Great Expectations Unfulfilled," review of *Pronto, Spectator*, November 27, 1993, p. 42.

Papineau, David, "When the Boiling Gets Soft," review of *Get Shorty, Times Literary Supplement*, November 30-December 6, 1990, pp. 1287-88.

Reed, J. D., "A Dickens from Detroit," *Time*, May 28, 1984, pp. 84-86.

Steinberg, Sybil, review of *Get Shorty, Publishers Weekly*, June 15, 1990, p. 55.

Taylor, Charles, review of *Out of Sight, Salon Magazine*, September 9, 1996.

Williams, John, "Gumshoes in Gridlock," review of *Rum Punch, New Statesman and Society*, November 13, 1992, p. 86.

■ For More Information See

BOOKS

Authors in the News, Volume 1, Gale, 1976.

Contemporary Literary Criticism, Gale, Volume 28, 1984, Volume 34, 1985, Volume 71, 1992.

Geherin, David, *Elmore Leonard*, Continuum, 1989.

PERIODICALS

American Film, December, 1984.

Armchair Detective, Winter, 1986; Spring, 1986; Winter, 1989.

Boston Globe, July 30, 1992, p. 80; November 14, 1993, p. 7.

Chicago Tribune, February 4, 1981; April 8, 1983; December 8, 1983; February 7, 1985.

Chicago Tribune Book World, April 10, 1983; October 30, 1983; May 21, 1995.

Christian Science Monitor, November 4, 1983.

Commentary, May, 1985, pp. 64, 66-67.

Detroiter, June, 1974.

Detroit News, February 23, 1982; October 23, 1983.

Esquire, April, 1987, pp. 169-74.

Globe and Mail (Toronto), December 14, 1985.

Library Journal, October 15, 1991, p. 140.

Listener, April 9, 1987, p. 28; October 4, 1990, pp. 30-31.

London Review of Books, September 5, 1985, p. 16.

Los Angeles Times, June 28, 1984; May 4, 1988.

Los Angeles Times Book Review, February 27, 1983; December 4, 1983; January 13, 1985; August 30, 1987, pp. 2, 8; April 23, 1989, p. 14.

Maclean's, January 19, 1987.

Michigan Magazine (Sunday magazine of the *Detroit News*), October 9, 1983.

New Statesman and Society, October 11, 1991, p. 25.

Newsweek, March 22, 1982; July 11, 1983; November 14, 1983; April 22, 1985, pp. 62-64, 67.

New York, May 2, 1988, p. 86.

New York Times, June 11, 1982; April 28, 1983; October 7, 1983; October 29, 1983; April 26, 1985; May 2, 1988; September 23, 1993, p. C18; May 11, 1995; August 16, 1996.

New York Times Book Review, May 22, 1977; September 5, 1982; March 6, 1983; December 27, 1983; January 4, 1987, p. 7; October 14, 1990, p. 1.

Observer, September 22, 1991, p. 59; August 16, 1992, p. 13.

People, March 4, 1985; October 25, 1993, p. 38.

Publishers Weekly, February 25, 1983.

Rolling Stone, February 28, 1985.

Times (London), April 23, 1987.

Times Literary Supplement, December 5, 1986, p. 1370; October 30, 1992, p. 21.

Tribune Books (Chicago), April 9, 1989, pp. 1, 4.

U.S. News and World Report, March 9, 1987.

Village Voice, February 23, 1982.

Voice Literary Supplement, February, 1985, p. 4.

Washington Post, October 6, 1980; February 6, 1985.

Washington Post Book World, February 7, 1982; July 4, 1982; February 20, 1983; November 13, 1983; December 28, 1986, p. 3; August 23, 1987, pp. 1-2; May 1, 1988; July 14, 1991, pp. 1-2.*

—Sketch by David P. Johnson

Gregory Maguire

■ Personal

Born June 9, 1954, in Albany, New York; son of John (a journalist) and Helen (Gregory) Maguire. *Education:* State University of New York at Albany, B.A., 1976; Simmons College, M.A., 1978; Tufts University, Ph.D., 1990. *Politics:* Democrat. *Religion:* Roman Catholic. *Hobbies and other interests:* Painting in oils or water colors, song writing, traveling.

■ Addresses

Home and office—63 Upland Rd., Concord, MA 01742. *Agent*—William Reiss, John Hawkins and Associates, 71 West 23rd St., Suite 1600, New York, NY 10010.

■ Career

Freelance writer, 1977—. Vincentian Grade School, Albany, NY, teacher of English, 1976-77; Simmons College Center for the Study of Children's Literature, Boston, MA, faculty member and associate director, 1979-87; Children's Literature New England, Cambridge, MA, co-director and consultant, 1987—.

■ Awards, Honors

100 Best Books of the Year citation, New York Public Library, 1980, for *The Daughter of the Moon;* Children's Books of the Year citation, Child Study Children's Books Committee, 1983, and Teachers' Choice Award, National Council of Teachers of English, 1984, both for *The Dream Stealer;* Best Book for Young Adults citation, American Library Association (ALA), and Choices award, Cooperative Children's Book Center, 1989, both for *I Feel Like the Morning Star;* Parents' Choice Award, 1994, and Children's Books of the Year citation, Child Study Books Committee, 1994, both for *Missing Sisters;* Notable Children's Book citation, ALA, 1994, for *Seven Spiders Spinning.* Fellow at Bread Loaf Writers' Conference, 1978; residencies at Blue Mountain Center, 1986-90 and 1995; artist in residence, Isabella Stewart Gardner Museum, 1994.

■ Writings

JUVENILE

The Lightning Time, Farrar, Straus & Giroux, 1978.
The Daughter of the Moon, Farrar, Straus & Giroux, 1980.

Lights on the Lake, Farrar, Straus & Giroux, 1981.

The Dream Stealer, Harper, 1983.

The Peace and Quiet Diner (picture book), illustrated by David Perry, Parents' Magazine, 1988.

I Feel Like the Morning Star, Harper, 1989.

Lucas Fishbone (picture book for young adults) illustrated by Frank Gargiulo, Harper, 1990.

Missing Sisters, McElderry, 1994.

Seven Spiders Spinning, Clarion, 1994.

(Contributor) *Am I Blue? Coming Out from the Silence,* HarperTrophy, 1994.

The Good Liar, O'Brien Press, 1995.

Oasis, Clarion, 1996.

FOR ADULTS

(Editor with Barbara Harrison) *Innocence and Experience: Essays and Conversations on Children's Literature,* Lothrop, 1987.

Wicked: The Life and Times of the Wicked Witch of the West, HarperCollins, 1995.

OTHER

Reviewer for *Horn Book, School Library Journal,* and *Christian Science Monitor.*

■ Sidelights

"Writing is for me simply recording the story which is currently playing in my head," Gregory Maguire once commented in *Something about the Author* (*SATA*). Nevertheless, he added, "sometimes I take a long time getting up the nerve to look in on it." From a reader's standpoint, Maguire has quite a bit of nerve—his stories range from fantasy to science fiction and from biting reality to fairy tales. His characters face crises and survive, and he always returns to the power of love. These features have made his work popular with children and young adults. Maguire has also written a novel for adults as well as a short story for young adults in a volume about growing up gay. To further confirm his versatility, Maguire has published a humorous story called *Seven Spiders Spinning.*

Maguire's childhood began with tragedy when his mother, Helen, died while giving birth to him. Shortly after his birth, one of his aunts took care of him to give his father a break with household responsibilities. Maguire's aunt became attached to him and wanted to adopt him. But Maguire's fa-

ther, John, refused and put him in an orphanage, expecting someday to reunite the family. After his father remarried, Maguire returned home. However, during his stay at the orphanage the nuns had dubbed him "Gregory the Executive" because he never smiled.

After Maguire rejoined his three siblings, the family grew as his father and his new wife, Marie, had three more children. Maguire remembered his childhood as being a happy one, generally. His parents, who had grown up during the Depression, scrimped by dressing the children in hand-me-downs and giving them home haircuts. Yet his parents were generous when it came to encouraging reading. "What we lacked in material luxury—bicycles, horseback-riding lessons, our own individual televisions or stereos, or even new clothes to show off—we made up in our reading lives. Our parents shared a love of reading and the written and spoken word, and the ceremony of a young Maguire getting his or her first library card was treated with as much solemn joy as a First Communion or a birthday," Maguire wrote in *Something about the Author Autobiography Series* (*SAAS*). At times, his parents would reward the children by giving them a nickel for each book they read. When the family moved to a house that was far from the library, Marie made special trips there and brought home books in a huge box.

It was hardly necessary to reward young Gregory for reading. He took to it easily. As he told J. Sydney Jones in an interview for *SATA*, "I learned my letters well before kindergarten and was reading simple stories to myself and to my younger brothers and sister with panache and invention if not with accuracy." Maguire's interest in reading later translated into his vocation: "I read like a fiend. This will not surprise any reader . . . it would be the rare writer who *hadn't* found the love of books while he or she was a child." At first he was indiscriminate, reading everything in sight. Later, after discovering four similar editions of James Barrie's *Peter Pan* and being disappointed that the different editions didn't yield different texts, he told Jones he made an important choice: "I then decided to read just what I wanted."

Surrounded by Wordsmiths

Several of Maguire's siblings have grown up to be professional writers. The roots of their talent

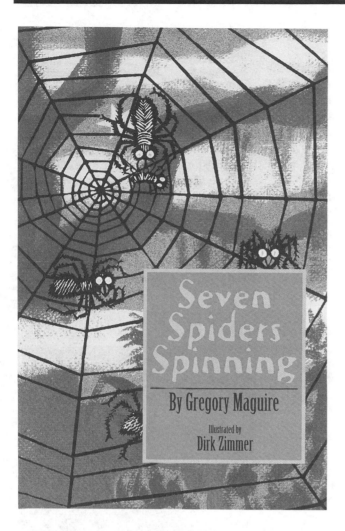

Baby Siberian snow spiders fall in love with a group of Vermont schoolgirls in this humorous 1994 work.

are perhaps traceable back to the Maguire family dinner table. Their father was a journalist, a speechwriter, and a great storyteller. Their mother was a poet. They kept a dictionary at the table in case anyone wanted to look up a word during a conversation. "We were all very interested in word derivation, spurred on by my father and mother," Maguire recalled in the *SATA* interview. "Our favorite family story revolves around that passion. One night at dinner someone asked to have the butter passed, and my three-year-old brother, seated in his high chair, cocked his head. 'Butter,' he said reflectively. 'Is that from the Latin or the Greek?' So I guess we all had a love for words instilled in us from the beginning."

Maguire found himself entranced with fantasy books, influenced by the magical stories about

saints he had heard growing up as a Roman Catholic. Maguire found that he was more inclined to believe in saints, angels, and the afterlife because of the inexplicable death of his mother. "I do cherish the religious teaching I received from Catholic schools for its emphasis on moral integrity, for its strong narrative traditions, and for its giving me a language and a grammar with which to consider the crises of everyday life," Maguire observed in *SAAS*. In another way, his religious background also played a role in his creative development. In fourth grade, he was asked to write a Thanksgiving play. In Maguire's version, the Catholic Pilgrims are taught how to make stuffing by an Indian chief. The play was staged with much success. "I didn't learn until I was in college that the Pilgrims weren't Catholic," he told Jones. The school didn't seem to mind, either, for when he returned there to teach twelve years later, he found they were still performing the play every Thanksgiving.

So concerned with magic was Maguire that he began searching for it in his everyday life in Albany, New York. "I poked around in improbable places looking for a bit of proof," he commented in *SAAS*. "I wanted to see some tiny hint of magic, some clue—it didn't need to be much!" One winter afternoon, while walking his sister to a ballet lesson, Maguire found his magic. He and a friend decided to explore a small strip of land between some stores and the Little League field. They found a frozen pond bordered by somewhat exotic-looking ferns that was hidden from sight of the busy road nearby. The discoverers named their land Fliaan, and set out naming and mapping its many features. The children also wrote Fliaan's national anthem, which they would sing upon departing from its boundaries. Maguire decided to write a novel about this mystical land. Although he had already written several stories, starting at about the age of seven, this was his first turn at writing a fantasy adventure. His multi-volume series, "The Chronicles of Fliaan," was populated with dragons, dwarves, and other fantastical characters, complete with illustrations. Although he admits "The Chronicles" were "not very good," he wrote in *SAAS* that "they were my first attempt at fantasy. They were also my first attempt to integrate into a story some atmosphere, some mood that I had experienced firsthand."

In high school, Maguire felt out of place, but he was eventually able to find some friends with whom he formed a folk quintet. He also was an avid journal writer, and he convinced many of his friends to take up the practice themselves. At one point, though, the members of a rock band he was playing with took him aside and encouraged him not to write because it was too "girlish." Luckily, Maguire did not take their advice. "Even if I was getting a reputation for being odd—there was no way I was going to change my habits for them. Writing was too much a part of me by then," he claimed in *SAAS*.

Birth of a Novel

Maguire attended State University of New York at Albany, primarily because his family couldn't afford to send him away to college. "I was a diligent and uninspired college student, increasingly shy in a class that numbered, I think, three thousand," he said in *SAAS*. He continued to write, however, and that provided him with hope for the future. "When I was a junior majoring in English and art, I wrote a book for independent study, throwing in lots of the places and characters from my own youth," he recalled in the *SATA* interview. "I went away to study in Dublin [Ireland] for a year, and when I came back I re-read the book and only then did I see it was probably a young adult title—the protagonist is 12."

"With great labor I typed up the manuscript and began to mail it to publishers who had brought out my favorite books," Maguire wrote in *SAAS*. Even when he suffered three rejections, he didn't lose hope. On the fourth try, he received a letter from the publisher saying they wanted to talk to him about the story. His editor gave him pages of suggestions, then asked him to rewrite and re-submit the story if he wished. At first, Maguire wasn't sure if they were kidding him or not, but he rewrote the manuscript anyway and sent it in. Shortly after beginning his studies at a children's literature program in Massachusetts, he learned the publishers wanted to print his novel. It was titled *The Lightning Time*.

The Lightning Time features Daniel Rider, who is sent to stay with his grandmother in the Adirondacks while his mother is in the hospital. At first he thinks his stay will be boring, but then he becomes friends with a mysterious female cousin. Controversy breaks out when a villainous developer comes to buy up property on the mountain to turn it into a cheap resort. Daniel, his cousin, and his strong-willed grandmother set out to thwart the developer's intent. Daniel has discovered that the mountain is magical—when lightning strikes, animals can talk. At the end of the story he also learns that his cousin is really the younger spirit-self of his grandmother. A critic in *Publishers Weekly* praised *The Lightning Time* for being written "with professional aplomb." Reviewing the novel in *Horn Book*, Ethel L. Heins observed that Maguire "creates tension successfully, and writes with conviction and style."

Daniel's real cousin, Erikka—not the grandmother's spirit-self—is featured in Maguire's next book, *The Daughter of the Moon*. In this story Erikka lives in

Thirteen-year-old Hand must deal with the sudden death of this father and the reappearance of his long-absent mother in this 1996 novel.

a crowded flat in Chicago with a very busy and serious stepmother. Bored by the predictability of her world, Erikka goes off into her neighborhood, seeking adventure. When she befriends a book-shop owner she finds that a painting left to her by her aunt is magical. With a candlestick given to her by her friend, she is able to enter into the world of the painting. While Erikka is in the magical world, she finds the long-lost lover of the bookstore owner. Maguire also peppered the plot with further twists and turns. Marjorie Lewis, writing in *School Library Journal*, commented that these subplots "clog the arteries" of the novel. Similarly, a reviewer for *Bulletin of the Center for Children's Books* felt that the novel was not well integrated: "The fantasy seems grafted rather than meshed. Too bad; Maguire almost carries it off." A *Horn Book* reviewer, while admitting that the novel was more complicated than necessary, suggested that Maguire "has created a fascinatingly complex heroine and a rich collection of adult and child characters."

Adirondack Adventures

In Maguire's next novel, *Lights on the Lake,* Daniel is on vacation in upstate New York, a setting Maguire often returns to in his fiction; as a child, he took annual trips with his family to the Adirondacks. When Daniel's friend, an Episcopalian priest, goes on vacation, Daniel is left alone. He soon finds that the mists off the lake are taking him back and forth in time. Encountering a poet devastated by the death of a friend, Daniel sees that he can help the poet by bridging space and time, thus uniting the living with the dead. Mary M. Burns, writing in *Horn Book*, praised Maguire's ability to "infuse the inexplicable with reality and conviction."

"I basically look at those first three novels as novice work . . . ," Maguire reflected in the interview with Jones. "But with my next book [*The Dream Stealer*], I created my own form. I wasn't imitating anything else I'd read." Set in a Russian village, *The Dream Stealer* portrays characters from early folktales: the Firebird, Vasillissa the Beautiful, and Baba Yaga and her chicken-footed house. Maguire created the Blood Prince, a terrible wolf who causes disaster in the village once each generation and steals the dreams of children. Heins commented in *Horn Book* that "both the tale and the telling are thoroughly original; the author

If you enjoy the works of Gregory Maguire, you may also want to check out the following books and films:

David Brin, *The Postman*, 1985.
Robert R. McCammon, *Boy's Life,* 1991.
Neal Shusterman, *The Eyes of Kid Midas,* 1992.
Jane Yolen, *Briar Rose,* 1992.
Jumanji, Tri-Star, 1995.

has his own way with words." Jill Paton Walsh, writing in *Twentieth-Century Children's Writers,* noted that the book was the work "of a writer finding his voice, and putting not a foot wrong."

In 1979 Maguire took a job as a teacher in the children's literature program at Simmons College. At the same time he was earning his doctorate at Tufts University. Because of these commitments, his next book was published ten years later. *I Feel Like the Morning Star*, a post-nuclear science fiction story, is quite different from Maguire's previous work. Three teenagers live in an underground colony, supposedly safe from the nuclear disaster that had taken place aboveground five years earlier. Bored with their existence, they band together to find their way back to the surface of the earth. "Ultimately, *Morning Star* is about bucking authority," Maguire admitted in the *SATA* interview. Jane Beasley, in a review for *Voice of Youth Advocates*, found the novel exciting, observing that it "builds to a 'can't-put-it-down' threshold." Pam Spencer, writing in *School Library Journal*, called the book "a top choice for young adults."

Gone Fishin'

With *Lucas Fishbone* Maguire tried his hand at a picture book. "I had jotted down the odd name in my journal several years earlier, but hadn't been able to make anything of it," he recalled in *SAAS*. One night, he was unable to sleep: "After tossing and turning, I got up and scribbled down at one sitting the text. . . ." In spite of Maguire's excitement about *Fishbone*, it was not well received by critics. A *Publishers Weekly* reviewer felt the book was "overwritten" and "the illustrations . . . unappetizing." Heide Piehler, writing in *School Library Journal*, concluded that the book was "overall, an artistic and sophisticated effort that isn't likely to connect with an audience."

In 1990 Maguire moved to London with his companion, Rafique Keshavjee. Stumped by the negative reception of *Fishbone,* he did not produce another book until 1994, when *Missing Sisters* was released. The novel tells the story of twin sisters, one adopted as a young girl and the other living in an orphanage. Through a series of coincidences, they meet and both of their lives are permanently changed. "*Missing Sisters* is, in many ways, my favorite of my children's novels," Maguire wrote in *SAAS.* "For the first time I was eschewing any fantasy overtone and relying on my memories of growing up Irish Catholic in the Albany area in the 1960s."

Seven Spiders Spinning was published shortly after *Missing Sisters.* Maguire wrote the novel to satisfy the legions of young adults he had spoken to during his career. "Over the years," he told Jones, "I've developed a very funny presentation. The kids usually howl at my speech, but when they learn that I don't have any humorous books, they're disappointed." *Seven Spiders Spinning* tells the tale of seven Siberian Spiders that were frozen prior to the ice age. They fall in love with girls from a small Vermont town. Before the spiders can sting the objects of their desire, however, they start dying off. When the sole surviving spider stings the teacher they all love, her students must come up with a quick cure. A *Kirkus Reviews* critic stated that the book is "a lighthearted fantasy that, while easily read, is as intricately structured as a spider's web." Hazel Rochman, writing in *Booklist,* considered the work a cross between "Roald Dahl and Mother Goose."

In *Oasis,* Maguire returned to his more serious themes. The main character, Mohandas "Hand" Gunther, finds that his father has been murdered in the Oasis motel they run together. Hand's estranged mother then comes to take care of him and run the business. Hand is helped through his grief by Uncle Wolfgang, who is dying of AIDS, along with a host of other assorted characters. Chris Crowe wrote in *Voice of Youth Advocates* that the book is "vague and slow-paced." A *Publishers Weekly* reviewer, though, found it to be "idiosyncratic and touching," and a critic writing in *Bulletin for the Center for Children's Books* described it as "a nuanced story about human fragility and hope."

Maguire has also written an adult novel, *Wicked: The Life and Times of the Wicked Witch of the West,* which is based on his imagined version of the witch from the *Wizard of Oz.* But he has not stopped publishing children's books. "Ideally," he stated in the *SATA* interview, "I'd like to continue writing for both children and adults."

■ Works Cited

Beasley, Jane, review of *I Feel Like the Morning Star, Voice of Youth Advocates,* June, 1989, p. 117.

Burns, Mary M., review of *Lights on the Lake, Horn Book,* April, 1982, pp. 167-68.

Crowe, Chris, review of *Oasis, Voice of Youth Advocates,* February, 1997, p. 330.

Review of *The Daughter of the Moon, Bulletin of the Center for Children's Books,* July-August, 1980.

Review of *The Daughter of the Moon, Horn Book,* June, 1980.

Heins, Ethel L., review of *The Lightning Time, Horn Book,* October, 1978, pp. 517-18.

Heins, Ethel L., review of *The Dream Stealer, Horn Book,* October, 1983, pp. 576-77.

Lewis, Marjorie, review of *The Daughter of the Moon, School Library Journal,* May, 1980, p. 69.

Review of *The Lightning Time, Publishers Weekly,* June 5, 1978, p. 89.

Review of *Lucas Fishbone, Publishers Weekly,* September 28, 1990, pp. 101-2.

Maguire, Gregory, comments in *Something about the Author,* Volume 28, Gale, 1982, pp. 148-49.

Maguire, Gregory, interview with J. Sydney Jones for *Something about the Author,* Volume 84, Gale, 1995, pp. 154-59.

Maguire, Gregory, essay in *Something about the Author Autobiography Series,* Volume 22, Gale, 1996, pp. 141-67.

Review of *Oasis, Bulletin of the Center for Children's Literature,* January, 1997, pp. 179-80.

Review of *Oasis, Publishers Weekly,* October 28, 1996, p. 82.

Paton Walsh, Jill, "Gregory Maguire," *Twentieth-Century Children's Writers,* 3rd edition, St. James Press, 1989, pp. 626-27.

Piehler, Heide, review of *Lucas Fishbone, School Library Journal,* December, 1990, p. 84.

Rochman, Hazel, review of *Seven Spiders Spinning, Booklist,* September 15, 1994, p. 136.

Review of *Seven Spiders Spinning, Kirkus Reviews,* July 15, 1994, p. 989.

Spencer, Pam, review of *I Feel Like the Morning Star, School Library Journal,* May, 1989, p. 127.

■ **For More Information See**

PERIODICALS

Booklist, June 1, 1994, p. 1798.

Bulletin of the Center for Children's Books, July-August, 1980, p. 219; February, 1982; May, 1989, p. 230; June, 1994, p. 327.

Horn Book, July-August, 1994, pp. 454-55.

Kirkus Reviews, July 15, 1978, p. 750; May 1, 1980, p. 585; February 1, 1982, p. 136; March 1, 1989, p. 380; February 15, 1994, p. 229; August 15, 1995, p. 1135.

New York Times, October 24, 1995, p. C17.

New York Times Book Review, November 26, 1995 p. 19.

Publishers Weekly, August 1, 1994, p. 80; September 4, 1995, p. 71.

School Library Journal, September, 1978, p. 143; May, 1994, p. 116.

Voice of Youth Advocates, April, 1995, p. 24.

Wilson Library Bulletin, December, 1989, p. 113; September, 1990, p. 12.*

—Sketch by Nancy Rampson

Carol Matas

■ Personal

Born November 14, 1949; married Per Brask; children: Rebecca and Sam. *Education:* University of Western Ontario, B.A. in English, 1970; graduate of Actor's Lab, London, England, 1972. *Hobbies and other interests:* Theater, reading, baseball.

■ Addresses

Office—c/o Writers' Union of Canada, 24 Ryerson Ave., Toronto, Ontario M5T 929, Canada. *Agent*—Ashley Grayson Literary Agency, 1342 18th St., San Pedro, CA 90732.

■ Career

Writer and actor. Creative writing instructor in Continuing Education Division of the University of Winnipeg; visiting professor at Bemidji State University in Minnesota; writer-in-residence at Centennial Library in Winnipeg, Manitoba. *Member:* International PEN, Writers' Union of Canada, Society of Children's Book Writers and Illustrators, Manitoba Writers Guild.

■ Awards, Honors

Geoffrey Bilson Award for Historical Fiction for Young Readers, 1988, for *Lisa;* Mr. Christie Honor Book, and Manitoba Book of the Year nomination, both 1989, Young Adults' Choices for 1991, International Reading Association, all for *Jesper;* Sydney Taylor Book Award Honor Book, Association of Jewish Libraries, 1989; Notable Children's Trade Book in the Field of Social Studies citation, National Council for the Social Studies and the Children's Book Council (NCSS/CBC), 1990, Young Adults' Choices for 1991, International Reading Association, all for *Lisa's War;* runner-up citation, Young Adult Canadian Book Awards, 1990, Notable Children's Trade Book in the Field of Social Studies citation, NCSS/CBC, 1991, both for *Code Name Kris;* Notable Book citation, Canadian Library Association, 1992, for *The Race;* Governor General's Award nomination, Ruth Schwartz Award nomination, Mr. Christie Honor Book, and Notable Children's Trade Book in the Field of Social Studies citation, NCSS/CBC, all 1993, Silver Birch Award, 1994, and 1994 Books for the Teen Age citation, New York Public Library, Manitoba Reader's Choice Award, 1996, all for *Daniel's Story;* Sydney Taylor Book Award, and Notable Book citation, Canadian Library Association, both 1993, Notable Children's Trade Book in the Field of Social Studies citation, NCSS/CBC, 1994, and 1994 Books for the Teen Age citation, New York Public Library, all for *Sworn Enemies;*

Quick Pick for Young Adults citation, American Library Association (ALA), and Governor General's Award nomination, both 1994, and 1994 Books for the Teen Age citation, New York Public Library, all for *The Burning Time;* Manitoba Book of the Year nomination, 1995, and Outstanding Book of the Year citation, Children's Book Centre, 1996, both for *The Primrose Path;* Quick Pick for Young Adults citation, ALA, Best Book of the Year for Young Adults citation, ALA, Best Book of the Year for Children nomination, McNally Robinson Book Award, and Ruth Schwartz Award nomination, all 1996, Notable Children's Trade Book in the Field of Social Studies citation, NCSS/CBC, 1997, and 1997 Books for the Teen Age citation, New York Public Library, all for *After the War.*

■ Writings

YOUNG ADULT NOVELS

The DNA Dimension, Gage Publishing, 1982.
The Fusion Factor, Fifth House, 1986, reissued as *It's Up to Us,* Stoddard, 1991.
Zanu, Fifth House, 1987.
Me, Myself and I, Fifth House, 1987.
Lisa, Lester (Canada), 1987, published in the U.S. as *Lisa's War,* Scribner, 1989.
Jesper, Lester, 1989, published in the U.S. as *Code Name Kris,* Scribner, 1990, reissued as *Kris's War,* Scholastic, 1992.
The Race, HarperCollins, 1991.
Daniel's Story (commissioned by U.S. Holocaust Memorial Museum), Scholastic, 1993.
Sworn Enemies, Bantam, 1993.
The Burning Time, Delacorte Press, 1994.
The Primrose Path, Bain & Cox, 1995.
After the War, Simon and Schuster, 1996.
The Garden, Simon and Schuster, 1997.
The Freak, Key Porter, 1997.

WITH PERRY NODELMAN

Of Two Minds, Bain & Cox (Canada), 1994, Simon and Schuster, 1995.
More Minds, Simon and Schuster, 1996.

CHAPTER BOOKS

Adventure in Legoland, illustrated by Mark Teague, Scholastic, 1992.
Safari Adventure in Legoland, illustrated by Elroy Freem, Scholastic, 1993.

The Lost Locket, illustrated by Susan Gardos, Scholastic, 1994.

PLAYS

(With husband, Per Brask) *Lisa* (adapted from the novel of the same name), first produced by the Prairie Theatre Exchange, 1991.
The Escape (adapted from the novel *Sworn Enemies*), commissioned by the Winnipeg Jewish Theatre, produced April, 1993.
Sworn Enemies, first reading at the Jewish Repertory Theatre, New York, 1994, staged reading at Barbara Striesand New Play Festival, 1997.
Telling (radio play), broadcast by CBC Manitoba, 1994.

Also author, with Per Brask, of *Jesper* (adapted from the novel of the same name), 1997.

■ Work in Progress

Contageon of Good, a young adult novel, Simon and Schuster, expected 1998; *Telling,* a young adult novel, Key Porter.

■ Sidelights

"I thought you were all dead. Didn't the gas ovens finish you all off?"

In *After the War,* this is the welcome a Jewish teenager, Ruth, receives from her now-dead family's former maid, who, Ruth notices, is wearing one of Mother's dresses. It is 1945, and Ruth, recently liberated from the Buchenwald concentration camp, has made her way back home to her village in Poland. She realizes home is now a memory, an idea—not a place. Young Daniel, in *Daniel's Story,* comes to a similar realization at a train station where Polish farm boys beat to death his friend Peter, while onlookers do nothing to help. Daniel, Peter, and Daniel's father have survived the Nazi death camps and are starting their lives over. Having witnessed and endured unspeakable acts, they are weak and numb but finally free. Yet their triumph is cut to the quick by the young thugs' menacing taunts: "What have we got here? Two Jews who escaped the gas?"

Ruth, Daniel, Peter, and Daniel's father—all characters in novels by Carol Matas—represent the minority of people who survived the Holocaust, Adolf Hitler's systematic elimination of some six million European Jews. More than one million of Hitler's victims were children. For many survivors who were liberated into a devastated Europe after World War II, anti-Semitism still prevailed and freedom was not about safety or happy homecomings. Such subject matter, for which Matas is best known, may seem unimaginable, but then, the author did not have to imagine it. The horror had already been imagined, had already been carried out, was real. Matas's goal as a novelist is to recreate actual human situations from the past and, through her storytelling, to challenge existing conditions and, perhaps, to bring about change.

Since the mid-1980s Matas has published some eighteen books for young readers. In addition to historical fiction, she has also written chapter books and fantasy-adventures, including two novels co-authored with her colleague Perry Nodelman. Yet for all her success as a novelist, Matas did not initially seek out a writing life. She wanted to be an actor, and studied English at the University of Western Ontario, from which she earned a bachelor's degree in 1969. At age twenty she traveled to England for theater training at the Actor's Lab in London. Returning home to Canada, she began a professional acting career in Toronto.

Writing stories was primarily a hobby Matas shared with friends, and it was not until after she married and had children that she began working seriously on book-length material. Her first books were action stories devoted to futuristic topics like genetic engineering (*The DNA Dimension*) and nuclear war (*The Fusion Factor*, reissued as *It's Up to Us*). Both featured a young character, Rebecca (named after Matas's daughter; the author also has a son, Sam). Matas did not plan to become a children's writer. I sort of stumbled into it, she explained in a conversation with Nodelman in *Canadian Children's Literature* (CCL). It wasn't until I wrote my first novel that I specifically focused on children as an audience. . . . I have to admit I wrote those books with children in mind and with their minds in mind, specifically. In fact, dare I admit this, I wanted to change them. . . . I wanted to make them into young people who would think for themselves."

Matas lives with her family in Winnipeg, Manitoba. When her children were both in school, she began working full time on her writing and research. She also tours frequently to speak about writing to children and adults. Though Matas is no longer acting on stage, she is still involved in theater. Some of her works, such as *Lisa*, have been adapted into plays and successfully staged. She has also written *Sworn Enemies*, a full-length adult play, *The Escape*, a young adult play based on the novel *Sworn Enemies*, and *Jesper*. Careful readers may detect elements of Matas's dramatic sense in her writing: she uses a straightforward, first-person narrative style, depicting strong main characters who figure prominently in every scene.

This 1993 novel focuses on the disturbing relationship between two young Jewish men in early nineteenth-century Russia.

"Matas proves to be a very visual writer, allowing the reader to easily see the action setting," Ronald Jobe wrote in the *Journal of Adolescent and Adult Literacy* (*JAAL*). Matas's historical fiction, in particular, has been noted less for its prose style than for the dramatic and emotional power of her subject matter. While oversimplification of complicated political situations is a risk in creating historical fictions, Matas's careful research and historical accuracy are often cited by reviewers.

Matas's novels address common themes: the human capacity for both good and evil, the misuse of authority, and the need to balance the roles of the individual and the community in society. Usually her young characters are involved in social conflict that causes them to discover personal strengths and to increase their self-awareness. "Often I place my characters in a situation where their assumptions are challenged, or where they are forced to challenge others. I hope their dilemma will challenge the reader in a similar way. And if my point of view does come through, then I hope it's one the reader at least finds interesting—maybe it's something that they hadn't considered before, a new, different way of seeing the world," Matas said in *CCL*.

Personal Path Leads to Holocaust Writing

A personal path led Matas to write about the Jewish experience in World War II. Her husband Per Brask's father and grandfather had participated in the resistance movement against the Nazis in Denmark during the war. Fascinated and inspired by their stories, Matas decided to write a book for young people about a boy who worked against the Nazis. But her novel *Lisa's War* (published in Canada as *Lisa*) came first, after she read about how the Nazis had planned to round up Danish Jews on Rosh Hashanah, the Jewish New Year. Their plans were thwarted, however, when the Danes saved nearly all of their Jewish countrymen by secretly spreading a warning. Of some 7,000 Danish Jews, about 500 were arrested and sent to concentration camps. The rest were led to safety in neutral Sweden.

Matas told Nodelman in *CCL* she had never heard this story before: "I figured, as a fairly well-educated Jew, if I hadn't heard it, probably most children hadn't heard it either. So I felt I *had* to write it. I must admit it was as much for the drama of

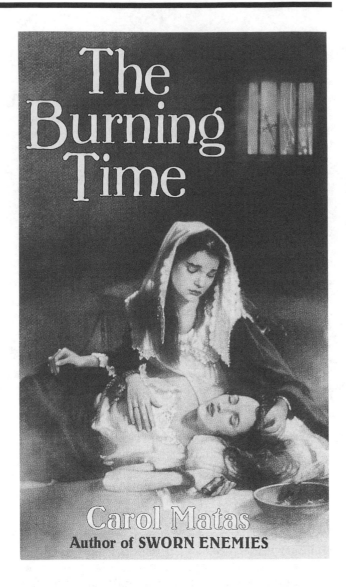

After her mother is accused of being a witch, fifteen-year-old Rose must hide herself in this 1994 work that examines witch burnings in France during the sixteenth century.

the story, as for the theme I wanted to explore. Also, it was an uplifting story, a story which said this didn't have to happen the way it did, look at what happened in Denmark. That's how I came to write *Lisa*."

The award-winning novel, described as "both realistic and poignant" by Margaret B. Shelley in the *English Journal*, is the story of Lisa, a Jewish girl living in Copenhagen in 1940. She comes of age during the German occupation of Denmark as her family is increasingly persecuted and placed in danger. Lisa follows her older brother Stefan into the resistance movement, distributing underground newspapers on trolley cars. At first she sees her efforts as simply an after-school adventure. But soon her involvement progresses to life-or-death exploits that lead to the climactic, secret evacuation of Jews to Sweden. "*Lisa* combines personal emotion with historical fact in just the right proportions to produce a first hand look into what it must have been like to be a Jew in occupied Europe during those dark years," wrote J. R. Wytenbrock in *Canadian Literature*. "There is nothing sentimental about this novel, and yet the heroine is very human, and thus engaging."

Code Name Kris (published in Canada as *Jesper*, and retitled in a later U.S. printing as *Kris's War*) is a sequel to *Lisa's War*. In this novel Matas continues the Danish resistance story through seventeen-year-old Jesper, the boyfriend Lisa had left behind. Jesper, whose code name is Kris, has been captured and tortured by the Nazis. As he awaits execution in a German prison he reflects on the events leading to his final capture: After joining the resistance, he engages in sabotage in order to antagonize and cripple the occupying German troops. At one point he is captured, yet he manages to escape and joins a group that publishes an underground newspaper.

When Lisa's brother Stefan returns from Sweden he teams with Jesper to work in the resistance. Before Jesper and Stefan are captured, they fall in love with the same girl. The climax of the story comes in a dramatic meeting between Jesper and his Nazi jailer, who is a fellow Dane and childhood friend. David A. Lindsey praised *Code Name Kris* in *School Library Journal*: "Matas, in sparse, understated, and somewhat dispassionate prose, effectively depicts what life was like in occupied Denmark and in the Danish resistance. . . . All of this is woven into an easily read, interest-holding story of bravery, loyalty, and patriotism."

Pictures Worth a Thousand Words

Matas's third novel, *Daniel's Story*, was commissioned by the United States Holocaust Memorial Museum to complement a children's exhibit in 1993. Matas wrote the story in the form of a traveler's journal, with teen-aged Daniel using his photo album—and later only his memory of its contents—to tell about his experiences. The photographs "show the deterioration of a world, a family, a way of life," Frances Bradburn wrote in the *Wilson Library Bulletin*. "Each [photograph] is a picture of horror, terror, and the wonderful will to survive."

Daniel engages in his mental storytelling exercises to pass the time as he and other family members undertake four harrowing train treks from their home in Frankfurt, Germany (where Daniel's family has lived for centuries), to Poland. Along the way, they experience barbarism and bribery, sickness and starvation. First they go to a Jewish ghetto in Lodz. Then they are transported to the death camp at Auschwitz, where Daniel's mother is killed and he is separated from his sister. Daniel and his father are later taken back Germany, to the Buchenwald camp. Finally, after the Jews are liberated at the end of the war, father and son return to Lodz to search for surviving family members and friends.

Matas recalled in *CCL* that *Daniel's Story* was "the most painful and difficult book I've ever had to research. In a way, although obsessed by the evil of the Holocaust, it was also a topic I actively avoided because I got depressed just thinking about it. This book forced me to look at the worst, most evil thoughts and deeds, and I could not flinch." In the end, hope and love prevail for Daniel, as he locates his girlfriend Rosa and the two plan a new life together in Palestine.

A nominee for Canada's prestigious Governor-General's Award, *Daniel's Story* "is the most powerful account of a teenager living through the Holocaust since *The Diary of Anne Frank*," according to Arlene Perly Rae in the *Toronto Star*. Kenneth Oppel, writing in *Quill and Quire*, noted that the "historical material itself is so powerful here that it's impossible not to become intensely emotionally involved . . .," and he concluded, "*Daniel's Story* is never less than gripping. It is a book all children should read." Ronald Jobe, writing in the *Journal of Adolescent and Adult Literacy*, found characterization to be the novel's strength: "Matas has created a memorable character in Daniel, surviving as he does during these terrible times. Her skill as a writer shows itself as the reader walks in Daniel's shoes." Discussing the work, Matas told *AAYA*: "*Daniel's Story* is being read and studied across North America, and children are deeply moved by it, as evidenced by all the letters I get."

Grief, Hope, Even Miracles

In *After the War* Matas takes up the question of what happened to children who survived the Holocaust. She stated in an author's comment for *JAAL* that the idea came to her after she had completed *Daniel's Story*. "I began to wonder what might happen to my characters Daniel and Rosa. . . . What was left for the children who survived? . . . Where could they go? What could they do?" Matas speculated that most young people, unaware of the anti-Semitism still rampant in Europe, thought they could return to a normal life after the war. Having researched the subject, Matas knew they would instead continue to encounter persecution and hardship. "A beast like that let loose cannot simply be put to sleep," Matas wrote in *JAAL*.

Ruth, the central character in *After the War*, joins an underground group devoted to smuggling Jews into Palestine, where they hope to create a Jewish homeland. She helps lead a band of orphans from Poland through Czechoslovakia and Austria to Italy, where they board a ship for illegal passage to Palestine. On the ship she is reunited with her brother Simon, who was believed dead. This is just the kind of miracle Matas said she found evidence of in her extensive research, which included interviews with survivors. "*After the War* may be a story filled with grief, but it is also a story filled with hope, even miracles," Matas said in *JAAL*.

Reviewers praised the work. Hazel Rochman, discussing the work in *Booklist*, wrote that "Matas has retold [the historical incidents] and shaped them into a tightly edited drama far from the rambling and repetition of authentic oral history." *School Library Journal* contributor Robyn Nicoline Ryan believed that the "use of descriptive language creates a mood of desperation and hope combined with a commitment to survival." In *Voice of Youth Advocates*, Marian Rafal declared, "Rich in texture and simple in its honesty, this story resonates with feeling."

Matas has written two other related novels, *Sworn Enemies* and *The Garden*. *Sworn Enemies* takes place in early nineteenth-century Russia when, under the rule of Czar Nicholas I, army quotas were filled by forcing Jewish men and boys—some as young as twelve years old—into military service. The underlying motive of the government was to as-similate the Jews by forcing them to convert to Christianity. The main characters in the novel are two Jewish boys, Aaron and Zev, who have been forced to join the army. They narrate the story in alternating chapters. Aaron comes from a prominent family, is a good student, and is engaged to a beautiful young woman named Miriam. Zev, on the other hand, is poor and works as a *khapper*, one who kidnaps boys for army service. Jealous of Aaron and also in love with Miriam, Zev kidnaps Aaron and hands him over to the army. But Zev soon finds himself kidnaped into the same troop, and the two enemies, each in his own way, must deal with identical hardships and moral quandaries as they try to escape.

Oppel noted in *Quill and Quire* that Matas "brings her historical material quickly to light. . . . This is a gripping, provocative novel for young adults that raises many issues and avoids pat solutions." Roger Sutton, writing in the *New York Times Book Review*, called Matas a "good storyteller." Whereas Aaron might be too obviously good and Zev too clearly a corrupted soul, Sutton observed, Matas has nevertheless succeeded in raising worthwhile philosophic questions in *Sworn Enemies*. A reviewer in *Bulletin of the Center for Children's Books* concurred, stating that the historical information "is only a background here for the moral dilemmas more fully developed through portrayals of each character's inner conflicts."

Matas's most recent book, *The Garden*, is a sequel to *After the War*, and follows the character Ruth to Palestine. Living on a kibbutz, she has been put in charge of the garden. She and her brother Simon are members of separate Zionist organizations, which hold different views about how to establish peace with both the Arabs and the British forces. "They must fight but at least now they *can* fight, they are no longer victims. And yet, having to kill as they were once killed is a terrible moral dilemma, so the questions raised here are all to do with idealism and what one must do to survive," Matas explained in *CCL*. She says she plans to write at least two more books set during World War II.

Young Women of Note

Characterization is a Matas strength in general, and in particular her novels portray strong female characters. Ruth is a survivor and a leader by

If you enjoy the works of Carol Matas, you may also want to check out the following books and films:

Lois Lowry, *Number the Stars*, 1989.
Chaim Potok, *The Chosen*, 1967.
Jane Yolen, *The Devil's Arithmetic*, 1988.
Schindler's List, Universal, 1993.

virtue of her own courage and character. Lisa's role in the Danish resistance is as important as that of her brother and boyfriend. Equally strong is Rose in *The Burning Time*, a novel in which Matas turns to a different chapter in history, telling a story about witch hunting in sixteenth-century France. Elizabeth Devereaux in *Publishers Weekly* called *The Burning Time* "feverish" and "extreme," concluding that "Matas limits her impact with her inability to convey historical drama through any but the crudest filters." Discussing this criticism with Nodelman, Matas stated, "some reviewers in the U.S. (the book got raves in Canada) were horrified. . . . And yet I had to leave the worst out—it was far too horrible." She added that "young women who write me now list it as one of their favourite books (my reward)."

It is volatile subject matter, to be sure. Yet other critics were impressed with the story of fifteen-year-old Rose and her widowed mother, Suzanne, who negotiate their way through the maze of their neighbors' malignant motives. For instance, a priest makes sexual advances toward Suzanne, and land-grabbing brothers-in-law are motivated by sex and the need to form marriages of convenience. Other characters are suspicious of Suzanne's healing and midwifery skills. By holding their ground, Rose and Suzanne make numerous enemies. They are finally accused of witchcraft, then imprisoned and tortured. With the help of a friend, Suzanne must take courageous action and persevere in the face of tragedy. Mary Hedge, writing in *Voice of Youth Advocates*, predicted that *Burning Time* would be much more popular than most other young adult historical fiction. . . . What jealousy, lust for flesh and money, and fear does to people's minds [in the novel] is just as true today as in the story."

Matas writes about lighter subject matter in her collaborative efforts with children's literature pro-

fessor and author Perry Nodelman. Their two fairy-tale-style novels, *Of Two Minds* and *More Minds*, are set in the fantasy land of Gepeth, where things can be imagined into being. The stories follow the adventures of the strong-willed Princess Lenora and her on-and-off fiancee, Prince Coren. Lisa Dennis praised *Of Two Minds* in *School Library Journal*, noting that Matas and Nodelman created a kaleidoscope of characters, cultures, and events that offers both entertainment and enrichment to young readers.

Matas has stated that her primary goal is to tell a good story. As someone who never intended to write for young people, she now has young people's books—and readers—very much in mind. As Matas said in *CCL*, "I have to have a reason for writing, and I desperately want to tell a story that is unputdownable! . . . I think there's a place for all kinds of books—young people should be no more confined in their choices than us old guys."

■ Works Cited

Bradburn, Frances, "Middle Books," *Wilson Library Bulletin*, December, 1993, p. 119.

Dennis, Lisa, review of *Of Two Minds*, *School Library Journal*, October, 1995, p. 136.

Devereaux, Elizabeth, review of *The Burning Time*, *Publishers Weekly*, October 17, 1994, p. 82.

Hedge, Mary, review of *The Burning Time*, *Voice of Youth Advocates*, October, 1994, p. 210.

Jobe, Ronald, review of *Daniel's Story*, *Journal of Adolescent and Adult Literacy*, October, 1995, p. 174.

Jobe, Ronald, "Canadian Connections," *Journal of Adolescent and Adult Literacy*, December, 1996/January, 1997, p. 325.

Lindsey, David A., review of *Code Name Kris*, *School Library Journal*, December, 1990, p. 122.

Matas, Carol, *Daniel's Story*, Scholastic, 1993.

Matas, Carol, *After the War*, Simon and Schuster, 1996.

Matas, Carol, "Author Comment: Why *After the War*?", *Journal of Adolescent and Adult Literacy*, December, 1996/January, 1997, p. 325.

Nodelman, Perry, "Good, Evil, Knowledge, Power: A Conversation between Carol Matas and Perry Nodelman," *Canadian Children's Literature*, Number 82, 1996, pp. 58-59, 61, 66, 67.

Oppel, Kenneth, review of *Sworn Enemies*, *Quill and Quire*, January, 1993.

Oppel, Kenneth, review of *Daniel's Story, Quill and Quire*, February, 1993, p. 35.

Rae, Arlene Perly, "And the Governor-General's nominees are . . . ," *Toronto Star*, November 6, 1993.

Rafal, Marian, review of *After the War, Voice of Youth Advocates*, August, 1996.

Rochman, Hazel, "Escape Stories," *Booklist*, April 1, 1996.

Ryan, Robyn Nicoline, review of *After the War, School Library Journal*, May, 1996, p. 136.

Shelley, Margaret B., review of *Lisa's War, English Journal*, February, 1992, p. 88.

Sutton, Roger, review of *Sworn Enemies, New York Times Book Review*, April 11, 1993, p. 30.

Review of *Sworn Enemies, Bulletin of the Center for Children's Books*, April, 1993.

Wytenbrock, J. R., "Trouble on Wheels," *Canadian Literature*, Spring, 1996, p. 198.

■ For More Information See

PERIODICALS

Bulletin of the Center for Children's Books, September, 1989, pp. 12-13; January, 1991, p. 124; May, 1993, p. 289; December, 1994, p. 139; April, 1996, p. 271.

English Journal, October, 1993, p. 81.

Kirkus Reviews, September 15, 1995, p. 1354.

Los Angeles Times Book Review, June 4, 1989, p. 13.

Publishers Weekly, October 12, 1990, p. 65; April 19, 1993, p. 63.

School Library Journal, May, 1996, p. 135.

Voice of Young Advocates, June, 1989, p. 104; February, 1991, p. 354; June, 1993, p. 92; August, 1993, pp. 153-54; April, 1996, p. 40; August, 1996, p. 158; June, 1997, pp. 110-11, 119.

—Sketch by Tracy J. Sukraw

Toni Morrison

■ Personal

Born Chloe Anthony Wofford, February 18, 1931, in Lorain, OH; daughter of George and Ramah (maiden name, Willis) Wofford; married Harold Morrison, 1958 (divorced, 1964); children: Harold Ford, Slade Kevin. *Education:* Howard University, B.A., 1953; Cornell University, M.A., 1955.

■ Addresses

Office—Department of Creative Writing, Princeton University, Princeton University, Princeton, NJ 08544-1099. *Agent*—Amanda Urban, International Creative Management, 40 West 57th Street, New York, NY 10019.

■ Career

Texas Southern University, Houston, TX, instructor in English, 1955-57; Howard University, Washington, DC, instructor in English, 1957-64; writer, 1965—; Random House, New York City, senior editor, 1965-89; State University of New York at Purchase, Purchase, NY, instructor in Afro-American literature and creative writing, 1969-70, associate professor of English, 1971-72; State University of New York at Albany, Albert Schweitzer Chair in the Humanities, 1984-89; Princeton University, Princeton, NJ, Robert F. Goheen Professor in the Council of the Humanities, 1989—. Visiting lecturer, Yale University, New Haven, CT, 1976-77, Bard College, Annandale-on-Hudson, NY, 1979-80, 1986-88, Rutgers University, New Brunswick, NY, 1983-84; Regents' Lecturer at University of California at Berkeley, and Santagata Lecturer at Bowdoin College, Brunswick, Maine, both 1987; Clark Lecturer at Trinity College, Cambridge, and Massey Lecturer at Harvard University, both 1990. National Council on the Arts (appointed by President Carter); National Humanities Center (trustee); Schomburg Commission for the Preservation of Black Culture (co-chair). *Member:* American Academy and Institute of Arts and Letters, American Academy of Arts and Sciences, Authors Guild (member of council), Authors League of America.

■ Awards, Honors

National Book Award nomination and Ohioana Book Award, both 1975, both for *Sula;* National Book Critics Circle Award and American Academy and Institute of Arts and Letters Award, both 1977, both for *Song of Solomon;* American Academy and Institute of Arts and Letters Award, 1978; New York Public Library's Books for the Teen Age selection, 1980 and 1981, for *Song of Solomon,* and 1982, for *Tar Baby;* New York State Governor's Arts Award, 1986; Book of the Month Club Award, 1986; Langston Hughes Festival Award, City College of New York, 1986; Anisfield Wolf Book Award, 1987; Washington College Literary Award (first recipient), 1987. National Book Award nomination and National Book Critics Circle Award nomination, both 1987, and Pulitzer Prize for Fiction and Robert F. Kennedy Award, both 1988, all for *Beloved;* Elizabeth Cady Stanton Award, National Association of Women, Melcher Book Award, Peggy V. Helmerich Distinguished Author Award, Before Columbus Foundation Award, Mayor's Award of Honor for Art and Culture, City of New York, all 1988; Commonwealth Award, 1989; Chianti Ruffino Antico Fattore International Literary Prize, 1990; Nobel Prize for Literature, 1993; Medal for Distinguished Contribution to American Letters, National Book Foundation, 1996. Honorary degrees from the University of Pennsylvania, the College of Saint Rose, Spelman College, University of Massachusetts at Amherst, Bard, Barnard, Morgan State University, Oberlin College, Dartmouth College, Wesleyan University, Georgetown University, Bryn Mawr College, Columbia University, and Yale University.

■ Writings

FICTION

The Bluest Eye (novel), Holt, 1969, published with a new afterword by the author, Knopf, 1993.
Sula (novel), Knopf, 1973.
(Editor) *The Black Book* (anthology), Random House, 1974.
Song of Solomon (novel), Knopf, 1977, published with an introduction by Reynolds Price, Knopf, 1995.
Tar Baby (novel), Knopf, 1981.
Dreaming Emmett (play), first produced in Albany, NY, 1986.
Beloved (novel), Knopf, 1987.
Jazz (novel), Knopf, 1992.
Toni Morrison Boxed Set: Song of Solomon, Beloved; Jazz, NAL/Dutton, 1994.
Dancing Mind, Random House, 1996.

OTHER

Playing in the Dark: Whiteness and the Literary Imagination (lectures), Harvard University Press, 1992.

(Editor) *Race-ing Justice, En-Gendering Power: Essays on Anita Hill, Clarence Thomas, and the Construction of Social Reality,* Pantheon, 1992.
Conversations with Toni Morrison, edited by Danille Taylor-Guthrie, University Press of Mississippi, 1994.
Nobel Prize Boxed Set, Alfred A. Knopf, Inc., 1994.
Lecture and Speech of Acceptance upon the Award of the Nobel Prize for Literature, Chatto and Windus, 1994.
(Contributor) Nicolaus Mills, editor, *Arguing Immigration: the Debate Over the Changing Face of America,* Simon & Schuster, 1994.
(Editor) *To Die for the People: The Writings of Huey P. Newton,* Writers and Readers, 1995.
Birth of a Nation'hood: Gaze, Script & Spectacle in the O.J. Simpson Trial, Pantheon Books, 1997.

Author of lyrics for "Honey and Rue," commissioned by Carnegie Hall for Kathleen Battle, with music by Andre Previn, 1992. Contributor of essays and reviews to numerous periodicals, including *Black World, New York Times Magazine, New York Times Book Review, Mademoiselle, Michigan Quarterly Review,* and *Thought.*

■ Adaptations

The Bluest Eye, "Nobel Lecture in Literature 1993," both for cassette by Ingram, 1994.

■ Work in Progress

A revision of *The Bluest Eye;* a novel to follow *Beloved* and *Jazz,* tentatively titled *Paradise.*

■ Overview

"When they say I'm a great American novelist," Toni Morrison commented to Gail Caldwell in an interview published in *Conversations with Toni Morrison,* "I say, 'Ha! They're trying to say I'm not black.' When they say I'm a wonderful woman novelist, I think, 'Aha, they think I don't belong.' So I've just insisted—insisted!—upon being called a black woman novelist. And *I* decided what that meant. . . ." Since the beginning of her career as a writer, Morrison has defined not only her own identity, but that of a group of people who had—she asserts—repressed their own. As Denise Heinze elaborated in *Dictionary of Literary*

Biography (*DLB*), "Morrison celebrates the rich heritage and language of the black community and the values it struggles to maintain in a predominantly white society whose own value system, she finds, has lost its collective way."

Morrison fought for, and restored, a vital part of the American experience in American literature: voices that had been lost suddenly emerged. She enchanted critics with her poetic prose and reminded scholars of ancient myths and classic tales with her outrageous plots. She also shocked and jarred readers, bringing them to tears with her morally ambiguous characters and heartrending situations. And she won immense success. "Apart from the briefest stutter at the very beginning of her writing life in the early Seventies, Toni Morrison's career as a novelist has been greeted with gathering superlatives," noted Jane Miller in *London Review of Books*. By the late 1980s, many of Morrison's novels were "required reading in Afro-American literature courses around the country," and included on "lists of standard English courses, Afro-American or otherwise," as Caldwell noted in *Conversations with Toni Morrison*. In addition to forging the path for other African American writers, Morrison has actively encouraged and assisted many of them personally. Over the years, she has worked as a scholar, a teacher, and a leading commentator on American culture and literature.

Morrison's maternal grandparents left a life of sharecropping in Greenville, Alabama, for a better life in Kentucky in 1912. Discouraged by the dismal prospect of educating their daughters in Kentucky, they moved on to Lorain, Ohio. One of their daughters, Ramah Willis, met and married George Wofford, who was originally from Georgia. They had four children, and Chloe Anthony Wofford—who later became Toni Morrison—was their second-born child. As Chloe grew up during the Great Depression, she watched her parents work hard to support the family. George Wofford usually held three jobs at once—he was a shipyard welder, construction worker, and car washer. Chloe was expected to work hard as well. By the age of thirteen, she was cleaning houses.

Morrison's parents insisted on the importance of education. An early reader, she enjoyed novels by Russian writers and the British author Jane Austen. As Denise Heinze observed in *DLB*, Morrison "did not suffer the effects of racism early on" because she excelled in school. By the fifth grade, when Morrison finally confronted racism, she gained strength from "her parents' emphasis on the value of African-Americans as a people, of their family as an inviolable unit, and of themselves as individuals. Heinze also pointed out the influence of environment on the author's writing: "Morrison's family and community held a remarkable wealth of music, storytelling, the supernatural, and black language."

"When they say I'm a great American novelist, I say, 'Ha! They're trying to say I'm not black.' When they say I'm a wonderful woman novelist, I think, 'Aha, they think I don't belong.' So I've just insisted—insisted!—upon being called a black woman novelist. And I decided what that meant. . . ."

—Toni Morrison

As Morrison stated in an interview with Marguerite Feitlowitz for *Authors and Artists for Young Adults* (*AAYA*), she "never lived in a black neighborhood. Poor neighborhoods, yes, black neighborhoods, no. People in small midwestern towns came from everywhere. . . . [While] Blacks were frequently barred from various spots in town. . . . I always thought that there was something wrong with adults who kept black people out of certain activities." Morrison stressed that she developed neither a hatred for whites nor "an absence of self-esteem."

Morrison graduated from Lorain High School with honors and then went on to Howard University. Her mother worked difficult jobs to help with college expenses. During this time Morrison changed her name from Chloe to Toni because many people found her given name too difficult to pronounce. She hoped to become a teacher, so she majored in English and studied the classics. Yet she was disappointed by two aspects of life at Howard. First, she had little opportunity to read literature by African American writers. "The bulk of the Howard English curriculum consisted of Shakespeare, Melville, Hawthorne and so on," Morrison told *AAYA*. The second problem was the constant socializing, which emphasized parties, finding a marriage partner, and wearing fashionable clothes. One benefit of her college career, however, was that as a member of the Howard University Players she was able to tour the South, which she had heard so much about from her grandparents.

After graduating from Howard, Morrison entered graduate school at Cornell University. Once again finding a lack of black literature in the curriculum, she wrote her master's thesis on suicide in the works of William Faulkner and Virginia Woolf. "Perhaps I was attracted to Faulkner because at least in his world there is the presence of blacks," she told Feitlowitz. After receiving a master's degree, Morrison began her professional career by teaching undergraduate English courses at Texas Southern University in Houston. After two years she took a job as an English instructor at Howard. There she met and influenced such prominent 1960s activists as Amiri Baraka, Andrew Young, and Claude Brown. Stokely Carmichael was a student in one of her classes.

Morrison Begins Her Writing Career

While teaching at Howard, Morrison married Harold Morrison, an architect from Jamaica. They had two sons, Harold Ford and Slade. She also began to write. "I never wanted to be a writer," she explained to Mel Watkins in an interview for the *New York Times Book Review,* but "I drifted into a writer's group while teaching. . . . I wrote a little story about a black girl who wanted blue eyes. It was written hurriedly and probably not very well, but I read it and some liked it." Morrison did not work on the story again for a few years. In 1964, after her marriage dissolved, she went to live with her parents. A year and a half later, she became a textbook editor in Syracuse, New York, for a Random House subsidiary. Morrison then began to revise the story about the black girl who wanted blue eyes, and it turned into the novel *The Bluest Eye.*

According to Susan L. Blake in *DLB, The Bluest Eye* is "the story of three young girls at the threshold of maturity in Lorain, Ohio—two who survive the assault of a racist world, and one who doesn't. . . . [It is] a novel of initiation, a microscopic examination of that point where sexual experience, racial experience, and self-image intersect." The main character, Pecola Breedlove, is

unloved and rejected, and she desperately wishes for blue eyes. After she is raped by her own father and gives birth to a baby that dies, she "retreats into madness, believing that her eyes are not simply blue but the bluest of all." Blake reported that *The Bluest Eye* "received moderate though appreciative critical notice, yet most reviewers noted the impact of [Morrison's] vision of black life, her poetic prose, and her construction of a narrative out of discrete scenes and stories."

"Yes, life can be complicated; it can be virtually unlivable. But you can use your mind to learn, to change things and to think things through. . . . Thinking and learning are what we are born for."

—Toni Morrison

The early 1970s was a busy and productive period for Morrison. She was a mother, an editor, a teacher, and a writer. Her editorial work particularly inspired her because she was able to edit the works of African American writers, among them Muhammad Ali, Angela Davis, Henry Dumas, Toni Cade Bambara, and Gayl Jones. Morrison also compiled a scrapbook she called *The Black Book,* which contains newspaper clippings, records, recipes, portions of slave narratives, and photographs illuminating the lives of African Americans over three hundred years. This work led Morrison to develop her strategy of literary archeology, in which she combines her own imagination and experience with information from historical documents. In addition, she wrote twenty-eight book reviews for the *New York Times Book Review* as well as an article entitled "What the Black Woman Thinks About Women's Lib," for the *New York Times Magazine.* During this time she rose each morning before the sun rose to write a second novel, *Sula.*

Sula is about "good and evil and about friendship" between women, Morrison explained to Claudia Tate in *Black Women Writers at Work.* Set in a small Midwestern town during the early 1940s, the novel tells the story of two best friends. One of them, Nel, stays in the town after she grows up, then marries and becomes a respected member of the community. The other, Sula, leaves town for college and the big city. When Sula returns, she engages in promiscuous sex and even seduces Nel's husband. In *Sula*, wrote Darwin T. Turner in *Black Women Writers (1950-1980)*, "Morrison demonstrates her ability to conjure the reader into suspension of disbelief. A woman cuts off her leg to feed her children and sets fire to her drug-dazed son. . . . Sula cuts off the tip of her finger to intimidate white boys into believing her fearlessness . . . [but] Morrison narrates [events] so vividly that readers accept them." *Sula* brought Morrison acclaim for its lyrical prose, surreal tone, and portrayal of friendship among black women. Yet the novel also created a controversy that lasted for years. "Some critics have balked at the sensational level of physical and emotional violence in *Sula*," Carol Iannone noted in *Commentary*, "but what is really disturbing is the author's determination to take no clear stand on the appalling actions she depicts."

Morrison Wins the Admiration of Critics

Morrison wrote her next novel, *Song of Solomon*, after the death of her father. As she explained in the *AAYA* interview, she worked "in a state of profound grief. In my earlier books, the main characters were women and while in *Solomon* there are three extremely strong females, I wanted the world of this novel to be predominantly male. . . . I also wanted to deal with a large time-span, covering several generations and the distances (physical, emotional, historical) they traveled." In a review of *Song of Solomon* in the *Concise Dictionary of American Literary Biography*, Elizabeth B. House characterized it as "the story of Milkman Dead's quest for identity. . . . As he travels southward from his Michigan home, he moves back through the generations in his family history. . . . To make sense of the clues he finds in each location, he must put himself imaginatively into the lives of his forebears, but to find the clues, and even to survive in these strange places, he must first put himself into the minds of the people he meets." In the novel Morrison utilizes myth and engages the fantastic as characters speak to the dead and even fly.

Song of Solomon has been compared to *One Hundred Years of Solitude*, the classic work by Gabriel García Márquez. Caldwell notes in *Conversations with Toni Morrison*, however, that Morrison "was well into *Song of Solomon* before she discovered Gabriel García Márquez." *Song of Solomon* was featured as a main selection for the Book-of-the-Month Club. It thus became the first novel written by an African American to be chosen in nearly forty years, since *Native Son* by Richard Wright. A paperback best-seller, *Solomon* won the award for fiction from the National Book Critics Circle. It also established Morrison as a great American writer. In the *New York Times Book Review*, Reynolds Price described the novel as "rich, slow enough to impress itself upon us like a love affair or a sickness." He went on to assert that "Few Americans know, and can say, more than she has in this wise and spacious novel."

By the late 1970s and early 1980s, Morrison had gained respect as a significant figure in American literature. She was invited as a visiting lecturer to Yale University, appointed by President Jimmy Carter to the National Council on the Arts, and elected to the American Academy and Institute of Arts and Letters. She also appeared in the Public Broadcasting System series "Writers in America." When Morrison's next novel, *Tar Baby*, was published, the event was a *Newsweek* cover story. In *Tar Baby* Morrison features major white characters for the first time. The story has numerous settings—the South, a Caribbean island, Paris, and New York. Jadine, a black fashion model, is the tar baby in a plot based on the story of Brer Rabbit and the Tar Baby. Despite her heritage, Jadine has been educated by whites, and she is determining whether or not to marry a rich white man. Her affair with a poor black man, Son Green, results from her efforts to regain her black heritage. The love between Jadine and Son is complicated by the cultural tension between them. The novel ends as Son runs toward a wilderness reputedly inhabited by wild black men.

Beloved Creates a Controversy

Morrison followed *Tar Baby* with *Beloved*, which is based on a 1855 newspaper account of an escaped slave named Margaret Garner. After Garner escaped from her owner with her children, she was discovered in Cincinnati, Ohio. Rather than let her children return with the owner into slavery, she decided to kill them and then commit suicide. Garner succeeded in killing one of the children before her captors subdued her. As

Morrison told *AAYA*, "In *Beloved* I wanted to look at the ways in which slavery affected women specifically, particularly the ways in which it affected the manner and the extent to which a slave woman could be a mother." She continued, "Now a woman killing her child is fearsome. But look at the ways in which slavery victimized women. Women could be punished twice—they could be worked to death *and* raped."

According to Caldwell, writing *Beloved* was a difficult process for Morrison. She spent two years thinking about the story and three years writing it. She found the effort so overwhelming that she hit a writing impasse in 1985 and was able to produce only one volume instead of the three she had promised her editor. *Beloved* is the surreal story of Sethe, a woman who killed her baby girl rather than let her live enslaved. It begins after the Civil War, when Sethe is living with one daughter, Denver, and a strange woman arrives. Sethe and Denver believe the woman embodies the spirit of Sethe's dead baby, and they call her "Beloved," which is the inscription on the baby's gravestone. Beloved, in turn, thinks of Sethe as the incarnation of her mother, who threw herself off the side of a slave ship into the ocean. Morrison dedicated *Beloved* to "Sixty Million and More," the estimated number of blacks who died as a result of slavery.

Beloved won immense praise from critics, many of whom demanded that the book be placed in the canon of American literature. In a review for *Studies in American Fiction*, Deborah Horvitz gave the novel symbolic significance: "The powerful corporeal ghost who creates matrilineal connection between Africa and America, Beloved stands for every African woman whose story will never be told. She is the haunting symbol of the many Beloveds—generations of mothers and daughters—hunted down and stolen from Africa. . . . " Walter Clemens wrote in *Newsweek* that *Beloved* evoked the lives of slaves and ex-slaves "with a moving intensity no novelist has even approached before." Clemens concluded, "I think we have a masterpiece on our hands here: difficult, sometimes lushly overwritten, but profoundly imagined and carried out with burning fervor."

Despite critical acclaim, however, Morrison did not receive the National Book Award for *Beloved*. This created a controversy: forty-eight black writers wrote a letter published in the *New York Times*

Book Review to thank Morrison for her work and to protest the failure of the literary world to recognize her contribution. When Morrison was awarded the Pulitzer Prize for Fiction later in 1988, the furor died down. Still, confessed Morrison in an interview with Dennis Hevesi for the *New York Times*, "I had dark thoughts about whether the book's merits would be allowed to be the only consideration of the Pulitzer committee. The book had begun to take on a responsibility, an extra-literary reputability, that it was never designed for."

Morrison did not rest on her laurels. In addition to continuing a series of novels begun by *Beloved*, she intended to revise some of her past work. She admitted to Feitlowitz in the *AAYA* interview: "Looking back on my early work, I can isolate technical things I would now handle differently. In *The Bluest Eye*, for example, I had some difficulty establishing and maintaining the proper tone. . . . The voice is too obviously adult and I think perhaps too close to the story's events."

■ Update

Quoting Morrison in an article for the *Journal of Ethnic Studies*, Susan Bowers says the author believes her "job as a writer in the last quarter of the 20th century, not much more than a hundred years after Emancipation, becomes how to rip that veil drawn over 'proceedings too terrible to relate.'" That is, Morrison has strived to relieve Americans, and African Americans, especially, from "forgetting." She has clearly achieved her goal. By the mid-1990s, Morrison's novels were appreciated as American classics, and Morrison herself was recognized as an important African American leader. "Some of us consider her our greatest living writer," stated the introduction to an interview with Morrison in *Essence* magazine. "Some of us say she is our greatest writer, period." Explaining the selection of Morrison as one of America's most influential people, *Time* magazine cited her "importance to and impact on her times transcend the literary." According to the *Time* article, Morrison has "inspired a generation of black artists,. . . produced seismic effects on publishing . . . [and] affected the course of black-studies programs across the U.S."

The success of *Beloved* in the late 1980s set the stage for Morrison's work and its reception in the

If you enjoy the works of Toni Morrison, you may also want to check out the following books and films:

Maya Angelou, *I Know Why the Caged Bird Sings*, 1974.
Paula Marshall, *Daughters*, 1991.
Alice Walker, *In Love and in Trouble*, 1973.
Roots, an epic mini-series that first aired on ABC-TV, 1977.
The Color Purple, Warner Bros., 1985.

early 1990s, when she published *Jazz*, her sixth novel. According to Denise Heinze in a review in *DLB*, "[In *Jazz*] Morrison continues her investigation of the debilitating impact of history on black families." Like *Beloved*, the idea for *Jazz* began with a clipping Morrison saw in an old newspaper. In the photo, which dated from the early twentieth century, a young woman lay in a casket. She had been murdered by her lover. Readers are confronted by this image in *Jazz* after Joe Trace commits adultery with a teenage girl named Dorcas and shoots her. Joe's wife Violet then attempts to mutilate the corpse during the funeral. Joe and Violet live on, without speaking much, obsessed with the dead girl. Violet even begins a relationship with Dorcas's care-taker aunt to learn more about the girl. Throughout the novel, Morrison returns to Joe and Violet's first moments in love, to their lives in the country, and to their experiences with life in the big city.

As Michael Dorris wrote in the Chicago *Tribune Books*, *Jazz* is more than the story of two people. "It is the drawn and exhaled breath of a city," he observed, "the blues song of people who understand suffering and survival . . . the complicated labyrinth that stretches from slavery to the Manhattan of the 1920s. . . . It is a marvel." Richard Eder's critique in the *Los Angeles Times Book Review* was equally enthusiastic. Eder claimed that *Jazz* was even better than *Beloved*: "Nearly as heart-stopping in its intensity, it is on the whole a freer and sunnier book. . . . From the darkness of slavery and its nightmare aftermaths, it moves into the glitter, the exaltation and the pain of the turn-of-the-century migration of black people from the rural South to the cities of the North." Miller observed in *London Review of Books* that Morrison "magically transformed" the melancholy pleasures of blues music into a novel. "More than that," Miller noted, "she has claimed new sources and new kinds of reading as the inspiration for a thriving literature."

In an interview with Elissa Shappell in *Paris Review*, Morrison elaborated on the links among jazz, the city, freedom, and romance in the novel. "With *Jazz*, I wanted to convey the sense that a musician conveys—that he has more but he's not gonna give it to you," she said. "It's an exercise in restraint, a holding back." Morrison was also interested in migration after the Civil War: "How classes and groups and nationalities had the security of numbers within their own turfs and territories. . . . I was interested in how music changed in this country."

In 1992 Morrison also published two important nonfiction collections. *Playing in the Dark: Whiteness and the Literary Imagination* is based on a series of lectures she gave at Harvard University. In the collection Morrison demonstrates how white writers have used black characters not only to express their own sexual anxieties, but to portray and identify whites by contrast. In a review in *Voice Literary Supplement*, Jane Mendelshon wrote that Morrison sheds light on American literature: "Morrison explores how the temptation to enslave others instead of embracing freedom has shaded our national literature, and how an acceptance of this truth will enable us to see that literature's struggles and fears, and so better understand her [Morrison's] exuberance." *Race-ing Justice, En-Gendering Power: Essays on Anita Hill, Clarence Thomas, and the Construction of Social Reality*, which Morrison edited, features essays by black authors who try to make sense of the controversial Thomas-Hill case.

Winning the Nobel Prize for Literature

Around seven o'clock one morning in 1993, as sixty-two-year-old Toni Morrison was writing, she received a telephone call. Fearing it was "terrible news," she answered the phone. However, the caller was one of her friends, who announced that Morrison had just won the Nobel Prize. Speaking with William Grimes for an article in the *New York Times*, Morrison said that after the news had finally sunk in she was ecstatic. "This is a palpable tremor of delight for me. It was wholly unexpected and so satisfying," she exclaimed.

Morrison was the first African American to win the Nobel Prize for literature. Moreover, she was the only American woman writer to be so honored since Pearl S. Buck received the award in 1938. Only the eighth woman ever to win the prize out of the ninety writers who have been received it, Morrison was given $825,000. Henry Louis Gates, Jr., the respected and influential African American scholar at Harvard University, told William Grimes in a *New York Times* report, "This is a great day for African-Americans, and for Americans in general. . . . Just two centuries ago, the African-American literary tradition was born in slave narratives," he said. "Now our greatest writer has won the Nobel Prize." Morrison herself was quoted in *Newsweek* as saying, "I hope it says something about the evolution of African-American writing, that it's no longer outside the central enterprise, that it speaks about things that matter to anyone."

John Darnton noted in the *New York Times* that Morrison's Nobel Prize acceptance speech "brought the crowd in the Swedish Academy . . . to a standing ovation" as she commented on the "value of language: not official language or the censoring language of the state or the trick language of journalism, but language as words, with the magic they contain when they are learned by children."

During the mid-1990s, Morrison continued to teach at Princeton University. She also started working on the third novel in the series she had begun with *Beloved*. Her next novel, she said, will be set in the 1970s and depict the African American experience during the Vietnam War. Morrison remained an authoritative voice in the dialogue' about the treatment of blacks in American popular discourse as well as in literature. In 1997, she published another nonfiction book. *Birth of a Nation'hood: Gaze, Script & Spectacle in the O.J. Simpson Trial* explores the media hype surrounding the O.J. Simpson criminal trial and the portrayal of black males as the trial progressed.

Morrison has faced significant changes in her life during the 1990s. As she told *Essence*, "two close cousins died, both of my brothers died, my mother died, my house burned down. . . . My faith is always being challenged, but that is good. You discover of what you are made." Morrison sees personal crises as "opportunities." She affirmed that "Yes, life can be complicated; it can

be virtually unlivable. But you can use your mind to learn, to change things and to think things through. . . . Thinking and learning are what we are born for."

■ Works Cited

Blake, Susan L., "Toni Morrison," *Dictionary of Literary Biography*, Volume 33: *Afro-American Fiction Writers After 1955*, Gale, 1984, pp. 187-99.

Bowers, Susan, "*Beloved* and the New Apocalypse," *Journal of Ethnic Studies*, Spring, 1990, pp. 59-77.

Caldwell, Gail, *Conversations with Toni Morrison*, edited by Danille Taylor-Guthrie, University Press of Mississippi, 1994, pp. 239-45.

Clemens, Walter, "A Gravestone of Memories," review of *Beloved*, *Newsweek*, September 28, 1987, pp. 74-75.

Darnton, John, "Accepting Nobel, Morrison Proves the Power of Words," *New York Times*, December 8, 1993, pp. B1, B6.

Dorris, Michael, "Singing the Big City Blues," review of *Jazz*, *Tribune Books* (Chicago), April 19, 1992, pp. 1, 5.

Eder, Richard, "Those Nights on the Harlem Rooftops," review of *Jazz*, *Los Angeles Times Book Review*, April 19, 1992, pp. 3, 5.

Gates, David, with Danzt Senna and Lynn James, "Keep Your Eyes on the Prize," *Newsweek*, October 18, 1993, p. 89.

Grimes, William, "Toni Morrison Is '93 Winner of Nobel Prize in Literature," *New York Times*, October 8, 1993, pp. A1, B10.

Heinze, Denise, "Toni Morrison," *Dictionary of Literary Biography*, Volume 143: *American Novelists Since World War II*, Gale, 1994, pp. 171-87.

Hevesi, Dennis, "Toni Morrison's Novel 'Beloved' Wins the Pulitzer Prize in Fiction," *New York Times*, April 1, 1988.

Horvitz, Deborah, "Nameless Ghosts: Possession and Dispossession in *Beloved*," *Studies in American Fiction*, Autumn, 1989, pp. 157-67.

House, Elizabeth B., "Toni Morrison," *Concise Dictionary of American Literary Biography, Broadening Views, 1968-1988*, Gale, 1989, pp. 200-15.

Iannone, Carol, "Toni Morrison's Career," *Commentary*, December, 1987, pp. 59-63.

Mendelsohn, Jane, "Harlem on Her Mind: Toni Morrison's Language of Love," review of *Jazz*, *Voice Literary Supplement*, May, 1992, pp. 25-26.

Miller, Jane, "New Romance," review of *Jazz*, *London Review of Books*, May 14, 1992, p. 6.

Morrison, Toni, interview with Marguerite Feitlowitz for *Authors and Artists for Young Adults*,
Volume 1, Gale, 1989, pp. 163-74.

Morrison, Toni, interview with Elissa Schappell,
Paris Review, Fall, 1993, pp. 82-125.

Morrison, Toni, "The World According to Toni
Morrison," *Essence*, May, 1995, p. 222.

Price, Reynolds, "The Adventures of Macon
Dead," review of *Song of Solomon*, *New York
Times Book Review*, September 11, 1977, repub-
lished, October 6, 1996, p. 93.

Tate, Claudia, editor, *Black Women Writers at Work*,
Continuum, 1983.

"Toni Morrison," *Time*, June 17, 1996, p. 73.

Turner, Darwin T., "Theme, Characterization, and
Style in the Works of Toni Morrison," *Black
Women Writers (1950-1980): A Critical Evaluation*,
edited by Mari Evans, Anchor Press/Doubleday,
1984, pp. 361-69.

Watkins, Mel, "Talk with Toni Morrison," *New York
Times Book Review*, September 11, 1977, p. 48.

■ **For More Information See**

BOOKS

Century, Douglas, *Toni Morrison*, Chelsea House,
1994.

Cooey, Paula M., *Religious Imagination and the Body*,
Oxford University Press, 1994.

Furman, Jan, *Toni Morrison's Fiction*, University of
South Carolina Press, 1996.

Harris, Trudier, *Fiction and Folklore: The Novels of
Toni Morrison*, University of Tennessee Press,
1991.

Kramer, Barbara, *Toni Morrison, Nobel Prize-Winning
Author*, Enslow Publishers, 1996.

Otten, Terry, *The Crime of Innocence in the Fiction
of Toni Morrison*, University of Missouri Press,
1989.

Reference Guide to American Literature, 3rd edition,
edited by Jim Kamp, St. James Press, 1994.

PERIODICALS

African American Review, Spring, 1992; Fall, 1992;
Fall, 1993; Winter, 1993; Summer, 1994; Fall,
1994; Winter, 1994; Winter, 1995; Spring, 1995;
Spring, 1996.

American Imago, Spring, 1990; Winter, 1994.

Atlantic, April, 1981.

Black Enterprise, October, 1992; April, 1993.

Booklist, March 1, 1992; December 1, 1992; March
15, 1993; February 15, 1994.

Chronicle of Higher Education, October 13, 1993.

Jet, October 25, 1993; November 15, 1993; December 27, 1993; February 12, 1996; February 19,
1996.

Library Journal, May 1, 1992; June 1, 1992.

Maclean's, June 1, 1992.

Monthly Review, April, 1994.

Ms., June, 1974.

Nation, May 25, 1992; December 21, 1992; January
17, 1994.

National Review, June 8, 1992; March 15, 1993.

New Republic, March 21, 1981; May 18, 1992; November 12, 1992; February 22, 1993; March 27,
1995.

Newsweek, April 27, 1992; October 18, 1993.

New York, May 4, 1992; December 21, 1992.

New York Review of Books, November 19, 1992.

New York Times Book Review, October 25, 1992;
December 6, 1992.

New York Times Magazine, September 11, 1994;
November 21, 1996.

Obsidian, spring/summer, 1979.

People Weekly, October 3, 1994; December 2, 1996.

Publishers Weekly, October 17, 1992; October 11,
1993; January 3, 1994; February 28, 1994; October 28, 1996; November 11, 1996.

Saturday Review, September 17, 1977.

School Library Journal, July, 1990; November, 1993.

Time, April 27, 1992; October 18, 1993.

Vogue, May, 1992.

Women's Review of Books, March, 1988, pp. 5-6.

Working Woman, November-December, 1996.*

—*Sketch by R. Garcia-Johnson*

Margaret I. Rostkowski

■ Personal

Surname is pronounced "Ros-*kow*-ski"; born January 12, 1945, in Little Rock, AR; daughter of Ralph Carlisle (a pathologist) and Charlotte (a registered nurse; maiden name, Leuenberger) Ellis; married Charles Anthony Rostkowski (a director of a shelter for the homeless), September 12, 1970 (divorced); children: David Lee, Diovannie. *Education:* Middlebury College, B.A., 1967; University of Kansas, M.A.T., 1971. *Politics:* Democrat. *Religion:* Society of Friends (Quakers).

■ Addresses

Home—2930 Marilyn Dr., Ogden, UT 84403. *Office*—Ogden High School, 2828 Harrison Blvd., Ogden, UT 84403. *Agent*—Ruth Cohen, P.O. Box 7626, Menlo Park, CA 94025.

■ Career

Teacher of English, French, and reading at middle schools in Ogden, UT, 1974-84; Ogden High School, Ogden, teacher of English and writing, 1984—. Member of advisory board, *Rough Draft;* member, Ogden City Arts and Friends of Weber County Library. *Member:* National Education Association, Society of Children's Book Writers and Illustrators, National Council of Teachers of English, League of Women Voters, Utah Education Association, Ogden Education Association, Delta Kappa Gamma, Phi Delta Kappa.

■ Awards, Honors

Golden Kite Award, Society of Children's Book Writers, 1986, Children's Book Award, International Reading Association, 1987, and Jefferson Cup, Virginia Library Association, 1987, all for *After the Dancing Days;* Best Books for Young Adults and Notable Children's Books citations, American Library Association, both 1986, both for *After the Dancing Days;* Sequoyah Young Adult Book Award Masterlist citation, Texas Lone Star Reading List selection, and New York Public Library Books for the Teen Age selection, all for *Moon Dancer.*

■ Writings

After the Dancing Days, Harper, 1986.
The Best of Friends, Harper, 1989.
Moon Dancer, Harcourt, 1995.

■ **Work in Progress**

A young adult novel.

■ **Sidelights**

"My books," Margaret Rostkowski comments in *Twentieth-Century Young Adult Writers*, "begin with questions, with things I want to explore and learn more about." In her three young adult novels, Rostkowski examines how young people react when history intrudes on their lives. Sometimes the intruding history is on a worldwide scale, such as World War I in *After the Dancing Days* and the Vietnam War in *The Best of Friends*. Sometimes it is on a smaller scale, as is the case with the Anasazi Indians and early settlers of southern Utah in *Moon Dancer*. In each case, however, Rostkowski's protagonists are changed by their contact with history. They grow and change on a personal level. Rostkowski's "powerful, thought-provoking books," writes Kathy Piehl in *Twentieth-Century Young Adult Writers*, "make young adults think about . . . causes and consequences."

Rostkowski's own life has been influenced by warfare and American history since her birth in 1945. "My parents are Kansans—they were from Kansas, not Arkansas," she explains in an interview with *Authors and Artists for Young Adults* (*AAYA*), "but they were stationed in Arkansas during World War II. My father was at Camp Robinson in Little Rock, serving as a doctor at the military base there. As soon as he was released from the army in the fall of 1945, he did a little training in the Chicago area. After the war they were wondering where to settle and my mother's family encouraged them to go west. My father was a pathologist, and when a position opened up in Ogden, Utah they decided to go there. We moved to Utah in 1947. I was only two at the time, but being in Utah has greatly influenced me.

"I have an older brother (two years older) and a younger sister (four years younger). *The Best of Friends* has a brother and sister in it, and *Moon Dancer* has two sisters in it. I thought a lot about that, because those books are about intense family relationships. My relations with my brother and sister were and continue to be very good, and the tensions that appear in the books are literary license. The funny thing is, everyone thinks that the characters are based on my family—my mother thinks that the fathers in *After the Dancing Days* and *The Best of Friends* are based on my father. I think they're two completely different fathers, but she sees them both as my father. I'm interested in family relationships because our family is so close—not geographically, but in other ways. There's a fair amount of my sister and me in *Moon Dancer*, which draws tensions between sisters. We played together when we were kids and spent a lot of time hiking in the mountains, which were literally in our back yard, so a lot of that came into the last two books."

Rostkowski's family moved to Seattle when she was in the eighth grade, where she attended high

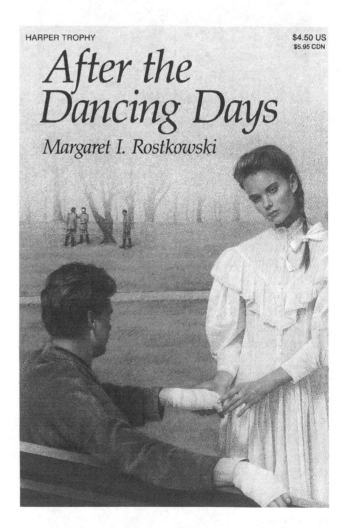

Thirteen-year-old Annie helps a bitter World War I veteran heal his physical and emotional wounds in this 1986 novel.

school. This was the point, she recalls in her *AAYA* interview, that writing became very important to her. "My mother has a couple of poems I wrote in second grade, but writing didn't really become important until I reached high school. Then I was fortunate enough to be in a school where writing was valued. One paper I wrote as a sophomore gave me a wonderful sense of power, of being able to create somebody out of nothing, and that's when I really started to get excited about it. During the summer of my junior year I took creative writing from George Taylor. For about three years in high school I was really active—editor of the school literary magazine.

"I was also an intense reader. My parents always read to us from *Peter Rabbit* and *Babar*, so I grew up surrounded by books. I loved historical fiction—I'd go to the library here in town and get titles like *Betsy in Philadelphia* and *Katherine of Boston*, and books like that. I read *Little Women* when I was ten and just loved it. I also loved dog and horse stories—I read all the *Black Stallion* books. (I was not allowed to read the 'Nancy Drew' series; my mother thought that they were trash.) In high school we read Faulkner, Hemingway, and Steinbeck. One teacher made me read Virginia Woolf's *Orlando*, which I just hated. I can remember throwing it across the room in disgust. Fortunately I was reintroduced to Woolf in my thirties and I just love her now. A writer who influenced me greatly in high school was Stephen Crane. *The Red Badge of Courage* just knocked my socks off. The images in that book still astound me. I read everything he ever wrote, would haunt used book stores to find his out of print poetry. I was very complemented when Mr. Taylor told me that a story I wrote sounded just like Stephen Crane.

"I don't remember a lot of the direct things George Taylor taught us; I remember writing sonnets because of his directions, but mostly it was reading a lot of material, listening to good music as you're writing; we formed response groups, in which we'd sit around and discuss each other's writing in good and productive ways. This was during the summer, all day sessions at the school. I remember a lot of time to write, and a lot of encouragement, and not much intervention on his part. Just giving me opportunities to write and models of great writing. I remember him playing Dylan Thomas for us—it was the first time I heard the poet reading 'Fern Hill' and 'Do Not Go Gentle into That Good Night.' I remember him playing a recording of the opening of *Twelfth Night*. Those are things that stick in my mind. That's the way I run my classes, so he really influenced me in those ways. We did a book of our writings at the end of the term. . . . One of my big regrets in life was that George Taylor died before I became a professional writer, so I never got a chance to tell him how much of an influence he was on me.

Higher Education

"I got my B.A. at Middlebury College in Vermont and did my master's work at the University of Kansas. Mr. Taylor told me that Middlebury had a great writing program and that I should consider going there. I planned to attend the Breadloaf School of Writing with the intention of being an English major but I switched to history because I loved how one of the professors there taught. And that really changed my direction—the kind of writing you do for history is different. When I first started teaching I taught history. I majored in Middle Eastern history, which was a very odd little major then. There were only five people not doing either European or American history then.

"At the University of Kansas I was getting my Masters of Arts in teaching, which was a degree to take all the liberal arts graduates and turn them into teachers. It was a sure way of getting my teaching certificate and still maintaining my concentration in history. I had resisted the idea of becoming a teacher because everybody had told me I would become one—my grandfather had been one, and my grandmother as well—but I ended up teaching just the same. I taught at a junior high in Kansas for three years and really loved it. The Kansas background influenced *After the Dancing Days* a lot; the story is based on stories of my mother's family, who came from that part of the country."

Rostkowski continued, "I met my former husband while we were in graduate school at the University of Kansas. He was also in the history program there. He was from Vermont, and that drew us together. We were married while we were still in graduate school. We had two sons, who are now twenty-one and nineteen, and we now have a grandson.

"I guess right now I'm a teacher who writes because so much of my time is taken up with teaching. I do all of my real thinking and composing during the summer. I love teaching, but I've had to come to terms with the fact that as long as I'm teaching I have to be a teacher who writes. To do either job well, I can't do them both at once. And certainly my writing has grown out of my teaching—that's why I write for the age group that I do. A lot of my ideas have come from my students; they asked me to write *The Best of Friends* because they wanted to know about that time period. And I've used some students as models [for my characters]. Although I never have specific students in mind, I watch their clothes and hair and language, particularly for something like *Moon Dancer*."

"I Fear Your Dancing Days Are Done"

After the Dancing Days is the story of thirteen-year-old Annie Metcalf, who lives with her parents near Kansas City in the year 1919. Annie and her mother Katherine are "puzzled and upset," reveals Piehl, by her father Lawrence's decision to work with the returning injured veterans of World War I rather than take a job at the county hospital. "Annie is torn between her desire for life to resume the shape of prewar days," Piehl continues, "and her growing knowledge that in many ways such an existence can never return." Annie visits her father's hospital and meets some of the injured men he treats. She is perhaps most impressed—and, at first, frightened—by Andrew, who has had his face destroyed by severe burns. "Yet, she comes to appreciate the person behind the frightening exterior," Piehl concludes, "and helps the embittered Andrew reach out to others."

"Andrew was the character who first came to me, and I kept thinking what it would be like to live like that, to have a face that people turned away from in horror," Rostkowski explains in her *AAYA* interview. "I knew that I couldn't write from that point of view and I really wanted to tell the story from a young person's point of view, and so I introduced Annie. The title *After the Dancing Days* is taken from a line in an old Irish song; in this country it became 'When Johnny Comes Marching Home.' It's a very bitter song; it's sung by a mother about her son, and the line 'I fear your dancing days are done' reflects that. It was brought to this country and jazzed up and made

happy—hurrah, hurrah, they're all coming home, isn't it great—but most of them didn't look so great when they got home.

"The story's specific genesis was the movie *Chariots of Fire*. There's a marvelous scene in that movie, which is set during the 1920s, in which two young athletes are going off to Cambridge. They're the athletes who will go to the Olympics, and as they're arriving at Cambridge they're helped into the cab by two veterans, young men about their own age, who have had their faces destroyed in various ways. I was struck with the irony of these beautiful athletes, who are going to go off to Paris and compete, while these other young men had been to France ten years before and had been destroyed. That was the immediate impulse."

Elements from Rostkowski's family history found their way into the book as well. "My mother always talked about her uncles who had been in the war," she tells *AAYA*. "All of them came back, but one had been gassed in the Argonne, and one caught measles on the troop ship and was quarantined at Gibraltar. There were all these stories and pictures of young men in uniform and that was all part of the family lore. It seemed very natural to set the story during that period. But part of the story also arose from what I was seeing in my own life about the war in Vietnam—my generation's war. Men in that war were not accepted when they returned either."

Some of Andrew's bitterness comes from the fact that he knows he is scarred for life, with no hope of good reconstructive surgery. "In the research I did I learned that the medical technology at that time was still primitive; it was right after the war that doctors began experimenting with reconstructive surgery," Rostkowski tells *AAYA*. "All they were really doing at that time was reconstructing a mouth so you'd have something to eat with, and a nose so you could breathe. Annie's father says in the book that Andrew will have surgery for years to come. My own father's work in medicine entered into the book; my father worked at a Catholic hospital in Ogden. But my father's work during World War II was mostly with soldiers about to be sent off and with prisoners of war; I don't think he ever had to see that."

One of the most popular themes of the story is the budding relationship between Annie and Andrew. "Annie's feelings toward Andrew is partly family related—she's reacting in part to the loss of her uncle," Rostkowski explains in her *AAYA* interview. "She idealizes and romanticizes him. I don't think she has much of an idea of what he's been through. At thirteen, she's not sure what she's feeling; she can probably feel what she calls love for him because he's unattainable—he's older and because of what has been done to him, he's safe.

"I think Andrew is very clear about the limits of their relationship. Almost every letter I get from kids about that book asks for a sequel in which Andrew and Annie get married. That's what they see in the book. I always write back and say No, it will not happen. For one thing, Andrew probably will not live very long. They think that he will be made all right, and everything will be fine, but he won't—he's going to have a really awful life. He will spend the rest of his life in great pain because of the damage to his lungs. He would never consider any kind of romantic relationship with Annie."

Dealing with the Consequences of War

After the Dancing Days also reflects a modern attitude toward war that historically only emerged after World War I. "I think that after the war there was a reaction about the real worthlessness of what had happened," Rostkowski explains to *AAYA*. "Annie sees what has happened to Andrew and she has to come to terms with the really ghastly way her uncle died. I've been influenced greatly by Wilfred Owen's poetry, which was being published even before his death—'Dulce et Decorum Est' and others. People were beginning to think this, although the official view hadn't changed yet. The book has been informed by the over-seventy years that have passed since then, and we've realized what a horrible thing it really was.

"I've always been interested in the impact of war on the people at home. I was in college, graduate school, and in my first years of teaching during the Vietnam war. My older boy was still young while I was writing *After the Dancing Days*, and I was quite horrified by the contrast between his 'G.I. Joe' action figures and the culture of violence, and the contrast between that and what really happened."

By the author of *After the Dancing Days*
MARGARET I. ROSTKOWSKI
MOON Dancer

In this 1995 work, Miranda experiences both love and conflict when she takes a backpacking trip in Southern Utah.

The Best of Friends is set in the Vietnam War era, during the 1960s. It tells the story of how two young friends, Dan and Will, and Dan's younger sister Sarah, come to terms with themselves, their families, and their time. Dan, a straight-A student, has frequent arguments with his demanding father, head of the local draft board and a former soldier himself. "Dan has made a hobby of parachute jumping," explains Nancy Vasilakis in *Horn Book*. "Only when he is up in the air alone, with nothing to push him, does he feel completely happy." Will, the reviewer explains, is much more relaxed and is "one of the few people willing to put up with the stubborn, moody Dan." Sarah, a budding antiwar activist, defies her father by opposing the war in Vietnam. Dan refuses to fight in the war or to go to school as his father wishes. Will volunteers for active duty. Sarah is torn between her antiwar feelings and her budding romance with Will. "Ultimately, Dan and Will choose very different options," writes Diane Roback in *Publishers Weekly*, "yet each wins independence." "*Best of Friends*," concludes Gerry Larson in *School Library Journal*, "adds a new dimension to the growing body of literature on the Vietnam era."

"*The Best of Friends*, since it deals with the subject of Vietnam, has not been widely read," Rostkowski explains to *AAYA*. "I think kids nowadays are a little more sophisticated about the culture of warfare and they recognize the horror of it. I've had some very interesting letters from kids about *After the Dancing Days*, but the issue of heroism has not been something that they've thought a lot about.

"I did a fair amount of activism against the war and the character of Chris is based on my activities. The whole atmosphere—every night seeing the body counts and the pictures of the soldiers on television—was so much a part of everyday life then. Being a teacher and a mother of boys, the war became something deeply personal for me. Another teacher confided in me that he felt that if he failed a boy, that boy would have to leave school and then be drafted, sent to Vietnam and killed. My own students ten years ago, when they found out I was writing a story about World War I, said, 'Why don't you write about Vietnam? We don't know anything about that war.' It's ten years later, and they now know even less."

The three major young people in *The Best of Friends* offer three distinct viewpoints about the Vietnam War. Sarah is vehemently opposed to the war on ethical grounds. Will sees entering the military as his only real hope for a good job. Dan has the option of deferring or avoiding military service altogether because of his scholastic record. "Sarah realizes that she cares for Will before he made the decision to go," Rostkowski tells *AAYA*. "Dan is really occupying the middle ground. At that time, if you were going to school you were F2, and you didn't have to be involved. It isn't until Dan realizes that Will's going to be over there that he realized that he can't continue his college career. Sarah really does feel angry toward

If you enjoy the works of Margaret I. Rostkowski, you may also want to check out the following books and films:

John Marsden, *So Much to Tell You*, 1987.
Bobbie Ann Mason, *In Country*, 1985.
The novels in Susan Beth Pfeffer's "Sebastian Sisters" series.
Born on the Fourth of July, Universal, 1989.

Will for his decision, and although the three of them meet again at the end of the story they aren't really reconciled. It's a very unhappy ending, but it seems to be a very realistic one."

Dan's final moment of revelation—the time he realizes that he will defy his father and refuse both the college deferment and the draft—comes during a parachute jump. "The parachute jump in *The Best of Friends* is based in part on one that I took at the age of nineteen," Rostkowski explains. "I had a friend who talked me into it. It was something I really wanted to do, and Will's experience was very much my own. I was absolutely terrified, but I really loved it once I got out of the plane and was on my way down. That became something I wanted to use in the book, and then it became a metaphor for Dan. The ending of that book was very difficult and I didn't know what was going to happen. I realized while he was falling that he wasn't focused on the jump and he was going to hurt himself on landing." "Dan and his father have a very uneasy relationship," the author continues. "Dan's very much like his father. He's very rigid, very demanding, he's quite cold—he's his father's son. I find it fun to write characters like Dan who aren't very nice, who are knotty. They're the ones that stick with me."

Athletics and Anthropology

Rostkowski's third novel for young adults, *Moon Dancer*, differs from *The Best of Friends* and *After the Dancing Days* in several ways; it is more contemporary and warfare is not a dominating theme in it. The story begins when four young people—fifteen-year-old athletic Miranda, her older sister Jenny, their cousin Emily, and her friend Max—make a backpacking tour of the southern Utah wilderness. The trip is Emily's idea: she is looking for some ancient Native American artwork discovered by a pioneer woman named Katie, who wrote about them in her diary. Emily hopes to discover the Anasazi artworks Katie talks about and document them for a school project. The search becomes special for Miranda when she begins to take an interest in Emily's project for her own sake. "Reality interrupts her daydreaming when she finds herself alone in the moonlight with Max," writes Lois Buckman in the *ALAN Review,* "and realizes that she doesn't have to live her life in her sister's shadow." "Rostkowski is wonderfully conscious of balance," declares *School Library Journal* contributor Vanessa Elder. "Her style is friendly, frank, and light, but it's also spiritual, physical, and intense. She celebrates what is natural and joyful, but also accepts what is awkward and painful." "This coming-of-age novel is truly refreshing," the reviewer concludes. "It's mystical, and yet it's down-to-earth at the same time."

"*Moon Dancer* is more contemporary and more personal, because I was trying to express my feelings about the wilderness and what being in the wilderness has meant to me," Rostkowski explains to *AAYA.* "I wanted to communicate two things in this book: Katie's story, and the sense of the wilderness being a refuge and a learning place for Miranda. I've never been an athlete, although I'm very physically active—I do a lot of walking and skiing, but I see that from observing my students. I've seen over the past twenty-five years the wonderful way in which girls have come into their own athletically, and how they're very proud of being strong and healthy. I saw Mira that way—athletic and enjoying it. You gain confidence in yourself when you use your body as an athlete and personal growth is a big part of that. Miranda's real delight in being able to do physical things is something I also enjoy, and I see my female students enjoying it too."

One of the major conflicts in *Moon Dancer* is between Mira and her older sister Jenny. Jenny is very attractive physically, and she is very aware of her attractiveness. Miranada feels dowdy by comparison, and it is a sign of her growth when by the end of the novel she begins to assert her own attractiveness. "Jenny, on the surface, is shallow, but there's more to her," Rostkowski states. "She's that pretty girl we all see and dismiss sometimes, but she has depth. Seventeen-year-olds are the most self-absorbed people on the planet.

That's the age I teach, and I see Jenny that way. She has been rewarded for being an attractive person, but she is sensitive to Miranda—she doesn't go on the evening hike with Miranda and Max, because she's very aware that's something Miranda would really like. She's strong in her own way, bright and funny, but she's very much obsessed with physical comfort and being pretty. Miranda's very much in Jenny's shadow."

The scenery of the book, the stories of the early settlers, and the Native American artwork are all taken from real, existing places and histories. "Everything in the book except for the figure of Walking Woman I have actually seen," Rostkowski states. "I've seen the breech birth and the Kokapelli figure, and I've done enough research to know that Walking Woman could have existed—there are figures holding hands and figures with their feet turned. I've seen a lot of them down there. I really wanted to transmit the mystery of seeing them into the book. Katie is not historical, but there were women who homesteaded all over the west, and I know of a women in Utah who lived alone until she was ninety years old.

"The finding of the drawings is based on the story of Richard Weatherall, who discovered Mesa Verde when he was out looking for cattle. The Navajo knew about them and were very afraid of them. They did not go into those areas. I had a Navajo student who told me I shouldn't go to those places. When I said, 'Why not?,' he said 'They're really dangerous and those were bad people.' When I came back he told me that he'd talked to his grandmother and she had told him that the reason they were bad people was because they did things with snakes. And the Navajo are very frightened of snakes. But the Hopi, who are descended from the Anasazi, do the Snake Dance carrying the snakes in their teeth. So there's still a lot of lore around those canyons.

"I find being in the wilderness very restorative, a place of refuge. I never felt frightened when I was in the wilderness. I've always felt safe. That was something I wanted to get across in the book. There are so few children's books that talk about nature in those ways. Nature in most children's books is an antagonist—something to survive. There's a very small number of books that feature nature—most of them are urban—and the ones that do show nature as the enemy, so I was very pleased that I could see this in a different way."

Rostkowski regards writing as one of the most difficult and, at the same time, one of the most rewarding of creative activities. "I teach an essay writing class, and I tell the kids, 'You're all looking at me as if you think there's something I can tell you that will make this easier, and there isn't,'" she tells *AAYA*. "I'll give them an assignment, and they'll say, 'It's hard,' and I say, 'Right.' There's no easier way to do it. You have do it, and you have to fail at it, and you have to try again. A lot of people don't have that patience; they want some kind of trick to make it easy, and there isn't one. All three of my books I wrote and rewrote and rewrote; I have three boxes in my basement full of manuscripts. It's like any art; it takes time, concentration and focus."

■ Works Cited

Buckman, Lois, review of *Moon Dancer*, *ALAN Review*, winter, 1996.

Elder, Vanessa, review of *Moon Dancer*, *School Library Journal*, September, 1995, p. 220.

Larson, Gerry, review of *The Best of Friends*, *School Library Journal*, September, 1989, pp. 276-77.

Piehl, Kathy, "Margaret I. Rostkowski," *Twentieth-Century Young Adult Writers*, St. James Press, 1994, pp. 566-68.

Roback, Diane, review of *The Best of Friends*, *Publishers Weekly*, October 13, 1989, pp. 54-55.

Rostkowski, Margaret I., comments in *Twentieth-Century Young Adult Writers*, St. James Press, 1994, pp. 566-68.

Rostkowski, Margaret I., interview with Kenneth R. Shepherd for *Authors and Artists for Young Adults*, February 10, 1997.

Vasilakis, Nancy, review of *The Best of Friends*, *Horn Book*, March, 1990, p. 210.

■ For More Information See

BOOKS

Gallo, Donald R., editor and compiler, *Speaking for Ourselves, Too*, National Council of Teachers of English, 1993.

PERIODICALS

English Journal, December, 1989, p. 76.
Horn Book, January/February, 1989.
Publishers Weekly, June 26, 1995, pp. 108-9.

—Sketch by Kenneth R. Shepherd

Gillian Rubinstein

cil, London, administrative officer, 1965-66; Tom Stacey Ltd., London, editor, 1969-71; freelance journalist and film critic, 1971-74; freelance writer, 1986—. Writer-in-residence, Magpie Theatre, 1989. *Member:* Australian Society of Authors, National Book Council (Australia).

Personal

Full name Gillian Margaret Rubinstein; born August 29, 1942, in Potten End, Berkhamstead, Hertfordshire, England; daughter of Thomas Kenneth (a research chemist) and Margaret Jocelyn (Wigg) Hanson; married Ion Will (marriage ended); married Philip Eli Rubinstein (a health educator), 1973; children: Matthew, Tessa, Susannah. *Education:* Lady Margaret Hall, Oxford, B.A. (with honors), 1964; Stockwell College, London, post-graduate certificate of education, 1973.

Addresses

Home—29 Seaview Road, Lynton, SA 5062, Australia. *Agent*—Caroline Lurie, Australian Literary Management, 2-A Armstrong St., Middle Park, VIC 3206, Australia.

Career

London School of Economics, London, England, research assistant, 1964-65; Greater London Coun-

Awards, Honors

Children's Book Council of Australia honour book, 1987, Children's Literature Peace Prize, 1987, Adelaide Festival of Arts National Children's Book Award, 1988, and Young Australians Best Book Award, 1990, all for *Space Demons;* Australia Council Literature Board senior fellowship, 1988, 1989-92; New South Wales Premier's Award, 1988, and Children's Book Council of Australia honour book, 1989, both for *Answers to Brut;* Children's Book Council of Australia honour book, 1989, and New South Wales Family Therapy Association Family Award for Children's Books—Highly Recommended, 1989, both for *Melanie and the Night Animal;* Children's Book Council of Australia Book of the Year for Older Readers, 1989, Adelaide Festival of Arts National Children's Book Award, 1990, and shortlisted for Victorian Premier's Award Alan Marshall Prize, all for *Beyond the Labyrinth;* shortlisted for Children's Book Council of Australia Book of the Year, 1990, and Children's Book Council of Australia notable book citation, both for *Skymaze;* Children's Book Council of Australia notable book citation, for *Flashback, the Amazing*

Adventures of a Film Horse; Children's Book Council of Australia notable book citation, 1992, for *Squawk and Screech;* Children's Book Council of Australia notable book citation, 1992, shortlisted for New South Wales State Literary Award, and shortlisted for Victorian Premier's Award Alan Marshall Prize, all for *At Ardilla;* shortlisted for Children's Book Council of Australia Book of the Year, 1992, and Children's Book Council of Australia notable book citation, both for *Dog In, Cat Out;* Children's Book Council of Australia honour book, 1993, Best Books for the Teen Age citation, New York Public Library, 1996, and shortlisted for Victorian Premier's Award Alan Marshall Prize, all for *Galax-Arena;* shortlisted for Children's Book Council of Australia Book of the Year, 1994, and Children's Book Council of Australia notable book citation, 1994, both for *The Giant's Tooth;* Children's Book Council of Australia Book of the Year, 1995, shortlisted for New South Wales State Literary Awards, 1995, and shortlisted for Victorian Premier's Award Alan Marshall Prize, all for *Foxspell;* Children's Book Council of Australia notable book citation, 1996, for *Jake and Pete.*

Writings

JUVENILE FICTION

Space Demons (novel), Omnibus/Penguin (Adelaide), 1986, Dial Books (New York), 1988.

Melanie and the Night Animal, Omnibus/Penguin, 1988.

Answers to Brut, Omnibus/Penguin, 1988.

Beyond the Labyrinth (novel), Hyland House (Melbourne), 1988, Orchard (New York), 1990.

Skymaze (second in the computer game trilogy), Omnibus/Penguin (Adelaide), 1993, Orchard (New York), 1991.

Flashback, the Amazing Adventures of a Film Horse, Penguin, 1990.

At Ardilla, Omnibus, 1991.

Squawk and Screech (chapter book), illustrated by Craig Smith, Omnibus, 1991.

Dog In, Cat Out, illustrated by Ann James, Omnibus, 1991, Ticknor and Fields (New York), 1993.

Keep Me Company, illustrated by Lorraine Hannay, Penguin, 1991.

Mr. Plunkett's Pool (picture book), illustrated by Terry Denton, Mark Macleod/Random House (Milson's Point), 1992.

Galax-Arena, Hyland House (Melbourne), 1992, Simon & Schuster (New York), 1995.

The Giant's Tooth (chapter book), Viking, 1993.

Foxspell, Hyland House, 1994, Simon & Schuster, 1996.

Jake and Pete (chapter book), illustrated by Terry Denton, Random House (Milson's Point), 1995.

Peanut the Pony Rat (chapter book), Heinemann (London), 1995.

Shinkei (third in the computer game trilogy), Omnibus, 1995.

Sharon Keep Your Hair On, illustrated by David Mackintosh, Random House (Milson's Point), 1996.

Witch Music (collected short stories), Hyland House, 1996.

Annie's Brother's Suit (collected short stories), Hyland House, 1996.

Jake and Pete and the Stray Dogs (chapter book), Random House, 1997.

Pure Chance (junior novel), Walker Books (London), 1998.

Hurray for the Kafe Karaoke, illustrated by David Mackintosh, Random House, 1998.

Under the Cat's Eye (novel previously called *Nexhoath Nine*), Hodder Headline (Sydney), 1997, Simon & Schuster (New York), 1998.

The Pirate's Ship (sequel to *The Giant's Tooth*), illustrated by Craig Smith, Viking, forthcoming.

The Fairy's Wings (sequel to *The Giant's Tooth*), forthcoming.

PLAYS

New Baby, for Magpie Theatre, 1989.

Alice in Wonderland (adaptation) for Magpie Theatre, 1989.

Melanie and the Night Animal (adaptation) for Patch Theatre, 1990.

Paula, for Patch Theatre, 1992.

Galax-Arena (adaptation) for Come Out 95, Patch Theatre, and Adelaide Festival Centre Trust (AFCT).

Wake Baby, for Out of the Box and Company Skylark, first presented at the Queensland Festival of Early Childhood, 1996.

Jake and Pete (adaptation) for Theatre of Image, first presented at the Sydney Theatre Company, 1997.

Each Beach (original play) for Patch Theatre, first presented at the Adelaide Festival Centre, 1997.

OTHER

(Compiler) *After Dark,* Omnibus/Penguin, 1988.

(Compiler) *Before Dawn,* Omnibus/Penguin, 1988.

Has also contributed numerous short stories to anthologies including *After Dark, State of the Heart, Dream Time, Bizarre, Landmarks, The Pattern Maker,* and *Celebrate,* and several articles for periodicals including *Magpies, Literacy for the New Millenium, Island Magazine,* and *Australian Magazine.*

Work in Progress

Across the Nightingale Floor, a fantasy with a Japanese historical setting; *South Road,* a novel about families and horses in the southern part of Adelaide.

Adaptations

Space Demons was adapted for the stage by Richard Tulloch and performed in Australia in 1989.

Sidelights

Although Australian author Gillian Rubinstein's best-known books are her science fiction and fantasy stories, her works attract readers who do not normally enjoy those genres. She also uses the genres to explore family and relationship issues as they affect children and young adults. In books such as *Space Demons* and its sequel *Skymaze, Beyond the Labyrinth, Galax-Arena,* and *Foxspell,* Rubinstein investigates the boundaries between childhood and adulthood as well as between imagination and reality. "Her tightly plotted narratives move seamlessly from reality to fantasy," *Twentieth-Century Young Adult Writers* contributor Agnes Nieuwenhuizen states, "and, while they incorporate tough issues, they do so in ways that seem to both entertain and empower readers."

Rubinstein's protagonists tend to learn cooperation and responsibility from their experiences. They confront strong emotions—including fear, love, and hate—and feelings such as insecurity. Her characters learn to confront these feelings in a forthright, positive, and constructive manner. "Many of my books," she tells *Something about the Author (SATA),* "have the underlying theme that 'we must love one another or die.' I don't think human beings have a very good track record in this area, and sometimes I despair of us ever getting it right, but I keep plugging away at the idea that if we love and respect the planet we live on, the other

species we share it with, and each other, then our lives won't have been wasted."

A Wartime Upbringing

Much of the material Rubinstein draws on comes from her own life. She was born in the village of Potten End, near Berkhamstead in Hertfordshire, England, during World War II. "My husband says that after I was born things started looking up for the Allies," the author writes in her essay in *Something about the Author Autobiography Series (SAAS).* "But it must have been an anxious time for my parents, starting a family. My father, as a research chemist, was considered to be on essential war work, so he stayed at home throughout the war. The only major excitement was when his laboratory was bombed by mistake by a German plane dropping its bombs too late and missing London." "As a child," she continues, "I was always in some dramatic state or other, either deliriously happy or desperately miserable. I cried easily and fell into terrible rages. My parents described me as exasperating, or more kindly, as highly strung."

Rubinstein describes her own family life as uneasy. Her parents were not well-matched, and they had many personality conflicts. Her father was a scholar who had entered Oxford University on scholarships and earned his Ph.D. degree there. He also, Rubinstein reveals in *SAAS,* had a serious drinking problem. Her mother, on the other hand, was a very social woman, partly handicapped by a childhood bout of osteomyelitis. "She had to undergo many painful operations and spend long periods in hospital, and had to wear a leg brace. She was left with a deep scar and ongoing arthritis," the author explains. "But her spirits were undamaged. She was a very attractive woman who loved company and parties. She was also strong willed and sharp tongued. . . . With only bridge and charity work for outlets, she had too much energy to be a comfortable person to live with. I spent a lot of time as a child studying her to find out what sort of mood she was in."

Gillian and her sister Jocelyn found additional support outside their immediate family. Lavendar Helen Hatt-Cook, her husband John, and her two children, Mark and Pippa, became close family friends. The two families originally met during

World War II, and formed a close attachment for each other. "When the war ended and we started going away on summer holidays," Rubinstein explains in *SAAS*, "we always went with the Hatt-Cooks, to Devon, Cornwall or Guernsey in the Channel Islands. Later when my mother and my stepfather went to live in Nigeria my sister and I made out home with the Hatt-Cooks, and they became like a foster family to us. I drew on this situation for some of the feelings Victoria has in *Beyond the Labyrinth*." The same summer holidays supplied memories that went into Rubinstein's 1991 novel *At Ardilla*. Later childhood memories of English village life inspired *Mr. Plunkett's Pool*, her 1992 picture book.

The tension between Rubinstein's parents led directly to their divorce in the mid-1950s. "Their

In this 1993 novel, four young people are drawn into a computer game's alternate reality.

relationship had deteriorated beyond saving," the author recalls in her *SAAS* entry, "and the fights and arguments had escalated." After her father left, she remembers, the tension in the house lessened, but other pressures emerged. "Even though the atmosphere in the house was better and my mother did all she could the soften the shock, I was devastated," she states. "No one else in my school, no one else I knew, had divorced parents. My strongest feeling was one of terrible shame. I couldn't bear to tell anyone." The shock of the revelation—divorce was regarded as disgraceful in England at that time—may have contributed to the strong stammer Rubinstein developed around this time. Both her parents later remarried. Her mother and stepfather accepted a position in Nigeria, and her father died in an automobile accident a few years after his remarriage. The two girls stayed at boarding school in England, dividing their holidays between visiting their mother in Africa and staying with the Hatt-Cooks. "My parents spent eight years in Nigeria and the pattern of my life," Rubinstein states in *SAAS*, "became one of spending the long summer holidays with them in Kano, and later Lagos, the school terms at Queen Anne's [boarding school], until I went to Oxford in 1961, and the holidays at Whiteparish with the Hatt-Cooks."

An Emerging Writer

Rubinstein did very well in her final exams at school, and won a place at Lady Margaret Hall at Oxford University to study modern language. She decided to read Spanish and French, influenced by the large French-speaking population she had met in Africa and the great love she developed for Spanish language and culture. At Oxford she was introduced to drama and began to work with the Worcester College Players and the Oxford University Dramatic Society as a props person and stage manager. "I enjoyed stage management for its own sake," she recalls in *SAAS*, "but I was also fired with ambition to write for the theatre, and did in fact write a one act play for an OUDS competition." After graduation she turned to a succession of jobs, finally "ending up as the Arts and Entertainment Editor on *Chambers's Encyclopaedia Year Book*" in London. During the early 1970s, she returned to school to earn her teaching certificate and "worked as a part-time cook in a 'stately home,' Oxenhoath in Kent, in return for a flat in the old servants' quarters. It was an extraordinary experience which I've always wanted to write about. My latest novel, *Nexhoath Nine*, is based on this house."

In 1973 Rubinstein married Philip Rubinstein and the couple relocated to Australia. They settled first in Sydney, then in Byron Bay, and finally in Adelaide. Their three children were born in Australia, and Rubinstein credits them for influencing her decision to become an author of juvenile and young adult fiction. "I didn't know anything about Australian adult culture," she says in her *SAAS* article, "but my children were growing up as young Australians and I knew their world. I wanted to write books that they would enjoy reading, that spoke to them about their concerns and their problems, that didn't shy away from describing the world they lived in with all its cruelties and dangers but that gave them hope and confidence in the abiding human virtues of courage, compassion and unselfishness."

The Australian culture also contributed to Rubinstein's development as a writer. "When my son was 11 he gave up reading novels—all he did was play computer games and read computer magazines," she tells *SATA*. "There were simply no books around that he thought looked interesting. I thought I could write something that would appeal to him and in 1985 I gave myself three months to see if I could write a novel. At the end of three months I had a manuscript of 42,000 words—the first version of *Space Demons*. The first publisher I sent it to rejected it, but the second, Omnibus Books, said they would be interested in it if I could rewrite it. I went through two more versions before it was accepted—and taught me the important lesson that books aren't written, they are rewritten!"

Negative Emotions

Space Demons was Rubinstein's first successful novel. It attracted critical attention after its publication in Australia for its forthright confrontation of hatred and fear, and for the ways four young people—Andrew, Ben, Mario, and Elaine—react to and deal with them. *Space Demons* opens with Andrew Hayford, the neglected son of well-to-do parents, receiving a new computer game. Although the game has no instruction manual, Andrew guesses that its object is to destroy the video demons with his laser gun. "What he discovers

later," says Susan Rogers in *School Library Journal*, "is that the game feeds on the preexisting alienation and hostility of its players in order to pull them into the reality level." Gradually Andrew and his companions are sucked into the reality of the "Space Demons" game, and it is only after they learn to overcome their hostility and work together that they manage to escape from the game's alternate reality. *Skymaze* is the sequel to *Space Demons*, and once again it takes the four young people into an alternate reality where they are forced to confront their weaknesses, prejudices, and fears. "Each book," writes John Foster in *Children's Literature in Education*, "illustrates the power of a negative emotion, hate in the former and fear in the latter."

All of the protagonists in *Space Demons* and *Skymaze* come from unhappy or broken families, like Rubinstein herself. "Andrew's parents break up in *Space Demons*," Foster explains, "and he lives uneasily with his mother, stepfather, and troublesome stepbrother in *Skymaze*; Ben's parents are teachers and seldom at home, while his older brother bullies him, especially in the second novel; Mario's parents wished he had been a girl and his older brother makes fun of him; and Elaine's father is a drifter while her mother has run away, so that she is insecure in *Space Demons* and left with a foster family in *Skymaze*." Each of them carries their emotional baggage into the gaming arena, where it can become deadly. "The growing understanding in the children that they must cooperate to defeat the dangerous game," Foster concludes, "leads inevitably to the improvement in their relationships in *Space Demons*." In *Skymaze*, timid Mario must overcome his fears in order to release himself and the other three from the game. "Rubinstein convincingly melds the two worlds of fantasy and reality, revealing how inner and outer selves connect," writes Cathi Dunn MacRae in *Wilson Library Bulletin*. "Her characters' authentic conflicts seem intense enough to set the maze in motion. Games are explored on several levels, from power struggles . . . to dance exercises probing inner fears."

Rubinstein uses another game motif to probe externalized fears, racism, and sexism in *Beyond the Labyrinth*. Fourteen-year-old Brenton Trethewan and his younger friend Victoria are the protagonists of the story. Brenton "is sharply different from his brothers and sister," states *Horn Book* reviewer Ann A. Flowers, "and has become the outsider, the scapegoat, in his heedless, noisy, materialistic family." Victoria is a visitor; she has been sent to board with the Trethewans while her parents work in Africa. Brenton expresses his alienation through devotion to a "Dungeons and Dragons"-like role-playing game called *Labyrinth of Dead Ends.* "He bases all his decisions on the fall of the dice that he always carries with him," Flowers explains, "and plays 'Choose Your Own Adventure' games constantly." Trouble arises when Vicky and Brenton discover Cal, an alien anthropologist, on a nearby beach. "What is interesting," declares Foster, "is that Cal is both female and black, factors that affect others' reactions to her. Through this ploy, Rubinstein demonstrates the racism and sexism which underlie much of Australian society." When Cal falls ill with a viral infection, Brenton and Vicky realize that they must return her to her home planet. In a finish reminiscent of the "Choose Your Own Adventure" books Brenton loves, Rubinstein confronts the reader with alternative endings that describe different futures for Cal, Brenton, and Vicky.

Beyond the Labyrinth attracted critical attention for its use of language as well as for its theme. While *Space Demons* and *Skymaze* are written in a relatively conventional format, *Beyond the Labyrinth* jumps backward and forward in time, mixing flashbacks with sections set in the current time—all of them written in present tense. The book also uses much controversial language. "After it won its award," Foster explains, "a reporter for a television current-affairs program read excerpts from the novel to startled (and often horrified) members of the public in the main shopping street of Rubinstein's hometown, Adelaide, and asked them whether they would allow *their* children to be submitted to such material." Many libraries refused to shelve the book, citing its language as a factor in their decision. Despite this critical uproar, all three of Rubinstein's early novels have been popular with young adult audiences. *Space Demons* in particular proved very popular with readers; it was dramatized and performed onstage throughout Australia in 1989.

Gaming, in the form of sports, again becomes an issue in *Galax-Arena*, Rubinstein's 1995 psychological thriller. *Galax-Arena* is the story of three young siblings, Peter, Joella, and Liane, who are kidnapped and taken by spaceship to the planet Vexa. Hythe, their trainer, begins preparing them for a life in the arena, where they will perform

If you enjoy the works of Gillian Rubinstein, you may also want to check out the following books and films:

Monica Hughes, *Invitation to the Game,* 1990.
William Sleator, *Interstellar Pig,* 1984.
Rosemay Wells, *Through the Hidden Door,* 1987.
WarGames, MGM, 1983.

dangerous gymnastics for the amusement of the native Vexans. "Peter soon shows unrivalled gymnastic skills," explains Flowers in her *Horn Book* review of the book, "and Liane somehow turns her toy puppet, Bro Rabbit, into a menacing prophet of things to come." Joella, however, proves incompetent at gymnastics and is placed in a tank, where she is destined to become a sort of pet for the Vexans. However, this "situation," explains Chris Sherman in *Booklist,* " . . . allows her to learn the truth about her captivity and acquire the courage and means to escape. Rubinstein's *Galax-Arena* is chillingly real—from the Peb pidgin language to the children's gradual loss of innocence," the reviewer concludes. Flowers also praises the book, comparing it to William Golding's *Lord of the Flies.*

Alienation takes a fantastic twist in *Foxspell.* Twelve-year-old Tod is caught in a difficult family life. His father has deserted the family and his mother has been forced to move in with her mother to save money. Tod is facing extreme pressure to join a local teenage gang, and he finds escape in the wildlife of a local quarry. "Eventually," writes Steven Engelfried in *School Library Journal,* "he meets a spirit fox that allows him to transform into an animal himself." Dan Russell, the fox spirit, "tempts Tod with an offer of peace and immortality if he will assume a fox shape forever," explains *Booklist* contributor Chris Sherman. Although Tod enjoys life as a fox, his human self is shaken by the animal violence that the shape unleashes in him. As a human, he enjoys the excitement and danger of gang life. "The harrowing climax takes place when one of his friends is accidentally killed during a gang escapade," declares Flowers in *Horn Book;* "the ending leaves the reader in doubt as to whether Tod can resolve the tension between a natural and a human life or escape permanently from his misery by becoming a fox." "Rubinstein does not depict one mode of existence as better than the other," states Christine Heppermann in *Five Owls.* "Hers is more a plea for sympathy between species." "Rubinstein intertwines the two stories with skill," writes *Voice of Youth Advocates* contributor Deborah A. Feulner, "developing her characters fully."

Rubinstein continues to follow her stated goal of writing stories that draw and speak to alienated young readers. Yet the books she writes also serve as a connection with her own past. "Most of all," she concludes in *SAAS,* "when I write I want to spin the spell of words that enthralls the reader and takes them into the magic world of the imagination that inspired and consoled me when I was young. When I look back over my life, I can see that everything I've ever felt, whether it's been good or bad at the time, has all contributed to the emotion that goes into my writing."

Works Cited

Engelfried, Steven, review of *Foxspell, School Library Journal,* September, 1996, p. 206.

Feulner, Deborah A., review of *Foxspell, Voice of Youth Advocates,* December, 1995, p. 282.

Flowers, Ann A., review of *Beyond the Labyrinth, Horn Book,* January-February, 1991, pp. 75-76.

Flowers, Ann A., review of *Galax-Arena, Horn Book,* November-December, 1995, p. 206.

Flowers, Ann A., review of *Foxspell, Horn Book,* November-December, 1996, p. 747.

Foster, John, "'Your Part in This Adventure Is Over, You Have Lost': Gillian Rubinstein's Novels for Older Readers," *Children's Literature in Education,* June, 1991, pp. 121-27.

Heppermann, Christine, review of *Foxspell, Five Owls,* January/February, 1997, p. 62.

Macrae, Cathi Dunn, "The Young Adult Perplex: Reading Teenagers Enjoy," *Wilson Library Bulletin,* March, 1994, pp. 124-25.

Nieuwenhuizen, Agnes, "Gillian Rubinstein," *Twentieth-Century Young Adult Writers,* 1st edition, St. James Press, 1994, pp. 568-69.

Rogers, Susan, review of *Space Demons* and *Skymaze, School Library Journal,* March, 1992, p. 177.

Rubinstein, Gillian, comments in *Something about the Author,* Volume 68, Gale, 1992, pp. 202-3.

Rubinstein, Gillian, essay in *Something about the Author Autobiography Series,* Volume 25, Gale, 1997.

Sherman, Chris, review of *Galax-Arena, Booklist,* October 15, 1995, p. 403.

Sherman, Chris, review of *Foxspell, Booklist,* October 15, 1996, pp. 414-15.

For More Information See

BOOKS

Children's Literature Review, Volume 35, Gale, 1995, pp. 207-13.

Twentieth-Century Children's Writers, 4th edition, St. James Press, 1995, pp. 844-45.

PERIODICALS

Bulletin of the Center for Children's Books, January, 1997, p. 184.

Horn Book, May-June, 1991, pp. 339-40.

Locus, February, 1989, p. 50.

New York Times Book Review, March 30, 1997, p. 18.

School Library Journal, April, 1991, p. 123.*

—Sketch by Kenneth R. Shepherd

Sir Walter Scott

■ Personal

Also wrote under name Jedediah Cleishbotham; born August 15, 1771, in Edinburgh, Scotland; died September 21, 1832, in Abbotsford, Scotland; buried in Dryburgh Abbey, Berwick, Scotland; son of Walter (a lawyer) and Anne (Rutherford) Scott; married Charlotte Carpenter (Anglicized from Charpentier), December 24, 1797 (died, 1826); children: Charlotte Sophia, Walter, Anne, Charles. *Education*: Attended University of Edinburgh, 1782.

■ Career

Novelist, poet, short story writer, biographer, historian, critic, and editor. Apprentice in law under his father; called to the bar, 1792; appointed sheriff-deputy, Selkirkshire, Scotland, 1799; appointed clerk of sessions court, Edinburgh, Scotland, 1806; silent partner, James Ballantyne Printing, Edinburgh, 1809-1826; writer, late 1700s to 1832. Cofounder of *Quarterly Review*, 1809.

■ Awards, Honors

Named a Baronet, 1819.

■ Writings

POEMS

The Lay of the Last Minstrel, Longman, Hurst, Rees & Orme, and A. Constable, 1805, I. Riley, 1806.
Ballads and Lyrical Pieces, A. Constable, 1806, Etheridge & Bliss, 1807.
Marmion: A Tale of Flodden Field, Hopkins & Earle, 1808.
The Lady of the Lake, W. Wells & T. B. Wait, 1810.
The Vision of Don Roderick, T. B. Wait, 1811.
Rokeby, J. Cushing, 1813.
The Bridal of Triermain, or The Vale of St. John. In Three Cantos, M. Thomas, 1813.
The Lord of the Isles, R. Scott, 1815.
The Field of Waterloo, T. B. Wait, 1815.
The Dance of Death, and Other Poems, M. Carey, 1816.
Harold the Dauntless, J. Eastburn, 1817.
Miscellaneous Poems, A. Constable, 1820.
Halidon Hill, S. Campbell, 1822.

NOVELS

Waverley, three volumes, A. Constable, 1814; one volume, Wells & Lilly, 1815; two volumes, Van Winkle & Wiley, 1815.
Guy Mannering, two volumes, West & Richardson, 1815.

The Antiquary, two volumes, Van Winkle & Wiley, 1816.

(Under pseudonym Jedediah Cleishbotham) *Tales of My Landlord, Collected and Arranged by Jedediah Cleishbotham, Schoolmaster and Parish-Clerk of Gandercleugh* (includes *The Black Dwarf* and *Old Mortality*), four volumes, William Blackwood and John Murray, 1816; one volume, M. Thomas, 1817.

Rob Roy, two volumes, J. Eastburn, 1818.

(Under pseudonym J. Cleishbotham) *Tales of My Landlord, Second Series, Collected and Arranged by Jedediah Cleishbotham, Schoolmaster and Parish-Clerk of Gandercleugh* (includes *The Heart of Mid-Lothian*), four volumes, M. Carey & Son, 1818.

(Under pseudonym J. Cleishbotham) *Tales of My Landlord, Third Series, Collected and Arranged by Jedediah Cleishbotham, Schoolmaster and Parish-Clerk of Gandercleugh* (includes *The Bride of Lammermoor* and *A Legend of Montrose*), four volumes, Charles Wiley, W. B. Gilley, and A. T. Goodrich, 1819.

Ivanhoe, two volumes, M. Carey & Son, 1820.

The Monastery, M. Carey & Son, 1820.

The Abbot, two volumes, J & J. Harper, 1820.

Kenilworth, S. G. Goodrich, 1821.

The Pirate, two volumes, Wells & Lilly, 1822.

The Fortunes of Nigel, two volumes, T. Longworth, 1822.

Peveril of the Peak, four volumes, A. Constable, 1822; three volumes, H. C. Carey & I. Lea, 1823.

Quentin Durward, H. C. Carey & I. Lea, 1823.

St. Ronan's Well, H. C. Carey & I. Lea, 1824.

Redgauntlet, two volumes, H. C. Carey & I. Lea, 1824.

Tales of the Crusaders (includes *The Betrothed* and *The Talisman*), four volumes, E. Duyckinck, Collins & Hannay, Collins, E. Bliss & E. White, and W. B. Gilley, 1825.

Woodstock; or, The Cavalier, two volumes, H. C. Carey & I. Lea, 1826.

Chronicles of the Canongate (includes *The Highland Widow, The Two Drovers*, and *The Surgeon's Daughter*), Carey, Lea & Carey, 1827.

Chronicles of the Canongate, Second Series (includes *The Fair Maid of Perth; or, St. Valentine's Day*), Carey, Lea, & Carey, 1828.

Anne of Geierstein, two volumes, Carey, Lea, & Carey, 1829.

(Under pseudonym J. Cleishbotham) *Tales of My Landlord, Fourth and Last Series, Collected by Jedediah Cleishbotham, Schoolmaster and Parish-clerk of Gandercleugh* (includes *Count Robert of Paris* and *Castle Dangerous*), three volumes, Carey & Lea, 1832.

OTHER

(Translator) *The Chase and William and Helen: Two Ballads from the German of Gottfried Augustus Burger*, Manners & Miller, 1796.

(Translator) *Goetz of Berlichingen, with the Iron Hand: A Tragedy. Translated from the German of Goethe*, J. Bell, 1799.

The Eve of Saint John: A Border Ballad, J. Ballantyne, 1800.

(Contributor) *Tales of Wonder; Written and Collected by M. G. Lewis* (includes Scott's "Glenfinlas," "The Eve of Saint John," "Frederick and Alice," and "The Wild Huntsman"), two volumes, J. Bell, 1801.

(Editor) *Minstrelsy of the Scottish Border*, two volumes, Manners & Miller, 1802; enlarged edition, three volumes, Manners & Miller, 1803, revised 1810, published by Carey, 1813; another edition, edited by Thomas Henderson, Harrap, 1931.

(Editor) Thomas of Ercildoune, *Sir Tristrem: A Metrical Romance of the Thirteenth Century*, A. Constable, 1804.

(Editor) Henry Slingsby, *Original Memoirs, Written during the Great Civil War; Being the Life of Sir Henry Slingsby, and Memoirs of Captain Hodgson*, A. Constable, 1806.

(Editor and author of biography) John Dryden, *The Works of John Dryden*, eighteen volumes, Miller, 1808.

(Editor) Joseph Strutt, *Queehoo-Hall, A Romance; and Ancient Times, A Drama*, four volumes, J. Murray, 1808.

(Editor) George Carelton, *Memoirs of Captain George Carelton, An English Officer. . . . Written by Himself*, A. Constable, 1808.

(Editor) Robert Carey, *Memoirs of Robert Carey, Earl of Monmouth*, A. Constable, 1808.

(Editor and author of introductory essay) Ralph Sadler, *The State Papers and Letters of Sir Ralph Sadler, Knight-Banneret*, A. Constable, 1809.

(Editor) *A Collection of Scarce and Valuable Tracts* (the Somers Tracts), second edition, thirteen volumes, T. Cadell & W. Davies, 1809-15.

(Editor) *English Minstrelsy; Being a Selection of Fugitive Poetry from the Best English Authors*, two volumes, J. Ballantyne, 1810.

(Editor) Anna Seward, *The Poetical Works of Anna Seward; with Extracts from Her Literary Correspondence*, three volumes, J. Ballantyne, 1810.

(Editor) *Secret History of the Court of James the First*, two volumes, J. Ballantyne, 1811.

Character of Lord Byron, [London], 1813.

(Editor and author of notes and biography) Jonathan

Swift, *The Works of Jonathan Swift,* nineteen volumes, A. Constable, 1814.

(Author of introduction) *The Border Antiquities of England and Scotland,* two volumes, Longman, Hurst, Rees, Orme & Brown, 1814, 1817.

(Editor) James, eleventh Baron Somerville, *Memorie of the Somervilles,* two volumes, A. Constable, 1815.

(With James Hogg) *The Ettricke Garland; Being Two Excellent New Songs on the Lifting of the Banner of the House of Buccleuch, at the Great Foot-Ball Match on Carterhaugh, December 4, 1815,* J. Ballantyne, 1815.

Paul's Letters to His Kinfolk, M. Thomas, 1816.

Description of the Regalia, J. Ballantyne, 1819.

Provincial Antiquities and Picturesque Scenery of Scotland, plates by J. M. W. Turner and others, ten parts, J. Ballantyne, 1819-26; two volumes, J. & A. Arch, 1826.

(Editor and author of biographical prefaces) *Ballantyne's Novelist's Library,* ten volumes, Hurst, Robinson, 1821-24.

(Editor) *Memorials of the Haliburtons,* J. Ballantyne, 1824.

Lives of the Novelists, A. W. Galignani, 1825; revised as *Lives of Eminent Novelists and Dramatists,* F. Warne, 1887; reprinted as *Biographical Memoirs of Eminent Novelists, and Other Distinguished Persons,* Books for Libraries, 1972.

Letter to the Editor of the Edinburgh Weekly Journal [and] A Second Letter to the Editor of the Edinburgh Weekly Journal, from Malachi Malagrowther, Esq.: On the Proposed Change of Currency and Other Late Alterations, As They Affect, or Are Intended to Affect, the Kingdom of Scotland, William Blackwood, 1826; reprinted together as *Thoughts on the Proposed Change of Currency,* Barnes & Noble, 1972.

A Third Letter to the Editor of the Edinburgh Weekly Journal, from Malachi Malagrowther, Esq.: On the Proposed Change in Currency, and Other Late Alterations, As They Affect, or Are Intended to Affect, the Kingdom of Scotland, William Blackwood, 1826.

The Life of Napoleon Bonaparte, nine volumes, Carey, Lea, & Carey, 1827.

Religious Discourses by a Layman, Collins & Hannay, 1828.

The Scottish Exiles, J. Field, 1828.

Tales of a Grandfather; Being Stories Taken from Scottish History, eight volumes, Carey, Lea, & Carey, 1828-1830; reprinted as *Stories from Scottish History,* edited by Madalen Edgar, T. Y. Crowell, 1906.

The History of Scotland, two volumes in *The Cabinet Cyclopedia, Conducted by Rev. Dionysus Lardner,* Longman, Rees, Orme, Brown & Green and John Taylor, 1830.

Letters on Demonology and Witchcraft, J. & J. Harper, 1830.

The Doom of Devorgoil (melodrama), J. & J. Harper, 1830.

Autobiography of Sir Walter Scott, compiled by Henry D. Gilpin, Carey, Lea, 1831.

Tales of a Grandfather; Being Stories Taken from the History of France, two volumes, Carey & Lea, 1831.

Catalogue of the Library at Abbotsford, T. Constable, 1838, reprinted, AMS Press, 1971.

(Supposed author) *Moredun: A Tale of Twelve Hundred and Ten,* S. Low, 1855.

Essays in Chivalry, Romance, and Drama, F. Warne, 1887, reprinted, Books for Libraries, 1972.

EDITIONS AND COLLECTIONS

The Works of Walter Scott, five volumes, J. Ballantyne, 1806.

The Novels, Tales, and Romances of the Author of Waverley, thirty-one volumes, S. H. Parker, 1820-34.

The Poetical Works of Sir Walter Scott, ten volumes, A. Constable, 1825.

The Miscellaneous Prose Works of Sir Walter Scott, six volumes, R. Cadell, 1827, Wells & Lilly, 1829.

Waverley Novels (with Scott's prefaces and final revisions), forty-eight volumes, R. Cadell, 1829-33.

Miscellaneous Prose Works, edited by John Gibson Lockhart, thirty volumes, R. Cadell, 1834-46.

The Selected Poetical Works of Sir Walter Scott, R. Griffin, 1838.

Critical and Miscellaneous Essays of Sir Walter Scott, three volumes, Carey & Hart, 1841.

Waverley Poetry; Being the Poems Scattered through the Waverley Novels, Monroe & Francis, 1851.

The Miscellaneous Works of Sir Walter Scott, thirty volumes, A. & C. Black, 1870-71.

The Illustrated Excelsior Edition of the Waverley Novels, six volumes, Excelsior Publishing, 1872.

Favorite Poems, J. R. Osgood, 1877.

The Complete Poetical and Dramatic Works of Sir Walter Scott, G. Routledge, 1883.

Tales of Chivalry and the Olden Times, Selected from the Works of Sir Walter Scott, edited by William J. Rolfe, Harper, 1887.

The Waverley Novels, border edition, edited by Andrew Lang, forty-eight volumes, J. C. Nimmo, 1892-94, Estes & Lauriat, 1893-94.

The Poetical Works of Sir Walter Scott, with the Author's Introductions and Notes, edited by J. Logie Robertson, H. Frowde, 1894.

Lives of the Novelists, Oxford University Press, 1906.

The Wisdom of Sir Walter Scott: Criticisms and Opinions Collected from the Waverley Novels and Lockhart's Life of Sir Walter Scott, edited by Owen Redfern, A. & C. Black, 1907; reprinted, B. Franklin, 1971.

Two Hours with Ivanhoe, Old Greek Press, 1907, also published as *An Evening with Scott*, Sherwin Cody School of English, 1927.

Selections from the Poems of Sir Walter Scott, edited by A. Hamilton Thompson, Cambridge University Press, 1922.

Selected Poems of Sir Walter Scott, edited by John Clark Jordan, Macmillan, 1929.

New Love Poems, B. Blackwell, 1932.

The Waverley Pageant: The Best Passages from the Novels of Sir Walter Scott, edited by Hugh Walpole, Eyre & Spottiswoode, 1932.

Sir Walter's Post-Bag: More Stories and Sidelights from His Unpublished Letter-Books, edited by Wilfred Partington, J. Murray, 1932.

Short Stories by Sir Walter Scott, Oxford University Press, 1934, reprinted, Scholarly Press, 1970.

The Journal of Sir Walter Scott, edited by John Guthrie Tait and W. M. Parker, three volumes, Oliver & Boyd, 1939-49; new edition, edited by W. E. K. Anderson, Clarendon Press, 1972.

Songs and Lyrics of Sir Walter Scott, edited by Herbert Grierson, Oliver & Boyd, 1942.

Private Letters of the Seventeenth Century, edited by Douglas Grant, Clarendon Press, 1947.

The Life of John Dryden, edited by Bernard Kreissman, University of Nebraska Press, 1963.

Selected Poems, edited by Thomas Crawford, Clarendon Press, 1972.

The Prefaces to the Waverley Novels, edited by Mark A. Weinstein, University of Nebraska Press, 1978.

The Letters of Malachi Malagrowther, edited by P. H. Scott, Blackwood, 1981.

Scott on Himself: A Collection of the Autobiographical Writings of Sir Walter Scott, edited by David Hewitt, Scottich Academy Press, 1981.

Contributor of articles to *Encyclopaedia Britannica*.

■ **Adaptations**

OPERAS AND PLAYS

Thomas J. Dibdin, *The Lady of the Lake* (three-act), [London], 1810; Edmund J. Eyre, *The Lady of the Lake* (three-act), W. H. Wyatt, 1811; Thomas Morton, *The Knight of Snowdoun* (three-act musical; adaptation of *The Lady of the Lake*), [London], 1811; John Roby, *Jokeby* (burlesque; adaptation of *Rokeby*), T. Tegg, 1813; Daniel Terry, *Guy Mannering; or The Gipsey's Prophecy* (three-act musical), [London], 1816; Isaac Pocock, librettist, *Rob Roy Macgregor; or, Auld Lang Syne* (three-act opera), [London], 1818; Terry, *The Heart of Mid-Lothian* (three-act musical), W. Stockdale, 1819; Dibdin, *The Heart of Mid-Lothian; or, The Lily of St. Leonard's* (three-act), R. Stodart, 1819.

Henry R. Beverly, *The Abbot; or, Mary Queen of Scots* (three-act historical burletta), J. Lowndes, 1820; Terry, *The Antiquary* (three-act musical), W. Stockdale, 1820; Dibdin, *Ivanhoe; or, The Jew's Daughter* (three-act), Roach & Co., 1820; William T. Moncrieff (pseudonym of William T. Thomas), *Ivanhoe! or The Jewess* (three-act), [London], 1820; George Soane, *The Hebrew* (five-act; adaptation of *Ivanhoe*), [London], 1820; Pocock, librettist, *Montrose; or, The Children of the Mist* (three-act opera; adaptation of *The Legend of Montrose*), W. Simpkin & R. Marshall, 1822; John W. Calecraft (pseudonym of John W. Cole), *The Bride of Lammermoor* (five-act), W. Simpkin & R. Marshall, 1823; James L. Huie, *Quentin Durward* (three-act), [Edinburgh], 1823; Soane, *Rob Roy* (three-act), J. Cumberland, 1829; Michael R. Lacy, *The Maid of Judah; or, The Knight's Templars* (three-act opera; adaptation of *Ivanhoe*), J. Cumberland, 1833; Gaetano Donizetti, *Lucia di Lammermoor* (three-act opera; adaptation of *The Bride of Lammermoor*), first produced in Naples, Italy, 1835; Dibdin, *Kenilworth* (two-act), J. Cumberland, 1836.

Robert Reece, *The Lady of the Lake* (three-act burlesque), T. H. Lacy, 1850; J. H. Thompson, *Rokeby; or, The Robber Chief,* [London], 1851; Henry M. Milner, *The Fair Maid of Perth; or, The Battle of the Inch* (three-act historical drama), T. H. Lacy, 1866; Joseph Barton, *The Lady of the Lake* (three-act military drama), Gazette Printing & Publishing, 1871; Frederick Fox Cooper, *Ivanhoe* (three-act), J. Dicks, 1883; John A. Copeland, *Louis the Eleventh* (adaptation of *Quentin Durward*), E. Stock, 1889; Julian R. Sturgis, *Ivanhoe* (opera), Chappell, 1891; Joseph Bennett, librettist, *Jeanie Deans* (four-act opera; adaptation of *The Heart of Mid-Lothian*), [London], 1894; Miriam Thomas and Margaret Dakin, *The Lady of the Lake*, Press of Ketterlinus, 1916; Elizabeth C. Abbott, *Scott's Woodstock*, H. Milford, 1925; Abbott, *Scott's Kenilworth*, H. Milford, 1925; Muriel Brown, *Ivanhoe* (four-act), Row, Peterson, 1930;

Charles H. Connell, *Ivanhoe*, Blackie & Son, 1950; Connell, *Quentin Durward*, Blackie & Son, 1957.

MOVIES AND FILMSTRIPS

Ivanhoe (motion picture), Big A. Features, 1913, Metro-Goldwyn-Mayer (MGM), 1952; *Ivanhoe* (television series), Screen Gems, 1957-59, and A & E/ BBC Productions, 1997; *Ivanhoe* (filmstrip), Brunswick Productions, 1968; *Bride of Lammermoor* (motion picture), Kennedy Features, 1914; *Richard the Lionhearted* (motion picture; adaptation of *The Talisman*), Associated Artists, 1923; *King Richard and the Crusaders* (motion picture; adaptation of *The Talisman*), Warner Brothers, 1954; *Quentin Durward* (motion picture), MGM, 1955; *Rob Roy* (filmstrip), Encyclopaedia Britannica Films, 1960; *Rob Roy, the Highland Rogue* (motion picture), Walt Disney Productions, 1961; *Rob Roy, the Highland Rogue* (filmstrip), Walt Disney Productions, 1971; *Rob Roy*, MGM-United Artists, 1995.

■ Sidelights

"Our wishes for riches are seldom satisfied by possessing more than we can use, enjoy or bequeath," Walter Scott once wrote in his journal. However, like much of Scott's life, this comment displays a contradiction between his life and his words, between the intellect and the heart. In reality, Scott—made a baronet in 1818 and thereafter known as *Sir* Walter Scott—had wishes that far exceeded personal use. After becoming a successful poet with publication of the fabulously popular *The Lay of the Last Minstrel* and *Lady of the Lake*, Scott purchased an estate on the banks of the Tweed which he called Abbotsford, and proceeded to build a fake medieval castle, complete with turrets, but also with such modern conveniences as toilets and gas lighting. He planted 500 acres of this domain with mature oaks to give it the appearance of age, and took up the life of the landed country gentry. Yet Scott was no more of the gentry than his ersatz castle, and he poured so much money into its building that when financial difficulties later arose, he would have to spend the rest of his life paying off debt, turning out book after book in the effort.

Scott continued to be fascinated with the lore and lure of bygone ages up unto his death in 1832. All his works are imbued with this antiquarian passion; indeed he single-handedly created the genre of historical fiction, bringing to vivid life not only Scottish history, but English as well. In his Scottish novels such as *Waverley, The Heart of Mid-Lothian, Rob Roy*, and *The Bride of Lammermoor*, Walter Scott displayed on paper the dichotomy at work in his own life: "the regret for the old days when Scotland was an independent but turbulent and distracted country," as the critic David Daiches put it in his *Literary Essays*, coupled with a "satisfaction at the peace, prosperity and progress which he felt had been assured by the Union with England in 1707 and the successful establishment of the Hanoverian dynasty on the British throne." In short, Scott wrote of medieval castles with modern plumbing. Always present in his work is the tension between the benefits of civilization and the sacrifice of heroic and chivalric values of another age which had to be made to attain such progress. Though Scott was, according to Gary Kelly in the *Concise Dictionary of British Literary Biography*, "the most influential novelist in world literature," he paid dearly for such personal progress.

Adversity in Youth

Scott was born in Edinburgh, Scotland, on August 15, 1771. His father was also named Walter, and was a solicitor with strong ties to the land, in particular the Scottish Border country where the Scott family had been known for generations. His mother was Anne Rutherford Scott, daughter of a professor of medicine. Scott was thus born into a prosperous middle-class family, though the family's status was no help for the child when he contracted infantile paralysis at eighteen months, leaving his right leg permanently crippled. His parents sent young Walter off to the country for long periods between 1773 and 1778, to a paternal grandfather, hoping that the fresh air and country living would help. His lameness could never be cured, though Scott did learn to compensate for it during this time, to hold his own against not only his infirmity but the cruel jests of others, as well.

Back in Edinburgh, Scott entered school at age eight, but he continued in the summers to visit the countryside, staying with an aunt in Kelso. "To this period I can trace the awakening of that delightful feeling for the beauties of natural objects which has never since deserted me," he is quoted as saying in John Buchan's *Sir Walter Scott.* "From this time the love of natural beauty, more especially when combined with ancient ruins, or remains of our fathers' piety or splendour, became with me an insatiable passion." Scott would feed off this vision for the rest of his life, never letting his bad leg hold him back from tramping the hills of the Border country.

In 1783 Scott entered Edinburgh University, and three years later signed an indenture as his father's apprentice. In 1792, Scott was admitted to the Bar, though his first love was and remained the countryside. He travelled a good deal as a young man in the Border counties, gathering folk ballads, revelling in the oral tradition of the simple farmers and shepherds. Interested in things literary, he came under the sway for a time of the German *Sturm and Drang* movement, and he translated poems and plays by Goethe. He also experienced an unhappy, unrequited love—one that seemed to affect him all his life. In 1797, one might say on the rebound, he married Charlotte Carpenter, with whom he had four children, two girls and two boys, but for whom he held fondness rather than passion. Meanwhile, he read widely in politics and history, and soon he was composing his own version of traditional oral ballads. In 1798 he was appointed sheriff of Selkirkshire in the Border country.

Scott as Poet

Scott's first publication was of the ballads he had been collecting over the years, *Minstrelsy of the Scottish Border.* The popularity of this collection and the prompting of friends encouraged Scott to publish his own version of ballads in 1805, *The Lay of the Last Minstrel,* a long narrative poem which illustrated the customs and manners of inhabitants on both sides of the border between Scotland and England in medieval times. Scott also entered into a long-time relationship with the printer James Ballantyne, purchasing a third share in the business which would over the years publish many of his works. The success of *The Lay of the Last Minstrel* was immediate and large. Large enough, in fact, for Scott to attempt to make his living from writing. As a contemporary reviewer, Francis Jeffrey, noted in the *Edinburgh Review,* Scott "has manifested a degree of genius which cannot be overlooked, and given indication of talents that seem well worthy of being enlisted in the service

WORLD'S CLASSICS

WALTER SCOTT

OLD MORTALITY

This 1816 novel depicts life in seventeenth-century Scotland during a period of rebellion known as the "killing time."

of the epic muse." With this first narrative, Scott had already set his writing career on course, for at the heart of the poem is a dramatization of a national culture and a mythologized and personalized vision of the people of Scotland—in fact the beginnings of a national literature for Scotland and England which Scott's entire body of work would continue to build.

Scott followed up this success with the poem *Marmion,* and a measure of his instant popularity was the fact that he was paid one thousand pounds for it—a sizeable sum in 1808—by the publisher Archibald Constable. Scott had established himself as a best-selling author in short order and was quickly becoming known for his political views, as well. His conservative Tory opinions were being disseminated in the *Quarterly Review*, which he helped to found. But he was no simple stodgy man of letters; he blended social and political conservatism with a progressive agenda. He saw the costs of progress, but championed it nonetheless.

In 1810 he published *The Lady of the Lake*, yet another best-selling poem, this one set in the Scottish Highlands concerning the adventures of the hero James Fitz-James, the villainous hero Roderick Dhu, and the love interest Ellen Douglas. Something of an Arthurian romance transposed to the Highlands, the poem narrates the attempts of Fitz-James to establish a Scottish kingdom and the ensuing conflict with the Dhu clan in this effort. It is generally regarded as his most accomplished poem in terms of plot, and though seven further verse narratives were to follow over the years, none gained such wide popularity as *The Lady of the Lake* and the two preceding it. While some contemporary reviewers, including Jeffrey, applauded Scott for his ability to reach such a wide readership, others, including the English poet Samuel Taylor Coleridge, thought the poem tedious and "endless," as Coleridge wrote to William Wordsworth. "I never remember a narrative poem in which I felt the sense of progress so languid."

Coleridge predicted that the poetry of Scott would not survive, and in this he proved correct. But verse came with ease to Scott, and he wrote quickly, bothering little with revision. "My connection with my poem drops as completely with its publication as that of the bird with her nestlings when she has turned them off," Scott is quoted as saying in Hesketh Pearson's *Sir Walter Scott*. "My poetry has always passed from the desk to the press in the most hurried manner possible, so that it is no wonder I am sometimes puzzled to explain my own meaning."

Scott would continue this "hurried manner" when later turning to fiction, and as he never plotted his novels, such unrevised publication became a problem with both story and character consistency in works encompassing three volumes. Such hasty publication was in part due to the necessity of earning money to support two households. Not only did he have a house in Edinburgh, but in 1811 he purchased the property along the Tweed, and the following year he moved his family to Abbotsford. However, with the rise in popularity of a new breed of poet, epitomized by Byron, Scott began to lose his loyal readership. It was time for him to move to new fields of literary endeavor.

The Waverley Novels

As early as 1804, Scott had begun a novel about the Jacobite revolution in Scotland, the attempt to restore the old Stuart throne. He put the unfinished novel aside for other matters, but in 1814 he returned to this story of an Englishman's journey to the north and of his temporary involvement with the Jacobite Rebellion of 1745. Waverley, the vacillating protagonist of the novel, goes to the Highlands out of romantic curiosity, but once there he is attracted to clan life and is seduced into joining the rebel cause for a time. His is an emotional surrender, though he sees clearly with his reason that the Jacobites are fighting a lost cause. As the critic Daiches has noted, "the essence of *Waverley* is the way in which the conflicting aims of the two worlds impinge on the titular hero."

Published in 1814 and anonymously—for novel-writing was not considered quite proper for a gentleman of the time—*Waverley* was an instant success. The next year was a particularly productive one for Scott. He published not only his first novel, but also edited *The Works of Jonathan Swift*, penned a narrative poem, *The Lord of the Isles*, and wrote—in a bare six weeks—a second novel, the three-volume *Guy Mannering*. That book firmly established "The Author of *Waverley*" as an institution. Indeed, Scott can be regarded as the world's first best-selling author. In quick succession, he wrote and published the core of his Scottish novels, all published under the rubric of the Waverley Novels. Though literary critics knew the secret of their authorship, Scott relished the mystery he felt he had created by keeping his anonymity.

Guy Mannering and Scott's third novel, *The Antiquary*, were set in the Scotland of Scott's childhood, while *Old Mortality*, published in 1816, dealt with the seventeenth-century strife between the Scottish peasants, strong Presbyterians, and the aristocracy—basically an opposition of two fanaticisms. With *Old Mortality*, included in the first of the series known as *Tales of My Landlord*, Scott invented a pedantic schoolmaster, Jedediah Cleishbotham, as narrator or editor of the supposedly discovered manuscript. This was another ruse to continue Scott's anonymity.

With *Rob Roy*, Scott returned to the Jacobite theme, this time to a rebellion in 1715, using as an historical centerpiece the Highland outlaw, Rob Roy Macgregor. Once again, a romantic young Englishman becomes embroiled in the plots, but with *Rob*

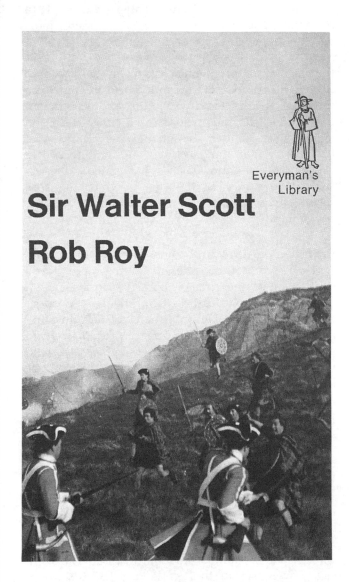

Everyman's Library

Sir Walter Scott

Rob Roy

Scottish Highland outlaw Rob Roy Macgregor is the centerpiece of this 1818 novel, which also featured an equally strong female protagonist in Diana Vernon.

Roy, Scott came up with a female protagonist full of temper and spirit, Diana Vernon, a sure pleaser for nineteenth-century readers—and for modern readers, as well. As John Buchan noted in his *Sir Walter Scott*, "Whatever she says or does, we are her devout henchmen, believing fiercely in her beauty, her goodness and her brains." This proved to be the most popular of Scott's romances to date, selling ten thousand copies in two weeks. However, Scott was so ill with gallstones during the composition of *Rob Roy* that he had to dictate most of the manuscript. But the book appeared on time, something Scott was famous for.

A Romantic Vision

Scott was learning the craft of novel-writing as he went along. There were, of course, models to follow, such as Henry Fielding, Tobias Smollett, Daniel Defoe, and Samuel Richardson. As Gary Kelly noted in *Concise Dictionary of British Literary Biography*, Scott borrowed a bit from each. "Like Fielding, Scott uses an omniscient third person narrator," Kelly observed. Scott also relied upon "picaresque adventures" to illustrate his themes, employed characters as "representative social types," and for overall structure used the "romance plot of testing a young man's character by experience of the contradictions and the relativities in the wider world."

A peculiarity of Scott's romances is the appearance of dual protagonists: a somewhat passive hero of virtuous and gentlemanly demeanor, and a more villainous hero who is the pragmatic man of action, and whose actions are sometimes for good, sometimes for ill. These two heroes represent for Scott the old and new world so often at conflict in his novels. Scott also was always conscious of blending the historical with the literary, and as such he can be seen to have influenced an entire century of writers from Honore de Balzac to Leo Tolstoy. Conscious also of narration and style, Scott was one of the first writers to use dialect in his novels, though this was generally reserved for dialogue. All of the narration was dealt with in standard English.

Throughout the second and third decades of the nineteenth century, Scott continued the production of his Waverley Novels, focusing initially on Scottish themes and history. Perhaps one of his most famous and critically acclaimed is *The Heart of*

Liam Neeson starred in the 1995 film version of Scott's swashbuckling work, *Rob Roy*, which was filmed on location in the Scottish Highlands.

Mid-Lothian, set in 1737 and utilizing a simple dairy woman, Jeanie Deans, as the protagonist. Based on an actual story, *The Heart of Mid-Lothian* has a "seriousness lacking elsewhere in Scott," according to the critic John Lauber in his *Sir Walter Scott.* Jeanie Deans's sister, Effie, the younger and more attractive of the pair, has been seduced and made pregnant by a young and dissipated Englishman, Sir George Staunton. Effie tries to hide her condition, but there are rumors, and once she gives birth, the baby is stolen from her by a former mistress of Staunton. Effie, unable to produce the living baby, is accused of infanticide and sentenced to be hanged. But Jeanie, with the help of Lord Argyle, travels to London to see the queen and win a pardon for her sister. Eventually Effie marries Staunton, and Jeanie—now married—lives on Argyle's estate, prospering over the years. However, in a final twist, Staunton is killed by his kidnapped son who has become

a Highland outlaw and is ignorant of his father's identity.

The reading public as well as critics reacted favorably to this novel that rewards virtue and that is anchored by a strong female protagonist. Robin Mayhead, in *Essays in Criticism,* while noting that Scott is usually guilty of loose plotting and inconsistencies of both story and character, commented that for at least the first half of *The Heart of Mid-Lothian,* Scott "is sufficiently mastered by a theme to be inspired to a piece of almost entirely consistent artistic achievement." Lauber, in his *Sir Walter Scott,* commented that the real significance of *The Heart of Mid-Lothian* "lies at least as much in its contribution to the development of the English novel as in its own achievement." According to Lauber, both George Eliot's *Adam Bede* and Thomas Hardy's *Tess of the D'Urbervilles* were heavily indebted to Scott's earlier novel.

The Bride of Lammermoor is another of the most popular Waverley titles, and one of the last of the author's Scottish novels. With this book, Scott created a darkly tragic vision, perhaps reflective of his own dark moods of the time, afflicted as he was with ill health. He was so sick at the time, in fact, that many in Edinburgh thought he was dying. As Edgar Johnson noted in his biography, *Sir Walter Scott: The Great Unknown*, page after page of this novel "was written in a blurred trance of suffering in which he did know what words he was putting down, images and dream-like actions rising somehow out of unconscious depths of the imagination." Set in the early eighteenth century, the book details the tragic love of Edgar Ravenswood and Lucy Ashton, something of a Scottish Romeo and Juliet, doomed by the opposite political and religious opinions of their families. The novel was adapted after Scott's death for an opera by Gaetano Donizetti, *Lucia di Lammermoor*, one of several of Scott's novels so adapted. It is the tragic element of the book that makes it work so well as opera, and as Lauber concluded, "Living in different worlds, Edgar and Lucy are drawn together by the very differences that make their union impossible, and their impossibility, sensed by readers from the outset, creates the deepest emotional effect of any of the Waverley Novels." Lauber also noted that with *The Bride of Lammermoor*, "the series of novels set in the Scotland of the preceding 150 years comes to a end, and with it Scott's most significant contribution to the English novel."

This 1957 television adaptation of *Ivanhoe*, Scott's popular 1820 novel, follows the exploits of Wilfrid of Ivanhoe, a dispossessed knight in twelfth-century England.

A Change of Scene

With publication in 1820 of *Ivanhoe*, Scott moved farther afield for both scene and historical epoch. Set in the England of Richard-the-Lion-Hearted and the twelfth century, *Ivanhoe* inaugurated a change for the rest of the Waverley series. Only once more, with *Redgauntlet* in 1824, would Scott return to purely Scottish themes. This change of setting, if anything, brought new readers to Scott, and the first printing of ten thousand copies quickly sold out. An index of how popular and successful Scott was is that the price of each copy of *Ivanhoe*, at thirty shillings, was the equivalent of a week's wage for a skilled workman. This book helped to spread Scott's fame to Europe, where Goethe—as quoted by Alan Massie in *Sir Walter Scott: The Long-Forgotten Melody*—declared that he found in Scott "a wholly new art which has its own laws." The story of Wilfred of Ivanhoe, a knight dispossessed by his own father, the novel employs the usual Scott theme of past versus present and future. In the work, a weak monarchy has resulted in a divided England, and it is Ivanhoe's father who is trying to turn the clock back to the days of Saxon power. There are heroines as well: the blond and very proper Rowena and the darkly beautiful Rebecca. Jousting and kidnapping and battle scenes have made this novel a perennial favorite, though as Kelly noted in *Concise Dictionary of British Literary Biography*, "*Ivanhoe* is now regarded as one of Scott's lesser novels." In quick succession, Scott published three more novels: *The Monastery*, *The Abbot*, and *Kenilworth*. Of the three, the last is best known, set in Elizabethan times and involving all manner of court intrigues. The other two both deal with the Protestant Reformation. Further Waverley Novels are depictions of both English and European history, as well as the Crusades.

The early 1820s were busy years for the Scott, with publication after publication, but in 1826 a two-fold tragedy struck: his wife Charlotte died in May of that year, and later came the bankruptcy of Ballantyne and financial ruin for the author. The following year, in order to begin putting his affairs in order, he publicly acknowledged authorship of the Waverley Novels. His debt was well over one hundred thousand pounds—an enormous sum in its day—but he stubbornly refused to sell off Abbotsford to pay for it. Instead he turned with renewed urgency to his pen. The remaining years of his life were ones of literary

Scott, who died in 1832, is buried at Dryburgh Abbey in Berwick, Scotland.

drudgery, as he wrote four more Waverley Novels, including *The Fair Maid of Perth, Anne of Geierstein, Count Robert of Paris*, and *Castle Dangerous*, as well as a nine-volume life of Napoleon and a collected edition of his works with new prefaces, notes, and some revisions. Eventually, the debt was paid off, but at a terrible cost to his health. Scott suffered a stroke in 1830 yet continued to write and travel. A navy ship was made available to him in late 1831 for a voyage to the Mediterranean in hopes that improved climate would help his failing health. Everywhere he traveled, Scott was received as a celebrity, one of the first authors to enjoy international fame. During his travels, however, he suffered another stroke, and quickly returned home to Abbotsford, where he died at age sixty-one, on September 21, 1832.

Scott's works have suffered from falling critical fortunes more so than those of many authors famous in their day. Critically, the books enjoyed fulsome success in their time, though contemporary reviewers noted the many inconsistencies and

If you enjoy the works of Walter Scott, you may also want to check out the following books and films:

Pamela Kaufman, *Banners of Gold*, 1986.
Judith Merkle Riley, *In Pursuit of the Green Lion*, 1990.
Rosemary Sutcliff, *The Shining Company*, 1990.
The Adventures of Robin Hood, Warner Bros, 1938.
Braveheart, 20th Century-Fox/Paramount, 1995.

organizational problems inherent in such sprawling romances. However, the later Waverley Novels were already being ignored by contemporary reviewers, as increased production by Scott decreased his literary quality. However, from 1815 to 1830, as Lauber noted, "Scott was the most widely read novelist in the world." For Scott, production was important. Thomas Carlyle commented in an essay on Scott collected in *Criticism and Miscellaneous Essays* that the great fact about the Waverley Novels "is that they were faster written and better paid for than any other books in the world," a charge Scott would most probably have taken delight in. Among nineteenth-century critics of Scott was Mark Twain, who blamed Scott—because of his idealization of the past—for many modern woes. Included in these was the cult of chivalry, responsible—as Twain saw it—for the mind-set of the American South. In his *Life on the Mississippi* and *The Adventures of Huckleberry Finn*, as well *A Connecticut Yankee in King Arthur's Court*, Twain mocked much of the code of chivalry which Scott developed in *Ivanhoe*. Twentieth-century criticism largely relegated Scott to the dust-bin of literature. The novelist E. M. Forster, in his *Aspects of the Novel*, declared that Scott displayed "a trivial mind and a heavy style."

However, with the English publication of the Marxist critic George Lukacs's book on the historical novel, Scott's critical assessment began to change. Lukacs pointed to Scott as a father of the genre and spurred renewed interest in the writer. It is now generally accepted that Scott's great contributions were in the development of the historical novel and in the depiction of regional characteristics such as dialect and class differences. Virginia Woolf, in her *Collected Essays*, once commented on Scott's abilities as a novelist, focussing on his use of dialogue, and concluded that "he is perhaps the last novelist to practice the great, the Shake-spearean art, of making people reveal themselves in speech." Walter Allen, in *The English Novel: A Short Critical History*, observed that Scott "made the European novel" and "revolutionized the writing of history." Whether skilled craftsman or literary artist, Scott made a defining contribution in the development of the novel. As John Lauber concluded in his *Sir Walter Scott*, "Scott enormously widened the range of fiction—certainly no other writer would deserve a longer chapter in any history of the English or world novel."

■ Works Cited

Allen, Walter, *The English Novel: A Short Critical History*, Phoenix House, 1954, p. 52.

Buchan, John, *Sir Walter Scott*, Cassell, 1932.

Carlyle, Thomas, "Sir Walter Scott," *Criticism and Miscellaneous Essays*, Scribner's, 1896, p. 83.

Coleridge, Samuel Taylor, *Collected Letters of Samuel Taylor Coleridge, Volume III: 1807-1814*, edited by Earl Leslie Griggs, Clarendon Press, 1959.

Daiches, David, "Scott's Achievement as a Novelist," *Literary Essays*, Philosophical Library Publishers, 1957.

Forster, E. M., *Aspects of the Novel*, Harcourt, 1927, p. 52.

Jeffrey, Francis, review of *The Lay of the Last Minstrel*, *Contributions to the Edinburgh Review*, D. Appleton and Co., 1860.

Johnson, Edgar, *Sir Walter Scott: The Great Unknown*, Volume 1, Macmillan, 1970, p. 646.

Kelly, Gary, "Sir Walter Scott," *Concise Dictionary of British Literary Biography*, Volume 3: *Writers of the Romantic Period, 1789-1832*, Gale, 1992, pp. 316-38.

Lauber, John, *Sir Walter Scott*, Twayne, 1989.

Massie, Alan, "Scott and the European Novel," *Sir Walter Scott: The Long-Forgotten Melody*, edited by Alan Bold, Vision, 1983, p. 95.

Mayhead, Robin, "*The Heart of Mid-Lothian*: Scott as Artist," *Essays in Criticism*, July, 1956, p. 266.

Pearson, Hesketh, *Sir Walter Scott*, Harper and Brothers, 1954.

Scott, Walter, *The Journal of Sir Walter Scott*, edited by W. E. K. Anderson, Oxford University Press, 1972.

Woolf, Virginia, *Collected Essays*, Volume 1, Harcourt, 1967, p. 143.

■ For More Information See

BOOKS

Brown, David, *Walter Scott and the Historical Imagination*, Routledge & Kegan Paul, 1979.

Cottum, Daniel, *The Civilized Imagination: A Study of Ann Radcliffe, Jane Austen, and Sir Walter Scott*, Cambridge University Press, 1985.

Crawford, Thomas, *Scott* (Scottish Writers Series), revised edition, Scottish Academic Press, 1982.

Grierson, Sir Herbert, *Sir Walter Scott, Bart.: A New Life Supplementary to and Corrective of Lockhart's Biography*, Constable, 1938.

Hart, Francis R., *Scott's Novels: The Plotting of Historic Survival*, University Press of Virginia, 1966.

Hayden, John O., editor, *Scott: The Critical Heritage*, Routledge & Kegan Paul, 1970.

Jeffares, A. Norman, editor, *Scott's Mind and Art*, Oliver & Boyd, 1969.

Johnson, Edgar, *Sir Walter Scott: The Great Unknown*, two volumes, Macmillan, 1970.

Kerr, James, *Fiction against History: Scott as Storyteller*, Cambridge University Press, 1989.

Lauber, John, *Sir Walter Scott*, revised edition, Twayne, 1989.

Lockhart, John Gibson, *Memoirs of the Life of Sir Walter Scott, Bart.*, seven volumes, Cadell, 1837-1838; revised, ten volumes, 1839.

McMaster, Graham, *Scott and Society*, Cambridge University Press, 1981.

Millgate, *Walter Scott: The Making of a Novelist*, University of Toronto Press, 1984.

Millgate, Jane, *Scott's Last Edition: A Study in Publishing History*, Edinburgh University Press, 1987.

Pearson, Hesketh, *Sir Walter Scott: His Life and Personality*, Harper, 1955.

Shaw, Harry E., *The Forms of Historical Fiction: Sir Walter Scott and His Successors*, Cornell University Press, 1983.

Tulloch, Graham, *The Language of Walter Scott*, Andre Deutsch, 1980.

Welsh, Alexander, *The Hero of the Waverley Novels*, Yale University Press, 1963.

Wilt, Judith, *The Novels of Sir Walter Scott*, University of Chicago Press, 1985.

PERIODICALS

Atlantic, March, 1994, p. 109.

Cambridge Journal, October, 1953, pp. 20-35.

Clio, Winter, 1976, pp. 181-92.

English Literary History, Fall, 1983, pp. 559-87.

House and Garden, June, 1992, pp. 136-44.

Journal of the History of Ideas, July, 1975, pp. 497-512.

New Republic, August 17, 1992, pp. 35-8.

Nineteenth-Century Fiction, September, 1951, pp. 80-95; December, 1951, pp. 153-73.

Studies in Scottish Literature, July, 1966, pp. 29-41; October, 1966, pp. 63-78; January, 1967, pp. 155-78; July, 1967, pp. 14-27; October, 1967, pp. 83-97; January, 1968, pp. 143-66; number 15, 1980, pp. 95-123.*

—Sketch by J. Sydney Jones

Ivan Southall

■ Personal

Born June 8, 1921, in Canterbury, Victoria, Australia; son of Francis Gordon (in insurance) and Rachel Elizabeth (Voutier) Southall; married Joyce Blackburn, September 8, 1945 (divorced); married Susan Westerlund Stanton, 1976; children: (first marriage) Andrew John, Roberta Joy, Elizabeth Rose, Melissa Frances. *Education:* Attended Melbourne Technical College, 1937-41. *Politics:* Independent. *Religion:* Methodist.

■ Addresses

Home and office—P.O. Box 25, Healesville, Victoria 3777, Australia.

■ Career

Herald and Weekly Times, Melbourne, Victoria, Australia, process engraver, 1936-41 and 1947; freelance writer, 1948—. Library of Congress, Whittall Lecturer, 1973; American Library Association, Arbuthnot Honor Lecturer, 1974. MacQuarie Uni-

versity, writer-in-residence, 1978. Community Youth Organization, past president; Knoxbrooke Training Centre for the Intellectually Handicapped, foundation president. *Military Service:* Australian Army, 1941; Royal Australian Air Force, 1942-46, pilot, 1942-44, war historian, 1945-46; became flight lieutenant, received Distinguished Flying Cross. *Member:* Australian Society of Authors.

■ Awards, Honors

Australian Children's Book of the Year Award, 1966, for *Ash Road,* 1968, for *To the Wild Sky,* 1971, for *Bread and Honey,* and 1976, for *Fly West;* Australian Picture Book of the Year Award, 1969, for *Sly Old Wardrobe;* Japanese Government's Children's Welfare and Culture Encouragement Award, 1969, for *Ash Road;* Carnegie Medal, Library Association (England), 1972, for *Josh;* Zilver Griffel (Netherlands), 1972, for *To the Wild Sky;* named member of Order of Australia, 1981; National Children's Book Award (Australia), 1986, for *The Long Night Watch.*

■ Writings

FICTION

Out of the Dawn: Three Short Stories, privately printed, 1942.

Third Pilot, Horwitz, 1959.
Flight to Gibraltar, Horwitz, 1959.
Mediterranean Black, Horwitz, 1959.
Sortie in Cyrenaica, Horwitz, 1959.
Mission to Greece, Horwitz, 1960.
Atlantic Pursuit, Horwitz, 1960.

NONFICTION

The Weaver from Meltham (biography), illustrated by George Colville, Whitcombe & Tombs (Christchurch), 1950.
The Story of The Hermitage: The First Fifty Years of the Geelong Church of England Girls' Grammar School, F. W. Cheshire (Harlow, Essex), 1956.
They Shall Not Pass Unseen, Angus & Robertson (London), 1956.
A Tale of Box Hill: Day of the Forest, Box Hill City Council, 1957.
Bluey Truscott: Squadron Leader Keith William Truscott, R.A.A.F., D.F.C. and Bar, Angus & Robertson, 1958.
Softly Tread the Brave: A Triumph over Terror, Devilry, and Death by Mine Disposal Officers John Stuart Mould and Hugh Randall Syme, Angus & Robertson, 1960.
Parson on the Track: Bush Brothers in the Australian Outback, Lansdowne (London), 1962.

"SIMON BLACK" SERIES FOR CHILDREN

Meet Simon Black, illustrated by Frank Norton, Angus & Robertson, 1950.
Simon Black in Peril, Angus & Robertson, 1951.
Simon Black in Space, Angus & Robertson, 1952, Anglobooks, 1953.
Simon Black in Coastal Command, Anglobooks, 1953.
Simon Black in China, Angus & Robertson, 1954.
Simon Black and the Spacemen, Angus & Robertson, 1955.
Simon Black in the Antarctic, Angus & Robertson, 1956.
Simon Black Takes Over: The Strange Tale of Operation Greenleaf, Angus & Robertson, 1959.
Simon Black at Sea: The Fateful Maiden Voyage of A.P.M.I. Arion, Angus & Robertson, 1961.

NONFICTION FOR CHILDREN

Journey into Mystery: A Story of the Explorers Burke and Willis, illustrated by Robin Goodall, Lansdowne, 1961.
Lawrence Hargrave (biography), Oxford University Press (Oxford), 1964.

Indonesian Journey (travel), Lansdowne, 1965, Ginn (Aylebury, England), 1966.
Bushfire!, illustrated by Julie Mattox, Angus & Robertson, 1968.
Seventeen Seconds (children's adaptation of *Softly Tread the Brave*; also see below), Macmillan (Basingstoke), 1973.
Fly West, Angus & Robertson, 1974, Macmillan (New York City), 1975.

FICTION FOR CHILDREN

Hills End, illustrated by Jim Phillips, Angus & Robertson, 1962, St. Martin's (New York City), 1963.
Ash Road, illustrated by Clem Seale, Angus & Robertson, 1965, St. Martin's, 1966.
To the Wild Sky, illustrated by Jennifer Tuckwell, St. Martin's, 1967.
The Fox Hole (also see below), illustrated by Ian Ribbons, St. Martin's, 1967.
Let the Balloon Go (also see below), illustrated by Ribbons, St. Martin's, 1968.
Sly Old Wardrobe (picture book), illustrated by Ted Greenwood, F. W. Cheshire, 1968, St. Martin's, 1970.
Finn's Folly, St. Martin's, 1969.
Chinaman's Reef Is Ours, St. Martin's, 1970.
Bread and Honey, Angus & Robertson, 1970, published as *Walk a Mile and Get Nowhere*, Bradbury (Scarscale, NY), 1970.
Josh, Angus & Robertson, 1971, Macmillan, 1972.
Over the Top (also see below), illustrated by Ribbons, Methuen (London), 1972, published as *Benson Boy*, illustrated by Ingrid Fetz, Macmillan, 1973.
Head in the Clouds, illustrated by Richard Kennedy, Angus & Robertson, 1972, Macmillan, 1973.
Matt and Jo, Macmillan, 1973.
Three Novels (contains *The Fox Hole*, *Let the Balloon Go*, and *Over the Top*), Methuen, 1975.
What about Tomorrow?, Macmillan, 1977.
King of the Sticks, Greenwillow (New York City), 1979.
The Golden Goose, Greenwillow, 1981.
The Long Night Watch, Methuen, 1983, Farrar, Straus (New York City), 1984.
A City out of Sight, Angus & Robertson, 1984.
Christmas in the Tree, Hodder & Stoughton (London), 1985.
Rachel, Farrar, Straus, 1986.
Blackbird, Farrar, Straus, 1988.
The Mysterious World of Marcus Leadbeater, Farrar, Straus, 1990.

Ziggurat, Viking Penguin, 1997.

OTHER

Woomera, Angus & Robertson, 1962.

Indonesia Face to Face (travel), Lansdowne, 1964.

(Editor) *The Challenge: Is the Church Obsolete?—An Australian Response to the Challenge of Modern Society* (essays), Lansdowne, 1966.

The Sword of Esau: Bible Stories Retold, illustrated by Joan Kiddell-Monroe, Angus & Robertson, 1967, St. Martin's, 1968.

A Journey of Discovery: On Writing for Children (lectures), Kestrel (London), 1975, Macmillan, 1976.

Also author, with others, of a screenplay titled *Let the Balloon Go*, 1976.

■ Sidelights

Ivan Southall's award-winning novels for young adults are often considered inappropriate by critics because of his serious topics and challenging literary techniques. However, none of this has altered Southall's style: he continues to treat his readers intelligently, regardless of their age. And the popularity of his books has increased, ever since he made the plunge into writing serious children's fiction.

Southall's own life story was peppered with tragedies, starting from before he was even born. His maternal grandmother lived in the harsh climate of a gold mining town in the Australian outback and died of pneumonia, leaving her aunt to raise the children. His mother's family never did strike it rich searching for gold, but they stayed on in the rough mining town. His father was so poor growing up that he had to trudge through the streets of his hometown, earning money by selling yeast. Eventually, half of his father's family died in a diphtheria epidemic. These events had a strong influence on Southall's writing. He commented in his essay in *Something about the Author Autobiography Series* (*SAAS*) that "all that family struggle, the deprivation, the gold never won— let me say it has lain heavily behind my work in more recent years."

Southall's life with his own parents was not much easier. He recalled that he was born during the Australian winter, and when the nurse opened the doors to his birth room, the view was of dead chrysanthemums. Southall has reminisced that this was a sign of foreboding for his life. He was the first born of five children. His father died of tuberculosis when Southall was in the ninth grade, and he had to go to work full-time to help support his family.

By then, Southall was already used to a difficult life—but only when it was self-imposed. As a youth he refused to wear slippers on the family's pine floor, which gave him frequent splinters. He wouldn't wear rain boots when it was raining. Southall also recalled to *SAAS* that "as a boy— because of the dedicated commitment to suffering that has added so much event to my life—I spent my sleeping time on the wired-in back verandah where the weather beat in round the edges of the homemade blinds, spattering my face with spray. There were mornings when the floor was awash and whole days when my mum was drying out the bedclothes in front of the kitchen stove, muttering to herself. But I wouldn't have surrendered the hardships of 'sleeping out' for worlds. It was a status symbol."

Southall's family was very religious, and they attended their Methodist church regularly, often giving away scarce family money to the church coffers. "Church was our way of life, religiously, intellectually, socially, and recreationally," he explained in *SAAS*. "It was the only way I knew." Later in life, people commented with pity on the strictness of his church upbringing. But Southall didn't feel that it had a negative affect on him at all. "I remember the church with gratitude. Over many years I listened to marvellous stories and received instruction from scholars and orators, some of the best of their day." He also realized that the church had a hand in his later writing success: "If I'm to claim any serious literary foundation," he recounted, "it has to be the influence of the King James Bible, absorbed (at times restlessly) during after-dinner readings at the kitchen table or in the sharp physical discomfort of the church during boyhood and adolescence. I was fortunate. I could've been born later and left to the ravages of some later translations that give new definition to the meaning of *deprivation*."

Story Spinning Begins

At school, Southall especially enjoyed writing stories, and completed his first at the age of nine.

Soon, he became fascinated with the *Herald Junior*, a newspaper that had story contests for children. The prize for winners was five shillings—the equivalent of one U.S. dollar—and it seemed to Southall to be a fortune. He quickly penned a story about a panther who kills a villain, and it was chosen as the top story. "The overnight notoriety! The Fame!," Southall wrote in *SAAS*. "The other face of which was the unflattering astonishment of parents, school-teachers, the parson, the Sunday School teacher, friends, neighbours, relations, and all the kids around."

Hooked on this contest, Southall continued to write and submit a story a week. Although many were ignored, a total of six of his stories were published. Southall was so involved with his writing that he wrote a book, which he submitted to the *Herald Junior*. They declined to publish it. Nevertheless Southall had gained enough fame and notoriety that he earned a half-scholarship to a local Methodist school. The family finances were taxed by having to pay the other half of the tuition. Southall's mother felt that he should know that writing was a difficult life and that writers usually starve. Southall wrote in *SAAS* that "she went on telling me [this] for years. Still tells me sometimes. I don't know where she got her information. She wasn't misinformed."

Soon after Southall entered this school his father died, and he began a full-time job as a laboratory assistant where he washed glassware. Southall claimed that he probably broke more glassware than he saved. At the age of sixteen, he became a copy boy at the Melbourne *Herald*. While his job consisted of tasks such as serving tea to the reporters and editors, he also made many friends there and had some of his writing published. He continued to ask his supervisor for a reporting apprenticeship, but he was turned down because he hadn't completed his education. After his copy boy apprenticeship was over, his supervisor suggested that he should try an apprenticeship as a process engraver, where he cleaned the glass used for photographic negatives with toxic chemicals. Southall gladly accepted, excited to stay in the newspaper field.

Several years after Southall's apprenticeship had started, World War II began. Although he wanted to join the war effort, at first his mother was against it. She knew she needed his income to support her large family. However, Southall de-

cided to apply for a spot in the Royal Australian Air Force. He was turned down because he was underweight and had a racing pulse. Southall tried gaining weight by eating huge quantities of bananas and drinking large quantities of water. He reapplied, only two pounds heavier. This time, his mother had consented to him joining the military, and he was accepted.

Southall spent a year in the army before he was called into the air force. There he was told that only the top-seated recruit would be able to pick his assignment. Ever since childhood, Southall had a fascination with airplanes and flying. He knew that being a pilot was the only assignment he wanted, and he plunged into his studies wholeheartedly. "To earn the right to choose, I had to

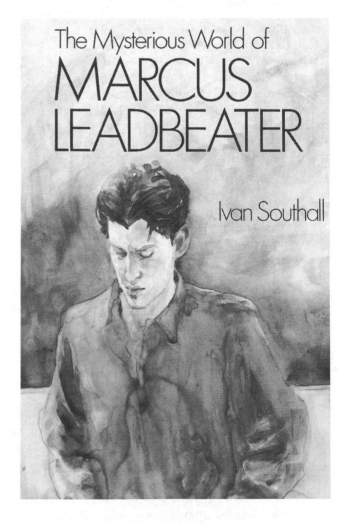

A young man struggles with his grief over his grandfather's death in this 1990 work.

top the flight in the examinations that concluded initial training," he told *SAAS*. "On ninth grade and no preparation except the artillery. . . . It's in the motivation. And the application. I topped it."

During Southall's military career, he flew fifteen-seven missions, each more difficult than the previous one. It turned him off on flying, but he was able to use his diaries as notes for many later works. He was posted in London, and there met and married Joy Blackburn, the daughter of one of the families he had befriended.

The Writing Life Calls

After the war, Southall returned to Australia, and continued his process engraving apprenticeship. When it was finished, he decided to quit the newspaper and try to make it as a full-time writer. His supervisor argued with him about it and even offered him a job with the literary staff, but Southall knew it was the right decision for him.

Life was still difficult, and Southall moved to various inexpensive farms around southern Victoria. The one his family lived in longest, Blackwood Farm, was without water or sewer or gas service. Southall constructed the entire estate by himself. Several of his children were born there. Unfortunately, his finances began to deteriorate, and he lost the farm shortly before his internationally-acclaimed novel *Hills End* was published in 1963.

Southall had previously published his "Simon Black" series for children, along with adult fiction and nonfiction, before he reached financial and critical success with *Hills End*. The novel, which tells the story of a cyclonic storm gone awry, advanced Southall's name worldwide. John Rowe Townsend wrote in *A Sense of Story: Essays on Contemporary Writers for Children* that "*Hills End* is almost a perfect novel of its kind. . . . The rapid character development and self-discovery of the children under stress are notable."

Southall followed the success of this book with the 1966 publication of *Ash Road*, which won the Australian Children's Book of the Year Award. *Ash Road* focuses on the effects of a fire that sweeps through the windy Australian foothills, as it comes close to an unprotected house that is filled with children. The narrative is an hour-by-hour telling of both the children who are trapped in the house and the boy who started the fire. The tension mounts just before a sudden storm stops the fire, leaving the children unscathed. "You could call this a formula novel," wrote a reviewer for *Virginia Kirkus' Service*, "But it's still a good formula, one which proves out to a sustaining sense of tension and an unusually forceful revelation of personality under stress."

Southall once again was awarded the Australian Children's Book of the Year award for his novel *To the Wild Sky* in 1968. In this work, six children are on their way to a birthday party in a private plane. The pilot has a mysterious health problem that causes him to collapse; one of the children is miraculously able to land the plane. They find themselves stranded on a remote island. The ending is ambiguous—although there are hints that the children may survive, there are also hints that they may not. "What makes *To the Wild Sky* such an outstanding book is that never for one moment does Ivan Southall forget that he is dealing with children," wrote a *Times Literary Supplement* reviewer. Virginia Haviland, critiquing the work in *Horn Book*, found that "the power of the writing lies in the author's avoidance of idealization." In 1984 Southall gave some answers about the characters' plight in the sequel *A City out of Sight*.

Mining His Memories

Southall won another award—the prestigious Carnegie Medal—for his semi-autobiographical work *Josh*. The story tells about an adolescent boy who visits his aunt in her country village. Southall himself used to make regular visits to his Aunt Susie in the bush country. Josh is a sensitive writer who finds himself at odds with the rough-and-tumble boys in the country community. They taunt him and toss him into a pond, although he is unable to swim. Scared, Josh realizes that the country is not the place for him. Gladys Williams, writing in *Books and Bookmen*, commented that the way the story is told "is original and compelling. . . . This makes the novel something more than an intriguing story—a deeply understanding character study."

In *Rachel*, published in 1986, Southall tells a story similar to his mother's harsh childhood. Set in a gold mining town in the late 1800s, the book de-

If you enjoy the works of Ivan Southall, you may also want to check out the following books and films:

Irene Bennett Brown, *Answer Me, Answer Me*, 1985.
Libby Gleeson, *Eleanor, Elizabeth*, 1990.
Michelle Magorian, *Good Night, Mr. Tom*, 1982.
Walkabout, 20th Century-Fox, 1971.

tails the difficult life of Rachel, who must circumvent the dangerous mining shafts and lives in fear of the Tantanoola Tiger. Amanda Swaney commented in the *Times Educational Supplement* that Southall "makes no compromises in his writing for children. . . . The style of *Rachel* is tough, few words of delicacy soften the writing." Alan Brownjohn, writing in the *Times Literary Supplement*, stated that Southall "has produced an unusual, oddly memorable tale."

Southall's 1988 release, *Blackbird*, chronicles the life of a boy named Will during World War II. The youth feels that it is his duty to protect his family from the Japanese army, who are threatening to invade his country. As his father goes to war, he becomes more and more reclusive, until his only companions are a blackbird and his cat. Through it all, Southall tells the story with dialogue fragments and stream-of-conscious narration. Roger Sutton, writing in the *Bulletin of the Center for Children's Books*, found the book interesting, but difficult: "A compellingly textured story is hidden in this book, but few young readers will have the patience to find it."

The Mysterious World of Marcus Leadbeater follows teenaged Marcus, whose life has been turned upside down ever since he witnessed the disappearance at sea of his beloved grandfather. His grandfather had held great expectations for Marcus, and he doesn't feel worthy of living up to them. When he visits his grandmother, he finds that all of his grandfather's possessions are going to be auctioned, even though his grandfather had promised them to him. Upset, Marcus has a glass of wine, falls into the arms of a woman, and has a dream that seems to put these events into place. *School Library Journal* reviewer Kenneth E. Kowen found the book imposing, and commented that "this

style, along with the Australian English, makes the book difficult for American young adults to follow." However, Lola H. Teubert praised the book in *Voice of Youth Advocates*, suggesting that adults should "purchase two copies of this book or read it before you circulate it; otherwise you may never get the chance."

"Ivan Southall's novels are very much 'for real'," wrote Geoffrey Fox in *Children's Literature in Education*. "He offers his readers a criticism of life which is often excruciating . . . in its insistence upon the pain, disillusionment and embarrassed failures which are integral to adolescence." Those elements are something the author has strived to put into his works. Southall remarked in *SAAS* that "life is everyone's undiscovered land coming little by little into view. The excitement of it all is why I've spent the last twenty-five years putting words around it. I've seen this kind of writing as a worthy pursuit and an accomplishment worth the striving. It's why I've gone on largely resisting the urge to write of wider adult experiences." "One of my objectives as a writer primarily for the young," he concluded, "has been to 'protect' the great moments of life, not to spoil them or 'give them away.' It's why so many of my endings are open and why I've brought the reader to bridges over which imagination has to cross."

■ Works Cited

Review of *Ash Road, Virginia Kirkus' Service*, February 15, 1966, pp. 187-88.
Brownjohn, Alan, review of *Rachel, Times Literary Supplement*, December 12, 1986, p. 1410.
Fox, Geoffrey, "Growth and Masquerade: A Theme in the Novels of Ivan Southall," *Children's Literature in Education*, APS Publications, Inc., 1971, pp. 49-64.
Haviland, Virginia, review of *To the Wild Sky, Horn Book*, August, 1967, p. 476.
Kowen, Kenneth E., review of *The Mysterious World of Marcus Leadbeater, School Library Journal*, October, 1990, pp. 144-5.
Southall, Ivan, essay in *Something about the Author Autobiography Series*, Volume 3, Gale, 1987, pp. 263-80.
Sutton, Roger, review of *Blackbird, Bulletin of the Center for Children's Books*, January, 1989, p. 135.
Swaney, Amanda, review of *Rachel, Times Educational Supplement*, November 28, 1986, p. 29.

T. H. White

■ Personal

Full name Terence Hanbury White; also wrote as James Aston. Born May 29, 1906, in Bombay, India; died January 17, 1964, in Piraeus, Greece; son of Garrick Hanbury and Constance Edith Southcote (Aston) White. *Education:* Queens' College, Cambridge, B.A. (first class honors), 1928.

■ Career

Writer. Teacher at Stowe School in England, resigned at age thirty to write full-time. *Member:* British Falconer's Club.

■ Writings

JUVENILES

The Sword in the Stone, illustrated by the author, Collins, 1938, Putnam, 1939, revised edition published in *The Once and Future King,* 1958.

The Witch in the Wood, illustrated by the author, Putnam, 1939, Collins, 1940, revised edition published as *The Queen of Air and Darkness* in *The Once and Future King,* 1958.

The Ill-Made Knight, illustrated by the author, Putnam, 1940, Collins, 1941, revised edition published in *The Once and Future King,* 1958.

Mistress Masham's Repose, illustrated by the author, Putnam, 1946.

The Master: An Adventure Story, Putnam, 1957.

The Once and Future King (includes *The Candle in the Wind* and revised versions of *The Sword in the Stone, The Witch in the Wood* and *The Ill-Made Knight*), Putnam, 1958.

The Book of Merlyn: The Unpublished Conclusion to The Once and Future King, introduction by Sylvia Townsend Warner, illustrated by Trevor Stubley, University of Texas Press, 1977.

NOVELS

(With R. McNair Scott) *Dead Mr. Nixon,* Cassell, 1931.

Darkness at Pemberley, illustrated by the author, Gollancz, 1932, Putnam, 1933.

(Under pseudonym James Aston) *They Winter Abroad,* Viking Press, 1932.

(Under pseudonym James Aston) *First Lesson,* Chatto & Windus, 1932, Knopf, 1933.

Farewell Victoria, Collins, 1933, Smith & Haas, 1934.

The Elephant and the Kangaroo, illustrated by the author, Putnam, 1947, Cape, 1948.

SHORT STORY COLLECTIONS

Earth Stopped; or, Mr. Marx's Sporting Tour, Collins, 1934.

Gone to Ground, Collins, 1935.

The Maharajah and Other Stories, edited by Kurth Sprague, Putnam, 1981.

POETRY

Loved Helen and Other Poems, Viking Press, 1929.

The Green Bay Tree; or, The Wicked Man Touches Wood, Heffer, 1929.

Verses, privately printed, 1962, published as *A Joy Proposed*, with introduction, afterword and notes by Kurth Sprague, Rota, 1980, University of Georgia Press, 1983.

OTHER

England Have My Bones (memoir), illustrated by the author, Macmillan, 1936.

Burke's Steerage; or, The Amateur Gentleman's Introduction to Noble Sports and Pastimes, Collins, 1938.

The Age of Scandal: An Excursion Through a Minor Period, Putnam, 1950.

The Goshawk (on falconry), illustrated by the author, J. Cape, 1951, Putnam, 1952.

The Scandalmonger (on English scandals), Putnam, 1952.

(Editor and translator) *The Book of Beasts, Being a Translation from a Latin Bestiary of the Twelfth Century*, Cape, 1954, Putnam, 1955.

The Godstone and the Blackymor (on Ireland), illustrated by Edward Ardizzone, J. Cape, 1959, published as *A Western Wind*, Putnam, 1959.

America at Last: The American Journal of T. H. White, Putnam, 1965.

The White/Garnett Letters, edited and with an introduction by David Garnett, Cape & Viking, 1968.

Letters to a Friend: The Correspondence Between T. H. White and L. J. Potts, edited by Francois Gallix, Putnam, 1982, Sutton, 1984.

■ Adaptations

Camelot, a stage musical by Alan Jay Lerner and Frederick Loewe based on *The Once and Future King*, was first produced in New York City in 1960, a film of the musical, starring Richard Harris and Vanessa Redgrave, was released in 1967, and a filmstrip was released by Educational Audio Visual, 1968; *The Sword in the Stone* was released as an animated film by Walt Disney Productions in 1963; *The Master* was filmed in 1966.

■ Sidelights

Socially awkward and largely reclusive, T. H. White managed to turn his obsession with King Arthur and his knights into one of the most popular and most critically acclaimed books of his generation, *The Once and Future King*. White was a prolific writer and a constant and voracious reader throughout his life. He balanced intellectual pursuits with a wide variety of sports and manual skills. He incorporated this store of knowledge into his work, enlivening his descriptions with sharply accurate descriptions of hunting and falconry. His strong, resilient character influenced all his writing, drawing comparisons to the person, though not the writings, of Hemingway.

In fact, White had far more in common with other scholarly writers of his generation. His work, like theirs, was written largely in response to the events that led to World War II. His gift was to breathe new life into the accepted legends and myths of England, to show the relevance of that history to World War II and the period that followed.

White was the sole child of terribly mismatched parents, both British citizens living in India. The daughter of an Indian judge, White's mother didn't marry his father until she was thirty. She chose him capriciously, knowing that his position as a district superintendent of police would enrage her parents. She soon found herself deeply unhappy. In Sylvia Townsend Warner's *T. H. White: A Biography*, she quotes White when he recalled one of the more dramatic moments in his parents' unpleasant marriage: "My mother and father were to be found wrestling with a pistol, one on either side of my cot, each claiming that he or she was going to shoot the other and himself or herself, but in any case, beginning with me. . . . It was not a safe kind of childhood."

White's father lapsed into serious, abusive alcoholism. Though gifted with a wild imagination and a great sense of drama, White's mother did not provide much stability either. Warner quotes him as saying, "Either there were the dreadful parental quarrels and spankings of me when I was tiny, or there were excessive scenes of affection during which she wooed me to love her—not her to love me."

By the time White was fourteen, his parents had divorced. In 1920 he was sent to Cheltenham College, a private school and military academy. White later blamed his masochistic tendencies partly on this brutalizing experience and on his confusing relationship with his mother, whom he adored for much of his childhood. White's sadistic tendencies took a personal toll; he did not successfully forge relationships with women and largely suppressed his homosexual feelings. On a less destructive note, Cheltenham was where he encountered C. F. Scott, a teacher who encouraged his writing and of whom White said, "I shall be grateful to him till I die."

To offset his tremendous lack of surety, self-confidence, and self-worth, White determined to excel academically and physically. He learned to hunt with a bow and arrow, to dive in an old-fashioned brass diving bell, to ride, to shoot, and to fish. He also learned falconry, a skill he used to great effect in his fictional writings, and to which he devoted an entire nonfiction book, *The Goshawk*. He was awarded first-class honors, with distinction, at Cambridge and went on to head the English department at Stowe School. He soon grew restless, says Warner, writing to a friend that he was anxious for the chance "to see a bit of the world while I am still young."

White balanced his booklearning with manual skills, with almost equal emphasis on intellectual and tactile abilities. Warner quotes him as saying at the time, "I am doing exactly three full-time jobs at the moment (a) being psychoanalyzed (b) being an author (c) being a schoolmaster. As relaxation I am learning to be a farmer." By 1935 he had already published two collections of poems, *Loved Helen and Other Poems* and *The Green Bay Tree* (or *The Wicked Man Touches Wood*), and four novels. An automobile accident in March of that year resulted in temporary blindness; he managed to earn enough with *England Have My Bones*, a collection of essays outlining the joys of English country life, that he resigned from Stowe to write full-time.

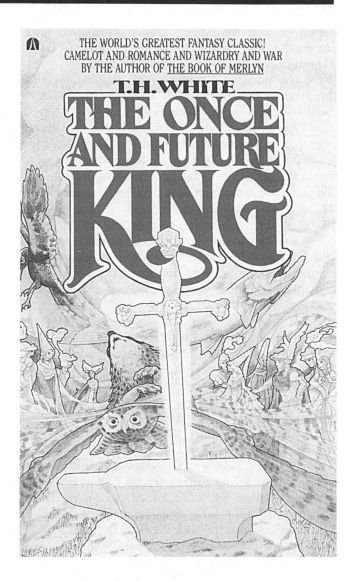

In this 1958 work, White recounts the epic adventures of King Arthur and the world of Camelot.

Reviving Arthurian Lore

White's books enjoyed a small following, but the publication of *The Sword in the Stone* brought him wide recognition, wealth, and freedom. Using Thomas Malory's fifteenth-century *Le Morte d'Arthur* as his inspiration, White traced the early years of King Arthur, focusing on his tutelage by the sorcerer Merlin—who, according to White, has been educated in the twentieth century and is now living backwards into the Middle Ages. Its famous opening line, "On Mondays, Wednesdays and Fridays it was Court Hand and Summulae Logicales, while the rest of the week it was the Organon,

Repetition and Astrology," immediately alerts readers to the dual sensibilities that guide the book. Although White drew on ancient legends for his story, the book was replete with autobiographical revelations and similarities. In particular, Merlyn expressed the author's notion that education is experience: in White's story, Merlyn turns his young charge into a fish, a hawk, a grass snake, an owl, and a badger so that he can recognize the restrictions of using force to solve problems (White was a dedicated pacifist) and understand the madness of war.

White's strength was to recreate medieval life in massive and believable detail while simultaneously poking fun at medieval concerns and beliefs. His wordplay takes the form of broad puns and complicated references to other literary, musical, and art works. He also scatters the story with symbols from children's literature, in particular the familiar fairy-tale use of animals as collaborators. Their assistance is necessary in helping Arthur to extract the sword from the stone.

Throughout, the novel draws from both realistic and fantastic elements. White lavished great detail on his hunting scenes. Arthur and his foster brother Kay speak and relate to one another like teenagers. Anachronisms, such as neon signs, and descriptions that rely on a knowledge of the twentieth century, play off quotations from Shakespeare and Latin poetry. In this sense, the book reflects its author's many scholarly accomplishments and his sense of humor.

For the most part, reviewers praised *The Sword and the Stone* highly. Typical was Vida D. Scudder's assessment in the *Atlantic Monthly* that it was "riotously funny. . . . If you are a boy, you can find here the best battles and enchantments going. . . . If you are just an ordinary person, it would be a pity for you to miss King Pellinore, blood-brother to the White Knight, and his household pet, the Blatant Beast; or Friar Tuck, turned into a pink china Cupid on Morgan le Fay's mantelpiece, or the living room of Madame Mim, B.A. Whoever you may be, don't miss this book." Writing in the *New Yorker*, Clifton Fadiman took issue with White's humor, terming his Twainian efforts "pretty dreadful," but he acknowledged that White knew whereof he spoke in matters of hunting and falconry. Fadiman concluded that the book was not meant to be taken seriously on any level but that White "wrote the book just for a lark, and a

very nice lark it turned out to be, too." The film rights to the work were acquired by Walt Disney Studios. By the time the film was produced, however, White had made heavy revisions to *The Sword in the Stone* in order to include it in *The Once and Future King*. He narrowed his focus to war's lunacy, removing many humorous references, and giving the book overall a graver, less exuberant tone.

Despite his professional success, White remained largely alone and lonely. He had friends, including the writer David Garnett, but was made terribly uncomfortable by his homosexual inclinations. He resorted to hormonal treatments in an attempt to deal with these feelings, and often turned to alcohol for relief.

Two More Installments in a Darker Vein

In 1939 White moved to Ireland, partly to find seclusion for his work and partly to avoid the stress of World War II England. During that time, he wrote the second and third installments of the Once and Future King tetralogy: *The Witch in the Wood*, later revised to *The Queen of Air and Darkness*, and *The Ill-Made Knight*. White showed a grimmer side to his characters in *The Witch in the Wood*, beginning a shift he would continue over the series. He did not leave absurdities out completely, but in this book he concentrated on Gawain, Gareth, and their brothers, showing how their problematic childhoods were marred by their mother. Alternating a complete lack of attention with an overbearing obsession, she leaves the boys reeling—much like White's own mother. The book also focuses on Arthur and Merlyn's attempts to define war and to debate whether it can ever be useful or justified.

Reviewers were generally critical of *The Queen of Air and Darkness*. Iris Barry wrote in the *New York Herald Tribune Books* that "a defiant minority refuses to succumb to Mr. White's entertaining but often outrageous volumes. The mixture of seriousness and levity, the occasional archness and buffoonery that follow beautiful and grave passages, even the ease of the writing all combine into a highly individual dish." One of that minority was *Commonweal* critic William J. Grace, who noted that "Mr. White in revising the Arthurian material for popular consumption succeeds admirably in completely failing to understand either its spiritual significance or its aristocratic wit . . . and reaches a very high degree of banality."

Again, White's own concerns are reflected in his work, despite the fact that the narrative is not directly autobiographical. The shadow of World War II looms over his later books. Warner quotes White as writing, "I have made up my mind about this war at last. I am not going to fight in it." His decision sprang from his belief in his writing project. "My most important business is to finish my version of Malory, and so I shall tell any tribunal which sits on me. I cannot finish it if dead; I am the only person who can finish it. I have been at it unconsciously ever since I was at Cambridge, when I wrote a thesis on Malory; anybody can throw bombs."

More Popularity, Further Seclusion

White's next novel was *The Ill-Made Knight* which dealt with Sir Lancelot—physically unattractive, but an adept knight and the most gifted jouster of his time. The focus of the story is Lancelot's love for Guenever. Their affair is an adulterous betrayal of Arthur, but, paradoxically, a pure love as well. Although Lancelot does not reach the Holy Grail—or even see it—he is redeemed by bringing about a partial healing.

Critics were favorably impressed with *The Ill-Made Knight*, including *Commonweal*'s Olive B. White, who found that it matched its predecessors in "virtuosity and wit, and it outdoes them in wisdom, swift, scalpel-sharp, of a kind infrequently

In 1963, Walt Disney Productions came out with a full-length animated feature based on *The Sword in the Stone*, featuring a screenplay by Bill Peet.

consorting with cleverness." Writing in the *New York Times Book Review,* Beatrice Sherman praised it as "a more thoughtful, adult and subdued piece of writing" than the first two novels. Summing up in the *New York Herald Tribune Books,* Florence Haxton Bullock described *The Ill-Made Knight* as managing "both to debunk and to build up again on a more likely, human basis, the life of a period which has been fairly glamorized out of existence."

White wrote these books in Ireland, in the house of the McDonagh family. Publication of *The Elephant and the Kangaroo,* a direct satire of the family inspired by Chaucer's *Miller's Tale,* brought his friendship with the McDonaghs to a close. Nor did it make many points with critics. Charles Lee's write-up in the *New York Times Book Review* stated flatly that "[it] is not entirely clear what *The Elephant and the Kangaroo* is all about," but that "whatever it is, it does not come off."

White returned to England after the war and settled in Yorkshire. While there, White fell in love with a thirteen-year-old farm girl. This attachment prompted him to write *Mistress Masham's Repose,* a children's novel of great complexity and multiple plot lines. Maria, the protagonist, is a ten-year-old orphan who lives in a derelict mansion in Northamptonshire with only her governess and a cook for company. The grounds include monuments of every sort, dedicated to figures of the eighteenth and nineteenth centuries, enough to give White ample opportunity to make reference to historical details, gossip, events, personalities, and literature of those periods.

In her exploration of her surroundings, Maria comes upon Mistress Marsham's Repose, a summer pavilion that houses five hundred Lilliputians. Eventually they, along with a Merlyn-like professor who is her only friend, help Maria to reclaim her rightful inheritance. *Commonweal's* Francis X. Connolly said that White "deserves to be mentioned in the company of Evelyn Waugh, C. S. Lewis, and George Orwell as one of the few fortunate possessors of a splendid prose style." He added that: "There are no sermons in the book, but one must be an irretrievable adult not to pick up some wisdom from this delightful story. . . . May it be read for the century to come."

Many of White's nonfiction writings dealt with human history, gossip, sports, and other pursuits

The final chapter to *The Once and Future King,* this work was published posthumously in 1977.

of the moneyed classes, but in *The Goshawk,* he detailed his own attempt to become a falconer using seventeenth-century handbooks. Ostensibly a book for children, *The Goshawk* is a chronicle of the struggles between man and bird, a relationship composed equally of love and hate. In the *New York Times,* Henry Morton Robinson felt that White "is grappling with a mysterious, ruthless power, embodied in a bird that never voluntarily stoops (unless killing be its mood) to the level of the earth-treading man." But the *New York Herald Tribune Book Review's* Joseph Wood Krutch interpreted this struggle quite differently, positing that readers might "suspect in Mr. White's glorification of violence something uncomfortably close to the kind of romanticism which inspired recent unsuccessful political experiments in certain parts of Europe."

The last book for young people that White wrote was *The Master: An Adventure Story*, which he set on an island midway between Russia and America. Believed to be drowned, twelve-year-old twins Nicky and Judy are given up for dead by their wealthy parents. They are in fact imprisoned, along with their dog, by the Master, a 157-year-old scientist, and his misfit staff. Eventually, it becomes clear that the Master is grooming Nicky to take over the world using techniques developed by the elder scientist. Filled with postwar warnings about militarism and the dangers of might-makes-right thinking, *The Master* was deemed a failure by many critics. Among the gentlest criticisms were those voiced by Maurice Richardson in the *New Statesman & Nation* who found that despite the work's ambitious scope, "it remains too much of a mish-mash of ideas and wheezes."

In 1958, White thoroughly revised his Arthurian novels and added to them *The Candle in the Wind*, which detailed the infighting that eventually undid Arthurian England. The entire saga appeared under the title *The Once and Future King*. In a journal entry, quoted by Warner, White noted on the day he completed the work that "I finished what I hope is my final revision of *The Once and Future King*, about twenty years after I started it, and believe and hope it is a great book. It sounds presumptuous to say so, but on a great subject, which is the epic of Britain, you have to write downright badly to make a mess of it."

Hailing White's achievement in *The Once and Future King*, a *Times Literary Supplement* reviewer said: "In three fields particularly the author excels. He can draw living people; he can describe a landscape; and he can enter into the inmost minds of birds and beasts. . . . This ambitious work, so long in the building, now stands complete. It will long remain a memorial to an author who is at once civilized, learned, witty and humane." In the *New York Herald Tribune Book Review*, Richard Winston rejoiced over "a whole stout volume of T. H. White's unique wit, vast and curious learning and brooding wisdom, a volume of levity and gravity for young and old." Erwin D. Canham echoed this in the *Christian Science Monitor*, where he declared "England's no-

If you enjoy the works of T. H. White, you may also want to check out the following books and films:

Stephen R. Lawhead, *Arthur*, 1989.
Marion Zimmer Bradley, *The Mists of Avalon*, 1982.
Welwyn Wilton Katz, *The Third Magic*, 1989.
Excalibur, Warner Bros., 1981.

blest tale, the composite memories of its golden age, have been put together by an expert medievalist who is also a brilliant storyteller, a wit, a master of romance and invention. . . . All this, and infinitely more, is woven together with literary genius, archaeological authority, and a freshness which is as bright as the dawn of history and the memories we associate with a golden age. It is hard to say at which level White's greatness is most special." In a critical discussion of the author's work titled *T. H. White*, John K. Crane stated that "White's masterpiece, *The Once and Future King*, is, ultimately, an examination of mankind's addiction to warfare and of his moral and physical destruction by it."

Camelot and a Love Affair with the U.S.

Alan Jay Lerner and Frederick Lowe adapted White's most famous work for their 1960 stage musical *Camelot*, which starred Julie Andrews and Richard Burton. The film version wasn't made until 1973, when Richard Harris, Vanessa Redgrave, and Franco Nero led the cast. In his journal, quoted by Warner, White wrote that he was "perfectly satisfied" with this version of his work. His early success with *The Sword in the Stone* had afforded him financial freedom. He described himself as "indifferent" to the added profits, "as I have no kith or kin to spend them on and no ambitions for myself."

White altered his accustomed pattern of solitude to make a lecture tour through the United States from 1963 to 1964. He had a wonderful time and wrote to a friend, as quoted by Warner, that "the students of La Salle College gave me, for the last time I shall get it, the stunning applause and affection which makes my heart turn over, and I am miserable that the tour is finished." He greatly enjoyed America, the landscape, the animals, and people that he met: "novelty, discovery, beauty, grandeur, simplicity, seriousness, youth, vigour, [the] enormousness of the United States combine to look over our shoulders and say, Don't go. In spite of the killing struggle, perhaps because of it, I have never been happier in my life." Later, his account of this trip appeared under the title *America at Last: The American Journal of T. H. White.*

White departed the United States in January, 1964, aboard the *S. S. Exeter*, bound for Europe. He visited Spain, Italy, Egypt, and Lebanon. Greece was the last stop on the tour. Enroute White died of acute coronary disease at the age of fifty-seven. Writing to a friend two years earlier, according to Warner, he grimly predicted that "I think I will go to Venice and Naples and perhaps do a Byron and never come back any more. I expect to make a rather good death. The essence of death is loneliness, and I have plenty of practice at this." White was buried in Athens, Greece. His papers are contained in the T. H. White Collection of the Harry Ransom Humanities Research Center, University of Texas at Austin.

White's final addition to the *Once and Future King, The Book of Merlyn*, was published posthumously in 1977. In it, he turned Merlyn into a pacifist philosopher, a didactic instrument for White's own desire to rid the world of war. White never submitted *The Book of Merlyn* for publication and the volume was deemed of inferior quality to the rest of the novels by several critics. Typical of the response was Harold C. Schonberg's article in the *New York Times Book Review* which stated that "all White loyalists will rush to read it, if only to savor the way their hero's mind works." A second posthumous publication, *The Maharajah and Other Stories*, garnered many of the same qualified responses. The stories dealt with many of the themes of White's longer works, in particular the tension between the world of feelings and the rational world. A reviewer for *Publishers Weekly* noted that "an inevitable sameness" weakened many of the stories, but that White's "superb storytelling" compensated for the similarities. Writing in *Best Sellers*, Frank Kelly compared White's best stories to those of Saki, but despite "a few gems" found the collection disappointing.

White was a prolific, dedicated writer. His work gave his life a much-needed center. As Crane writes, "T. H. White was a man who despised life as it was made for him by his mother, his homosexuality, organized religion and world politics." Yet, he continues, White was able "to fashion his life into a meaningful existence in which his own standards and personal morality replaced those which would otherwise have been imposed upon him by the modern world's manufactured machinery, manufactured war, manufactured god, and manufactured Hell." Similarly, Schonberg assessed White as "a wonderful writer and . . . a man who so desperately wanted the world to live up to his dream: a dream in which the state never exceeds the individual, and in which the future lies with the personal soul." Fortunately for White's readers, he dealt constructively with his disappointments and failings, using literature to compensate for what he missed out on in life.

■ Works Cited

"Arthurian Achievement," *Times Literary Supplement*, April 25, 1958, p. 224.

Barry, Iris, "More Moonstruck Madness," *New York Herald Tribune Books*, November 5, 1939, p. 6.

Bullock, Florence Haxton, "Meet Lancelot and His Lady," *New York Herald Tribune Books*, November 17, 1940, p. 6.

Canham, Erwin D., "'A Yankee's Odyssey'—Far Frontiers—'The Once and Future King': Arthur and the 'Matter of Britain,' *Christian Science Monitor*, August 28, 1958, p. 11.

Connolly, Francis X., review of *Mistress Masham's Repose, Commonweal*, November 15, 1946, p. 125.

Crane, John K., *T. H. White*, Twayne, 1974, pp. 18, 186-88.

Fadiman, Clifton, "Three Novels to Open," *New Yorker*, January 7, 1939, pp. 45-46.

Grace, William J., review of *The Queen of Air and Darkness, Commonweal*, November 24, 1939, pp. 121-22.

Kelly, Frank, review of *The Maharajah and Other Stories, Best Sellers*, November, 1981, pp. 292-93.

Krutch, Joseph Wood, "The Violent Taming of a Violent Hawk," *New York Herald Tribune Book Review*, March 23, 1952, p. 4.

Lee, Charles, "Ould Sod, Trampled," *New York Times Book Review*, April 13, 1947, p. 18.

Review of *The Maharajah and Other Stories, Publishers Weekly*, July 31, 1981, p. 47.

Richardson, Maurice, review of *The Master, New Statesman & Nation*, March 9, 1957, p. 316.

Robinson, Henry Morton, "Dominating the Hawk," *New York Times*, March 23, 1952, p. 6.

Scudder, Vida D., review of *The Sword in the Stone*, *Atlantic Monthly*, February, 1939, pp. 3, 5.

Schonberg, Harold C., "Unhappy Ending," *New York Times Book Review*, November 27, 1977, pp. 15, 46.

Sherman, Beatrice, "T. H. White's New Spoof on the Arthurian Legend," *New York Times Book Review*, November 10, 1940, p. 6.

Warner, Sylvia Townsend, *T. H. White: A Biography*, Viking Press, 1967.

White, Olive B., review of *The Ill-Made Knight*, *Commonweal*, December 20, 1940, p. 235.

White, T. H., *The Sword in the Stone*, illustrated by the author, Collins, 1938, Putnam, 1939.

Winston, Richard, "T. H. White's Arthurian Omnibus Rolls to a Triumphant Conclusion," *New York Herald Tribune Book Review*, August 24, 1958, p. 3.

■ For More Information See

BOOKS

Carter, Lin, *Imaginary Worlds: The Art of Fantasy*, Ballantine Books, 1973.

Contemporary Literary Criticism, Volume 30, Gale, 1984.

Gallix, Francois, editor, *Letters to a Friend: The Correspondence between T. H. White and L. J. Potts*, Putnam, 1982.

Gallix, Francois, *T .H. White: An Annotated Bibliography*, Garland, 1986.

Garnett, David, editor, *The White/Garnett Letters*, Viking, 1968.

Silvey, Anita, editor, *Children's Books and Their Creators*, Houghton, 1995, p. 678.

Meynell, Viola, editor, *The Best of Friends: Further Letters to Sydney Carlyle Cockerell*, Hart-Davis, 1956.

Reference Guide to English Literature, St. James Press, 1991.

St. James Guide to Fantasy Writers, 1st edition, edited by David Pringle, St. James Press, 1996.

■ Obituaries

Illustrated London News, January 25, 1964.
Newsweek, January 27, 1964.
New York Times, January 18, 1964.
Publishers Weekly, January 27, 1964.*

—Sketch by C. M. Ratner

Rita Williams-Garcia

■ Personal

Born April 13 in Jamaica, Queens, NY; father was in the U.S. Army; mother was a domestic servant; married Peter Garcia; children: Michelle, Stephanie. *Education:* Graduated from Hofstra University; pursuing a master's degree in creative writing, Queens College; also studied dance under Alvin Ailey and Phil Black. *Hobbies and other interests:* Chess, playing Tetris, jogging, sewing.

■ Addresses

Home—Jamaica, NY.

■ Career

Writer; Interactive Market Systems, New York City, manager of software distribution and production. Has also worked as a dancer and reading teacher. *Member:* Authors Guild, Society of Children's Book Writers and Illustrators.

■ Awards, Honors

Notable Books for Children and Young Adults citation, American Library Association (ALA), 1991, for *Fast Talk on a Slow Track; Booklist* Editors' Choice selection, 1995, Best Books for Young Adults citation, ALA, and Coretta Scott King Honor Book selection, ALA, both 1996, all for *Like Sisters on the Homefront;* PEN/Norma Klein Award for Children's Fiction, 1997.

■ Writings

Blue Tights, Lodestar, 1988.
Fast Talk on a Slow Track, Lodestar, 1991.
Like Sisters on the Homefront, Lodestar, 1995.

■ Work in Progress

Every Time a Rainbow Dies, a novel about a young boy who falls in love with a rape victim.

■ Sidelights

"Focusing her attention on contemporary African American youth," writes Susan P. Bloom in *Twentieth-Century Young Adult Writers,* "Rita Williams-Garcia informs her fictional teenagers with her own experiences as student, as teacher, as dancer." Her three young adult novels to date show young black men and women living and coping with difficulties in an honest, uncontrived manner. "Williams-Garcia's portrayal of these urban black adolescents and their worlds feels genuine, neither sensationalized nor romanticized," declares *Horn Book* contributor Rudine Sims Bishop. "Her work is marked by an authentic rendering of the styles and cadences of urban black language, some touches of humor, and strong, dynamic characterization." Together with such African American writers as Jacqueline Woodson, Dolores Johnson, and Angela Johnson, says Bishop, Williams-Garcia "show[s] great promise, and with continuing support and nurturing, . . . may well turn out to be among the most prominent African-American literary artists of the next generation."

"I was born in Queens, New York, at the tail end of the fifties," Williams-Garcia tells Susan Pais, Phyllis Brown, Ann Gartner, and Kay E. Vandergrift in a specially-conducted interview posted on their web page, "Learning about Rita Williams-Garcia." "My father was in the army so we traveled by car across the country. Our first stop was to Arizona when I was three—a sweeping contrast to our Far Rockaway projects" The family then settled in the California town of Seaside, where Rita and her siblings spent their childhood. "We played a lot outdoors; we were very athletic children," she explains to *Booklist* interviewer Hazel Rochman. "We were always doing things. My sister was an artist. My brother was into math. I loved words; I just thought that was normal. To characterize me as a kid, you could say that I was definitely a geek."

Perhaps the most important influence on Williams-Garcia's life, she says, was her mother, whom she calls "Miss Essie." "My sister, brother and I grew up thinking our mother, `Miss Essie,' discovered Pop Art," the author states in a publisher's biography released by Penguin Books. "When she wasn't cleaning, working or in school, Miss Essie painted every little thing that needed color."

Development

Williams-Garcia developed her reading skills early in life. She recalls in her "Learning about Rita Williams-Garcia" interview that she taught herself to read at age two by learning to associate letters

with their sounds, partly through looking at billboards and partly through the efforts of her older sister, who would often share her books with young Rita. By the time she entered school, Williams-Garcia was already an accomplished reader and a writer of poetry and stories, "mostly adventures that involved the heroic exploits of my sister Rosalind, brother Russell and I."

> *"None of my characters are truly me, although there is always some aspect of me in each and every one."*
>
> —Rita Williams-Garcia

Williams-Garcia was exposed to racial issues while growing up during the 1960s. She remembers discussing race relations and racism in the classroom in the aftermath of the 1968 riots, the assassination of Dr. Martin Luther King, Jr., and the militant political views of the Black Panthers. At the age of twelve, she left California for Georgia for six months, then settled in Jamaica, New York. In the sixth grade, she reports in her "Learning about Rita Williams-Garcia" interview, she went looking for literature for young adults that featured black protagonists. She discovered biographies of historical figures, such as Harriet Tubman and Sojourner Truth, and a single novel (*Mary Ellen, Student Nurse*), but little else. "When I brought this up to the school librarian . . . she gave me three books about a West African girl who would rather hunt with her father, the chief, than do traditional girl things," the author recalls. "I'll pay a king's ransom to know the title and author of the aforementioned books!" Her teachers encouraged her to write for herself, and at age fourteen she published her first story in *Highlights* magazine.

"None of my characters are truly me," Williams-Garcia states in her interview, "although there is always some aspect of me in each and every one. Joyce in *Blue Tights* is a voluptuous teen with dance inside of her. Denzel in *Fast Talk* is a bright young man who must face himself. Gayle in *Like Sisters on the Homefront* has lived through a lot of pain but refuses to acknowledge it. That's where similarities between myself and my characters pretty much end. Outside of watching football and baseball with my sister, my adolescence was uneventful."

Dance

When Williams-Garcia enrolled in Hofstra University, she temporarily dropped writing for other activities. "In college, real life seemed to displace my need to `make' stories," she explains in the Penguin publishers biography, "so I didn't write for nearly three years. (Real life was running my dance company and being political)." She declared a major in economics, auditioned for dancing roles in musicals, and performed community outreach work through her sorority, Alpha Kappa Alpha. In her senior year in college, Williams-Garcia enrolled in a creative writing class. She combined her outreach work—teaching high school girls remedial reading—with her writing workshop training and penned an early version of the story that became *Blue Tights*.

Blue Tights is partly based on Williams-Garcia's own experiences, but it is mostly a conglomeration of the stories of many young women. The book tells the tale of Joyce Collins, an ambitious African American girl who loves to dance and exhibits great talent. However, Joyce finds that she is shut out of her school's European-oriented dance program because the dance instructor believes her body shape is not suited to ballet. Besides dealing with this great disappointment, Joyce has to come to terms with her home life—she has been raised by an often absent mother and a religiously fanatic aunt—and her identity. "A volatile combination of worldliness and innocence," Bishop states, "Joyce seeks love and popularity in all the wrong places and with all the wrong people." "Williams-Garcia does not shy away from the harsh circumstances that define Joyce and her family," explains Bloom. "Aunt Em's severe treatment of Joyce stems from a horrific self-induced coat hanger abortion she suffered in her adolescence. Williams-Garcia provides less sensational, daily evidence of the grinding poverty that eats at this family." "Through her work with an African-American dance troupe," Bishop concludes, Joyce "discovers her own special talents as a dancer and achieves a new appreciation of her own self-worth."

It took Williams-Garcia almost ten years to get *Blue Tights* published. While she worked on the book, revising and collating the stories she had assembled from her own life and the lives of her reading students, she went to work for a marketing company in Manhattan, churning out manuscripts on an IBM typewriter in the company mailroom. The manuscript of *Blue Tights* (originally titled *Blue Tights, Big Butt*), however, kept returning to the author with depressing regularity. Editors complained that the protagonist had a poor self-image and was too focused on her appearance. "The letters I got back from editors and agents were more or less on the same lines," the author explains to Rochman. "Can you make the

Denzel Watson takes a door-to-door sales job when he finds the going at Princeton University too tough in this 1991 work.

girl older, about 17, if there's going to be any kind of sexual content in the book? Or, this is not a good role model; she's not positive; she doesn't have anything uplifting to offer to young African American women growing up; can you do something about her attitude? Can you do something about all these references to black culture? Readers aren't going to understand them. Can you make it more universal?" Williams-Garcia put the manuscript away after three years of marketing it unsuccessfully.

Williams-Garcia continued to write and submit stories during the 1980s until her job was cut in a company restructuring. In the meantime she had married and given birth to two daughters. She brought the *Blue Tights* manuscript to Lodestar Books, a publishing house known for its history of publishing challenging books. The novel was released in 1988 and won recognition from many reviewers. "By writing about urban black teenagers and a young girl who aspires to be a dancer," Nancy Vasilakis states in *Horn Book*, "Rita Williams-Garcia incorporates a setting and a subject that she obviously knows well." "The novel vividly evokes [Joyce's] neighborhood and the rigor and joy of her dancing," writes a *Booklist* critic, adding, "Joyce's sexual conflicts are treated with candor." "Joyce's understanding is believably paced and powerfully realized," declares a *Publishers Weekly* reviewer, "and her story is uplifting."

Success out of Failure

While Joyce Collins's story becomes uplifting through her realization of her own potential and self-respect, Denzel Watson's story becomes uplifting in the way he deals with failure while moving from high school to college. Denzel, the smooth-talking valedictorian of his high school, attends a summer program for minority students at Princeton University. Denzel had relied on his winning personality throughout high school, but he quickly discovers that he cannot use the same tricks in college. "While he is involved with the summer program, he struggles with the feeling of inadequacy and decides not to return to Princeton in the fall," writes Jo Holtz in *Voice of Youth Advocates*. "For the first time in his life, he feels like a failure." Denzel turns to a part-time job as a door-to-door salesman to regain his self-esteem, and experiments briefly with the world of black

---

If you enjoy the works of Rita Williams-Garcia, you may also want to check out the following books and films:

Rosa Guy, *The Music of Summer*, 1992.
Walter Dean Myers, *Hoops*, 1981.
Cynthia Voight, *Come a Stranger*, 1986.
Fame, MGM, 1980.

---

street culture. Finally, however, he bows to family pressure and resolves to enter Princeton in the fall, "to find that, with a little humility and some serious study, he *can* hack it," explains a *Kirkus Reviews* contributor. "The author puts it to her college-bound readers: When the time comes, will *they* have what it takes to step up to a new, very challenging world?"

Fast Talk on a Slow Track won as much attention from reviewers as *Blue Tights* had. It was cited on the American Library Association's Notable Books for Children and Young Adults list. "Williams-Garcia writes just as authoritatively about teenage boys as she did about girls in her first novel," states Nancy Vasilakis in *Horn Book*. "She understands the forces and fears driving a young man in search of his true self." "Teens everywhere," writes Hazel Rochman in *School Library Journal*, "will be able to identify and commiserate with Denzel as he goes through his options, gains confidence, and matures."

The heroine of *Like Sisters on the Homefront*, fourteen-year-old Gayle, also has her own set of problems and needs to gain maturity in order to cope with them. After she becomes pregnant for a second time (her first pregnancy resulted in a son, Jose, now seven months old), her mother takes her to an abortion clinic and then ships her off to the family home in Georgia. At first Gayle feels uncomfortable in the rural environment; she is away from her boyfriend and homegirls and has to cope with her uncle's disapproval, her aunt's insistence on proper child care for her young son, and her cousin Cookie's religious standards. She begins to change when her aunt gives her the responsibility for caring for her great-grandmother, Great, who is sick and near death. The relationship between Great and Gayle deepens as the old woman's condition worsens. Great "exhibits a strength of spirit and a stubbornness that Gayle recognizes in herself," writes reviewer Nancy Vasilakis in *Horn Book*. "Great understands Gayle, too. `When you lay down your deviling,' she tells her great-granddaughter, `you'll be stronger than those who lived by the rule all their lives.'"

Great finally chooses Gayle to receive the Telling, the source of family history that keeps the family together. "Strong-willed, self-absorbed, and impulsive," states Vasilakis, Gayle "is not unlike the heroine of Williams-Garcia's earlier novel, *Blue Tights*, imbued with a lively mix of naivete and worldliness, particularly in sexual matters, that gives her characterization depth and vibrancy." "Painting Gayle as a hard-edged, high-spirited young woman clearly headed for either trouble or triumph," states Deborah Stevenson in the *Bulletin of the Center for Children's Books*, "Williams-Garcia breathes life into what could have been a stereotypical portrait of a trash-talking, streetwise city teen, and while its scales are tipped in favor of a responsible life, the book is honest enough to acknowledge the pleasures of the other kind."

Williams-Garcia plans to continue her pattern of writing strong, hard-hitting books about African-American teens living in the modern world—not in times of great crisis, but in the small crises of everyday life. "I really don't think we deal with the complex issues of our young people's lives," she tells Rochman. "We tell them about racism and those kinds of things, . . . but then there's that real person who has to deal with the fact that he is not a symbol, he is not a model, he is a real, flesh-and-blood person who makes mistakes and has to keep moving and learning and accepting all these things as part of life. . . . It's what you come to know about yourself that is more important than any big thing that might happen to you."

■ Works Cited

Bishop, Rudine Sims, "Books from Parallel Cultures: New African-American Voices," *Horn Book*, September-October, 1992, pp. 616-20.

Bloom, Susan P., "Rita Williams-Garcia," *Twentieth-Century Young Adult Writers*, 1st edition, St. James, 1994, pp. 709-10.

Review of *Blue Tights, Booklist*, December 15, 1987, pp. 696-97.

Review of *Blue Tights, Publishers Weekly*, November 13, 1987, p. 73.

Review of *Fast Talk on a Slow Track, Kirkus Reviews*, February 1, 1991, pp. 179-80.

Holtz, Jo, review of *Fast Talk on a Slow Track, Voice of Youth Advocates*, June, 1991, pp. 104-5.

Pais, Susan, Phyllis Brown, Ann Gartner, and Kay E. Vandergrift, compilers and interviewers, "Learning about Rita Williams-Garcia," http://www.scils.rutgers.edu/special/kay/williamsgarcia.html.

"Rita Williams-Garcia" (publishers' release), http://www.penguin.com/usa/childrens/bios/garcia.htm.

Rochman, Hazel, review of *Fast Talk on a Slow Track, School Library Journal*, April, 1991, p. 143.

Rochman, Hazel, "The Booklist Interview: Rita Williams-Garcia," *Booklist*, February 15, 1996, pp. 1002-3.

Stevenson, Deborah, review of *Like Sisters on the Homefront, Bulletin of the Center for Children's Books*, September, 1995, p. 34.

Vasilakis, Nancy, review of *Blue Tights, Horn Book*, March-April, 1988, pp. 215-16.

Vasilakis, Nancy, review of *Fast Talk on a Slow Track, Horn Book*, July-August, 1991, p. 466.

Vasilakis, Nancy, review of *Like Sisters on the Homefront, Horn Book*, November-December, 1995, pp. 748-49.

■ For More Information See

BOOKS

Children's Literature Review, Volume 36, Gale, 1995, pp. 202-6.

PERIODICALS

ALAN Review, winter, 1996.

Booklist, April 1, 1991, p. 1561.

Bulletin of the Center for Children's Books, January, 1988, p. 106; June, 1991, pp. 253-54; September, 1995, p. 34.

Dance, November, 1993, p. 81.

Kirkus Reviews, December 1, 1987, p. 1680.

Publishers Weekly, February 8, 1991, pp. 58-59.

School Library Journal, June-July, 1988, p. 120.

Voice of Youth Advocates, August, 1988, p. 136.*

—*Sketch by Kenneth R. Shepherd*

Jane Yolen

■ Personal

Born February 11, 1939, in New York, NY; daughter of Will Hyatt (an author and in public relations) and Isabelle (a social worker and homemaker; maiden name, Berlin) Yolen; married David W. Stemple (a professor of computer science), September 2, 1962; children: Heidi Elisabet, Adam Douglas, Jason Frederic. *Education:* Smith College, B.A., 1960; University of Massachusetts, M.Ed., 1976. *Politics:* Liberal Democrat. *Religion:* Jewish-Quaker. *Hobbies and other interests:* Folk music and dancing, reading, camping, politics, all things Scottish.

■ Addresses

Home—Phoenix Farm, 31 School Street, Box 27, Hatfield, MA 01038; and Wayside, 96 Hepburn Gardens, St. Andrews, Fife, Scotland KY16 9LN. *Agent*—Marilyn Marlow, Curtis Brown Ltd., 10 Astor Place, New York, NY 10003.

■ Career

Saturday Review, New York City, production assistant, 1960-61; Gold Medal Books (publishers), New York City, assistant editor, 1961-62; Rutledge Books (publishers), New York City, associate editor, 1962-63; Alfred A. Knopf, Inc. (publishers), New York City, assistant children's book editor, 1963-65; full-time professional writer, 1965—. Editor of imprint, Jane Yolen Books, for Harcourt Brace Jovanovich, 1988-96. Teacher of writing and lecturer, 1966—. Chairman of board of library trustees, Hatfield, MA, 1976-83; member of Arts Council, Hatfield. *Member:* International Kitefliers Association, Society of Children's Book Writers and Illustrators (member of board of directors, 1974—), Science Fiction Writers of America (president, 1986-88), Children's Literature Association (member of board of directors, 1977-79), Author's Guild, Science Fiction Poetry Association, National Association for the Preservation and Perpetuation of Storytelling, Western New England Storytellers' Guild (founder), Bay State Writers Guild, Western Massachusetts Illustrators Guild (founder), Smith College Alumnae Association.

■ Awards, Honors

Boys' Club of America Junior Book Award, 1968, for *The Minstrel and the Mountain;* Lewis Carroll Shelf Award, 1968, for *The Emperor and the Kite,* and 1973, for *The Girl Who Loved the Wind; The Emperor and the Kite* was selected as one of the *New York Times*'s Best Books of the Year and as a Caldecott Honor Book, both 1968; *World on a String: The Story of Kites* was named an American

Library Association (ALA) Notable Book, 1968; Chandler Book Talk Reward of Merit, 1970; *The Girl Who Loved the Wind* was selected for the Children's Book Showcase of the Children's Book Council, 1973, and *The Little Spotted Fish*, 1976; Golden Kite Award from the Society of Children's Book Writers, 1974, ALA Notable Book and National Book Award nomination, both 1975, all for *The Girl Who Cried Flowers and Other Tales*; Golden Kite Honor Book, 1975, for *The Transfigured Hart*, and 1976, for *The Moon Ribbon and Other Tales*; Christopher Medal, 1978, for *The Seeing Stick*.

Children's Choice from the International Reading Association and the Children's Book Council, 1980, for *Mice on Ice*, and 1983, for *Dragon's Blood*; LL.D. from College of Our Lady of the Elms, 1981; Parents' Choice Award from the Parents' Choice Foundation, 1982, for *Dragon's Blood*, 1984, for *The Stone Silenus*, and 1989, for *Piggins* and *The Three Bears Rhyme Book*; *The Gift of Sarah Barker* was selected one of *School Library Journal*'s Best Books for Young Adults, 1982, and *Heart's Blood*, 1985; Garden State Children's Book Award from the New Jersey Library Association, 1983, for *Commander Toad in Space*; CRABerry Award from Acton Public Library (MD), 1983, for *Dragon's Blood*; *Heart's Blood* was selected one of ALA's Best Books for Young Adults, 1984; Mythopoeic Society's Fantasy Award, 1984, for *Cards of Grief*; Daedelus Award, 1986, for "a body of work—fantasy and short fiction"; *The Lullaby Songbook* and *The Sleeping Beauty* were each selected one of Child Study Association of America's Children's Books of the Year, 1987; Caldecott Medal, 1988, for *Owl Moon*; World Fantasy Award, 1988, for *Favorite Folktales from Around the World*; Kerlan Award for "singular achievements in the creation of children's literature," 1988; Parents' Choice Silver Seal Award, Jewish Book Council Award, and Association of Jewish Libraries Award, all 1988, Judy Lopez Honor Book and Nebula Award finalist, both 1989, Maud Hart Lovelace Book Award, 1997, all for *The Devil's Arithmetic*; Golden Sower Award from the Nebraska Library Association, 1989, and Charlotte Award from New York State Reading Association, both for *Piggins*.

Smith College Medal for body of work, 1990; Skylark Award, New England Science Fiction Association, 1990; Regina Medal for body of writing in children's literature, 1992; Mythopoeic Fantasy Award for Adult Literature, Mythopoeic Society, 1993, for *Briar Rose*; Notable Book for Children se-

lection, ALA, and Blue Ribbon Book selection, *Bulletin of the Center for Children's Books*, both 1995, both for *The Ballad of the Pirate Queens*; Notable Book for Children selection, ALA, 1996, for *O'Jerusalem*; Children's Book of Distinction Award, Hungry Mind Review, for *Passager*, 1997; thirteen of Yolen's books have been selected by the Junior Literary Guild.

■ Writings

YOUNG ADULT FICTION

The Magic Three of Solatia, illustrated by Julia Noonan, Crowell, 1974.
The Gift of Sarah Barker, Viking, 1981.
Dragon's Blood: A Fantasy (first volume in trilogy), Delacorte, 1982.
Neptune Rising: Songs and Tales of the Undersea Folk (story collection), illustrated by David Wiesner, Philomel, 1982.
Heart's Blood (second volume in trilogy), Delacorte, 1984.
The Stone Silenus, Philomel, 1984.
Children of the Wolf, Viking, 1986.
Spaceships and Spells, Harper, 1987.
A Sending of Dragons (third volume in trilogy), illustrated by Tom McKeveny, Delacorte, 1987.
The Devil's Arithmetic, Viking, 1988.
The Faery Flag: Stories and Poems of Fantasy and the Supernatural, Orchard Books, 1989.
The Dragon's Boy, Harper, 1992.
Here There Be Dragons, illustrated by David Wilgus, Harcourt, 1993.
Here There Be Unicorns, illustrated by David Wilgus, Harcourt, 1994.
Here There Be Witches, illustrated by David Wilgus, Harcourt, 1995.
Here There Be Angels, Harcourt, 1996.
Passager (first volume in "Young Merlin Trilogy"), Harcourt, 1996.
Hobby (second volume in "Young Merlin Trilogy"), Harcourt, 1996.
Twelve Impossible Things before Breakfast, Harcourt, 1997.
Merlin (third volume in "Young Merlin Trilogy"), Harcourt, 1997.

ADULT FICTION

The Lady and the Merman, illustrated by Barry Moser, Pennyroyal, 1977.
Tales of Wonder (story collection), Schocken, 1983.
Cards of Grief (science fiction), Ace Books, 1984.

Merlin's Booke, Steel Dragon Press, 1984.

Dragonfield and Other Stories (story collection), Ace Books, 1985.

Sister Light, Sister Dark, Tor Books, 1988.

White Jenna, Tor Books, 1989.

Briar Rose, Tor Books, 1992.

Storyteller, New England Science Fiction Association, 1992.

The Books of Great Alta, Tor Books, 1997.

The One-Armed Queen, Tor Books, 1998.

ADULT NONFICTION

Writing Books for Children, The Writer, 1973, revised edition, 1983.

Touch Magic: Fantasy, Faerie, and Folklore in the Literature of Childhood, Philomel, 1981.

Guide to Writing for Children, Writer, 1989.

JUVENILE FICTION

The Witch Who Wasn't, illustrated by Arnold Roth, Macmillan, 1964.

Gwinellen, the Princess Who Could Not Sleep, illustrated by Ed Renfro, Macmillan, 1965.

(With Anne Huston) *Trust a City Kid*, illustrated by J. C. Kocsis, Lothrop, 1966.

The Emperor and the Kite, illustrated by Ed Young, World Publishing, 1967.

The Minstrel and the Mountain: A Tale of Peace, illustrated by Anne Rockwell, World Publishing, 1967.

Robin Hood (musical), first produced in Boston, MA, 1967.

Isabel's Noel, illustrated by Roth, Funk, 1967.

Greyling: A Picture Story from the Islands of Shetland, illustrated by William Stobbs, World Publishing, 1968.

The Longest Name on the Block, illustrated by Peter Madden, Funk, 1968.

The Wizard of Washington Square, illustrated by Ray Cruz, World Publishing, 1969.

The Inway Investigators; or, The Mystery at McCracken's Place, illustrated by Allan Eitzen, Seabury, 1969.

Hobo Toad and the Motorcycle Gang, illustrated by Emily McCully, World Publishing, 1970.

The Seventh Mandarin, illustrated by Ed Young, Seabury, 1970.

The Bird of Time, illustrated by Mercer Mayer, Crowell, 1971.

The Girl Who Loved the Wind, illustrated by Ed Young, Crowell, 1972.

The Girl Who Cried Flowers and Other Tales, illustrated by David Palladini, Crowell, 1974.

The Boy Who Had Wings, illustrated by Helga Aichinger, Crowell, 1974.

The Adventures of Eeka Mouse, illustrated by Myra McKee, Xerox Education Publications, 1974.

The Rainbow Rider, illustrated by Michael Foreman, Crowell, 1974.

The Little Spotted Fish, illustrated by Friso Henstra, Seabury, 1975.

The Transfigured Hart, illustrated by Donna Diamond, Crowell, 1975.

Milkweed Days, photographs by Gabriel A. Cooney, Crowell, 1976.

The Moon Ribbon and Other Tales, illustrated by David Palladini, Crowell, 1976.

The Seeing Stick, illustrated by Remy Charlip and Demetra Maraslis, Crowell, 1977.

The Sultan's Perfect Tree, illustrated by Barbara Garrison, Parents Magazine Press, 1977.

The Giants' Farm, illustrated by Tomie de Paola, Seabury, 1977.

The Hundredth Dove and Other Tales, illustrated by David Palladini, Crowell, 1977.

Hannah Dreaming, photographs by Alan R. Epstein, Museum of Fine Art (Springfield, MA), 1977.

Spider Jane, illustrated by Stefan Bernath, Coward, 1978.

The Simple Prince, illustrated by Jack Kent, Parents Magazine Press, 1978.

No Bath Tonight, illustrated by Nancy W. Parker, Crowell, 1978.

The Mermaid's Three Wisdoms, illustrated by Laura Rader, Collins, 1978.

Dream Weaver and Other Tales, illustrated by Michael Hague, Collins, 1979.

The Giants Go Camping, illustrated by Tomie de Paola, Seabury, 1979.

Commander Toad in Space, illustrated by Bruce Degen, Coward, 1980.

Spider Jane on the Move, illustrated by Stephan Bernath, Coward, 1980.

Mice on Ice, illustrated by Lawrence DiFiori, Dutton, 1980.

The Robot and Rebecca: The Mystery of the Code-Carrying Kids, illustrated by Jurg Obrist, Knopf, 1980.

Shirlick Holmes and the Case of the Wandering Wardrobe, illustrated by Anthony Rao, Coward, 1981.

The Robot and Rebecca and the Missing Owser, illustrated by Lady McCrady, Knopf, 1981.

The Acorn Quest, illustrated by Susanna Natti, Harper, 1981.

Brothers of the Wind, illustrated by Barbara Berger, Philomel, 1981.

Sleeping Ugly, illustrated by Diane Stanley, Coward, 1981.

The Boy Who Spoke Chimp, illustrated by David Wiesner, Knopf, 1981.

Uncle Lemon's Spring, illustrated by Glen Rounds, Dutton, 1981.

Commander Toad and the Planet of the Grapes, illustrated by Bruce Degen, Coward, 1982.

Commander Toad and the Big Black Hole, illustrated by Bruce Degen, Coward, 1983.

Commander Toad and the Dis-Asteroid, illustrated by Bruce Degen, Coward, 1985.

Commander Toad and the Intergalactic Spy, illustrated by Bruce Degen, Coward, 1986.

Owl Moon, illustrated by John Schoenherr, Philomel, 1987.

Commander Toad and the Space Pirates, illustrated by Bruce Degen, Putnam, 1987.

Piggins, illustrated by Jane Dyer, Harcourt, 1987.

(Reteller) *The Sleeping Beauty,* illustrated by Ruth Sanderson, Knopf, 1987.

Picnic with Piggins, illustrated by Jane Dyer, Harcourt, 1988.

Piggins and the Royal Wedding, illustrated by Jane Dyer, Harcourt, 1989.

Dove Isabeau, illustrated by Dennis Nolan, Harcourt, 1989.

Dream Weaver, Putnam, 1989, reissued with new book jacket by Michael Hague.

Baby Bear's Bedtime Book, illustrated by Jane Dyer, Harcourt, 1990.

Sky Dogs, illustrated by Barry Moser, Harcourt, 1990.

Tam Lin, illustrated by Charles Mikolaycak, Harcourt, 1990.

Elfabet: An ABC of Elves, illustrated by Lauren Mills, Little, Brown, 1989.

Letting Swift River Go, illustrated by Barbara Cooney, Little, Brown, 1990.

Wizard's Hall, Harcourt, 1991.

Eeny, Meeny, Miney Mole, illustrated by Kathryn Brown, Harcourt, 1992.

Encounter, illustrated by David Shannon, Harcourt, 1992.

Hands, illustrated by Chi Chung, Sundance Publishing, 1993.

All Those Secrets of the World, illustrated by Leslie Baker, Little, Brown, 1993.

Beneath the Ghost Moon, illustrated by Laurel Molk, Little, Brown, 1993.

Grandad Bill's Song, illustrated by Melissa B. Mathis, Putnam, 1993.

Mouse's Birthday, illustrated by Bruce Degen, Putnam, 1993.

Honkers, illustrated by Leslie Baker, Little, Brown, 1993.

(Compiler) *Weather Report,* illustrated by Annie Gusman, Boyds Millss Press, 1993.

And Twelve Chinese Acrobats, illustrated by Jean Gralley, Putnam, 1994.

Good Griselle, illustrated by David Christiana, Harcourt, 1994.

The Girl in the Golden Bower, illustrated by Jane Dyer, Little, Brown, 1994.

Old Dame Counterpane, illustrated by Ruth T. Councell, Putnam, 1994.

Little Mouse and Elephant: A Tale from Turkey, illustrated by John Segal, Simon & Schuster, 1994.

The Musicians of Bremen: A Tale from Germany, illustrated by John Segal, Simon & Schuster, 1994.

The Ballad of the Pirate Queens, illustrated by David Shannon, Harcourt, 1995.

Before the Storm, illustrated by Georgia Pugh, Boyds Mills Press, 1995.

A Sip of Aesop, illustrated by Karen Barbour, Scholastic, 1995.

Merlin and the Dragons, illustrated by Ming Li, Dutton, 1995.

The Wild Hunt, illustrated by Mora Francisco, Harcourt, 1995.

(With Edith E. Y. Stemple) *Meet the Monsters,* Walker & Co., 1996.

Nocturne, illustrated by Anne Hunter, Harcourt, 1996.

Wings, Harcourt, 1997.

Child of Faerie, Child of Earth, illustrated by Jane Dyer, Little, Brown, 1997.

Miz Berlin Walks, illustrated by Floyd Cooper, Philomel, 1997.

Once upon a Bedtime Story (retellings), illustrated by Ruth T. Councell, 1997.

King Long Shanks, illustrated by Victoria Chess, Harcourt, 1998.

The Mystery of the Mary Celeste, Simon & Schuster, forthcoming.

Commander Toad and the Voyage Home, Putnam, forthcoming.

The Sea Man, Putnam, forthcoming.

JUVENILE NONFICTION

Pirates in Petticoats, illustrated by Leonard Vosburgh, McKay, 1963.

World on a String: The Story of Kites, World Publishing, 1968.

The Fireside Song Book of Birds and Beasts, musical arrangements by Barbara Green, illustrated by Peter Parnall, Simon & Schuster, 1972.

Friend: The Story of George Fox and the Quakers, Seabury, 1972.

The Wizard Islands, illustrated by Robert Quackenbush, Crowell, 1973.

Ring Out! A Book of Bells, illustrated by Richard Cuffari, Seabury, 1974.

Simple Gifts: The Story of the Shakers, illustrated by Betty Fraser, Viking, 1976.

(Compiler) *Rounds about Rounds*, illustrated by Gail Gibbons, F. Watts, 1977.

Lullaby Song Book, musical arrangements by Adam Stemple, illustrated by Charles Mikolaycak, Harcourt, 1984.

The Lullaby Songbook, musical arrangements by Adam Stemple, illustrated by Charles Mikolaycak, Harcourt, 1986.

The Lap-Time Song and Play Book, musical arrangements by Adam Stemple, illustrated by Margot Tomes, Harcourt, 1989.

Jane Yolen's Mother Goose Song Book, musical arrangements by Adam Stemple, illustrated by Rosekrans Hoffman, Boyds Mills Press, 1992.

A Letter from Phoenix Farm, illustrated with photographs by Jason Stemple, Richard C. Owen, 1992.

Jane Yolen's Songs of Summer, musical arrangements by Adam Stemple, illustrated by Cyd Moore, Boyds Mills Press, 1993.

Welcome to the Green House, illustrated by Laura Reagan, Putnam, 1993.

Jane Yolen's Old MacDonald Songbook, illustrated by Rosekrans Hoffman, Boyds Mills Press, 1994.

Sing Noel, musical arrangements by Adam Stemple, illustrated by Nancy Carpenter, Boyds Mills Press, 1996.

Welcome to the Sea of Sand, illustrated by Laura Regan, Putnam, 1996.

JUVENILE POETRY

See This Little Line?, illustrated by Kathleen Elgin, McKay, 1963.

It All Depends, illustrated by Don Bolognese, Funk, 1970.

An Invitation to the Butterfly Ball: A Counting Rhyme, illustrated by Jane B. Zalben, Parents Magazine Press, 1976.

All in the Woodland Early: An ABC Book, illustrated by Jane B. Zalben, Collins, 1979.

How Beastly!: A Menagerie of Nonsense Poems, illustrated by James Marshall, Philomel, 1980.

Dragon Night and Other Lullabies, illustrated by Demi, Methuen, 1980.

Ring of Earth: A Child's Book of Seasons, illustrated by John Wallner, Harcourt, 1986.

The Three Bears Rhyme Book, illustrated by Jane Dyer, Harcourt, 1987.

Best Witches: Poems for Halloween, illustrated by Elise Primavera, Putnam, 1989.

Bird Watch, illustrated by Ted Lewin, Philomel, 1990.

Dinosaur Dances, illustrated by Bruce Degen, Putnam, 1990.

(Compiler) *Street Rhymes Around the World*, Boyds Mills Press, 1992.

Raining Cats and Dogs, illustrated by Janet Street, Harcourt, 1993.

What Rhymes with Moon?, illustrated by Ruth T. Councell, Philomel, 1993.

Sleep Rhymes Around the World, Boyds Mills Press, 1993.

(Compiler) *Alphabestiary: Animal Poems from A to Z*, illustrated by Allan Eitzen, Boyds Mills Press, 1994.

Sacred Places, illustrated by David Shannon, Harcourt, 1994.

Animal Fare: Zoological Nonsense Poems, illustrated by Janet Street, Harcourt, 1994.

Three Bears Holiday Rhyme Book, illustrated by Jane Dyer, Harcourt, 1995.

Water Music: Poems for Children, illustrated with photographs by Jason Stemple, Boyds Mills Press, 1995.

(Compiler) *Mother Earth Father Sky: Poems of Our Planet*, illustrated by Jennifer Hewitson, Boyds Mills Press, 1996.

Oh, Jerusalem, illustrated by John Thompson, Scholastic, 1996.

Sea Watch: A Book of Poetry, illustrated by Ted Lewin, Putnam, 1996.

(Compiler) *Sky Scrape: City Scape Poems of City Life*, illustrated by Ken Condon, Boyds Mills Press, 1996.

(Compiler) *Once upon Ice and Other Frozen Poems*, illustrated with photographs by Jason Stemple, Boyds Mills Press, 1997.

The Originals, illustrated by Ted Lewin, Putnam, forthcoming.

EDITOR

Zoo 2000: Twelve Stories of Science Fiction and Fantasy Beasts, Seabury, 1973.

Shape Shifters: Fantasy and Science Fiction Tales about Humans Who Can Change Their Shape, Seabury, 1978.

(With others) *Dragons and Dreams: A Collection of New Fantasy and Science Fiction Stories*, Harper, 1986.

Favorite Folktales from Around the World, Pantheon, 1988.

(With Martin H. Greenberg) *Werewolves: A Collection of Original Stories*, Harper, 1988.

(With Martin H. Greenberg) *Things That Go Bump in the Night*, Harper, 1989.

2041 AD (science fiction anthology), Delacorte, 1990.

(With Martin H. Greenberg) *Vampires*, Harper, 1991.

Xanadu, Tor Books, 1993.

Xanadu Two, Tor Books, 1994.

Xanadu Three, Tor Books, 1995.

Camelot: A Collection of Original Arthurian Tales, illustrated by Winslow Pels, Putnam, 1995.

(With Greenberg) *The Haunted House: A Collection of Original Stories*, illustrated by Doron Ben-Ami, HarperCollins, 1995.

OTHER

(Author of introduction) *Best-Loved Stories Told at the National Storytelling Festival*, National Storytelling Association, 1996.

Also author of *The Whitethorn Wood*, a chapbook. Contributor to books, including *Dragons of Light*, 1981; *Elsewhere*, Volume 1, 1981, Volume 2, 1982; *Hecate's Cauldron*, 1982; *Heroic Visions*, 1983; *Faery!*, 1985; *Liavek*, 1985; *Moonsinger's Friends*, 1985; *Imaginary Lands*, 1985; *Don't Bet on the Prince: Contemporary Feminist Fairy Tales in North America and England*, 1986; *Liavek: Players of Luck*, 1986; *Liavek: Wizard's Row*, 1987; *Visions*, 1987; *Liavek: Spells of Binding*, 1988; *Invitation to Camelot*, 1988; *The Unicorn Treasury*, 1988, and dozens more. Some of Yolen's manuscripts are held in the Kerlan Collection at the University of Minnesota.

Author of column "Children's Bookfare" for *Daily Hampshire Gazette* during the 1970s. Contributor of articles, reviews, poems, and short stories to periodicals, including *Writer, Parabola, New York Times, Washington Post Book World, Los Angeles Times, Parents' Choice, New Advocate, Horn Book, Wilson Library Bulletin, Magazine of Fantasy and Science Fiction, Isaac Asimov's Science Fiction Magazine*, and *Language Arts*. Member of editorial boards of *Advocate* (now *New Advocate*) and *National Storytelling Journal* until 1989. Some of Yolen's books have been published in England, France, Spain, Brazil, Germany, Austria, Norway, Sweden, China, Korea, South Africa (both in Afrikaans and Xhosa), Australia, Japan, and Denmark.

■ Adaptations

The Seventh Mandarin was filmed by Xerox Films, 1973; *The Emperor and the Kite* is available as a filmstrip with cassette, Listening Library, 1976; *The Bird of Time* was produced as a play in Northampton, MA, 1982; *The Girl Who Cried Flowers and Other Tales* was taped by Yolen by Weston Woods, 1983; *Dragon's Blood* was made into an animated television movie, *CBS Storybreak*, 1985; *Commander Toad in Space* was taped by Listening Library, 1986; *Touch Magic . . . Pass It On*, a selection of Yolen's stories told by Milbre Burch, was taped by Weston Woods, 1987; *Owl Moon* is available as a filmstrip with cassette, Weston Woods, 1988; *Piggins and Picnic with Piggins* was taped by Caedmon, 1988.

■ Work in Progress

Novels, *Many Mansions* and *Armageddon Summer*; picture books *The Traveler's Rose, Raising Yoder's Barn, Harvest Home*, and *Enough*; anthologies *Gray Heroes* and *Pandora's Box*.

■ Overview

Since Jane Yolen has an impressive catalogue of books, it is hard to believe that her first work was not published until 1963. Having written books of poems, fiction, and non-fiction for children, young adults, and adults alike, Yolen would seem to have had little time for anything else. Yet she still managed to have three children while establishing herself as the "American Hans Christian Andersen," as she was dubbed by publisher Ann K. Beneduce. Such acclaim, however, is not what Yolen wants for herself. In an essay in *Something about the Author Autobiography Series* (*SAAS*) she says, "I just want to go on writing and discovering my stories for the rest of my life because I know that in my tales I make public what is private, transforming my own joy and sadness into tales for the people." Yolen's massive collection has earned her numerous honors, most notably the Christopher Medal in 1978 for *The Seeing Stick* and the Caldecott Medal for *Owl Moon* in 1988. Her books continue to be enjoyed by adults as well as children.

It was not until 1980 that Yolen was "discovered" by the general reading public and her work began being published in anthologies, collections, magazines, and textbooks. Her fairy tales and mythological stories captured the popular imagination at a time when the art of storytelling experienced a massive rebirth in America. Suddenly people were gathering together to listen to someone tell stories, and Yolen's were among the favorites. On the basis of this experience, she comments in *SAAS*, she has "two pieces of advice for young people interested in writing: read and write. Read and read and read. It's the only way you'll discover what great stories have been told, and what stories you want to tell better."

Yolen's life can be summed up in one word: "imagination." She is the eldest of two children of William Hyatt Yolen, an author and pioneer of the resurgence of kite-flying in America, and Isabelle Berlin Yolen, herself a writer who constructed crossword puzzles for magazines. Yolen was born in New York, New York, in 1939, but she claims in *SAAS*, "I remember practically nothing about my early childhood." With her father stationed in Europe during World War II, Jane went to live with her grandparents in Hampton Roads, Virginia. After the death of her grandfather (one of many deaths in Yolen's life that would later affect her writings), she recalls that "the house seemed haunted and cold." The family returned to New York City, where Jane began her education. "I was in half a dozen schools by second grade, both public and private, as my mother looked for the best school for me," she remarks in *SAAS*. Yolen was not detoured by the rapid change of scenery, however, and she soon discovered her love for reading. "When I read our semester's reading book overnight, the teacher had no alternative but to skip me into second grade." At school she excelled beyond any expectations. The teachers took it upon themselves to nurture her budding abilities. Fueled by the desire to get as many gold stars as she could for her work, Yolen wrote the lyrics and music for the school musical, in which everyone was a particular vegetable. She played the lead carrot, and the finale was a salad.

Yolen's early educational experiences (at least those she can remember) have greatly influenced her writing. When she was appointed class secretary three years in a row, she memorized all the names of the children in the class, in alphabetical order, a trick she can still perform to this day. This ability later provided a large number of the character names that appear in her books. By the time Yolen reached sixth grade, her talent for reading, writing, music, and leadership was apparent, and

she was tested for one of the New York special schools for gifted students. She was accepted to Hunter, an all-girl's school, where she felt she would excel just as she had in public school. "To my surprise—and horror—I was barely in the middle of my class and managed to stay there only by studying extremely hard," Yolen confesses in *SAAS*.

> *"I just want to go on writing and discovering my stories for the rest of my life because I know that in my tales I make public what is private, transforming my own joy and sadness into tales for the people."*
>
> —Jane Yolen

Feeling humbled, Yolen turned her attention to her the real sources of her talent—music and writing. Playing the piano, performing ballet, singing, and writing poems and stories brought Yolen praise at school. She wrote an essay in rhyme for an eighth-grade social studies class, and she completed her first two books: a nonfiction book about pirates and a seventeen-page novel about life in the old West. Yolen feels that a novel should be short. "I have come to writing full-scale novels almost reluctantly," she writes in *SAAS*, "and it is always a struggle for me to make them long enough. Somehow, seventeen pages still seems about right!"

When Yolen was twelve and thirteen, she spent two summers at a camp in Vermont that was run by Quakers. Having been born Jewish, she was exposed to new ideas about pacifism and love. At camp she also discovered the impact that storytelling can have on the life of both the listener and the storyteller. After her second year, Yolen's parents unexpectedly bought a house in Westport, Connecticut. She and her brother Steve were unable to say goodbye to their friends in New York, a reality that had a unsettling affect on her. She was unable to attend the Arts and Music High School as she had hoped, and she was separated from her best friend. In Westport, however, she found a new best friend who was Catholic, a religion Yolen had had little contact with in her previous friendships. Attending mass with her friend, she was captivated by the rites and rituals performed in the Catholic service. This exposure influenced her later book *Cards of Grief*, which utilized elements of Mass, communion, confession, and other Catholic traditions.

The greatest influence on Yolen's life during this period, however, was her cousin-in-law Honey Knopp, who stimulated her interest in the life of George Fox, founder of the Quaker movement. This led her later to write a biography of Fox, *Friend: The Story of George Fox and the Quakers*. Recounting Knopp's impact on her life in *SAAS*, Yolen says, "Her [Honey's] influence can be seen in many of my books: *The Minstrel and the Mountain*, *The Boy Who Sang for Death*, *The Transfigured Hart*, *The Hundredth Dove*, *The Gift of Sarah Baker* among them."

Into Journalism

After graduating from high school, Yolen decided to attend Smith College, an all-woman's school in western Massachusetts, where she began to nurture her love for singing and started writing copious amounts of poetry and fiction. She found it difficult to make and sustain friendships with women, as most of her friends in high school had been males. Not letting this detour her from the immense possibilities that Smith had to offer, Yolen became friends with members of the faculty. She also worked on the school newspaper and became convinced she wanted to be a journalist. Remarking on this decision in *SAAS*, Yolen reports, "The summer of my freshman/sophomore year, I worked as a cub reporter for the *Bridgeport Sunday Herald*. It was there I wrote my first pieces for a newspaper. My first byline read 'by Joan Yolen.'"

Yolen continued to hold internships and jobs with other publications. But feeling unsatisfied, she decided she was better suited to be a writer, not a fact-checker or a mail room worker. "I spent the first few months of 1961 trying to make a living as a free-lance writer. I researched and helped write a book for my father who had been asked to do *The Young Sportsman's Guide to Kite Flying*." Her father's efforts almost single-handedly led to the rebirth of kite-flying as a sport, resulting in Yolen's first book. During this period she was also a freelance writer—a difficult way to make a living because jobs were short-term and low in pay.

Yet Yolen continued to write, hoping that one day her work would be published.

In 1962, after a long courtship, Jane married David Stemple. As she wrote in *SAAS*, "I realized that my fairy tale *The Girl Who Loved The Wind*, which is dedicated to David, is about our meeting. In it a Persian girl is kept in a walled-in palace by her overprotective father until the day the wind leaps over the garden wall and sweeps her away into the wide, everchanging world." Shortly after her marriage she received a letter that would forever change the course of her life. A publisher from A. A. Knopf named Judith Jones had been visiting college campuses to find students who might have publishable manuscripts. At Smith, Jones was told there was only one recent graduate who had any hope at all as an author, a young woman named Jane Yolen. When Jones approached Yolen about her writings, Yolen did the only thing she felt she could to get her foot in the door: she lied, saying she had completed several books. At the time, Yolen thought she might use Jones as a future reference when she had completed more work and had published some articles.

One can imagine Yolen's surprise when Jones wrote back and requested to see her manuscripts. Yolen wrote about this precarious situation in her *SAAS* autobiography. "Caught in the web of deceit I, who had always prided myself on my honesty, realized there was nothing to do but sit down at my typewriter and get something done quickly. Children's books!" Yolen was about to discover, however, that children's books are among the most difficult kind of literature to write. The stories have to be concise, yet still be just as involved and interesting as full-blown adult novels. Yolen was so eager to get published, though, that she took what little she associated with children's books (pictures, the alphabet, and of course her father's favorite, kite-flying), teamed up with an illustrator, and whipped out a few books. Along with these manuscripts, she was armed with a proposal for a book on lady pirates, taken from the idea she had in the eighth grade.

When she went in for her interview, however, Yolen's attempts were not received well. The editor was expecting a full-length novel, not a children's book, and Yolen's manuscripts were simply not very good. Yolen then decided to send her manuscripts around to other publishers. Al-

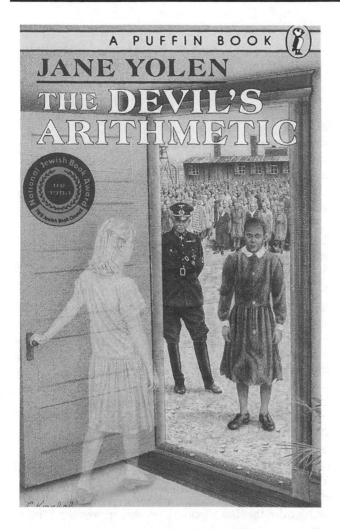

This 1988 work, concerning a girl who travels back in time to a Nazi concentration camp, was a finalist for the Nebula Award.

unknown writer that Dobbs hired, but also the first to receive a cash advance for work not yet written. The relationship between Dobbs and Yolen lasted for one more book, *See This Little Line*, before their inability to see eye-to-eye on the visual packaging for the book led Yolen to look for another publisher.

Serious Publishing

During this time Yolen worked at Gold Medal Books. Afterward she left for a job at Rutledge, a publisher of children's literature, where she met the editor Francis Keene. Keene would later publish many of Yolen's book and provide her with direction in her writing. Yolen eventually concluded that Rutledge was not a good place to learn the ins and outs of children's literature, so she went to Knopf. She worked there happily for three years while continuing to write. In August 1965 Yolen and her husband set sail to travel around Europe for a year. Yolen left her business ventures in the hands of a woman named Marilyn Marlow. While in Europe, Yolen found out that she was pregnant. Completing their trip, she and David returned to the United States. David took a job at the University of Massachusetts Computer Center in Amherst, and they purchased a house. Heidi Elisabeth was born on July 1, 1966.

While the Yolens were traveling Marlow had not been able to sell any of Jane's books. Nevertheless, Yolen continued to place her trust in Marlow, and it paid off. Two days after she returned home, Yolen was called to Marlow's office and informed that three books had been sold—all on the same day! The first, *It All Depends*, which Yolen had written in Israel, was sold to her former editor, Frances Keene. The other two books, *The Minstrel and the Mountain* and *The Emperor and the Kite*, were sold to an editor who would have a great affect on Yolen's life, Ann K. Beneduce of the World Publishing Company. Together they have published nearly thirty books.

After Heidi, the Yolens had two sons, Adam and Jason. Yolen says her children provide her with plenty of inspiration and characters, which can be seen in such books as *The Lullaby Songbook, Milkweed Days, No Bath Tonight,* and *The Stone Silenus.* Shortly after Jason was born, Yolen's mother died from cancer. Greatly shaken, Yolen dealt with her grief through her stories. *The Bird of Time*, for instance, expressed her desire to slow down time

though she received masses of rejection letters, she refused to be discouraged. "Of course I was crushed," she admits in *SAAS*. "Rejection, in person or by rejection letter, is never easy to take. But it is one of the constants in the world of publishing and anyone too shaken in confidence by a first refusal (or a second or a twenty-second) will never make it in the writing world." Finally, Yolen was introduced to Rose Dobbs, an editor at David McKay Publishing Company, who showed some interest in her work. Not liking the actual books Yolen had written, Dobbs was intrigued by the proposed book, *Pirates in Petticoats*. She said that McKay usually did not buy work from unknown writers, but she asked Yolen to leave the proposal for consideration. Sure enough, two months later Yolen became not only the first and stop her mother's gradual demise. *Cards of Grief*, a book that paints grieving as the highest art form, comes straight from Yolen's own pain and realizations about death.

With a growing family, Yolen and her husband decided to move to Hatfield, Massachusetts, where they have a fourteen-room farmhouse. Here Yolen became involved in the Society of Children's Book Writers (now the Society of Children's Book Writers and Illustrators) and has since served on the board of directors. She also teaches children literature at Smith College and gives numerous seminars. It was not until 1980, however, that she was discovered by the general audience. Her stories were being published in numerous magazines as well as being at the forefront of the storytelling revival taking place in the United States. From 1966 to 1990 Yolen wrote dozens of books. She attributed her productivity to her passion for writing. Her average day starts at eight in the morning and does not end until four or five in the afternoon. Many found it difficult to believe that she could keep her focus and generate such a large amount of material. For Yolen, however, it is simply a way of life. "For me," she stated, "writing is work and pleasure. I am very focused."

■ Update

Since 1990 Yolen has continued to edit and write prolifically. Her subjects have remained as diverse as her previous writings, ranging from Arthurian legend to dragon fantasies to cosmic events that affect the changing of the seasons. She has also selected stories and poems by some of the best fantasy writers in the business (some of them relatively unknown) and presented them in an anthology series entitled *Xanadu*. The first installment of *Xanadu* was released in 1993, and subsequent editions were published in 1994 and 1995.

One of Yolen's most ambitious projects has been the "Here There Be" series, which is written for younger children but can be enjoyed by readers of all ages. Each book is illustrated by David Wilgus, giving the series a feeling of unity. The first book, *Here There Be Dragons*, which was published in 1993, contains five poems and eight stories celebrating the mythical creatures. Yolen's style and subject matter differ greatly within the book, which includes tales of heroic battles, romance,

and the science fiction of other-world dragons. Like many of Yolen's books, some of the stories are laugh-out-loud funny, while others are moving and poignant. Yolen opens each selection with an introduction that explains its evolution (where, why, and how she wrote it) and what she is trying to express through the tale. *Here There be Dragons* was praised by critics. Among them was Susan L. Rogers, who writes in *School Library Journal*: "after experiencing [the dragons'] variety and might, readers won't be able to help echoing the author's hopes that they will return some day."

The next installment in the "Here There Be" series deals with another mythical creature loved by adults and children alike—the unicorn. *Here There Be Unicorns* draws on both Western and Eastern unicorn legends, weaving the two folkloric traditions into one masterful volume. As in *Here There Be Dragons*, each piece is prefaced by an explanation of the folklore surrounding the tale. Some of the stories have a present-day setting, but most have a traditonal "fairy tale feel," such as "The Unicorn in the Pool," which shows the protective power of the unicorn's horn against poisons. "The Boy Who Drew Unicorns" tells the tale of a traumatized boy who is unable to speak, yet is healed by the power of the unicorn's horn. Once again Yolen earned critical acclaim. In a review for *Booklist* Chris Sherman observes, "Yolen lends insight into the background of the myths and into her own creative process."

Yolen followed the two previous volumes with *Here There Be Witches*. With seven poems and ten short stories, she provides a diverse look at witches, from the humorous to the dramatic. The book addresses the fear people have of witches, and the hysteria that can result, much like the Salem witch trials in Massachusetts. "Weird Sisters," a poem about the power of the average person to cast spells, and the effects they can have, is one of the book's high points. Karen Hutt notes in *Booklist* that the "intriguing and entertaining compilation . . . will appeal to young adolescent readers" who enjoy works dealing with the supernatural.

Yet another "Here There Be" book was released in 1996. *Here There Be Angels* contains over a dozen stories and poems, featuring angels from both the Old and New Testaments as well as modern times. Angels appear in settings throughout the world—Greece, Russia, and New York

David Wilgus illustrated Yolen's 1996 collection of stories and poems titled *Here There Be Angels*.

If you enjoy the works of Jane Yolen, you may also want to check out the following books and films:

Joan Aiken, *Give Yourself a Fright: Thirteen Stories of the Supernatural*, 1989.
Allen Appel, *Time After Time*, 1985.
M. E. Kerr, *Gentlehands*, 1978.
Annette Curtis Klause, *The Silver Kiss*, 1990.
Excalibur, Warner Bros., 1981.
Interview with the Vampire, Geffen, 1992.

City—and touch people's lives in differing ways. Shirley Wilton, writing for the *School Library Journal*, comments that the book will influence aspiring younger writers, calling *Here There Be Angels* "A welcome addition to an interesting series."

Another of Yolen's achievements during the 1990s has been her dedication to keeping Arthurian legend alive, fresh, and accurate. Along with writing her own Arthurian stories, including a trilogy about Merlin, Yolen has also edited *Camelot: A Collection of Original Arthurian Stories*. For this project she gathered stories by some notable children's writers, including Nancy Springer, James B. MacDonald, and Debrah Doyle. Yolen then wove together a book that puts a new spin on old tales, and created some new ones, as well. Helen Gregory, writing in *School Library Journal*, remarks, "The women who appear in these stories tend to be stronger than in Malory's or other versions of the familiar tales."

Yolen's book on Arthurian legend, *The Dragon's Boy*, was published in 1990. Utilizing extensive research, the book is a coming-of-age tale of Artos (Arthur) and his teacher, Old Linn (Merlin). The story begins with Old Linn doubting his ability to get young Artos's attention, which causes him to construct a fire-breathing dragon to hide behind. Using the dragon, Old Linn convinces Artos to become his student. But when Artos finds out the dragon's true identity, he is furious. Old Linn is then able to persuade Artos to realize his own importance and the role of his lineage. When Artos recognizes the truth, he becomes a full disciple of Merlin. *The Dragon's Boy* is a valuable source of information as well as entertainment for children interested in Arthurian legend. As Vir-

ginia Golodetz observes in *School Library Journal*, that the author "skillfully develops those aspects of Artos character that will guide him in his adult life—courage, compassion, and fairness."

Introduces Merlin Trilogy

Along with *The Dragon's Boy*, Yolen also published *Passager*, the first book in the "Young Merlin Trilogy." Released in 1996, *Passager* is an unusual Arthurian tale. It operates on the human level, dealing with the emotions of Merlin rather than his magical capabilities. The tale begins with eight-year-old Merlin living alone in the forest and surviving off the land. After alienating himself from the rest of the world, Merlin begins to forget the customs and languages used by society. One day a man comes along hunting, and Merlin is captivated by him and his hunting hawk. Merlin follows the man out of the forest and is exposed to the comforts and confines of society. At first Merlin rebels, but he eventually grows to love and trust the man. "There is no magic or fantasy in Yolen's stark, poignant, and absorbing tale. Readers feel the sun, rain, hunger, and fear as the child does, . . ." Susan L. Rogers comments in *School Library Journal*.

The second book in the trilogy is *Hobby*, also published in 1996. The book opens with the now twelve-year-old Merlin burying his foster family, who were killed in a fire. Feeling guilt and shame for not comprehending a prophetic dream, Merlin leaves the farm where he had lived with the family and sets out on his own. As he wanders about the countryside, his dreams continue to come true in strange and mysterious ways. Merlin meets a traveling magician and his companion. The two men name him Hobby, after a small species of hawk. The three end up in the town of Carmarthen. The trip proved to be a fateful one for Merlin, who announces one of his dreams to an audience in the palace at Carmarthen. While the magician interprets the dream to have a happy ending, Merlin knows it is a prophecy of the death of the duke of Carmarthen. Abandoned by his companions, Merlin attempts to tell the duke about his dream, but the duke refuses to believe him. As Mary Jo Drungil notes in *School Library Journal*, *Hobby* provides an important link with adult Arthurian tales: "Though little information about Merlin's childhood appears in legend, this tale weaves in names and details that appear in adult versions of the wizard's story." *Merlin,* the third book in the trilogy, was published in 1997.

Another book of not by Yolen is *Briar Rose,* published in 1992, which is part of the "Fairy Tale" series created by Teri Windling. In *Briar Rose,* Yolen connects the traditional tale of Briar Rose (also known as Sleeping Beauty) with the Holocaust. It becomes the story of Becca Berlin who, through the Briar Rose legend told to her by her grandmother Gemma, discovers her grandmother's past in Poland during World War II. In a review of *Briar Rose* in *School Library Journal,* Cathy Chauvette writes that "Yolen once again demonstrates her facility in blending history and fantasy, reworking the terrors of the Holocaust that she explored so successfully in *The Devil's Arithmetic,*" an acclaimed 1988 work involving a young girl's horrific journey into the past. Sybil Steinberg, critiquing the work in *Publishers Weekly,* states, "By interpreting Gemma's vivid and imaginative story into the larger narrative, Yolen has created an engrossing novel."

Throughout the 1990s, Yolen has continued to maintain her position as the "American Hans Christian Anderson" and to adhere to the high standard she has set for children's literature. Because of her efforts, the field of juvenile fiction has become a much richer playground for the minds of young readers.

■ Works Cited

Chauvette, Cathy, review of *Briar Rose, School Library Journal,* April, 1993, p. 150.

Drungil, Mary Jo, review of *Hobby, School Library Journal,* September, 1996, p. 208.

Golodetz, Virginia, review of *The Dragon's Boy, School Library Journal,* October, 1990, p. 122.

Gregory, Helen, review of *Camelot: A Collection of Original Arthurian Stories, School Library Journal,* January, 1996, p. 127.

Hutt, Karen, review of *Here There Be Witches, Booklist,* October 15, 1995, p. 397.

Rogers, Susan L., review of *Here There Be Dragons, School Library Journal,* January, 1994, p. 117.

Rogers, Susan L., review of *Passager, School Library Journal,* May, 1996, pp. 118-19.

Sherman, Chris, review of *Here There Be Unicorns, Booklist,* November 4, 1994, pp. 492-93.

Steinberg, Sybil, review of *Briar Rose, Publishers Weekly,* July 20, 1992.

Wilton, Shirley, review of *Here There Be Angels, School Library Journal,* November, 1996, p. 119.

Yolen, Jane, essay in *Something About the Author Autobiography Series,* Volume 1, Gale, 1986, pp. 327-46.

■ For More Information See

BOOKS

Authors and Artists for Young Adults, Volume 4, Gale, 1990, pp. 229-41.

Children's Literature Review, Volume 4, Gale, 1982, pp. 255-69.

de Montreville, Doris, and Elizabeth D. Crawford, editors, *The Fourth Book of Junior Authors and Illustrators,* H. W. Wilson, 1978.

Dictionary of Literary Biography, Volume 52: *American Writers for Children since 1960: Fiction,* Gale, 1986, pp. 398-405.

Pringle, David, editor, *St. James Guide to Fantasy Writers,* 1st edition, St. James Press, 1996.

Roginski, Jim, *Behind the Covers: Interviews with Authors and Illustrators of Books for Children and Young Adults,* Libraries Unlimited, 1985.

PERIODICALS

Analog Science Fiction and Fact, March, 1993, p. 164.

Booklist, February 15, 1992, p. 1117; March 1, 1992, p. 1281; March 15, 1992, p. 1391; May 15, 1992, p. 1684; August, 1992, pp. 2008, 2020; September 15, 1992, p. 125; December 15, 1992, p. 740; January 15, 1993, pp. 872, 905, 925; April 1, 1993, p. 1435; June 1, 1993, p. 1846; November 1, 1993, p. 533; December 1, 1993, p. 696; December 15, 1993, pp. 741, 760; February 1, 1994, p. 1009; February 15, 1994, p. 1086; June 1, 1994, pp. 1814-15; September 15, 1994, p. 146; October 1, 1994, p. 335; October 15, 1994, p. 440; November 15, 1994, p. 609; December 15, 1994, p. 755; January 1, 1995, p. 804; March 15, 1995, p. 1331, 1332; April 15, 1995, p. 1501; June 1, 1995, p. 1755; September 1, 1995, p. 77; September 15, 1995, p. 164; November 15, 1995, p. 558; February 1, 1996, pp. 929, 931; April 15, 1996, pp. 1444-5; May 1, 1996, p. 1508; May 15, 1996, p. 1587; June 1, 1996, pp. 1716, 1749; July, 1996, p. 1828; October 1, 1996, pp. 337, 339; October 15, 1996, p. 425.

English Journal, April, 1991, p. 84; October, 1991, p. 96; March, 1994, p. 96.

Entertainment Weekly, April 10, 1992, p. 71.

Horn Book, January/February, 1990, pp. 73, 90; January/February, 1991, pp. 62, 72, 78, 80; September/October, 1991, p. 590; September/October, 1992, p. 581; March/April, 1993, p. 216; September/October, 1993, p. 594; January/February, 1995, p. 81; March/April, 1996, p. 202; July/August, 1996, p. 466; November/December, 1996, p. 741.

Library Journal, September 15, 1992, p. 97; October 1, 1995, p. 88.

Magazine of Fantasy and Science Fiction, December, 1991, p. 80; April, 1996, p. 28.

New York Times Book Review, May 19, 1991, p. 30; November 1, 1992, p. 25; November 8, 1992, p. 54; March 14, 1993, p. 14; March 15, 1995, p. 25.

People Weekly, December 23, 1996, p. 49.

Plays, October, 1994, p. 64.

Publishers Weekly, September 28, 1990, p. 101; October 26, 1990, p. 71; November 2, 1990, pp. 73, 74; March 22, 1991, p. 80; April 19, 1991, p. 66; June 7, 1991, p. 64; September 6, 1991, p. 102; September 20, 1991, p. 132; February 3, 1992, p. 79; March 9, 1992, p. 57; April 27, 1992, pp. 270-71; July 20, 1992, pp. 231-32, 248; October 5, 1992, p. 72; December 7, 1992, pp. 57-58; March 8, 1993, p. 76; April 19, 1993, p. 60; July 19, 1993, p. 252; October 11, 1993, p. 87; November 1, 1993, p. 81; December 20, 1993, pp. 55-56; May 23, 1994, p. 87; August 15, 1994, p. 95; September 19, 1994, p. 25; October 17, 1994, p. 81; November 28, 1994, p. 46; December 19, 1994, p. 54; February 13, 1995, p. 78; April 17, 1995, p. 59; May 22, 1995, p. 60; August 7, 1995, p. 460; October 16, 1995, p. 62; June 24, 1996, pp. 61-62; July 14, 1997, p. 82.

School Library Journal, March 30, 1990, p. 60; May, 1990, p. 94; July, 1990, pp. 79-80; October, 1990, p. 70; November, 1990, pp. 100-101; January, 1991, pp. 84, 109; July, 1991, pp. 66, 75, 91-92; August, 1991, p. 158; October, 1991, p. 35; November, 1991, p. 125; December, 1991, p. 132; May, 1992, pp. 72, 95, 110, 117; August, 1992, p. 153; September, 1992, p. 214; January, 1993, p. 95; March, 1993, pp. 188, 217; April, 1993, pp. 116, 150; August, 1993, pp. 162, 206; December, 1993, pp. 110, 118; January, 1994, p. 102; March, 1994, p. 219; April, 1994, p. 123; July, 1994, p. 92; September, 1994, p. 202; October, 1994, pp. 40, 45, 106; January, 1995, p. 110; February, 1995, p. 89; March, 1995, p. 236; April, 1995, pp. 120, 129; June, 1995, pp. 115-16, 126, 134; September, 1995, p. 198; November, 1995, pp. 108, 116; December, 1995, p. 110; February, 1996, p. 72; March, 1996, pp. 198, 217; May, 1996, pp. 109, 118; June, 1996, pp. 119, 149; July, 1996, p. 81; November, 1996, pp. 95.

Wilson Library Bulletin, March, 1990, p. S6; June, 1990, p. 119; September, 1990, pp. BT6-7; June, 1992, p. 130; March, 1993, p. 91; May, 1993, p. 94; March, 1994, p. 102; October, 1994, pp. 119-20.*

—Sketch by Peggy Saari

Acknowledgments

Acknowledgments

Grateful acknowledgment is made to the following publishers, authors, and artists for their kind permission to reproduce copyrighted material.

MICHAEL BEDARD. Bedard, Michael, photograph by Merrilee Brand. Reproduced by permission.

MARY CASSATT. "Boating Party," painting by Mary Cassatt. The Granger Collection, New York. Reproduced with permission./ "Mary Cassatt," painting by Edgar Degas. National Portrait Gallery, Smithsonian Institution. Reproduced by permission./ "Mother and Infant," painting by Mary Cassatt. Giraudon/Art Resource, NY. Reproduced by permission./ Cassatt, Mary, photograph. Archive Photos, Inc. Reproduced by permission.

JOHN CHRISTOPHER. Christopher, John, photograph by A. Vaughan Kimber. Reproduced by permission of the Literary Estate of A. Vaughan Kimber.

JAMES FENIMORE COOPER. Blakelock, Ralph Albert, illustrator. From a cover of *The Deerslayer*, by James Fenimore Cooper. Bantam Books, 1982. Reproduced by permission of Bantam Books, a division of Bantam Doubleday Dell Publishing Group, Inc./ Sharp, Joseph Henry, illustrator. From a cover of *The Last of the Mohicans*, by James Fenimore Cooper. Bantam Books, 1989. Reproduced by permission of Bantam Books, a division of Bantam Doubleday Dell Publishing Group, Inc./ Day-Lewis, Daniel, in a scene from *The Last of the Mohicans*, photograph by Frank Connor. fotos international/Archive Photos, Inc. Reproduced by permission./ "Leatherstocking Meets the Law," painting by John Quidor, photograph. New York State Historical Association, Cooperstown. Reproduced by permission./ Manuscript from *The Pathfinder*, by James Fenimore Cooper, photograph. Source unknown./ Cooper, James Fenimore, drawing by Cacilie Brandt. National Portrait Gallery, Smithsonian Institution. Reproduced by permission.

KAREN CUSHMAN. Rosenfeld, Stephanie, illustrator. From a cover of *Catherine, Called Birdy*, by Karen Cushman. HarperTrophy, 1995. Cover art © 1995 by Bryan Leister. Cover © 1995 by HarperCollins Publishers. Reproduced by permission of HarperCollins Publishers, Inc./ Hyman, Trina Schart, illustrator. From a jacket of *The Midwife's Apprentice*, by Karen Cushman. Clarion Books, 1995. Jacket illustration copyright © 1995 by Trina Schart Hyman. Reproduced by permission of Houghton Mifflin Company./ Cushman, Karen, photograph by Fred Mertz. Reproduced by permission of Curtis Brown, Ltd.

EMILY DICKINSON. Cover of *Selected Poems*, by Emily Dickinson. Dover Publications, 1990. Reproduced by permission./ Heinze, Mitchell, illustrator. From a cover of *Selected Poems of Emily Dickinson*, by Emily Dickinson. Tor Books, 1993. Reproduced by permission./ Dickinson, Emily, photograph. The Granger Collection, New York. Reproduced by permission.

WALT DISNEY. Chernabog in a scene from "Fantasia," photograph. Archive Photos, Inc. Reproduced by permission./ Mickey Mouse with young fans at Walt Disney World Resort, photograph. AP/Wide World Photos, Inc. Reproduced by permission./ Women in animation department painting Snow White, photograph. AP/Wide World Photos, Inc. Reproduced by permission./ Disney, Walt, photograph. Archive Photos, Inc. Reproduced by permission.

E. L. DOCTOROW. Jacket of *Lives of the Poets: A Novella and Six Stories*, by E. L. Doctorow. Random House, 1984. Reproduced by permission of Random House, Inc./ Bacon, Paul, illustrator. From a jacket of *World's Fair*, by E. L. Doctorow. Random House, 1985. Reproduced by permission of Random House, Inc./ Jacket of *Billy Bathgate*, by E. L. Doctorow. Random House, 1989. Reproduced by permission of Random House, Inc./ Rollins, Howard (and two unidentified men), in the film *Ragtime*, photograph. Archive Photos, Inc. Reproduced by permission./ Doctorow, E. L., photograph. AP/Wide World Photos, Inc. Reproduced by permission.

ALEXANDRE DUMAS. "Portrait of the Sculptor, Paul Lemoyne," painting by Jean Auguste Dominique Ingres. From a cover of *The Count of Monte Cristo*, by Alexandre Dumas. Bantam Books, 1981. Reproduced by permission of Bantam Books, a division of Bantam Doubleday Dell Publishing Group, Inc./ Reed, Oliver, with Michael York, Richard Chamberlain, and Frank Finlay, in a scene from "The Three Musketeers," photograph. Archive Photos, Inc. Reproduced by permission./ Dumas, Alexandre, photograph.

NIKKI GIOVANNI. Crampton, Nancy, photographer. From a cover of *Those Who Ride the Night Winds*, by Nikki Giovanni. Quill, 1983. Cover photograph copyright © 1983 by Nancy Crampton. Reproduced by permission of William Morrow & Company, Inc./ Ford, George, illustrator. From a jacket of *Ego-Tripping and Other Poems for Young People*, by Nikki Giovanni. Lawrence Hill Books, 1993. Illustrations copyright 1973, 1993 by George Ford. All rights reserved. Reproduced by permission of Lawrence Hill Books, an imprint of Chicago Review Press, Incorporated./

Giovanni, Nikki (reading book at microphone), photograph. AP/Wide World Photos, Inc. Reproduced by permission./ Giovanni, Nikki, photograph. AP/Wide World Photos, Inc. Reproduced by permission.

AMY HECKERLING. Scene from *Clueless*, photograph by Elliott Marks. Elliott Marks/fotos international/Archive Photos, Inc. Reproduced by permission./ Scene from *Fast Times At Ridgemont High*, photograph. Archive Photos, Inc. Reproduced by permission./ Travolta, John, with Kirstie Alley and Jason Schaller in a scene from *Look Who's Talking*, photograph. TriStar Pictures/Archive Photos, Inc. Reproduced by permission./ Chase, Chevy, in a scene from *National Lampoon's European Vacation*, photograph. Popperfoto/Archive Photos, Inc. Reproduced by permission./ Heckerling, Amy, photograph. AP/Wide World Photos, Inc. Reproduced by permission.

ALFRED HITCHCOCK. Scene from *The Birds*, photograph. Archive Photos, Inc. Reproduced by permission./ Scene from *Dial M for Murder*, photograph. Warner Bros./Archive Photos, Inc. Reproduced by permission./ Scene from *Psycho*, photograph. Archive Photos, Inc. Reproduced by permission./ Stewart, James, in a scene from *Rear Window*, photograph. Archive Photos, Inc. Reproduced by permission./ Hitchcock, Alfred, photograph. Archive Photos, Inc. Reproduced by permission.

JAN HUDSON. Cover of *Sweetgrass*, by Jan Hudson. Scholastic Inc., 1991. Illustration copyright © 1991 by Scholastic Inc. POINT is a registered trademark of Scholastic Inc. Reproduced by permission./ Hudson, Jan, photograph.

ELMORE LEONARD. Cover of *52 Pick-Up*, by Elmore Leonard. Avon Books, 1983. Reproduced by permission of Avon Books./ Cover of *LaBrava*, by Elmore Leonard. Avon Books, 1984. Reproduced by permission of Avon Books./ Cover of *Stick*, by Elmore Leonard. Avon Books, 1984. Reproduced by permission of Avon Books./ Ziemienski, Dennis, illustrator. From a cover of *Freaky Deaky*, by Elmore Leonard. Warner Books, 1989. Reproduced by permission of Warner Books, Inc./ Leonard, Elmore, photograph by Jerry Bauer. © Jerry Bauer. Reproduced by permission.

GREGORY MAGUIRE. Zimmer, Dirk, illustrator. From a jacket of *Seven Spiders Spinning*, by Gregory Maguire. Clarion Books, 1994. Jacket illustration copyright © 1994 by Dirk Zimmer. Reproduced by permission of Houghton Mifflin Company./ Hunt, Paul, illustrator. From a jacket of *Oasis*, by Gregory Maguire. Clarion Books, 1996. Reproduced by permission./ Maguire, Gregory, photograph by Debbie Kirsch. Reproduced by permission of Debbie Kirsch.

CAROL MATAS. Cover of *Sworn Enemies*, by Carol Matas. Dell, 1994. Reproduced by permission of Dell Books, a division of Bantam Doubleday Dell Publishing Group, Inc./ Cover of *The Burning Time*, by Carol Matas. Bantam Doubleday Dell, 1996. Copyright © 1994 by Carol Matas. Reproduced by permission of Delacorte Press, an division of Bantam Doubleday Dell Publishing Group, Inc./ Matas, Carol, photograph by Peter Tittenberger. Reproduced by permission.

TONI MORRISON. Morrison,Toni, photograph. AP/Wide World Photos, Inc. Reproduced by permission.

MARGARET ROSTKOWSKI. Benson, Linda, illustrator. From a cover of *After the Dancing Days*, by Margaret I. Rostkowski. HarperTrophy, 1988. Cover art © 1988 by Linda Benson. Cover © 1988 by HarperCollins Publishers. Reproduced by permission of HarperCollins Publishers, Inc./Akopyan, Loudvik, illustrator. From a cover of *Moon Dancer*, by Margaret I. Rostkowski. Browndeer Press, 1995. Cover illustration copyright © 1995 by Loudvik Akopyan. Reproduced by permission of Loudvik Akopyan./ Rostkowski, Margaret, photograph by Kent Miles. Reproduced by permission.

GILLIAN RUBINSTEIN. Weiman, Jon, illustrator. From a jacket of *Skymaze*, by Gillian Rubinstein. Orchard Books, 1991. Jacket illustration copyright © 1991 by Jon Weiman. Reproduced by permission of the publisher, Orchard Books, New York./ Rubinstein, Gillian, photograph. Doug Nicholas Photography. Reproduced by permission of Gillian Rubinstein.

SIR WALTER SCOTT. Jacket of *Rob Roy*, by Sir Walter Scott. J. M. Dent & Sons, 1975. Reproduced by permission./ Walker, Robert, illustrator. From a cover of *Old Morality*, by Sir Walter Scott. World's Classics, 1993. Cover photo © Christie's Images, London. Cover reproduced by permission of Oxford University Press. Cover photo reproduced by permission of Christie's Images, London./ Scene from *Ivanhoe*, photograph. Archive Photos, Inc. Reproduced by permission./ Neeson, Liam, in a scene from *Rob Roy*, photograph. fotos international/Archive Photos, Inc. Reproduced by permission./Scott, Walter (Sir), illustration. AP/Wide World Photos, Inc. Reproduced by permission./ Tomb of Sir Walter Scott, Dryburgh Abbey, photograph.

IVAN SOUTHALL. Cole, Brock, illustrator. From a jacket of *The Mysterious World of Marcus Leadbeater*, by Ivan Southall. Farrar Straus and Giroux, 1990. Copyright © 1990 by Ivan Southall. Illustration copyright © 1990 by Brock Cole. Reproduced by permission of Farrar, Straus and Giroux, Inc./ Southall, Ivan, photograph. Reproduced by permission of Ivan Southall.

T. H. WHITE. Cover of *The Book of Merlyn*, by T. H. White. Ace Books, 1987. Reproduced by permission of The Berkley Publishing Group./ Cover of *The Once and Future King*, by T. H. White. Ace Books, 1987. Reproduced by permission of The Berkley Publishing Group./ Scene from *The Sword in the Stone*, photograph. Walt Disney Productions/Archive Photos, Inc. Reproduced by permission./ White, T. H., photograph. Source Unknown.

RITA WILLIAMS-GARCIA. Baker, Garin, illustrator. From a cover of *Fast Talk on a Slow Track,* by Rita Williams-Garcia. Bantam Books, 1992. Cover art copyright © 1992 by Garin Baker. Reproduced by permission of Bantam Books, a division of Bantam Doubleday Dell Publishing Group, Inc./ Williams-Garcia, Rita, illustration by Bourne Graphics. Gale Research.

JANE YOLEN. Knabel, Lonnie, illustrator. From a cover of *The Devil's Arithmetic,* by Jane Yolen. Puffin Books, 1990. Copyright © 1990 by Lonnie Knabel, cover illustration. Reproduced by permission of Puffin Books, a division of Penguin Books USA Inc./ Wilgus, David, illustrator. From an illustration in *Here There Be Angels,* by Jane Yolen. Harcourt Brace & Company, 1996. Illustrations copyright © 1996 by David Wilgus. Reproduced by permission of Harcourt Brace & Company./ Yolen, Jane, photograph by Shulamith Oppenheim. Reproduced by permission of Jane Yolen and Curtis Brown, Ltd.

Cumulative Index

Author/Artist Index

The following index gives the number of the volume in which an author/artist's biographical sketch appears.